# Praise for *Get Better Faster 2.0*

"*Get Better Faster* has been a game-changer in shaping my practice as an instructional leader. It has allowed me to focus my observations when visiting multiple classrooms across multiple schools and to formulate specific action steps to enhance teachers' practice. One of its most significant impacts has been in norming instruction among a cluster of schools, leading to a noticeable improvement in teachers' practice and student achievement as a direct result."

—**Dr. Tenia Pritchard,** Instructional Superintendent, District of Columbia Public Schools

"*Get Better Faster 2.0* provides a powerful, actionable road map for improving instruction, grounded in Paul Bambrick-Santoyo's proven expertise in leadership practices that improve engagement and drive student achievement. His deep insights, built from years of coaching and studying effective leaders across the globe, offer instructional leaders clear step-by-step guidance that will transform teaching and learning."

—**Beth Grabois,** Director, Mathematics and Science, Jefferson County Public Schools, Colorado

"Having had the privilege of working closely with Paul, I've seen how his approach transforms not just classrooms but entire schools. *Get Better Faster 2.0* captures the precision, clarity, and heart of his leadership style, making it an invaluable resource for anyone serious about improving teacher performance and student outcomes."

—**Dr. Brandon Clay,** Principal, George Washington Carver Elementary School, St. Louis Public Schools, Missouri

"*Get Better Faster 2.0* is an essential guide for every education leader tasked with developing teachers in the post-COVID era. Never before has the urgency to 'get better faster' been so critical, nor the challenges for educators so steep. Fortunately, Paul Bambrick-Santoyo offers clear, proven, and easily replicable strategies to lead the way. With teacher turnover at an all-time high and a younger, less experienced workforce, school leaders and coaches need this

resource now more than ever. Our children's success depends on how quickly we can support and grow our teachers, and *Get Better Faster 2.0* provides the road map to do just that."

**—Kathryn Anstaett,** President and Chief Schools Officer,
United Schools, Columbus, Ohio

"*Get Better Faster* has been an anchor to our work, securing so much of how we think about instruction in the classrooms we support around the world. For many of those classrooms—and the schools and systems in which they're situated—it's also been a springboard to greatness, focusing attention and action on what is most important: student learning. This updated edition embodies Paul's belief that there's always more to learn and that our best can be better yet; we're grateful to have a stronger anchor and a springboard that will take us ever higher."

**—Mark Gregory** and **Colin Smith,** Regional Directors,
One World Network of Schools, England

"Paul Bambrick-Santoyo's *Get Better Faster 2.0* stands out as an indispensable guide for educators, offering a concrete, data-driven approach to rapidly improving instruction that has been proven effective in schools across the country. Drawing from his extensive experience as a successful school leader, Bambrick-Santoyo provides actionable strategies and scaffolded steps that empower teachers and administrators to create measurable, transformative change in their classrooms and schools."

**—Dr. Windy Dorsey-Carr,** Assistant Superintendent of Curriculum,
Instruction, and Accountability, Robeson County Public Schools, North
Carolina and **Amanda Graham,** Relay-Leverage Leadership Coach, Robeson
County Public Schools, North Carolina

"*Get Better Faster 2.0* gives leaders and teachers the specific observable actions that move teachers at exponential speed. Leaders will learn the language and skills that will take a new teacher from good to great within one year, and progress will be seen in a matter of days. The key skills are broken down into bite-sized actionable moves that anyone can master if followed well."

**—Lindsey Robinson,** Superintendent, Chicago
International Charter School, Illinois

"Paul Bambrick-Santoyo's work has revolutionized my approach to coaching teachers, replacing overwhelming and ineffective feedback with manageable action steps that teachers can realistically implement. *Get Better Faster 2.0* distills Paul's decades of experience into the EXACT book every instructional leader should have within arm's reach."

—**Janet Thorton,** Instructional
Leadership Coach, Texas

"*Get Better Faster* has been an invaluable resource in our work with schools in Chile. Paul Bambrick-Santoyo offers a practical vision and an actionable blueprint for supporting school leaders and teachers to develop the key practices that enhance student learning."

—**Maria Luis Valdes,** Head of Teacher and
Leadership Development, Aptus, Chile

"Once again, Paul has lit a fire within educators! Whether turnaround, overcoming a plateau, or maintaining strong student outcomes, *Get Better Faster 2.0* and its resources are the gold standard for impact and innovation within schools. Run (don't walk!) to read *Get Better Faster 2.0*! Our children are counting on us!"

—**Tameka Royal,** Former Principal and
Superintendent, Newark, New Jersey

"Rarely does a resource come along that empowers leaders with a proven blueprint for driving meaningful change in our classrooms. Paul Bambrick-Santoyo's *Get Better Faster 2.0* equips instructional leaders with the tools they need to think bigger, lead with purpose, and cultivate a culture of excellence. It's a practical road map for those ready to make a lasting impact on both their teams and students."

—**Eric Sanchez,** Chief Executive Officer and **Carice Sanchez,** Chief
Academic Officer, Henderson Collegiate, North Carolina

# GET BETTER FASTER 2.0

A 90-Day Plan for Coaching New Teachers

Paul Bambrick-Santoyo

Copyright © 2025 by Paul Bambrick-Santoyo. All rights reserved.
Videos © 2025 by Uncommon Schools. All rights reserved.

Published by John Wiley & Sons, Inc., Hoboken, New Jersey.
Published simultaneously in Canada.

Except as expressly noted below, no part of this publication may be reproduced, stored in a retrieval system, or transmitted in any form or by any means, electronic, mechanical, photocopying, recording, scanning, or otherwise, except as permitted under Section 107 or 108 of the 1976 United States Copyright Act, without either the prior written permission of the Publisher, or authorization through payment of the appropriate per-copy fee to the Copyright Clearance Center, Inc., 222 Rosewood Drive, Danvers, MA 01923, (978) 750-8400, fax (978) 750-4470, or on the web at www.copyright.com. Requests to the Publisher for permission should be addressed to the Permissions Department, John Wiley & Sons, Inc., 111 River Street, Hoboken, NJ 07030, (201) 748-6011, fax (201) 748-6008, or online at http://www.wiley.com/go/permission.

All of the print-ready materials available online and certain pages from this book (except those for which reprint permission must be obtained from the primary sources) are designed for educational/training purposes and may be reproduced. These pages are designated by the appearance of copyright notices at the foot of the page. This free permission is restricted to limited customization of these materials for your organization and the paper reproduction of the materials for educational/training events. It does not allow for systematic or large-scale reproduction, distribution (more than 100 copies per page, per year), transmission, electronic reproduction or inclusion in any publications offered for sale or used for commercial purposes—none of which may be done without prior written permission of the Publisher.

**Trademarks:** Wiley and the Wiley logo are trademarks or registered trademarks of John Wiley & Sons, Inc. and/or its affiliates in the United States and other countries and may not be used without written permission. All other trademarks are the property of their respective owners. John Wiley & Sons, Inc. is not associated with any product or vendor mentioned in this book.

**Limit of Liability/Disclaimer of Warranty:** While the publisher and author have used their best efforts in preparing this book, they make no representations or warranties with respect to the accuracy or completeness of the contents of this book and specifically disclaim any implied warranties of merchantability or fitness for a particular purpose. No warranty may be created or extended by sales representatives or written sales materials. The advice and strategies contained herein may not be suitable for your situation. You should consult with a professional where appropriate. Further, readers should be aware that websites listed in this work may have changed or disappeared between when this work was written and when it is read. Neither the publisher nor author shall be liable for any loss of profit or any other commercial damages, including but not limited to special, incidental, consequential, or other damages.

For general information on our other products and services, please contact our Customer Care Department within the United States at (800) 762-2974, outside the United States at (317) 572- 3993. For product technical support, you can find answers to frequently asked questions or reach us via live chat at https://support.wiley.com/s/.

If you believe you've found a mistake in this book, please bring it to our attention by emailing our reader support team at wileysupport@wiley.com with the subject line "Possible Book Errata Submission."

Wiley also publishes its books in a variety of electronic formats. Some content that appears in print may not be available in electronic formats. For more information about Wiley products, visit our website at www.wiley.com.

*Library of Congress Cataloging-in-Publication Data is Available:*

ISBN 9781394300167 (Paperback)
ISBN 9781394300174 (ePub)
ISBN 9781394300181 (ePDF)

Cover Design: Wiley
Cover Image: © JJ Ignotz

SKY10100573_032125

# Contents

| | |
|---|---|
| Online Content | ix |
| Acknowledgments | xxviii |
| About the Author | xxx |
| Get Better Faster Scope and Sequence | xxxi |

| | |
|---|---|
| **Introduction** | **1** |
| Changing the Game | 3 |
| Why Focus on New Teachers? | 7 |
| Myths and Realities of Coaching New Teachers | 11 |
| What Is "Better," and What Is "Faster"? | 13 |
| How This Book Is Structured | 14 |
| How to Use This Book | 18 |
| Dive in—Meet Your Teachers Where They Are | 21 |
| Ready to Dive in! | 22 |

| | |
|---|---|
| **Principles of Coaching** | **23** |
| Principle 1: Make It Bite-Sized | 25 |
| Principle 2: Practice What You Value | 51 |
| Principle 3: Give Feedback Frequently | 64 |
| Start Here Quick Reference Guide | 80 |

| | | |
|---|---|---|
| **1** | **Pre-teaching (Summer PD)** | **81** |
| | Phase 1 Coaching Blueprint: Lead PD | 83 |
| | Phase 1 Management—Develop Essential Routines and Procedures | 91 |
| | Phase 1 Rigor—Develop Content Expertise and Lesson Plans | 105 |
| | Conclusion | 144 |

| | | |
|---|---|---|
| **2** | **Instant Immersion** | **145** |
| | Phase 2 Coaching Blueprint: Make Time For Feedback | 147 |
| | Phase 2 Management—Roll Out and Monitor Routines/Build Trust and Rapport | 159 |
| | Phase 2 Rigor—Roll Out Academic Routines | 201 |
| | Conclusion | 244 |
| **3** | **Cleared For Takeoff** | **245** |
| | Phase 3 Coaching Blueprint: Look at Student Work | 246 |
| | Phase 3 Management—Engage Every Student | 259 |
| | Phase 3 Rigor—Activate Knowledge and Model | 282 |
| | Conclusion | 308 |
| **4** | **Go Deeper** | **309** |
| | Phase 4 Coaching Blueprint: Respond to In-the-Moment Data | 310 |
| | Phase 4 Management—Increase Classroom Energy | 315 |
| | Phase 4 Rigor—Deepen Discourse | 336 |
| | Conclusion | 358 |
| | Closing: The Pursuit of Excellence | 359 |
| | Appendix: Get Better Faster Coach's Guide | 363 |
| | Phase 1: Pre-Teaching | 364 |
| | Phase 2: Day 1–30 | 376 |
| | Phase 3: Day 31–60 | 398 |
| | Phase 4: Day 61–90 | 409 |
| | Notes | 419 |
| | Index | 431 |

# Online Content

Note: Online content will be posted at https://www.wiley.com/go/getbetterfaster2. The password for the online content is *moment*.

## PRINT-READY MATERIALS

These online resources are ready for you to print and use in your classroom:

| Resource | Description |
|---|---|
| Get Better Faster Scope and Sequence of Action Steps | A printable version of the sequence of all the action steps in one document. Ideal for carrying around with you when observing classes and trying to identify the highest leverage action step. |
| Get Better Faster Coach's Guide | The all-in summary document of the entire book: each action step with proven coaching resources for live models, scenarios for practice, and cues for real-time feedback. This is the best guide to have by your side when planning feedback meetings with teachers. |
| Leader Resources to accompany Coach's Guide | Latest version of guides to accompany the coaching principles/tips throughout the book:<br>• Living the Learning PD Cycle<br>• Instructional Leadership Team Meetings<br>• Leading Practice Clinics<br>• Giving Effective Feedback<br>• Weekly Planning Meetings<br>• Real-Time Feedback<br>• Weekly Data Meetings<br>• Monitoring for Learning While Observing |

*(Continued)*

| Resource | Description |
|---|---|
| Teaching Resources to accompany coaching of specific skills | Useful materials for teachers to accompany the coaching of specific skills in the Get Better Faster sequence:<br>• Habits of Academic Discourse Guide<br>• K-12 Universal Discourse |

## VIDEOS

Here is an overview of the video clips available as part of the online content for your quick reference (you can click on the QR code next to each video or find them online at https://www.wiley.com/go/getbetterfaster2).

Introduction

| Clip | Teacher Action Step | Key Leadership Move | Description |
|---|---|---|---|
| 1 | What to Do Directions | Do It | "Once you say, 'Eyes on me,' look for it."<br><br>Jaz Grant coaches his teacher to scan for observable behaviors. |

Principle of Coaching #1: Make It Bite-Sized

| Clip | Teacher Action Step | Key Leadership Move | Description |
|---|---|---|---|
| 2 | What to Do Directions | See It | "As I model What to Do directions, I want you to take note of two things. . . ."<br><br>Erica Lim models a new skill before asking teachers to practice. |

Online Content

Principle of Coaching #2: Practice What You Value

| Clip | Teacher Action Step | Key Leadership Move | Description |
|---|---|---|---|
| 3 | Academic Monitoring— Pen in Hand | Do It | "You gave the monitoring codes. Now make sure students know what you're looking for in that first lap."<br><br>Trennis Harvey coaches his elementary school teacher as she practices giving in-the-moment feedback to students. |
| 4 | Academic Monitoring— Gather Data | Do It | "Let's do two rounds of practice. In the first one, students miss the moment in the text."<br><br>Na'Jee Carter plays the role of student to help his elementary school teacher refine her feedback. |

Principle of Coaching #3: Give Feedback Frequently

| Clip | Teacher Action Step | Key Leadership Move | Description |
|---|---|---|---|
| 5 | Stretch It— Sophisticate | Real-Time Feedback | "Can I ask a question? Does that show progress over time?"<br><br>Art Worrell asks his teacher's students an important critical thinking question at the end of a social studies discussion; then, the two debrief. |
| 3 | Academic Monitoring— Pen in Hand | Do It | "You gave the monitoring codes. Now make sure students know what you're looking for in that first lap."<br><br>Trennis Harvey coaches his elementary school teacher as she practices giving in-the-moment feedback to students. |

*(Continued)*

Online Content **xi**

| Clip | Teacher Action Step | Key Leadership Move | Description |
|---|---|---|---|
| 6 | Academic Monitoring—Gather Data | Real-Time Feedback | (Silent signal to start writing)<br><br>Ashley Martin uses nonverbal signs to guide her teacher to get students writing. |
| 7 | Guide Discourse—Stamp Understanding | Real-Time Feedback | "What question are you going to ask students to get them to close the gap?"<br><br>Taro Shigenobu pushes the rigor of his science teacher's questioning during an observation. |
| 8 | Academic Monitoring—Gather Data | Real-Time Feedback | "Why did I stop the class and address the students?"<br><br>Ashley Martin debriefs with her math teacher after she pauses independent work time to address a trending error. |

Phase 1: Pre-Teaching (Summer PD)

| Clip | Teacher Action Step | Key Leadership Move | Description |
|---|---|---|---|
| 9 | Routines and Procedures 101—Practice the Rollout | Do It | "What feedback would you give?"<br><br>Kelly Dowling has new and returning high school staff practice the morning arrival routine. |
| 2 | What to Do Directions | See It | "As I model What to Do directions, I want you to take note of two things. . . ."<br><br>Erica Lim models a new skill before asking teachers to practice. |

xii   Online Content

| Clip | Teacher Action Step | Key Leadership Move | Description |
|---|---|---|---|
| 10 | Narrate the Positive | Do It | "First, script out academic narration you could use in your lesson. Then we'll jump into practice." <br><br> Annie Murphy and Ben Carman-Brown hold a morning practice clinic to improve teacher actions. |
| 11 | Routines and Procedures 101—Practice the Rollout | See It | "What did you notice about how [the teacher] intervened in that whole school moment?" <br><br> Kelly Dowling models the morning arrival routine for staff. |
| 12 | Routines and Procedures 101—Practice the Rollout | Do It | "Try rephrasing one of the things you want Daniel to do in the affirmative." <br><br> Amy Gile and senior leaders give feedback as teachers practice recess routines. |
| 13 | Routines and Procedures 101— Practice the Rollout | Teaching Clip | "Put your homework in your folder and then write it in your agenda." <br><br> Brittany Hollis practices the end-of-class agenda routine with students. Elirah Rice checks agendas as she monitors work. |
| 14 | Confident Presence | Do It | "I want you to square up and speak louder." <br><br> Lisa Hill coaches a new teacher on his class entry routine. |

*(Continued)*

Online Content **xiii**

| Clip | Teacher Action Step | Key Leadership Move | Description |
|---|---|---|---|
| 15 | Develop Understanding of Content— Analyze End Goals | See It | "To finetune the rigor of the standard, let's look at how it's assessed on the state exam."<br><br>Na'Jee Carter works with his math teacher to identify the essential concepts that students need to know to demonstrate mastery of an upcoming standard. |
| 16 | Develop Understanding of Content— Internalize Unit Plans | See It | "When you were thinking about the big idea of the text, you focused on the ending. What did I do differently?"<br><br>Na'Jee Carter coaches his teacher's ability to identify the central message in a text. |
| 17 | Develop Understanding of Content— Internalize Unit Plans | See It | "When you look at the arc of this unit, why is this lesson so important for students?"<br><br>Katie Abrams works with her math teacher to identify the major skills and ideas that students need to be successful in the unit. |
| 18 | Develop Understanding of Content— Internalize Unit Plans | See It | "What is the historical pattern happening here?"<br><br>Jesse Corburn and his history teacher unpack the conceptual takeaways of an upcoming lesson. |

| Clip | Teacher Action Step | Key Leadership Move | Description |
|---|---|---|---|
| 19 | Internalize Existing Lesson Plans—ID Key Tasks | See It | "What makes the big ideas difficult when considering the complexity of the text?"<br><br>Kelly Dowling and her literacy teacher identify the most productive struggle within a section of a novel. |
| 20 | Develop Effective Lesson Plans | Do It | "So, the first question is: modeling or guided discourse?"<br><br>Chi Tchsang works with a grade level team to plan an upcoming math lesson. |
| 21 | Internalize Lesson Plans—ID Productive Struggle | Do It | "What's stronger about that [version]?"<br><br>Zach Roach and his literacy teacher refine the end goal of the lesson. |
| 22 | Internalize Lesson Plans–Adjust | See It | "To make time for what matters, what can we cut?"<br><br>Katie Abrams works with her math teacher to adjust the lesson plan to focus on what matters most. |
| 23 | Write the Exemplar | Do It | "If they get this question right and we ask them 'why?,' what do we want them to say?"<br><br>Paul Bambrick-Santoyo works with a teacher to identify what she expects to see in an exemplar response. |

Online Content **XV**

Phase 2: Instant Immersion

| Clip | Teacher Action Step | Key Leadership Move | Description |
|---|---|---|---|
| 24 | What to Do—Check for Understanding | See It | "I want you to listen carefully to what the teacher says and does to make sure that students have clear expectations for the model." |
| | | | Susan Hernandez debriefs an exemplar video with a teacher to help her improve her What to Do directions. |
| 2 | What to Do Directions- | See It | "As I model What to Do directions, take note of two things. . . ." |
| | | | Erica Lim models a new skill before asking teachers to practice. |
| 25 | See Your Students—Make Eye Contact | Do It | "Every few seconds, glance up and scan the room to make sure all students are on task." |
| | | | Denarius Frazier coaches his math teacher to make eye contact while he teaches to ensure that all students are with him. |
| 26 | See Your Students—Circulate | Do It | "What is the drawback of that position?" |
| | | | Erica Lim and her teacher rehearse the way he will circulate during independent practice. |
| 27 | Routines and Procedures 201—Do It Again | Real-Time Feedback | "You don't have a 100% turn and talk. Let's try it again." |
| | | | Ashley Martin whisper prompts her math teacher to reset turn and talk expectations. |

xvi    Online Content

| Clip | Teacher Action Step | Key Leadership Move | Description |
|---|---|---|---|
| 28 | Make Authentic Connections | Teaching Clip (Literacy) | "So, what aspects of the argument do you need help with?"<br><br>Danny Murray checks in with an uncertain student during independent work time. |
| 29 | Independent Practice—Write First, Talk Second | Teaching Clip (Literacy) | "Flip to the first prompt. Take the next three minutes to write."<br><br>Vy Graham has students write before launching discourse. |
| 30 | Academic Monitoring— Pathway | Teaching Clip (Math) | "I'm noticing that four students are not creating three equal parts."<br><br>Christina Fritz and her co-teacher discuss trends in student work during independent practice. |
| 31 | Academic Monitoring— Pen in Hand | Teaching Clip (Math) | "How can you use your cubes to prove that?"<br><br>Brittany Hollis reviews student work as she monitors. |
| 3 | Academic Monitoring— Pen in Hand | Do It | "You gave the monitoring codes. Now make sure students know what you're looking for in that first lap."<br><br>Trennis Harvey coaches his elementary school teacher as she practices giving in-the-moment feedback to students. |
| 32 | Academic Monitoring— Pen in Hand | See It | "Watch what I say and do to respond to error. What makes it effective?"<br><br>Na'Jee Carter models a targeted response to a trending error for his literacy teacher. |

*(Continued)*

| Clip | Teacher Action Step | Key Leadership Move | Description |
|---|---|---|---|
| 33 | Academic Monitoring—Pen in Hand | Real-Time Feedback | "How do you want to respond to the data you're seeing?"<br><br>Kristen McCarthy observes math independent practice alongside her elementary school teacher. |
| 34 | Academic Monitoring—Gather Data | Do It | "What are they missing?"<br><br>Tera Carr and her math teacher review recent exit tickets to identify the conceptual error. |
| 4 | Academic Monitoring—Gather Data | Do It | "Let's do two rounds of practice. In the first one, students miss the moment in the text."<br><br>Na'Jee Carter plays the role of student to help his elementary school teacher refine her feedback. |
| 35 | Guide Discourse 101—Show-Call | Teaching Clip (Math) | "Take a look at his work. What did he do to figure out the area?"<br><br>James Cavanaugh uses an exemplar student response to launch a mathematical discussion. |
| 36 | Guide Discourse 101 | Real-Time Feedback | "How do you want to respond to the data you're seeing?"<br><br>Kristen McCarthy observes math independent practice alongside her elementary school teacher. |

| Clip | Teacher Action Step | Key Leadership Move | Description |
|---|---|---|---|
| 37 | Guide Discourse 101—Show-Call | Real-Time Feedback | "It would be powerful to do a show-call of two student responses, one with the common distractor and one with the right evidence." <br><br> Jen Petrosino guides her teacher's selection of student work for the show-call. |
| 46 | Weekly Data Meetings—Practice the Reteach | Do It | "After the turn and talk, what do we need to do?" <br><br> Jaz Grant finetunes his teacher's delivery of the reteach lesson. |
| 38 | Guide Discourse 101—Habits of Discussion | Teaching Clip | "We revoice so that we can understand someone else's opinion before adding our own." <br><br> Brittany Wolf introduces the discourse technique of revoicing to students. |
| 39 | Guide Discourse 101—Habits of Discussion | See It | "As I model, think about the language I use and the at-bats I give students to practice the skill." <br><br> Na'Jee Carter models the rollout of a discourse habit for his teacher. |
| 40 | Stretch It—Sophisticate | Teaching Clip (History) | "Did the developments between 1860–1877 constitute a social and/or constitutional revolution?" <br><br> Art Worrell launches debate with a broad, open-ended question. |

*(Continued)*

Online Content  **xix**

| Clip | Teacher Action Step | Key Leadership Move | Description |
|---|---|---|---|
| 41 | Guide Discourse 101 —Stamp the Understanding | Do It | "That 'why' gets to the heart of the inference you want them to make."<br><br>Zach Roach and his high school teacher make sure that the lesson ends on the big idea. |
| 7 | Guide Discourse 101 —Stamp the Understanding | Real-Time Feedback | "What question are you going to ask students to get them to close the gap?"<br><br>Taro Shigenobu pushes the rigor of his science teacher's questioning. |
| 42 | Guide Discourse 101 | Teaching Clip | "What if we didn't just have x and y?"<br><br>Ebonee Johnson challenges students to complicate their thinking. |

Phase 3: Cleared for Takeoff

| Clip | Teacher Action Step | Key Leadership Move | Description |
|---|---|---|---|
| 43 | Weekly Data Meetings—See the Exemplar | See It | "Based on our understanding of the teacher exemplar, is there anything we need to add to the know-show chart?"<br><br>Jaz Grant and his math teacher check for alignment among the standard, the teacher exemplar, and the know-show chart. |

| Clip | Teacher Action Step | Key Leadership Move | Description |
|---|---|---|---|
| 44 | Weekly Data Meetings— See the Gap | See It | "What is the gap between the work from these students and what we saw in our student and teacher exemplar?"<br><br>Na'Jee Carter and his grade level team look for key differences between student work and student and teacher exemplars. |
| 45 | Weekly Data Meetings— Plan | Do It | "Should we reteach with modeling or guided discourse? Why?"<br><br>Jaz Grant and his teacher use recent student data to choose the reteach method for the lesson. |
| 46 | Weekly Data Meetings— Practice | Do It | "After the turn and talk, what do we need to do?"<br><br>Jaz Grant finetunes his teacher's delivery of the reteach lesson. |
| 47 | Weekly Data Meetings— Practice | Do It | "Based on the student work we have here, who would you call on to stamp this idea?"<br><br>Julia Dutcher encourages her teacher to batch-call during the reteach lesson to stamp the new understanding. |
| 48 | Activate Knowledge— What Do We Know About? | Teaching Clip (Science) | "We're going to take what you know about energy conservation and apply it to a new scenario—the pendulum."<br><br>Emelia Pelliccio asks students to apply prior knowledge to a new situation. |

*(Continued)*

Online Content **xxi**

| Clip | Teacher Action Step | Key Leadership Move | Description |
|---|---|---|---|
| 49 | Engage all Students | Teaching Clip (Math) | "What do you need to remember?"<br><br>Jessica Rabinowitz coaches a student to recall the steps of a procedure during independent practice. |
| 50 | Individual Student Correction | See It | "What is the impact of precise What to Do directions and naming the behaviors students need to change?"<br><br>Nikki Bridges leads a staff PD session on What to Do directions and individual student correction. |
| 51 | Individual Student Correction | Do It | "If the scholar is not meeting your direction, what are you going to do?"<br><br>Jaz Grant adds off-task behavior to the final round of practice. |
| 52 | Activate Knowledge—Resource | Teaching Clip (Literacy) | "Look back at your notes to create a solid definition."<br><br>Danny Murray directs students to their notes to clarify the meaning of a key term. |
| 53 | Activate Knowledge—Resource | See It | "Can you restate that using one of the words from our word wall?"<br><br>Paul Bambrick-Santoyo role plays as a teacher who pushes students for more sophisticated vocabulary. |
| 54 | Activate Knowledge—Organizer | Teaching Clip (History) | "Use your reference sheet to quiz your partner."<br><br>Rachel Blake encourages students to use the knowledge organizer for individual and partner study. |

| Clip | Teacher Action Step | Key Leadership Move | Description |
|---|---|---|---|
| 55 | Activate Knowledge—Apply It | Teaching Clip (Math) | "What is the measure of my third angle?"<br><br>Jesse Rector leads a class oral review at the start of a lesson. |
| 56 | Activate Knowledge—Apply It | Teaching Clip (Literacy) | "Should Victor [Frankenstein] be in prison right now?"<br><br>Zach Roach's class oral review includes factual recall and evaluation. |
| 57 | Activate Knowledge—Apply It | Teaching Clip (History) | "What is the benefit of remembering events in chronological order when it comes to understanding history?"<br><br>Neha Marvania prompts students to connect chronology and causation to their analysis of Enlightenment-era revolutions. |
| 58 | Activate Knowledge—What Do We Know About? | See It | "What steps did I take to activate student learning and make connections to previous understandings?"<br><br>Equel Easterling models a knowledge retrieval activity for his math teacher to practice. |
| 59 | Activate Knowledge—Drop Knowledge | Teaching Clip (Literacy) | "So, how does knowing this add to the evidence we've seen so far?"<br><br>Sarah Schrag introduces new information to complicate an initially superficial reading of Jay Gatsby. |

*(Continued)*

| Clip | Teacher Action Step | Key Leadership Move | Description |
|------|---------------------|---------------------|-------------|
| 60 | Model—Narrow the Focus | See It | "Remember to include those three look fors' in the model."<br><br>Susan Hernandez coaches her elementary school teachers to emphasize the key thinking steps of analyzing a nonfiction text. |
| 61 | Model—Model the Thinking | Do It | "Every time you point out a text feature, you need to emphasize why you're doing this for your students."<br><br>Susan Hernandez gives her teacher feedback to make her model more exaggerated and precise. |
| 62 | Model—Check for Understanding | Teaching Clip (Math) | "What is the misconception in that case?"<br><br>Anushae Syed probes student understanding with a deliberate error. |

Phase 4: Go Deeper

| Clip | Teacher Action Step | Key Leadership Move | Description |
|------|---------------------|---------------------|-------------|
| 7 | Guide Discourse 101—Stamp Understanding | Real-Time Feedback | "What question are you going to ask students to get them to close the gap?"<br><br>Taro Shigenobu pushes the rigor of his science teacher's questioning. |
| 33 | Academic Monitoring—Pen in Hand | Real-Time Feedback | "How do you want to respond to the data you're seeing?"<br><br>Kristen McCarthy observes math independent practice alongside her elementary school teacher. |

| Clip | Teacher Action Step | Key Leadership Move | Description |
|---|---|---|---|
| 63 | Pacing—Give Time Stamps | Real-Time Feedback | "When there are five minutes left, tell them they should be on number 3."<br><br>Owen Losse coaches his teachers to give time stamps during independent practice. |
| 64 | Engaged Small Group Work—Directions | Teaching Clip | "Rows 1 and 3, silently transition."<br><br>Julia Dutcher cues students to rearrange desks in preparation for group discussion. |
| 40 | Stretch It—Sophisticate | Teaching Clip | "Did the developments between 1860–1877 constitute a social and/or constitutional revolution?"<br><br>Art Worrell launches debate with a broad, open-ended question. |
| 65 | Universal Prompts—Revoice | Teaching Clip (Literacy) | "Can someone revoice the point of disagreement?"<br><br>Danny Murray checks for understanding by asking a student to summarize the two conflicting readings of a character. |
| 66 | Universal Prompts | Real-Time Feedback | "So, we need to figure out what prompts to ask to get them to these key points."<br><br>Nikki Jones offers real-time feedback that helps her teacher swap overly-scaffolded questions for open-ended prompts. |

*(Continued)*

Online Content **XXV**

| Clip | Teacher Action Step | Key Leadership Move | Description |
| --- | --- | --- | --- |
| 67 | Universal Prompts—Press for Reasoning | Teaching Clip (Literacy) | "Why would she use that word? What two ideas is she trying to connect here?"<br><br>Hadley Westman guides students toward a more complex argument by prompting them to analyze word choice. |
| 35 | Guide Discourse 101—Show-Call | Teaching Clip | "Take a look at his work. What did he do to figure out the area?"<br><br>James Cavanaugh uses an exemplar student response to launch a mathematical discussion. |
| 53 | Activate Knowledge—Resource | See It | "Can you restate that using one of the words from our word wall?"<br><br>Paul Bambrick-Santoyo role plays as a teacher who pushes students for more sophisticated vocabulary. |
| 68 | Stretch It—Sophisticate | Do It | "Before you answer, see if anyone in the room can provide the answer. Push the thinking back on them."<br><br>Paul Bambrick-Santoyo encourages his teacher to complicate thinking through peer-to-peer conversation. |
| 41 | Strategic Calling | Do It | "That 'why' gets to the heart of the inference you want them to make."<br><br>Zach Roach and his high school teacher make sure that the lesson ends with an emphasis on a big idea. |

| Clip | Teacher Action Step | Key Leadership Move | Description |
|---|---|---|---|
| 69 | Stretch It—Problematize | Teaching Clip (Literacy) | "Is [the character] Etta a womanist? Why or why not? Or is she simultaneously both?"<br><br>Danny Murray offers a third option to two contrasting readings of a character. |
| 5 | Stretch It—Sophisticate | Real-Time Feedback | "Can I ask a question? Does that show progress over time?"<br><br>Art Worrell asks his teacher's students an important critical thinking question at the end of social studies discussion; then, the two debrief. |
| 70 | Stretch It—Sophisticate | Do It | "Before you answer, see if anyone in the room can provide the answer. Push the thinking back on them."<br><br>Paul Bambrick-Santoyo encourages his teacher to complicate thinking through peer-to-peer conversation. |

# Acknowledgments

On October 12, 2024, I lost my brother Peter to a house fire that destroyed our family home. Peter and I were just a year apart, and we were inseparable growing up as kids. Decades went by, and we went through periods of struggle, but in the latter half of our lives we found a beautiful reconciliation. And on that day in October, I lost my first best friend.

In the process of healing—and finishing this book—I was overwhelmed by the support I received, and it taught me a very powerful lesson. Sooner or later, when each of us faces the inevitable end of life, we won't focus on everything we accomplished or what we did. Rather, we will focus on the family and community we loved and, even more importantly, on the people who loved us. We will remember the people who believed in us even more than we believed in ourselves.

As *Get Better Faster 2.0* arrives nine years after the original, many parts of the education landscape have shifted dramatically. But one thing hasn't: the need for educators who believe so deeply in children (and love them) that they will do everything to achieve the best learning outcomes for every student who walks through their doors. With that comes the need for school leaders who will coach and support teachers— seeing the greatness in them—to make this possible. The school leaders featured in this book have done just that, and their work provides a road map that any inspired educator can follow. Writing this book is a chance for me to thank each of them for transforming the lives of so many teachers and students—leaving a legacy that matters most.

Thank you to my fellow educators from across the globe—we had contributions to this book from 17 different states and four different continents. Many of you participated in the Leverage Leadership Institute (LLI), co-led so capably by Kathleen Sullivan. Kathleen, you embody the sort of love for every LLI fellow that leaves a lasting impact—thank you! Thank you particularly to those leaders who filmed themselves and with their videos transported us to coaching sessions and classrooms across the globe (in the order that they appear in the book): Jaz Grant, Erica Lim, Trennis Harvey, Na'Jee Carter, Art Worrell, Ashley Martin, Taro Shigenobu, Kelly Dowling, Annie Murphy, Ben Carman-Brown, Amy Gile, Brittany Hollis, Lisa Hill, Katie Abrams, Jesse Corburn, Chi Tschang, Zach Roach, Susan Hernandez, Denarius Frazier, Danny Murray, Vy Graham, Christina Fritz, Kristen McCarthy, Tera Carr, James Cavanaugh, Jen Petrosino, Brittany Wolf, Ebonee Johnson, Julia Dutcher, Emelia Pelliccio, Jessica Rabinowitz, Nikki Bridges, Rachel Blake, Jesse Rector, Neha Marvania, Equel Easterling, Sarah Schrag, Anushae Syed, Owen Losse, Nikki Jones, and Hadley Westman.

I also want to thank my peers at Uncommon Schools, starting with the HS leaders that I've worked closely with for more than a decade—Mike Mann, Ted Eckert, Sean Gavin, Syrena Burnam, Chelsea McWilliams, Sarah Sladek, Justin Salvador, Kim Jerome, and Emma Simmons. And to our principal supervisors for creating conditions for coaching for all our K-12 teachers: Kelly Dowling, Nikki Bascombe, Eric Diamon, Denarius Frazier, Tera Carr, Nilda Velez Solomon, Jaz Grant, Kristen McCarthy, Brianna Riis, Na'Jee Carter, and Kris Hirsch. Thank you as well to the Content Development Team (David Deatherage, Jacque Rauschuber, Laura Fern, Jessica Rabinowitz, Natalie Bethea) and the senior leadership team (Julie Jackson, Brett Peiser, Michael Blake, Cyndi Leger, and Juliana Worrell) who made this all possible.

Writing can often be a solitary journey, but I have the gift of being able to benefit from a companion. Morayo Faleyimu, our writer, has been with me through so many projects over the last few years. Morayo, your leadership was fundamental to getting this done. Thank you!

I opened my acknowledgements with family, and I close with it. When I first wrote *Get Better Faster*, my three children were in the hands of educators themselves—one in elementary school, one in middle school, and one in high school. They gave me a front-row view of what it's like to be educated by extraordinary teachers and what happens when you don't have that. Incredibly, they are all grown now, and they now teach me what it means to love and be a constant source of support. Ana, Maria, and Nico—you are my purpose. You remind me of who I am and who I can be. The anchoring center of my life has been my wife Gaby. Through the most challenging times of my life, including my brother's death, you helped me encounter a deeper part of myself and taught me what concrete love looks like. Thank you, sweetie. Without you, I wouldn't be where I am today.

To my brother Peter: thank you for your unwavering love—for knowing me better than I know myself, for forgiving me, and for helping me fly. I dedicate this book to you.

# About the Author

**Paul Bambrick-Santoyo** is the Chief Schools Officer for Uncommon Schools and the Founder and Dean of the Leverage Leadership Institute, creating proofpoints of excellence in urban schools worldwide. Author of multiple books, including *Leverage Leadership 2.0, Driven by Data 2.0, A Principal's Guide to Leverage Leadership 2.0, Make History,* and *Love & Literacy,* Bambrick-Santoyo has trained more than 40,000 school leaders worldwide in instructional leadership, including multiple schools that have gone on to become the highest gaining or highest achieving schools in their districts, states, and/or countries. Prior to these roles, Bambrick-Santoyo cofounded the Relay National Principal Academy Fellowship and led North Star Academies in Newark, New Jersey, whose academic results rank among the highest in urban schools in the nation.

# Get Better Faster Scope and Sequence

You can find a printer-friendly version here: www.wiley.com/go/getbetterfaster2

| Phase | Management Trajectory | Rigor Trajectory |
|---|---|---|
| **Phase 1: Pre-Teaching (Summer PD)** | **DEVELOP ESSENTIAL ROUTINES & PROCEDURES**<br>1. **Routines & Procedures 101:** Design and Roll out<br>• Plan & practice critical routines and procedures moment-by-moment:<br>  ○ Explain what each routine means and what it will look like.<br>  ○ Write out what teacher and students do at each step, and what will happen with students who don't get it right at first.<br>• Plan & practice the roll out: how to introduce routine for the first time:<br>  ○ Plan the "I Do": how you will model the routine.<br>  ○ Plan the practice and what you will do when students don't get it right the first time. | **DEVELOP CONTENT EXPERTISE & LESSON PLANS**<br>1. **Develop Understanding of the Content:**<br>• Analyze end goal assessments: identify the most rigorous end goal assessment (AP items, SAT, state test, etc.) and name what students need to know and show to complete the tasks.<br>• Develop/internalize unit plans: sequence the big ideas of the content into a logical progression/story<br>  ○ Identify and name the key concepts/enduring understandings.<br>  ○ Describe the relationships between the concepts within the grade span and across preceding and upcoming grades. |

*(Continued)*

| Phase | Management Trajectory | Rigor Trajectory |
|---|---|---|
| | 2. **Confident Presence:** Stand and speak with purpose<br>• Confident stance: when giving instructions, stop moving and strike a formal pose.<br>• Warm-demander register: when giving instructions, use a warm but firm register, including tone and word choice.<br><br>*Note: Many other topics can be introduced during August training. What are listed above are the topics that should be addressed to reach proficiency. Other topics to introduce—even if the teachers will not yet master them—could be:*<br>• *What to Do*<br>• *See your Students*<br>• *Narrate the Positive*<br>• *Individual Student Correction*<br>• *Do It Again: have students do routines again if not done correctly* | 2. **Develop Effective Lesson Plans 101:** Build the foundation of an effective lesson rooted in what students need to learn:<br>• Write precise learning objectives that are:<br>   ○ Data-driven (rooted in what students need to learn based on end-goal assessments & analysis of assessment results)<br>   ○ Centered on enduring understandings of the unit<br>• Plan a launch: Use of Do Now, oral review, etc.<br>• Create/identify key tasks for students that lead to the most important conceptual understanding of the lesson.<br>• Plan the basic structure of the lesson (e.g., direction instruction, inquiry).<br>• Design an exit ticket (brief end assessment) aligned to the objective. |

xxxii    Get Better Faster Scope and Sequence

| Phase | Management Trajectory | Rigor Trajectory |
|---|---|---|
| | | **3. Internalize Existing Lesson Plans:** Make existing plans your own<br>• Identify the moment of most productive struggle in the lesson—articulate what students need to know/be able to do to master it.<br>• Internalize & rehearse key parts of the lesson.<br>• Build time stamps into the lesson plan.<br>• Adjust the lesson plan to target the knowledge/skills students need.<br><br>**4. Write an Exemplar: Set the bar for excellence**<br>• Script the ideal written responses you want students to produce throughout the arc of the lesson.<br>  ○ Humanities: includes key evidence, inferences, arguments<br>  ○ STEM: if they get this right and you ask them why, what do you want them to say? |

*(Continued)*

| Phase | Management Trajectory | Rigor Trajectory |
|---|---|---|
| **Phase 2 (Days 1–30)** | **ROLL OUT & MONITOR ROUTINES** <br><br> 3. **What to Do:** Use economy of language when giving directions: <br> • Make them bite-sized (e.g., 3–5 words) and observable. <br> • Chunk your directions: give them one by one in sequential order. <br> • Check for understanding on complex instructions. <br><br> 4. **See your Students:** Know when students are engaged or unengaged <br> • Make eye contact: look at all students for on-task engagement: <br>    ○ Choose 3–4 focus areas (places where you have students who often get off task) to look toward consistently. <br> • Circulate the room with purpose (break the plane): <br>    ○ Move among the desks and around the perimeter. <br>    ○ Stand at the corners: identify three spots on perimeter of the room to which you can circulate to stand and monitor student work. <br>    ○ Move away from the student who is speaking to monitor the whole room. | **ROLL OUT ACADEMIC ROUTINES** <br><br> 5. **Independent Practice:** Set up daily routines that build opportunities for students to practice independently <br> • Write first, talk second: give students writing tasks to complete prior to class discussion, so that every student answers independently before hearing their peers' contributions. <br> • Implement a daily entry prompt (Do Now) to either introduce the day's objective or review material from the previous day. <br> • Use an exit ticket (brief final task) to assess end-of-class mastery |

| Phase | Management Trajectory | Rigor Trajectory |
|---|---|---|
| | **5. Routines & Procedures 201:** Revise and perfect them<br>• Revise any routine that needs more attention to detail or is inefficient, emphasizing what students and teachers are doing at each moment.<br>• Do It Again: have students do the routine again if initially incorrect.<br><br>**BUILD TRUST & RAPPORT**<br>**6. Narrate the Positive**<br>• Warm welcome: make eye contact, smile, and greet students.<br>• Narrate what students do well, not what they do wrong.<br>  ○ "Table two is ready: their books are open and all are reading."<br>  ○ "I like how Javon has anticipated a counter-argument to strengthen his thesis."<br>• Praise intellect, not just behavior—reinforce students getting smarter:<br>  ○ Affirm the effort, not just the outcome: "Your diligence on revising your thesis really paid off here."<br>• While narrating the positive, look at student(s) who are off-task. | **6. Academic Monitoring 101:** Check students' independent work to determine whether they're learning and what feedback is needed<br>• Create & implement a monitoring pathway:<br>  ○ Name the lap: Announce what you will be looking for and how you will code work/give feedback as you circulate.<br>  ○ Monitor the fastest writers first to gather trends, then the students who need more support.<br>• "Pen in hand": Give written feedback to student work.<br>  ○ Compare answers to the exemplar: what are they missing?<br>  ○ Give quick feedback (star, circle, pre-established code).<br>  ○ Cue students to revise answers using minimal verbal intervention (affirm the effort, name error, ask to fix it).<br>• Gather data while monitoring & prepare to respond:<br>  ○ Track student responses: ideal, almost there, further off.<br>  ○ Determine how to respond: stop the class for a quick fix, activate knowledge, model, or discourse. |

*(Continued)*

Get Better Faster Scope and Sequence **XXXV**

| Phase | Management Trajectory | Rigor Trajectory |
|---|---|---|
| | **7. Make Authentic Connections:**<br>• Memorize student names & use them each time you call on them.<br>• Make self-to-student connection when they share a struggle, interest, or passion ("I struggled when. . ." or "I love that, too!").<br>• Show genuine concern: keep a tracker of important details and dates for each student to follow up with them; check in with them after class when something is off. | **7. Guide Discourse 101:** Launch the discourse cycle around the productive struggle:<br>• Everybody writes or Show-Call (post student work for students to analyze—exemplars, non-exemplars or both).<br>• Turn and talk.<br>• Cold call, then volleyball (multiple students speak before teacher).<br>• Prompt for & praise basic Habits of Discussion to strengthen conversation & listening skills (i.e., build, evaluate, agree/disagree, etc.).<br>• Stamp the key understanding: "What are the keys to remember?" |

| Phase | Management Trajectory | Rigor Trajectory |
|---|---|---|
| **Phase 3 (Days 31–60)** | ENGAGE EVERY STUDENT:<br>**8. Whole-Class Reset**<br>• Implement a planned whole class reset to re-establish student expectations when a class routine has slowly weakened over previous classes.<br>  ○ "I've noticed that only 40% of us are writing end notes. These are important because they demonstrate your understanding of the text as a whole. Today I'll be looking for end notes in all your annotations."<br>• Implement an "in-the-moment reset" when a class veers off task during the class period.<br>  ○ Example: Stop teaching. Confident stance. Clear What to Do: "Pencils down. Eyes on me in 3-2-1. Thank you: that's what Harvard looks like." Pick up tone & energy again. | ACTIVATE KNOWLEDGE & MODEL:<br>**8. Activate Knowledge:** Prompt students to access their knowledge<br>• Point students to resources (word wall, notes, texts).<br>• "What do we know about __?"<br>• Use a knowledge organizer (cheat sheet)—all key points on 1–2 pages.<br>• Retrieve knowledge by applying it—give a simple task (e.g., organize events in chronological order, quick math fluency).<br>• "Drop" knowledge:<br>  ○ Give them knowledge in the middle of the lesson when it will unlock understanding (e.g., stating definition of a vocab word that cannot be understood with context). |

*(Continued)*

| Phase | Management Trajectory | Rigor Trajectory |
|---|---|---|
|  | **9. Engage All Students:** Make sure all students participate:<br>• Cold Call: record which students participate in each class; cold call those who don't to ensure everyone participates.<br>• Pre-call/warm call: let a student who needs more time know you're calling on them next.<br>• Turn and talk: implement briefly (15–60 seconds) and frequently<br>• Intentionally alternate among multiple methods in class discussion: cold calling, all hands, and turn and talks.<br>• Provide supports to students with pre-identified needs:<br>  ○ Executive functioning (e.g., checklist, written steps, timer)<br>  ○ Social supports (e.g., communication strategies, strategies for resolving conflict)<br>  ○ Stress (e.g., strategies for naming and managing) | **9. Model:** Model for students the thinking behind the doing<br>• Narrow the focus to the thinking students are struggling with.<br>• Give students a clear listening/note-taking task that fosters active listening.<br>• Model the thinking, not just the procedure:<br>  ○ Model replicable thinking steps that students can follow (e.g., "Hmm . . . . so what is this prompt asking me to do?" OR "So, what do I already know about this time period?")<br>  ○ Vary your tone and cadence from the normal teacher voice to highlight the thinking skills.<br>  ○ Make your thinking visible (anchor chart, annotations).<br>• Check for understanding after the model:<br>  ○ Debrief the model by asking students to identify the thinking skills.<br>  ○ Stamp the key points/steps to make sure you draw out the aspects you want students to focus on.<br>  ○ Give students additional "at-bats" to practice independently. |

| Phase | Management Trajectory | Rigor Trajectory |
|---|---|---|
| | **10. Individual Student Corrections**<br>• Anticipate unengaged student behavior and rehearse the next two things you will do when that behavior occurs. Redirect students using the least invasive intervention necessary:<br>  ○ Proximity<br>  ○ Eye contact<br>  ○ Use a nonverbal<br>  ○ Say student's name quickly<br>  ○ Small consequence<br>• Engage in "close the loop" conversations with students to process what happened and improve for next time. | |

*(Continued)*

| Phase | Management Trajectory | Rigor Trajectory |
|---|---|---|
| **Phase 4 (Days 61 and beyond)** | INCREASE THE ENERGY OF THE CLASSROOM:<br>**11. Build the Momentum**<br>• Give the students a simple challenge to complete a task:<br>  ○ Example: "Now I know you're only 4th graders, but I have a 5th grade problem that I bet you could master!"<br>• Warm energy: speak faster, walk faster, vary your voice, and smile. | DEEPEN DISCOURSE:<br>**10. Universal Prompts:** Push the thinking back on the students through universal prompts that can be used at any point:<br>• Revoice: Prompt students to paraphrase others' reasoning<br>  ○ "If I hear you correctly, you seem to say X. Is that right?"<br>  ○ "Are you really saying [paraphrase or re-work their argument to see if they still defend it]?"<br>• Press for reasoning: Prompt students to elaborate or justify their answer with evidence:<br>  ○ "Tell me more." "Why/why not?"<br>  ○ "How do you know?" "Prove it." "Why is that important?" |

| Phase | Management Trajectory | Rigor Trajectory |
|---|---|---|
|  | **12. Pacing:** Create the illusion of speed so students feel constantly engaged<br>• Use a hand-held timer to stick to the time stamps in the lesson and give students an audio cue that it's time to move on.<br>• Increase rate of questioning: no more than two seconds between when a student responds and a teacher picks back up instruction.<br>• Use countdowns to work the clock ("do that in 5..4..3..2..1").<br>• Use Call and Response for key words. | **11. Strategically Call on Students** based on learning needs<br>• Create a sequence of students to call on based on the rigor of each prompt and a review of student work (e.g., first ask a student who is struggling, then one who is partially there, then almost there).<br>• Launch discourse by calling on a student with a limited answer.<br>• Call on students whose responses are closer to the exemplar when the class is struggling.<br>• Call on student with originally limited response to stamp new understanding. |

*(Continued)*

| Phase | Management Trajectory | Rigor Trajectory |
|---|---|---|
| | **13. Engaged Small Group Work:** Maximize the learning for every student during group work:<br>• Deliver explicit step-by-step instructions for group work:<br>  ○ Make the group tasks visible/easily observable (e.g., a handout to fill in, notes to take, product to build).<br>  ○ Create a role for every person (with each group no larger than the number of roles needed to accomplish the tasks at hand).<br>  ○ Give timed instructions, with benchmarks for where the group should be after each time window.<br>• Monitor the visual evidence of group progress:<br>  ○ Check in on each group every 5–10 minutes to monitor progress.<br>• Verbally enforce individual and group accountability:<br>  ○ "You are five minutes behind; get back on track."<br>  ○ "Lorena: focus." | **12. Stretch It:** Prompt to push for depth and conceptual understanding<br>• Problematize: Create tension<br>  ○ Name the debate: "Some of you say X. Some of you say Y. What do you think?"<br>  ○ Provoke debate: "[Name] would say [counter-argument]. How would you respond?"<br>  ○ Play devil's advocate: "I disagree. I actually think . . ." or "Who can play devil's advocate?"<br>  ○ Feign ignorance: "I don't understand. I was thinking . . ."<br>• Sophisticate: add complexity<br>  ○ Apply within different or new context/perspective: "Consider $2x + 5y = 4$. Does our rule still apply?"<br>  ○ Give a hypothetical: "What if . . ."<br>  ○ Consider alternatives: "What's another way to interpret this?"<br>  ○ Generalize: "So what's the emerging rule we could apply to all problems like this one?" |

# Introduction

Jaz's new kindergarten grade teacher Jade is stumped. He leafs through the stack of student work in front of him that he collected from last period. Despite his best efforts, his lesson hadn't gone as he had hoped. A number of the student worksheets were blank, others were only partially filled in, and few students had the correct answers. He's not sure what went wrong.

Across from him sits his principal, Jaz Grant. Jaz knows what it takes to produce incredible results for students. Most of the students who pass through the doors of his Brooklyn school qualify for free and reduced lunch and often struggle with the foundations of Literacy and Math. Challenges like these might overwhelm another leader, but they spur Jaz on. In 2023, the third graders at Excellence Boys Elementary School outperformed their peers by double-digit margins in the New York State math and ELA exams, and their math results placed them in the top 3% of the state. Yet this success doesn't belong to Jaz alone. For results like these, he needs every teacher to fly. That's where Jade comes in.

"You've got a great lesson design," Jaz says, "now we just have to help the students to be able to follow it." Instead of giving Jade a completed professional development rubric or rattling off multiple pieces of feedback, Jaz rises to his feet. "Jade, I want you to role play the student, and I'll play the teacher. Watch what I say and do."

For the next few minutes, Jaz models what it looks like to give clear directions, "Scholars, we have been learning about tribes. Before we start today's lesson, let's sit up nice and tall in learner's position. Nice, Lucas. Turn and talk: what do you know about tribes?

And then he pauses. "What did you notice?" he asks Jade.

The two go on to debrief Jaz's actions. Jade starts, tentatively at first, and then adds on more eagerly as the conversation continues. "You gave clear and concise cues."

After he jots a final note, Jaz gestures toward the front of the room. "Your turn," he says. A small smile tugs at the corners of Jade's mouth. He stands and, for the next several minutes, practices giving directions from an upcoming lesson. Here's what it looked like:

 WATCH Clip 1: **What to Do**[1] **Directions**
(Key Leadership Move: Do it)

In one short meeting, Jade has become a better teacher. He's internalized a new teaching skill that he will be able to access immediately when he returns to his classroom tomorrow morning. What's more, he's learned this skill after teaching for an incredibly short time. Jaz didn't wait until a mid-year review of Jade's teaching to coach him on this skill; instead, he practiced it with him in depth just a handful of weeks into his career. The result? Jade got better faster than he could have without Jaz's guidance.

It would be easy to underplay the impact of Jade learning such a small skill. Teaching is a vast, complex art—there's still so much more for Jade to learn! He still doesn't know how to respond to student error or how to lead a discussion. Considering this long path ahead, Jaz could have given Jade a long list of broadly-worded feedback, leaving him with 15 things to work on at once on the grounds that each is too important to implement later. Despite the good intentions of both leader and teacher, Jade would be incredibly hard put to respond to all this feedback at once; the likely result would be all 15 pieces of teaching wisdom falling through the cracks. Or just as dangerously, Jaz and Jade could throw up their hands in discouragement, foregoing coaching and leaving Jade to learn almost exclusively by trial and error as many teachers commonly do.

Yet Jaz shows us another way: Skill-by-skill and week-by-week, teachers can get better far faster through targeted, effective coaching. Over the course of Jade's first year, improvements like these, ones that look microscopic on their own, had an enormous impact. Jade's results match those of a seasoned virtuoso even though it would take many more years for him to reach that level of artistry himself. He's like a violinist who wouldn't yet book a solo concert but who can certainly contribute great music to an orchestra of other musicians who are among the most skilled in the nation.

This book tells the story of how school leaders guide new teachers to success. It reveals the practices of master teaching that every new teacher can learn and replicate within a few months of beginning to teach, and it breaks down the tools great leaders use to pass those practices on. More importantly, it will show you how you can use these tools, too.

## CHANGING THE GAME

Closing out the practice, Jaz asks Jade to name the impact of their work together. "Before, I was just following a lesson," he says. "Now I'm thinking about what it takes to break down directions so that they are clear enough for all my students to follow."

Imagine if Jaz had instructed Jade simply to "be clear in your instructions." This seemingly straightforward instruction is fairly abstract in execution. What does it look like to do it well? But giving bite-sized directions, looking at all students and narrating those on task—those are all moves that Jade could, and did, master with incredible precision. And more importantly still, he was able to master them in an empty classroom in the isolated space between one school day and the next. By practicing the concrete actions that would improve his ability to lead his class, Jade gave his students the gift of not having to wait for him to grow as a teacher. He returned to them the next day already measurably better.

It's this focus on the actionable—the practice-able—that drives the success of Jaz's coaching.

---

### Core Idea

Focus on the actionable—the practice-able—to drive effective coaching.

---

When Jaz works with his teachers, his focus is not merely on motivating and inspiring them (though he's more than capable of that, too): it's on teaching them concrete skills they can practice, perfect, and put into action. That's how he ensures that the time

Introduction    3

he dedicates to leading professional development sessions, supporting lesson planning, and observing classes is time well spent: time that has a direct impact on what teachers do and how well students learn. It's how he boils down the wisdom of his own experience as an educator into concrete skills any new teacher can practice—and perfect—one by one.

Jaz's approach is a great departure from what teacher training usually looks like. In 2022, the National Council for Teacher Quality reported that, on average, new teachers were observed about one to two times per year. Once the evaluation cycle ended, most received written a feedback report and a single meeting with the evaluator.[2] The bottom line is clear: Teachers aren't receiving much coaching. As a consequence, educators are very rarely asked to practice the micro-skills that will make them better at teaching—especially not under the supervision of an expert who can help them get better on the spot. Unlike soccer players, actors, or doctors, teachers tend to have to learn on their own. And when they do get some attention, it comes in the form of a single annual observation and a multi-page list of written feedback: an evaluation rather than a coaching session.

Jaz gets in the game with his teachers, focusing relentlessly on the specific, crucial actions he knows will win them the championship.

> ## Core Idea
> The purpose of instructional leadership is not to evaluate teachers but to coach them.

The challenge of such microscopic coaching is that in addition to boiling down the wisdom of his experience into specific, practice-worthy actions, Jaz must engineer his feedback to land like a perfectly placed set of dominoes. Going into immense depth on one skill at a time, each building on the last, is precisely what makes Jaz's approach to coaching effective. Pile on too many skills at once, and the chain of dominoes will tumble and scatter: the teacher will run out of both the time and the energy to internalize them all the way we saw Jade do as he practiced giving directions. But teach the right skill at the right time, and the result is a chain reaction of success.

The short-term result looks like incredibly slow growth. But what would have happened if Jaz had asked Jade to practice several different teaching moves during their meeting—if he'd attempted to provide a fully outfitted teaching toolkit instead of a single helpful strategy? The same thing that usually happens when you give someone a large box of unfamiliar tools. At worst, the box will go unopened. At best, the person will eventually figure out how to use the most essential tools but not as many of them, as quickly, or with as rich a level of understanding as if you'd introduced them to each tool one by one.

This book is far from the first to attest to the power of isolating and practicing individual skills in depth. Among the most significant has been Daniel Coyle's groundbreaking *The Talent Code*, which sets out to identify the secrets of the most successful professionals in fields from athletics to astronautics and regions from Japan to Brazil. What, Coyle asks, do top-20 Russian tennis players, pop stars from Dallas, and the Brontë sisters—three canonized writers all from the same "poor, scantily educated British family"—have in common?[3]

The answer is not in-born talent, but practice. At Moscow's Spartak Tennis Club, trainees hold their racquets in just the right position for untold hours before they even try swinging completely or hitting a ball. At the Septien Vocal Studio in Texas, singers spend years perfecting their vocal technique piece by piece—a pre-teenage Jessica Simpson worked for two years specifically to eliminate the vibrato from her voice. And in the small British town of Haworth, the seeds of *Jane Eyre* were planted as young Charlotte Brontë and her siblings entertained themselves by scribbling fantastical tales in the series of notebooks scholars call "the tiny books," giving each other an unconscious but highly intensive training in the art of building a story. Olympic athletes, chart-topping pop stars, and literary giants alike became great not through innate gift but through hard, smart work: by practicing minute aspects of their craft over, and over, and over again.

What Jaz accomplishes in the field of education is no less remarkable than what the athletes and artists Coyle observed have done, and his methods are no different. In the moment we just witnessed, Jade rehearsed like those Olympic tennis players with their frozen racquets: He practiced one essential component of teaching a great lesson until it was cemented into his muscle memory so deeply that tomorrow, when he returns to his students, he'll put it into action almost automatically. And over the course of his first year, Jade will repeat this process with dozens of other skills. His newly improved ability to get students working quickly and correctly will make it far easier for him to, for example, scan students' independent assignments as they work on them so that he can give them the in-the-moment support they need. The one skill he learned today will make an immediate impact on his teaching, will pave the way for him to grow even more as a teacher, and—above all—will stick. That's what makes that skill powerful.

Introduction     5

> ## Core Idea
>
> Great instructional leadership isn't about finding master teachers.
> It's about coaching new teachers until the masters emerge.

This book is based on the success not just of Jaz and Jade but of a growing community of educators like them. From coast to coast (and beyond the sea), thousands of educators are finding extraordinary achievement as a result of building, not just finding, great teachers. Some of these are individuals you'll get to know over the course of this book: they hail from the following cities (listed from west coast to east):

- Portland, OR
- Loveland, CO
- Denver, CO
- Pueblo, CO
- San Antonio, TX
- Corpus Christi, TX
- Dallas, TX
- Richardson, TX
- Shreveport, LA
- Kansas City, MO
- St. Louis, MO
- Memphis, TN
- Indianapolis, IN
- Atlanta, GA
- Columbus, OH
- Greensboro, NC
- Lumberton, NC
- Henderson, NC
- Washington, DC
- Camden, NJ
- Newark, NJ
- Brooklyn, NY
- Albany, NY
- Springfield, MA
- Providence, RI
- Boston, MA
- Santiago, Chile
- Birmingham, United Kingdom
- Pune, India

These teachers and leaders come from nearly every type of public school: small, large, district, charter, turnaround, startup, and many other designations unique to their cities. They have pioneered the practices in this book and have either provided their testimonials or graciously (courageously) volunteered to have some of their best work filmed to show what truly exemplary coaching looks like.

Since I first began to study and compile the work of successful school leaders more than 15 years ago, a collective of hundreds of instructional leaders have continued to refine and iterate the best practices shared within *Get Better Faster 2.0*. The guidance I share here is the result of working alongside these remarkable leaders and learning from their successes and challenges. May their experiences benefit you and your staff as well.

Throughout the book, we will break down the most critical actions leaders and teachers must enact to achieve exemplary results. We'll show what skills new teachers must learn to ensure student learning never has to wait and separating what's important generally for them to know from what's urgent for them to know now. We'll also reveal the coaching techniques school leaders use to teach them those skills. And perhaps most important of all, we'll provide every tool you need to make all these strategies work for you so that you can guide your own cohort of teachers to the same levels of success.

## WHY FOCUS ON NEW TEACHERS?

Teacher coaching is a vast topic. Yet in recent years, teacher attrition has come to dominate the conversation. Schools are losing educators at a steady clip.[4] Stagnant teacher pay, a rising cost of living, and political debates over what to teach and how to teach it have only made this worrying trend worse, especially for schools serving low-income students that need effective teaching the most. In this context, we need good coaching more than ever. Moreover, the first few years of a teacher's career matter more than ever and may be key to keeping them in the profession. *Get Better Faster 2.0* focuses heavily on a trajectory for new teacher development that responds to the urgency to develop them more efficiently and effectively.

### Success for All Students

First and foremost, focusing on new teachers matters because they are on the frontlines immediately. Unlike in a team sport like basketball, where you can sit on the bench and learn before entering the game, first-year teachers are professionals in action, doing the urgent daily work of teaching. They are entrusted with students who will only be in first-grade language arts or tenth-grade chemistry once. It may be their teacher's first year of delivering instruction, but it's students *only* year to learn the content.

The risk that great teaching won't happen that year, then, is one those students can't afford for us to take. It's all too likely that the result will be a year of learning lost to them forever. And while this would be an intolerable outcome in any circumstances, it would be nothing short of disastrous at this moment in the United States because more classrooms than ever are being led by new teachers.

As Richard M. Ingersoll has put it, our nation is currently experiencing an overall "greening" of its teaching workforce; that is, more teachers have fewer years of experience than was the case in previous decades. The most common teacher in 1988 had 15 years of teaching experience; but by 2008, the most common teacher was a first-year teacher. Fast forward 10 years to 2018, and the most common teachers were still in their first year of instruction.[5]

So, if we leave the development of new teachers to chance, we're putting a greater-than-ever proportion of our students at an unacceptable disadvantage. This book is about our best and only other option: embracing the task of getting new teachers better faster with determination and focus, so that they and their students both thrive. It's about passing down whatever we can of our experience as educators because, if we leave our new teachers to learn exclusively from their own experience, we're leaving students in a position where they might or might not get great instruction this year. Instead, we must insist that they *will*. As the leaders cited throughout the book will testify, the work with new teachers is fundamental for guaranteeing consistent student achievement from year to year.

## Success for New Teachers

Giving quality guidance to new teachers is critical for the development not only for the students but also of the new teachers themselves. In fact, coaching may be one of the most important factors that determines not only how successful a teacher's career is, but whether the teacher chooses to continue along that career path at all.

Prominent sources such as the Consortium for Policy Research in Education at the University of Pennsylvania have chronicled a worrying trend: more U.S. teachers than ever before—about 44%—are leaving the profession within the first five years of teaching.[6] These sky-high attrition rates often peak at schools that can least afford to spend time hand-picking a new crop of teachers every year and, when combined with an on-going teacher shortage, set a perfect storm into motion. A report by the Economic Policy Institute describes the trouble currently facing many school districts:

> "The teacher shortage is real, large, and worse than [previously thought]. When indicators of teacher quality (certification, relevant training, experience, etc.) are taken into account, the shortage is even more acute than currently estimated, with high-poverty schools suffering the most from the shortage of credentialed teachers."[7]

With many schools chronically understaffed and new teachers cycling out of the profession, students fare worst of all.

Is there any way to stem the mass exodus? Research has shown that several factors make retention more likely, yet one of the most impactful ones—quality professional development—is not widely available.[8] When new teachers take on their first teaching jobs, they too often land in much less collaborative communities than the ones they thrived in while earning their college degrees. In college, they were open to a constant stream of insights from both leaders and peers. When they reach the school classroom, however, they are asked to do the real work behind closed doors that give them nowhere to turn when challenges arise. When they need guidance the most, it's hard to find it.

Many school systems have implemented teacher mentoring programs to combat isolation and increase guidance and support for new teachers, but these programs vary in effectiveness. Some function more like "buddy systems" with little accountability or coaching, while others offer few touchpoints for teachers and mentors.[9] Josh Barnett of the National Institute for Excellence in Teaching says, "We know from research and experience that high-quality mentoring programs lead to better performance in the classroom, increased student achievement, and high teacher retention. The challenge is that not enough schools and districts are implementing comprehensive approaches to get the results all teachers and students deserve."[10] Few new teachers are receiving the high-quality, high-touch coaching they need to be successful in the earliest years of their career. With ineffective coaching, as with no coaching at all, new teachers tend to jump ship.

But with *good* coaching on their side, new teachers stick around. Research shows that when schools provide new teachers with meaningful leadership and partnership, new teachers are significantly more likely to remain in the profession. In fact, education researcher Richard Ingersoll discovered the more support we provide, the more new teachers we tend to hang onto. Teachers who receive just one or two basic forms of support—such as "regular supportive communication" with a school leader—are only slightly more likely to continue teaching than their peers who aren't given any support at all; those who receive a comprehensive induction package that also includes professional development and lesson planning support are dramatically less likely to leave. [11]

Why would coaching teachers make them want to stay—more even than financial incentives do? Because by and large, teachers are motivated by their desire to do well by their students. When they're left floundering, they see little hope of accomplishing

Introduction 9

what they set out to do. But when, with the help of a leader, their start-of-year anxieties are swiftly transformed into triumphs, and their desire to teach is fueled rather than diminished. They're working hard either way, but this way, they're working smart, making progress that's just as visible to them as it is to their coaches. They see their success reflected in that of their students, and they remain eager to do more.

What all this means is that if we want to keep new teachers teaching—if we want to build a generation of educators who will do their work well and passionately for many years to come—we must reach them when they come to us, not a few years down the road. We must spend the first year guiding every teacher to build outstanding teaching habits by trying the right strategies and watching them work. If we don't, they're likely to leave us; but when we do, they can become the all-stars our children need.

## Success for All Teachers—and School Leaders

Not only new teachers can benefit from the guidance in this book. Given that most teachers were not supported effectively in the early stages of their career, many of the skills and practices in this book apply to them as well. In fact, when we piloted this sequence of skills in our schools, we noticed that most teachers had areas where they could improve their instruction, and these skills helped close that gap. In the end, great coaching works for all teachers, and getting better at coaching new teachers makes you better at coaching any of your teachers.

Over more than two decades, we have coached more than 40,000 school leaders. When discussing the challenges of leadership, we have seen an overwhelmingly common pattern emerge: The classrooms of a small handful of teachers create 80% of the problems for a leader. They contribute to more discipline problems, more office referrals, more disgruntled parents, and disproportionately more work. Just as teachers fail to stay in the profession when they struggle, so do leaders: According to data from the National Center for Education Statistics, 10% of principals left their roles between the 2020–21 and 2021–22 school year, a higher rate of turnover than when data were last tracked five years prior.[12] Other studies echo these findings: Principals, stressed by heavy workloads and staffing shortages, are leaving the profession. Many flee specifically because they hunger to spend more meaningful time on instructional leadership tasks than is typical in the culture of our nation's schools today. [13] Learning to target your coaching on these teaching "focus areas" can dramatically improve not only a leader's success but also your satisfaction as an instructional leader. Successful coaching has a positive ripple effect on every aspect of school leadership.

# MYTHS AND REALITIES OF COACHING NEW TEACHERS

Every action recommended in this book emanates from an unshakeable core belief: Effective coaching makes people better at what they do. This may sound like something it would be easy for any educator—anyone who believes in the power of teaching—to agree with, but the rarity with which coaching is used effectively to train teachers reveals that's not necessarily the case. What follows are a few common myths that frequently prevent school leaders from using coaching to drive teacher development—and the realities that debunk them.

## Myth 1: Practice Doesn't Make Perfect—Experience Does

How long does it take to become proficient at teaching? Many in the profession would say that the answer is 10 years. In this view, it's only experience that can teach you how to teach.

Yet that commonplace answer isn't sustained when looking at the teaching profession. Ten-year teachers are not all alike: Some are vastly more developed and successful than others by any measure.[14] Teachers develop at vastly different rates for many reasons. The one thing we do know, however, is that effective coaching can greatly accelerate that growth. Great teaching isn't limited to those who have a certain amount of experience or some innate, undefinable spark of talent. It's accessible to those who can learn what makes great teaching, and practice it until it becomes their teaching.

## Myth 2: Just Any Practice Will Make Perfect

In the 2010s, a widely accepted truism about practice came under debate. Known as the 10,000-hour rule and popularized by Malcolm Gladwell, this common wisdom held that it takes 10,000 hours of practice to master any given skill. Get thousands of hours of practice in, and virtuoso-level success is all but guaranteed.

Since then, several studies have debunked this belief. The findings have been displayed in many publications with titles like "Practice Doesn't Always Make Perfect."[15] The number of hours logged practicing, this study finds, is erratic at best as a predictor of future success. The popular conclusion many professionals have drawn from this information is that innate talent must be a better indicator of success than practice.

In fact, both versions oversimplify the reality: Practice does make perfect, but it has to be *quality* practice. The quality of the time you spend practicing a skill, rather than the sheer quantity of time, is what affects your results. We'll describe in detail what quality practice looks like in "Principle 2: Practice What You Value" of the Principles of Coaching. For now, however, suffice it to say that perfect practice does make perfect, and a knowledgeable coach can make sure perfect practice happens all the time.[16]

> ## Core Idea
>
> Practice doesn't make perfect, but perfect practice does.

## Myth 3: Teachers Need to Master Management Completely Before They Can Focus On Learning

Too many educators assume that an early focus on school culture and classroom management must trump student learning altogether—you must wait for months to think about learning. But in reality, fostering student learning is like planting a seed. It's true that certain environmental factors need to be in place for what you're trying to grow to become strong and thrive: Students need an ordered classroom to learn just as seeds need water, air, and the proper temperature to sprout. But a seed doesn't magically shoot up into a fully grown plant all at once when the seed has been nourished by a set amount of water and air at the right temperature. Instead, you water it for a few days, and its roots emerge. You continue a bit longer, and the plant begins poking up out of the soil. Keep watering and place the new sprout in the right spot on the windowsill, and leaves appear. The creation of the right environment and the growth of the plant are ongoing processes that happen side by side.

In just the same way, student learning can't wait to take root until after the perfect classroom environment has been established. That's why we've set up the management and rigor skills we believe teachers must learn within the first few months of the school year to be mastered in tandem. They're two separate threads of teacher development, to be sure, and are presented in this book accordingly; but our students cannot afford for us to wait even a few weeks to begin attending to their learning, regardless of whether flawless classroom management is in place. Management needs to be a greater focus in the earliest days of the year than it will need to be after the first 90 days, but rigor is a focus at all times, and the results of the teachers in this book show that making room for learning from the beginning pays off.

# WHAT IS "BETTER," AND WHAT IS "FASTER"?

## Better: A Scope and Sequence of Skill

We set out to determine what teachers need *first* in order to be better at their job as quickly as possible. What do we mean by "better"? More able to meet students' most immediate needs. If we do our work with new teachers well, their students should be able to learn as effectively as those of more experienced teachers, never having the chance to fall behind.

There are many others who have documented the skills of better teaching: in particular, Doug Lemov in *Teach Like a Champion* and Jon Saphier in *The Skillful Teacher*. These books (and subsequent editions) are valuable for any educator interested in *Get Better Faster*; many of the skills that appear in this book are ones that could never have been identified without these books.

But neither book will tell an overwhelmed new teacher what's most important to master first. Prioritizing all these incredibly important teaching skills is the goal of this book. *Get Better Faster 2.0* orders essential teaching skills by what is most important for new teachers to learn first. These skill areas are then broken down into even more specific actions a teacher needs to take to be performing each skill effectively. As you'll see, those specific actions are the types of things a leader practices with a teacher as Jaz did with Jade. This level of specificity is what made Jade's practicing effective. Determining those types of actions for all these most highly prioritized skills is what this book does for you, so that you can get to the work of coaching teachers around those actions.

## Faster: 90 Days

*Get Better Faster 2.0* also proposes a 90-day timeline for mastering the skills. This book is far from the first to zoom in on this period of time. In his professional handbook *The First 90 Days*, Michael D. Watkins claims that close to 75% of leaders he interviewed agreed with the statement: "Success or failure during the first few months is a strong predictor of overall success or failure in the job."[17]

*Get Better Faster 2.0*, however, focuses on the first 90 days with a slightly different philosophy. For a teacher, succeeding early is more than a predictor of the trajectory their career will take. It's a matter of immense urgency because the more quickly a teacher masters the most important skills of teaching, the more quickly students get to develop the skills of being students. Getting to that level of competence within your first three months of teaching is an extraordinarily ambitious feat—but it's possible for a teacher who follows the methods in these pages, and for the sake of our students, it's well worth striving for.

While most applicable to the first 90 days of school, this sequence of skills and trainings can be started at any time. If a teacher starts later or develops less rapidly, this 90-day plan can be used to close the gap. More experienced teachers could pick a later starting point on the trajectory (if they've mastered everything listed in the first 30 days, they could start with the next 30 days). The coaching techniques presented here will help a teacher to develop at an accelerated rate wherever they begin and can help throughout the year.

## HOW THIS BOOK IS STRUCTURED

This book is divided into two basic parts: an introductory guide to the leadership principles that make coaching powerful, and a breakdown of the skill-by-skill coaching that is most urgent for a new teacher to receive during each of four phases. Let's take a more detailed look at what each part of the book will include.

### Coaching Principles

The following are the core principles of coaching described in the first major section of the book:

- **Make It Bite-Sized**—Coaching new teachers on just one or two skills at a time and polishing those skills down to the smallest detail may feel tedious, but it's the key to dramatic, lasting growth. This section will show why precise feedback is so powerful—and how to tell if your bite-sized feedback is bite-sized enough.

- **Practice What You Value**—When you value something, you devote time to it. In a nutshell, the cycle of planning, practicing, and repeating is the essence of getting better faster. Once you have the right piece of bite-sized feedback in hand, the key is perfect practice: planning the execution, implementing the plan, and repeating until mastered. This part of the book explains how.

- **Give Feedback Frequently**—The more immediate the feedback, the quicker the turnaround. This section shows the value of a practice already embraced in disciplines from medicine to music: giving real-time feedback. The section also provides a guide for bringing real-time feedback to the classroom while still respecting the teacher's role as the class leader.

14    Get Better Faster 2.0

## Phase 1 (Pre-Teaching)—Summer PD

Phase 1 takes place in the summer before students even enter the classroom. Summer professional development incorporates as many opportunities for new teachers to practice new skills as possible, culminating in an all-staff dress rehearsal of the first day of school from start to finish.

- **Coaching Blueprint:** Phase 1 focuses on leading summer professional development and particularly the final PD before school starts: the dress rehearsal.
- **Management Skills: Routines and Procedures:** New teachers will design, to the smallest possible detail, the routines and procedures that will keep their classrooms running smoothly, so that they can roll them out when students arrive.
- **Rigor Skills: Develop Content Expertise and Lesson Plans:** Just as the design of routines is the foundation for engagement, the understanding of unit and lesson plans is the foundation for teaching the content. In Phase 1, teachers set the foundation for rigor by deepening their understanding of the content area within the unit and learning the basics of designing and/or revising lesson plans: starting from the end goal (assessment and objective) and building the most essential pieces.

## Phase 2—Instant Immersion

School has started! While a few new skill areas will be introduced to new teachers during Phase 2, the major focus will be on getting new teachers to perfect what they began learning during Phase 1, now in the context of having their students on board as well.

- **Coaching Blueprint:** Phase 2 focuses on building an observation and feedback schedule and planning the first feedback meeting.
- **Management Skills: Roll Out and Monitor Routines and Build Trust and Rapport:** Having designed their classroom routines and procedures during Phase 1, new teachers must now roll them out with students and polish them so that they work just as well in practice with the students as they did when planned during the summer. This is also the time to build trust and rapport with students that will form the foundation of a safe, collaborative classroom.
- **Rigor Skills: Rollout Academic Routines:** The teacher builds on the management routines to lay the framework for the academic routines that will shape learning in the classroom: what happens during independent practice and discourse. Setting up effective independent practice—and monitoring what happens—gives students time

Introduction    15

to practice new concepts and get targeted feedback, while a solid foundation for discourse creates a space for students to build shared understanding.

## Phase 3—Getting into Gear

By the second month of the year, new teachers have enough foundations in their class to start pushing for 100%: 100% of students on task, 100% intellectually engaged, and 100% learning.

- **Coaching Blueprint:** Phase 3 focuses on using student work to drive teaching and a powerful way for leaders and teachers to support each other in doing so: the weekly data meeting.

- **Management Skills: Engage Every Student:** At this phase, management is in a place where most students are on task and the classroom generally looks well managed, and the new teacher's focus is on bringing any remaining students into the fold. Purposeful engagement techniques invite every student to participate and allow learning to take off.

- **Rigor Skills: Activate Knowledge and Model:** With academic routines in place, the teacher can focus on making sure every student has access to the content: guiding students to activate or acquire the knowledge they need or modeling to make visible the key thinking that can unpack the learning.

## Phase 4—Go Deeper

With lessons now highly attuned to the needs of every student, a teacher can start to turn the heaviest intellectual work over to the students: building momentum to foster rigorous student-driven discourse.

- **Coaching Blueprint:** Phase 4 focuses on giving real-time feedback, a natural but often overlooked tool for the instructional leader to increase achievement in the classroom.

- **Management Skills: Increase Classroom Energy:** A rigorous learning environment hums with energy. In this phase, the focus turns to cultivating this energy by actively managing the perception of time.

- **Rigor Skills: Deepen Discourse:** Leading class discussions effectively is one of the greatest art forms of instruction—and one of the most difficult. Here teachers will learn how to accelerate and target learning through the fine art of asking the right student the right question at the right time.

# Get Better Faster Overview

**Coaching Principles**

| Technique | Description |
|---|---|
| Make It Bite-Sized | Lasting growth doesn't come from trying to learn everything at once: It comes from working on just one or two skills at a time and polishing those skills down to the smallest detail. |
| Practice What You Value | The plan-practice-repeat cycle—planning how teachers will implement a piece of feedback, guiding them in practicing, and repeating this with the next piece of feedback—is the essence of getting better faster. |
| Give Feedback Frequently | Some feedback is best delivered in the moment. The section on principle 3 describes how to give teachers real-time feedback—a practice already embraced in disciplines from medicine to music. |

**The First 90 Days in Four Phases**

| Phase: Date | Coaching Blueprints | Management Trajectory | Rigor Trajectory |
|---|---|---|---|
| Phase 1: Pre-Teaching | Leading Professional Development, including the final PD before school: the "Dress Rehearsal" | Develop Routines and Procedures | Develop Content Expertise and Lesson Plans |
| Phase 2: Day 1–30 | Make Time for Feedback and First Feedback Meeting | Roll Out and Monitor Routines Build Trust and Rapport | Roll Out Academic Routines |
| Phase 3: Day 31–60 | Weekly Data Meeting | Engage Every Student | Activate Knowledge and Model |
| Phase 4: Day 61–90 | Monitoring the Learning | Increase Classroom Energy | Deepen Discourse |

Introduction    17

# HOW TO USE THIS BOOK

This book is designed to be a toolbox you reach for again and again in your work as a leader and coach—to give you all the materials you need to build a cohort of successful new teachers in 90 days. It strives to pass on the expertise of educators who are scaling the greatest heights in teacher coaching and student achievement on a national level. In theory, a written instruction manual for school leaders should be sufficient. But our experience in coaching tells us there will always be more to perfecting a skill than reading about it. Leaders learn much more when they can "see" it, and they become masters by doing.

To that end, *Get Better Faster 2.0* is designed to help you see it *and* do it. Each phase described previously includes not only text (naming each skill) but also a selection of videos of leaders in action (letting you see it). The final step—doing it—falls to you. With the right guidance included, you will know you are not alone in achieving this level of success!

Here are a few guidelines for using all this material to your advantage.

## Have Your Phone and Pencil Ready

The goal of *Get Better Faster 2.0* isn't just to read about all this—it's to be able to put it into action. So, the text is broken up by tools that will help you see, plan, and implement each technique that is being described. These include the following:

- **Videos:** Scan the QR codes throughout the book and you can immediately access the video of effective coaching and teaching (or go online at *https://www.wiley.com/go/getbetterfaster2*). These videos show the *how* of coaching the skills presented. Just like a student (or a new teacher) needs modeling, we also benefit from seeing what coaching a skill really looks like in action in order to do it. These clips capture the coaching and techniques we're describing better than words ever could. They take you directly into the classrooms of the top teachers and leaders in the nation who are getting the results that show these techniques work.

- **Stop and Jots:** Moments to process, think critically, and develop conclusions on your own before reading on. We remember more when we write while we read; this is a way to "learn by doing" even as you're reading this book.

These are meant not as bonuses but as core aspects of the book—the thinking and planning you get to do yourself as you go. The book is written, but you're writing the story of your school—so keep a pencil in hand and use it!

18    Get Better Faster 2.0

## Don't Skip the Coaching Principles and Blueprints

The coaching principles that launch this book—and the Coaching Blueprints found in each phase—aren't the cherry on top to the specific coaching actions recommended in each phase. Rather, they're essential techniques without which the coaching actions will be much less likely to bring about lasting change. If you skip ahead to one of the phases, you will be missing the coaching foundation that will allow you to dive effectively into the specific coaching techniques listed for each teaching skill.

We recommend this even for readers who already know about the coaching techniques from a workshop or from the observation and feedback chapter of *Leverage Leadership 2.0*. Here, each principle has been honed to focus on specific, critical aspects of teacher development in more detail. Making it bite-sized, practicing purposefully and consistently, and giving feedback more frequently are practices we always knew were powerful, but we have learned more recently exactly how much they determine the impact of observation and feedback, and why.

In addition to those blueprints, there are more than 50 "Findings from the Field" or "Tips from a Coach" embedded throughout the text from educators just like yourself: coaches, principals, and even teachers sharing their own tips based on using this material. Enjoy each unique nugget of wisdom!

## Use It—Your "Blueprints"

Once you've read the book, it will be easy to pick it off the shelf and turn to the most important sections for your use. To make these sections even more accessible, we have consolidated the key points of the book into a few documents that can be printed and carried around as you walk the school. You can find the list of resources that follows in the print-ready materials online. For your convenience, the Coach's Guide is also located at the back of this book.

Here's an overview of the most critical ones:

- **Get Better Faster Scope and Sequence:** This document is the most frequently referenced throughout *Get Better Faster 2.0*, and the summary Scope and Sequence breaks down every action new teachers must perform in order to master each of the teaching skill areas this book presents. This is the perfect resource to have at hand when observing classrooms.

- **Get Better Faster Coach's Guide:** The Get Better Faster Coach's Guide in this book's appendix takes the Get Better Faster Scope and Sequence and adds the key see-its or models, scenarios for practice, and cues for real-time feedback. This is the go-to

Introduction    **19**

guide for planning your feedback meetings with your teachers. (Please note that both the Get Better Faster Scope and Sequence and the Coach's Guide are designed to be printer friendly, which means the information they provide will be slightly more concise than the longer sections in the book.)

- **Living the Learning PD Cycle:** Use effective modeling and concrete, specific practice to help teachers develop the most important instructional skills.

- **Weekly Planning Meetings:** Identify and plan for the most important thinking that students must do to understand the objective or standard in a lesson or series of lessons.

- **Giving Effective Feedback:** First introduced in *Leverage Leadership*, the one-page Effective Feedback has been revised and improved to reflect the best practices of the highest-achieving leaders. Use this handout to make the most of debrief meetings with teachers.

- **Real-Time Feedback—Making It Stick:** This handy sheet outlines effective techniques to deliver in-the-moment feedback without interrupting the flow of instruction.

- **Weekly Data Meeting:** A protocol to analyzing student work that guides teachers and instructional leaders to spot academic gaps and create a response-to-data plan.

- **Monitoring the Learning with Teacher:** A simple set of questions asked while observing alongside teachers make instructional time a ripe opportunity to change student outcomes.

---

### Findings from the Field: Create a Rainbow Guide

"When I first read *Get Better Faster*, it was difficult to hold onto all the good ideas. Then I printed a "rainbow guide": a simple spiral bound version of all the concise guides in the book, each printed on paper of a different color. It was easy to carry around with me and use when I observed and coached. What was complicated became simple, and it made it easier to build effective habits of instructional leadership. Try it yourself!"

—*Trennis Harvey, Principal, Atlanta, GA*

# DIVE IN—MEET YOUR TEACHERS WHERE THEY ARE

Once you internalize the coaching principles and move on to the part of this book that breaks down the Get Better Faster Scope and Sequence piece by piece, it's less crucial to read straight through the book from beginning to end. If you have time to do this, then by all means do so! If, however, you're in the midst of coaching a teacher and need to dive right in, the book is set up to accommodate that. Simply begin by reading over the Scope and Sequence itself, then jump to the part of the book that specifically addresses what your teachers need the most.

Here's the best way to navigate this part of the book.

**If you are using the Scope and Sequence before the school year begins. . . .**

- **Read the Coaching Principles and the Phase 1 Coaching Blueprint:** The Phase 1 coaching tips will help you prepare summer PD sessions that train teachers in the skills they'll need most from the first day of school onward.

- **Start from the top—the first Phase 1 action step:** A strong foundation is critical to beginning the year. Therefore, start with the first action steps in Management (Routines and Procedures and Confident Prescence) and Rigor (Develop Content Expertise and Lesson Plans). Do not move forward until a teacher is proficient in these areas!

**If you are using the Scope and Sequence at any other point in the year. . . .**

- **Read the Coaching Principles.**

- **Identify your teacher's action step:** Go to the Get Better Faster Scope and Sequence (first pages of the book; a printable version is online) and determine the highest-leverage action step for your teacher. Remember: think waterfall—start from the top and stop as soon as you hit the highest-leverage problem area for the teacher.

- **Go to the appropriate Phase and read the Coaching Blueprint:** For example, if your teacher is struggling with getting all students engaged, jump to Phase 3 and start with the Coaching Tips.

- **In that same Phase, jump to the Rigor or Management section (depending on your action step), and go to the page that matches your teacher's struggle:** Use the Quick Reference Guide that appears at the beginning of each Management and Rigor section to identify the challenges that the teacher is most struggling with, and skip to the corresponding section that presents the skills that will help them overcome those specific challenges.

Introduction    21

## READY TO DIVE IN!

Every school year will bring new challenges and opportunities that are unique to each school. But one thing is constant worldwide: A legion of new teachers will enter schools, fresh from college or other jobs, ready to make a difference but not sure how. That's where you step in.

Let's begin the journey of serving each of our teachers to maximal impact! Time to turn the page.

# Principles of Coaching

What do professional soccer players, emergency room doctors, and stand-up comics all have in common? They all make their living in what we could call "adaptive performance" professions: jobs that require them to perform tasks in the moment with perfect precision, even in changing conditions. Soccer players has to score the winning goal, but to do so they have to decide where to cut and how to angle their shot based on where the defenders and goalie are located. And they have to do so precisely even with fans screaming in the stands. The best stand-up comics must respond to what the audience gives them, adjusting their jokes or creating new ones on the fly night after night, with just as much passion and humor each time. ER doctors often have just one chance to respond to the patient in front of them—they have to diagnose the problem and act immediately, where in some cases a delay in seconds can make the difference between life or death. Each of these individuals spends years learning and honing their craft, but their job is defined by how well they can channel that learning at the most important time.

Teaching is an adaptive performance profession, too. Just like the soccer player, stand-up comic, and ER doctor, teachers have to deliver excellent instruction *live*: not only delivering on a great lesson plan but also modifying it swiftly and surely in response to whatever challenges or triumphs the students bring to the classroom that day. Every moment in the classroom is one irreplaceable chance to teach your students what they need to learn, just as every second in the ER can be irrevocable.

Because of this, teachers can be trained more effectively by following the lead of their fellow adaptive performance professionals: with an eye to preparing them for the live game. Athletes, performance artists, and doctors all receive tons of information and knowledge to bolster their formation, but the magic occurs in the coaching. Great coaching gives them as many opportunities as possible to practice the tasks they'll need to complete when the stakes are high, so that when the critical moments come, they're ready.

There's a great deal of focus in the field of education on how leaders should *evaluate* their teachers. But when we view teaching as an adaptive performance profession, we see that what's more important than assessing how teachers did yesterday is making sure they will succeed today, tomorrow, and throughout their careers. Like any great soccer coach or orchestra conductor, we must shift our focus from *evaluating* to *coaching*—making sure our teachers will do dazzling work in the moments that matter most, when their classrooms are packed with students and the clock is ticking.

> ## Core Idea
>
> Lead like a maestro: Evaluate less and coach more.

The Principles of Coaching covers the essential techniques of great teacher coaching, revealing what every leader needs to know to train teachers as performance professionals. It includes three principles:

1. **Principle 1: Make It Bite-Sized**—break down teaching into discrete skills to be practiced successively and cumulatively.

2. **Principle 2: Practice What You Value**—coach a teacher through effective practice of the highest-leverage skill.

3. **Principle 3: Give Feedback Frequently**—give teachers regular feedback on their teaching.

These three topics don't comprise everything there is to know about coaching, but they cover all the most basic foundational skills: everything you need to shift the paradigm around teacher development so that teachers receive the training and guidance they deserve to thrive. In our discussion of the subsequent phases, we'll dive even deeper into these principles with concrete Coaching Blueprints relevant to that stage in a teacher's development. But first let's dive into the principles that can transform not only your approach to developing teachers but also your whole role as a school leader. Following these three principles ensures your work with teachers has a direct and consistent impact on student achievement.

## PRINCIPLE 1: MAKE IT BITE-SIZED

In 1990, NASA launched the Hubble Space telescope, the largest and most versatile space telescope at the time. It revolutionized our understanding of the universe for more than 30 years: pinpointing the age of the universe, identifying the rate of the universe's expansion, and discovering thousands of previously unknown galaxies. But the telescope was not without flaws. Despite its groundbreaking discoveries, the Hubble was still limited in what it could see. Its relatively small mirror relied on visible light, making it impossible to capture the infrared rays of light that could give scientists more information about the earliest days of the universe. There was also a technical error: a mirror that was off by less than a hair, which made the resulting images fuzzy.

NASA knew that it could build a bigger and better telescope than the Hubble. So, in 1989, it began dreaming. This new infrared telescope would be much larger and travel much farther from Earth. It would use a primary and secondary mirror to capture infrared light that the Hubble couldn't and allow scientists to look further back in time. But a telescope of this size would be too large to launch fully assembled; it would have to be folded into a rocket and unfolded in space without human guidance. In systems design, a "point of failure" occurs when a single nonworking component triggers a total system collapse. The new telescope had 344 components.

If even one of the components failed to work properly, the $10 billion telescope, now decades in the making, would be useless. But scientists were undeterred.[1] In July 2022, the telescope [eventually named the James Webb Space Telescope (JWST)] sent back the first set of images: ghostly swirls of interstellar gas in the Carina Cliffs, the glowing Southern Ring Nebula, and a deep field of shining, faraway galaxies. The difference between the JWST's images and the Hubble's was like night and day (visit the Webb Images gallery at science.nasa.gov to see for yourself!).

So, what made this incredible success possible? Scientists didn't just create a big design; they focused on perfecting it, one point of failure at a time. They worked their way through 344 of them until they were sure that none would fail.

What works for a telescope also works for a teacher. There are likely 344 single points of failure that could make a classroom go wrong (maybe even more). Trying to fix them all at once is an impossible task. But fixing them one at a time? Transformative. A steady, methodical process makes the improbable possible: start with a shift in a teacher's tone, then move on to positive narration, and so on. If you want to go big, think small. Use bite-sized moves to build better teachers.

> ## Core Idea
> If you want to go big, think small.
> Build better teachers with bite-sized moves.

Sounds simple. Yet we are often the most significant barrier to the change we wish to see. The perfect teachers we dream of eclipses the teachers who stand before us. And so we note the multitude of limitations and try to give them all to the teacher, often in the form of an infrequent, lengthy evaluation.

Yet coaching them effectively on this journey doesn't require the biggest moves or sweeping feedback. The power lies in thinking small: giving bite-sized feedback on the specific skills a teacher most needs to work on right now. Polish each foundational skill of teaching until it is locked in. Then introduce the next one.

The most successful leaders I've worked with give feedback in this way: They observe teachers frequently and assign them just one or two action steps per week. It feels excruciatingly slow at first—like the work on the JWST—but little by little, the steps build momentum, unfolding to reveal a stronger, more effective teacher. That is a teacher who will shine as brightly as any solar system seen by the JWST.

## Action Steps: The Bite-Sized View

The art of delivering the right bite-sized action step to a teacher at the right time is the heart of thinking small—and often, it's incredibly challenging. How can you know the right step? If we only choose one, it had better count!

We'll look at four case studies in this section all around a common challenge—off-task students. While it would be tempting to give them all the same action step, the underlying issue in each case is different.

We'll read each case study, name criteria for effective action steps, and then apply those criteria to the next case study. Step-by-step, we'll get better at the practice.

### The Right Action Step—Case Study #1

Anthony is a first-year teacher, and his instructional leader Danielle is coaching him. Here's what Danielle saw during yesterday's observation.

## Case Study #1: The Observation

Danielle slips into Anthony's middle school social studies class a few minutes after lunch. The class is several lessons into a unit on Ancient Greece. An excerpt from Pericles's 431 BCE speech "Funeral Oration" is projected onto the whiteboard.

"Ok, class, eyes up front," Anthony states, standing still at the front of the room and making sure students are with him. As he does so, nearly all students turn their attention to him as he starts speaking. "I'm really excited for us to work on this speech by Pericles. We're going to look at this on our own and then talk about it. So, take a few minutes to look it over and figure it out. You've got resources to help you. Go ahead."

Students look around at each other and they look back at their papers. Some start reading the passage; others notice the handout on their desk and see that there are questions they are supposed to answer. The first line has some complex vocabulary, and a few start whispering to each other, asking what that means or what they are supposed to do. Another subset of students stops reading after a moment and just stares straight ahead.

Anthony looks around the room and sees that most students aren't reading, so he intervenes. "I don't see people reading. Remember, you are going to read the speech, and there are questions on the handout." A student quietly asks him a question, and he shares out to the whole group, "Yes, you need to answer the questions that are in the handout. You can only do that by reading the passage. Remember your resources if you need help!"

A few more students start reading, but many still don't look at the questions in the handout. Students have their hand raised, and Anthony goes to talk with each of them. After a few more questions, he states, "Class, remember the resource. In your textbook you have vocabulary that could help with this passage. It's at the start of the unit."

Some students open the textbook, but many don't find the right section. Most students are reading at this point, but they aren't doing what the first question asked them—to highlight the key line of the opening paragraph and summarize what it means.

Principles of Coaching    27

Anthony notices the blank answers to #1, so he once again shares out to the class. "Remember that you have to answer the questions. Number 1 asks you to highlight the key line. So, don't forget to do that."

By now, some students are highlighting a key line, but some are doing that in different paragraphs. Most are looking at the questions in the handout, but they are not answering them correctly.

At this point Danielle steps out of the classroom and contemplates what should be Anthony's next step for improvement.

---

Imagine you are Danielle. How would you assess Anthony's performance? There is good news in this observation: When Anthony calls the class together, nearly all of them start listening. That in itself can be an accomplishment for a newer teacher. There is evidence of some procedures in place: classwork was already set out with materials and helpful resources, and Anthony speaks with a warm, confident tone. What could Danielle ask Anthony to do that would be sure to increase learning for everyone in his classroom?

## Stop and Jot

Before reading on, what would be your action step for Anthony?

_____

_____

_____

_____

Perhaps Danielle's first instinct is to say:

## Danielle's Action Step, Version 1

"Be clearer."

---

You can probably immediately see the flaw in Danielle's advice. For people who aren't clear, telling them to "be clearer" will not help (if they knew how, they would already do so!). This action step doesn't give Anthony any more guidance on what to do—and if Danielle observed his class again a week later, it would probably look exactly the same.

What if Danielle gave Anthony this feedback instead?

---

## Danielle's Action Step, Version 2

"When giving directions, make sure students understand what you want them to do. This helps students get right to work so that they spend more time practicing."

---

Danielle's second attempt is definitely stronger. She has narrowed her focus to the moment when the problem becomes visible: when students are sent off to work. She has selected a more specific aspect of great classroom management: making sure students know what to do before practice begins. Considering how vaguely Anthony introduced the activity, Danielle has correctly identified directions as an important next step for him.

Yet Danielle still hasn't guaranteed improvement in Anthony's classroom next week. Many questions remain. What do understandable directions look like? And, perhaps more importantly, what does it sound like to deliver them in class? Anthony needs to know the answers to these questions to improve his teaching craft—and Danielle will need to recognize them when she observes his class again, so that she can tell for sure if the change she identified has taken place.

How could Danielle further improve her feedback? Let's see what her action steps for Anthony look like when she re-writes them to be even narrower:

---

## Danielle's Action Step, Version 3

**What to Do:** Use economy of language when giving directions:

- Make them bite-sized (e.g., 3–5 words) and observable.
- Chunk your directions: give them one by one in sequential order.
- Check for understanding on complex instructions.

---

Principles of Coaching    29

---

## Stop and Jot: Danielle Gets Bite-Sized

What makes Danielle's third attempt at an action step more effective?

_____

_____

_____

_____

### Criteria for Effective Action Steps

These final action steps are much more likely to improve Anthony's classroom management than the others Danielle considered. Why? Three big characteristics made the difference.

- **Observable and practice-able.** The final action steps are unmistakably clear. What makes them clear is that you could observe them in action: make the directions bite-sized, give them one at a time, and check for understanding. The next time Danielle returns to Anthony's classroom, she can check immediately whether he has implemented the steps. She'd be able to tell right away whether he needed more coaching around those actions or whether he's ready to learn another habit of great teaching. Being observable also makes the action step practice-able: If teachers can see it, they can practice it. Anthony could easily practice any of these moves prior to teaching again.

- **Highest-leverage.** In the beginning, it may be difficult to figure out which action step has the highest leverage. Here's a helpful tip: an action step is highest-leverage if it will have the biggest impact on improving student learning—and will do so the most quickly. There are many other action steps Danielle could have considered: focusing on the handful of students who weren't paying attention at the very beginning or the small number who were completely staring into space without working. This would have been helpful, but if Anthony doesn't get the majority of the class on track first, he won't move the needle as quickly. Moreover, so many classroom management challenges are solved by clearer directions. Students will go off-task because they don't understand. That's why Danielle targeted her feedback at the most urgent challenge in this moment: the lack of clear directions. After that is solved, she can move on to other aspects of the class.

30    Get Better Faster 2.0

- **Bite-sized.** An action step is right-sized if a teacher can work on all of it at once and begin to practice immediately. Consider this from an overwhelmed teacher's point of view. Working on an action step for weeks before seeing any improvement isn't motivating. But seeing a shift in a week? That's enough to keep a teacher going. To determine whether an action step is bite-sized enough, ask yourself, "Could this action step be accomplished in one week?" If not, the action step isn't small enough. (I'll explain more about the value of the weekly action step in a moment.)

---

### Criteria for the Right Action Step

1. Is it observable and practice-able?
2. Is it the highest-leverage action you could ask the teacher to perform?
3. Is it bite-sized enough that the teacher could accomplish it in one week?

---

### Findings from the Field: Celebrate Progress, Step-By-Step

> "Meet people where they are. Do not bombard or overwhelm them with unrealistic implementation outcomes. Instead, stay the course with bite-sized feedback, high expectations, and unrelenting monitoring and celebrations of their progress. This allows for a more perfected outcome, buy-in, and an opportunity to celebrate them along their implementation journey."
> —Susan Hernandez, Principal Supervisor, Richardson, TX

---

### The Get Better Faster Scope and Sequence of (Bite-Sized) Action Steps

If this was your first time generating a specific action step, you might have found it difficult to create an action step that met these three criteria. If you did, you are not alone! Most leaders we have worked with are uncertain, at first, about identifying the right bite-sized action step during each observation. It can feel overwhelming to imagine choosing the single task that will drive the most learning in a teacher's classroom in the course of a single week, particularly when you have to do it for dozens of teachers at a time.

Principles of Coaching     31

But you don't have to dive blindly into the process of observation and feedback. As the team behind the JSWT would agree, a project of that magnitude would never come together without a blueprint to guide the way. And while there's no perfect blueprint for developing a teacher—no single document could ever account for the vast variety of paths different professionals follow when they set out to master a craft—there's still an extent to which you can foresee what will help a new teacher the most.

We have spent the past two decades bringing together thousands of instructional leaders to learn how to give action steps to teachers. We've culled through countless videos of teaching (as well as observing instruction live) and studied the observation notes of their instructional leaders. In that process, we looked most closely at principals who had the strongest track record of developing new teachers—leaders like Jaz Grant. These are principals where we observed that their newer teachers' growth outpaced those of schools around them. When we walked around the schools of principals like Jaz, we were stunned at the development of their teachers: None of the new teachers looked like new teachers!

As we looked at their observation notes and their action steps, we noticed patterns that distinguished their feedback from other, less effective school leaders. Their action steps were not only more precise, high leverage, and bite-sized (meeting the aforementioned three criteria) but also followed a similar order. Although not every teacher's feedback was the same, these leaders maintained an eerie level of consistency in the order to which they worked on actions with teachers. They consistently followed sequences—for example, developing a teacher's ability to see student behavior before teaching them how to re-direct a student and working on independent practice before managing a class discussion.

The fruit of this investigation was the development of a scope and sequence of action steps for new teachers that has since been used by tens of thousands of leaders. Continuously refined each year to reflect the latest best practices, this latest version is the 70th draft at the time of this writing (and we will continue to refine as more leaders use it and apply it!). This resource gives you a blueprint—and order—to help you in choosing and developing the right action steps.

Here is an overview of the sequence (specific action steps will be addressed within each phase):

---

### Get Better Faster Scope and Sequence of Action Steps to Launch a Teacher's Development

Note: This is a general summary of the topics—the precise, comprehensive list of action steps starts on page xxxi, and a printer-friendly version can be found in the online resources: *www.wiley.com/go/getbetterfaster2*.

| Phase | Management Trajectory | Rigor Trajectory |
|---|---|---|
| Phase 1 | Develop Essential Routine and Procedures | Develop Content Expertise and Lesson Plans |
| Pre-Teaching (Summer PD) | 1. **Routines and Procedures:** Plan and practice critical routines and procedures moment by moment.<br>2. **Confident Presence:** Stand and speak with purpose. | 1. **Develop Understanding of the Content:** Analyze end goal assessments: identify the most rigorous end goal assessment and name what students need to know and show to complete the tasks.<br>2. **Develop Effective Lesson Plans 101:** Build the foundation of an effective lesson rooted in what students need to learn.<br>3. **Internalize Existing Lesson Plans:** Break down existing lesson plans to make them your own.<br>4. **Write an Exemplar:** Script the ideal written responses you want students to produce throughout the arc of the lesson. |

*(Continued)*

---

Principles of Coaching **33**

| Phase 2 | Roll Out and Monitor Routines<br>Build Trust and Rapport | Roll Out Academic Routines |
|---|---|---|
| **Instant Immersion (Days 1–30)** | 3. **What to Do:** Use economy of language when giving directions.<br>4. **See your Students:** Know when your students are engaged or unengaged.<br>5. **Routines and Procedures 201:** Revisit and perfect existing procedures.<br>6. **Narrate the Positive:** Tell students what they are doing right.<br>7. **Make Authentic Connections:** Build a relationship with every student. | 5. **Independent Practice:** Set up daily routines that build opportunities for independent practice.<br>6. **Academic Monitoring 101:** Check students' independent work to see whether they're learning and what feedback is needed.<br>7. **Guide Discourse 101:** Launch the discourse cycle around the productive struggle. |
| Phase 3 | Engage Every Student | Activate Knowledge and Model |
| **Cleared for Takeoff (Day 31–60)** | 8. **Whole-Class Reset:** Reestablish student expectations when routines weaken.<br>9. **Engage All Students:** Make sure all students participate.<br>10. **Individual Student Corrections:** Quickly and discreetly reengage off task students. | 8. **Activate Knowledge:** Prompt students to access their knowledge.<br>9. **Model:** Model for students the thinking behind the doing. |

| Phase 4 | Increase the Energy of the Classroom | Deepen Discourse |
|---|---|---|
| Go Deeper (Days 61–90) | 11. **Build the Momentum:** Bring challenge and energy to your teaching.<br>12. **Pacing:** Create the illusion of speed to engage students.<br>13. **Engaged Small Group Work:** Maximize the learning for every student during group work. | 10. **Universal Prompts:** Push student thinking with universal prompts.<br>11. **Strategically Call on Students:** Choose students based on learning needs.<br>12. **Stretch It:** Prompt to push for depth and conceptual understanding. |

The Get Better Faster Scope and Sequence is divided into four phases of teacher development to mirror the first months of a teacher's career (thus the four sections that drive this book!). Each phase has a core focus—the major areas in which a teacher needs to develop—and bite-sized action steps listed with each action area. For example, the focus of Phase 1 Rigor is developing content and lesson plans, and the fourth action step is writing an exemplar. The following are two of the bite-sized action steps listed for this area:

- Script an ideal written response you want students to produce throughout the arc of the lesson

  o Humanities: include key evidence, inferences, arguments

  o STEM: if they get this right and you ask them why, what do you want them to say?

Every step of the way, you have an action step to use with teachers to help them get better faster.

### What's New About this Sequence?

If you have used an earlier version of the Get Better Faster Scope and Sequence, you will notice several changes in the sequence listed previously. These changes were created by the leaders who have put this sequence into practice—as they noticed a missing action step or one that was better to do earlier than we originally thought.

Principles of Coaching

Here is a high-level overview of the changes (see the end notes for a more in-depth explanation)[2]:

- **Building Content Knowledge (Phase 1 Rigor):** Developing the understanding of the content you teach is a lifelong journey (as you already know). This section identifies the highest-leverage action steps we have seen leaders use to accelerate that development, especially early in a teacher's career.

- **Build Trust and Rapport (Phase 2 Management):** Thanks to the work of Zaretta Hammond in *Culturally Responsive Teaching and the Brain* and many others, we have been able to expand on the techniques teachers use to strengthen the relationship with their students. We particularly added how to make connections with students during class.

- **Early Habits of Discourse (Phase 2 Rigor):** Originally, all discourse action steps were at the end of the GBF Sequence. But leaders quickly realized that you cannot build good discourse later without rolling out essential routines early on. So, "Guide Discourse 101" was moved to Phase 2 as it's really about creating a habit—get students to write, turn and talk, and share out in a large group. While the nuances of managing the discourse and pushing it further wait until Phase 4, placing this action step here gets students talking right away—even if it won't be totally fruitful initially.

- **Activate Knowledge (Phase 3 Rigor):** One of the biggest aha moments we have had in reteaching (i.e., designing lessons that respond to student error) is that models and discourse are limited without adding another tool—how to activate student knowledge. Knowledge retrieval is a burgeoning field of research, and we will discuss the highest-level takeaways for instructors in Phase 3.

- **Deepen Discourse (Phase 4 Rigor):** As we studied good discourse and connected it to the research in the field, we have sharpened the key action steps for discourse and put them in order of complexity. In doing so, we've absorbed the separate section that was originally "Stretch It" (after Phase 4) and consolidated it here to make a more seamless connection between the action steps.

- **Changes in language (throughout):** Finally, you'll see some similar action steps that now have new names. In building this collectively, we identified that certain language could be made clearer and could better avoid incorrect interpretations. For example, "aggressive monitoring" was always meant to emphasize the relentlessness with which teachers pay attention to the learning, but "aggressive" has negative connotations and could be misconstrued to refer to how to handle students.

The new language of "academic monitoring" better states the original intent—and effectiveness—of this action step.

Whether in its original sequence or this newly revised one, the action steps in the Scope and Sequence do not constitute an exhaustive list of everything a new teacher needs to master at every point in the year: rather, they focus on the highest-leverage steps based on the on-the-ground observation of exceptional leaders. Moreover, you might discover effective action steps yourself that aren't in this guide. If so, please pass them on! This guide has evolved and improved because of input from thousands of instructional leaders. You can help make it stronger as well.

We should also note that not all teachers will develop at the pace the Scope and Sequence proposes. But if they follow the sequence, the ultimate measure of their success will be the improvement you see in their classroom.

What the Scope and Sequence offers, then, is not an end-point evaluation tool but a Coaching Blueprint—it shows the granular increments by which to measure success and the ideal order in which to put each piece in place.

### Core Idea

The Get Better Faster Scope & Sequence is not an evaluation tool but a blueprint: a guide to building better teachers.

Take this example from instructional coach Erica Lim. Here she is leading a workshop for high school teachers who are struggling to give concise directions. The precision of her action step—what to do directions—leads to the clarity of her model, which makes it easier for teachers to grasp.

 WATCH Clip 2: **What to Do Directions**
(Key Leadership Skill: See it)

The action step itself doesn't address the "how" of coaching (that's the next principle!), but we cannot have effective leadership without it. Usually, when a feedback session goes poorly, the trouble is rooted in a weak action step. When you don't know where you're headed in a coaching meeting, neither will the teacher!

With this tool in hand, let's see how it influences our ability to generate high-leverage, bite-sized, doable action steps. Let's practice with three more case studies, all still dealing with students who are off task for one reason or another.

To guide you, you can use the Scope and Sequence on pages xxxi to xlii or you can use the printable version located online (www.wiley.com/go/getbetterfaster2). Get ready to practice identifying the right action step!

**Putting It into Practice—Case Study #2**

Jonathan is the instructional leader for Sophie, who teaches third grade. Here is a summary of what he observed in her classroom. What do you think is the highest-leverage, measurable, bite-sized action step?

---

## Case Study #2: Management

Jonathan worked closely with Sophie at the beginning of the school year to launch her routines and procedures effectively. In the summer professional development, she designed an opening routine that would get them right to work. As her elementary students cross the threshold into her classroom, she greets them at the door. A blue in-box on her desk is where they head next to drop off the previous night's homework. Lastly, they sit in assigned seats, take out their pencils, and immediately start the Do Now (a short written task).

This routine went very smoothly at the start of the school year. Jonathan began to notice some hiccups a few weeks later, and he is now observing her in the fifth week of school. Jonathan arrives before class starts to observe her launch.

Sophie is already at the door. The first student looks up at her with a big grin on his face.

"Good morning," Sophie says. "Homework in the bin." The smiling student walks directly to the bin; however, the next few students walk to their seats instead and begin rifling through their backpacks. Sophie peeks her head into the classroom. "Homework in the bin, please." Students look her way for a moment and then return to what they were doing. Two students swap seats, giggling.

More students line up at the doorway. A few don't greet Sophie and they all bypass the homework bin. They chatter quietly as they take their seats. Sophie hears this and calls into the room, "Remember, this is silent work time! I want that homework in the bin. Juan, head back to your seat. Lilly, pencil moving on your Do Now." Juan and Lilly follow directions, but other students continue to whisper. As some students go over to the homework bin, they use that time to chat and stay

38    Get Better Faster 2.0

standing. "Guys—get back to work please! This isn't time to talk." Students slowly head back to their seats and most begin the Do Now.

The final students enter class, and Sophie closes the door. "Three minutes left on the Do Now. We've got a busy day ahead."

---

Pull out your Get Better Faster Scope and Sequence. What would be the observable and practice-able, highest-leverage, bite-sized action step you could give her?

---

## Stop and Jot: Case Study #2

Write down the bite-sized action steps you would give to Sophie to improve her teaching next week:

_____

_____

_____

_____

_____

_____

**Stop Here**

Keep reading only after you've drafted the action step!

Here is the thinking that we did to approach this case study. From the start, we asked the question: Is this a management issue or rigor? Given that we were observing the entry routine and students weren't getting to work, we know we have to address management before we can get to rigor.

Starting from the top of the Get Better Faster Sequence with Phase 1, we ask the question: Is Sophie lacking a basic routine (Step 1) or a confident presence (Step 2)? From the information presented, Sophie has already designed and rolled out a routine that should work; the problem is that students have stopped following it. She also seems to have decent implementation of confident presence (granted that in a written case study it is much more difficult to ascertain her posture and register than in a real classroom observation!). So, Phase 1 action steps don't seem to be the highest-leverage issue. Moving to Phase 2, we continue to ask which is the root of the problem?

Principles of Coaching    **39**

- A lack of clear instructions in what students need to do in the procedure? (Step 3—What to Do).
  - Doesn't seem to be the case. Sophie reminds students of the expectations with bite-sized directions (turn in homework, working silently on the Do Now). While she doesn't check for understanding, we are not sure that by itself will address the issue. So, we keep exploring.
- Sophie's ability to see the problem? (Step 4—See Your Students)
  - Although Sophie doesn't catch every off-task behavior, she is aware that the class is not following the opening routine as she keeps calling on students to remind them. So we keep moving.
- An imperfect procedure? (Step 5—Routines and Procedures 201).
  - No, the routine as originally designed seems like it would be effective. (One way to ask the question is this: Would this routine work for a teacher with stronger classroom management? We think so.) The real issue is that students no longer follow it. Will Do it Again solve it? Perhaps. Let me note that for potential coming back to and keep reading.
- Sophie's ability to narrate the positive (Step 6) and make authentic connections (Step 7)?
  - At this stage, the students are happy to see her when they line up for class as evidence by the student's big grin at the beginning. This doesn't appear to be the gap (of course, if we had more evidence from observing the teacher over multiple weeks, we could answer that more definitively).
- Sophie's ability to reset the class once the routine has failed? (Step 8—Whole Class Reset)?
  - This feels like another stronger contender. It addresses the root cause—a routine that students do not follow—and gives clear guidance for Sophie that is directly connected to what she's not doing.
- Engage all students (Step 9) or Individual Student Correction (Step 10)?
  - The issue now seems to be class-wide, not individual students. As such, Step 5 or Step 8 seem more targeted to the highest-leverage action that will make the biggest impact right away.

So, we have two strong possible action steps: Do it Again or Whole Class Reset. The only real difference is that Do it Again assumes that if you simply ask them to do it again they will reset themselves without much guidance. That doesn't feel like the case anymore, which lands us on the following action step for Sophie:

---

## Case Study #2: Action Step

**Whole class reset:** implement a planned whole class reset for classroom entry;

- Use a warm-demander register: a warm but firm register, including tone and word choice.
- Issue clear What to Do directions ("Everyone in a line. All eyes on me. As you enter, you need to do three things: 1. Enter silently. 2. Immediately take your seat. 3. Work on your Do Now until the timer sounds.")
- Narrate the positive: 1–2 students who are doing it.
- Every third student greeted: Look around the room to see that they are following directions.

---

How did my thought process compare to yours? If you found yourself struggling to get to the same action step, here's a tip for you: think like a waterfall. Flow from top to bottom of the Get Better Faster Sequence until you locate the first major struggle and stop there—that's the action step.

> ## Core Idea
> When picking an action step, think of a waterfall.
> Start from the top, and stop when you hit the first major growth area.

Look more closely at Sophie's action step. What do you notice about it?

- It takes the language of the action steps in the Scope and Sequence and tailors it to Sophie's specific needs.
- It is cumulative: It remains centered on the whole class reset (Action Step 8) but includes elements from previous action steps Sophie has already worked on and

Principles of Coaching    **41**

been proficient in other settings (in this case, What to Do directions and Circulating with Purpose). Just as a piano players will keep practicing their posture, hand location, and chords with each new thing they learn, so too the teacher will continue to practice earlier action steps as she learns new ones.

- It remains bite-sized: Sophie could clearly practice and implement this immediately, mastering it in the upcoming week. This is the heart of building an effective action step.

As you work to identify the right action step, keep the following in mind:

- The Get Better Faster Scope and Sequence was written in priority order. Keep the waterfall image in mind: Start from the beginning, and stop when you hit the area where the teacher is starting to struggle.
- The action steps in the Scope and Sequence are written generally for any teacher. You should adapt them to even more specifically target the teacher in question.
- What makes an action bite-sized in not the number of words but whether or not you can accomplish it in one week. Sometimes, being more detailed adds clarity and precision.

Now that you've taken a crack at management, let's try rigor. For some, this will be easier; for others, harder. Let's give it a try!

**Putting It into Practice—Case Study #3**

## Case Study #3: Rigor

Edgar walks into Justine's geometry class at a moment of independent practice: They are working on a problem set on linear equations. As Edgar reviews the handout, the questions are strong and are aligned to the end-of-year assessment, particularly the later questions in the problem set. As he observes, he notices that Justine is crouched down by a student's desk to review his work. As Edgar leans in to listen to the conversation, he can tell that Justine has a great sense of the ideal answers she is looking for with each question. While she remains working with this student for a few minutes, Justine makes sure to look up periodically and scan the room to make sure students are working. While she occasionally redirects a student to get back to work, the students are largely on-task. The student she is working with is struggling: She coaches him through a problem step-by-step.

As she continues working with the student, Edgar begins to walk around the classroom. Most students have questions one to five correct. Their struggles begin with questions six through eight. A few students raise their hands to ask for help but Justine signals to them to keep working. Eventually after a few more minutes she moves onto another student to provide support.

Justine gets to two more students before the timer goes off, signaling the end of work time.

"Great focus today, class—you stayed working the whole time!" she affirms. "Let's review the work. Let's start with number one. What is the solution to this linear equation?"

Many hands go up. Justine calls on one who raised their hand, and that student begins to walk through his thinking and final answer. The class nods in agreement.

"Great," Justine says. "Who can explain number two?" More hands go up and she calls on another raised hand.

Justine continues to work her way through the assignment. The bell rings as she begins to go over number five. She tells students they will finish their review tomorrow and asks them to write down their homework.

---

Referring to your Scope and Sequence and remembering the tips from the previous case study, write down your action step. Again, start from the top and stop where the first major error occurs.

---

### Stop and Jot: Case Study #3

Write down the bite-sized action steps you would give to Justine to improve her teaching:

_____

_____

_____

_____

**Stop Here**

Turn the page only **after** you've drafted your action step!

As we look at this case study, so many things are going well for Justine. Students are fully engaged, and they remain working even during extended independent practice, which is a clear sign that her management routines and procedures are on point. So,

Principles of Coaching    43

we can shift to the rigor section, starting from the top of the sequence. If we look at Phase 1, she seems to have proficiency: She has a quality objective aligned to her upcoming assessments and a quality task that is also aligned (Step 1 and 2). She is using a timer to pace herself (Step 3). She understands what she is looking for in student responses (Step 4). Moving forward to Phase 2, independent practice is well set up, with an appropriate amount of time and on-task behavior (Step 5). Students seem excited and ready to share their thinking, and Justine calls on different students during the review (Step 7). However, she doesn't use a turn and talk and only calls on raised hands, so launching class discussion (Step 7) could still be a key action step. Or you might even jump to the discourse action steps later in the sequence (Steps 10–12). Given that the student she is working with is struggling, you might also focus on activating knowledge or modeling (Steps 8 and 9). She ran out of time to get to questions six through eight, where the struggle really occurred. As a result, you could be tempted to choose pacing (Step 12).

Yet jumping to these later action steps would miss a crucial point: She didn't realize where students were struggling with their work. By reviewing questions 1–5—which students largely mastered—she spent most of the class on what students needed the least. But she didn't know what they were struggling with because she didn't look at more than a few students' work.

Justine didn't see the student gap, and until you can see it, you cannot address it. You can't correct what you don't detect.

> ### Core Idea
>
> You can't correct what you don't detect.

Because she only looked at a few students' work during independent practice, she had no idea that the majority of the class already showed mastery of several concepts. If she had walked around the room and paid attention to more students, she could have seen their errors and coached them in the moment. She also could have diagnosed the class's struggles and targeted the discussion to address it.

Knowing what students get and don't get is key to successful, responsive instruction. And the best way to build that awareness is by monitoring student work.

By targeting the root cause of the problem—where it began—we landed on the following top action step:

## Case Study #3: Action Step

**Phase 2—Academic Monitoring:** Check students' independent work to determine whether they're learning what you're teaching.

- Create a monitoring pathway:
  - Name the lap: Announce what you will be looking for and how you will give feedback.
  - Monitor the fastest writers first, then the students who need more support.
- Pen in hand: Give written feedback to student work
  - Compare answers to the exemplar. What are they missing?
  - Give quick feedback (star, circle, pre-established code).
  - Cue students to revise answers, using minimal verbal intervention.
- Gather data while monitoring and prepare to respond
  - Track student responses: ideal, almost there, further off.
  - Determine how to respond: Stop the class for a quick fix, activate knowledge, model, or discourse.

---

Did you come up with a similar action step? If so, congratulations! If not, here are some final takeaways that could help:

- If we go in order from top to bottom (the waterfall approach), academic monitoring (Step 6) is the first area of error. If you chose an aspect of discourse or pacing, you are right that this is a key area! But if we don't get monitoring right first, we won't be giving students what they need. Use the order of the sequence to your advantage.

- Every one of us has "go-to" areas of instruction that we are naturally drawn to giving feedback. Because of this, we have also become quite adept at giving feedback in these areas. Yet these areas are not always the highest-leverage for that teacher. Using the Get Better Faster Scope and Sequence can open our horizons to giving feedback about other areas of instruction that normally haven't been our forte, and in turn, that develops our expertise to serve even more teachers.

Continue to sharpen your skills with the following case study. Keep in mind the final takeaways from Case Study 3. Use the waterfall method to help you identify the highest-leverage action step.

Principles of Coaching    **45**

**Putting It into Practice—Case Study #4**

For this case study, you need some context on what is happening in the lesson. The students in Roger's high school English class have just begun Nobel Prize winner Toni Morrison's novel *The Bluest Eye*. The opening of the novel is quite provocative. It takes the text of the *Dick and Jane* early reading series that was popular in the early 20th century and displays it three times: first with its original punctuation, second with the punctuation and capitalization removed, and third without spacing, punctuation or capitalization. The words all run together and look like this:

> Hereisthehouseitisgreenandwhiteithasareddooritisveryprettyhereist
> hefamilymotherfatherdickandjaneliveinthegreenandwhitehousethey
> areveryhappyseejanehasareddressshewantstoplaywhowillplaywithj
> aneseethecatitgoesmeowmeowcomeandplaythekittenwillnotplaysee
> mothermotherisverynicemotherwillyouplaywithjanelaughmotherla
> ughseefatherheisbigandstrongfatherwillyouplaywithjanefatherissmi
> lingsmilefathersmileseethedogitgoesbowwowlooklookherecomesaf
> riendthefriendwillplaywithjanetheywillplaygoodgamejaneplay.[3]

This opening has received substantial literary analysis over the years, where a common understanding is that Morrison is setting up the juxtaposition of the American Dream and the purported ideal family of the 1940s (Dick and Jane, blond-haired, blue eyed brother and sister) against the struggles and experiences of Black families that are central to the rest of the novel.

Roger has already launched the unit by sharing background knowledge about Morrison and the setting of the story— segregated 1940s Ohio. In today's conversation, Roger wants students to discuss Morrison's use and manipulation of the Dick and Jane text.

Maria, his principal, gets ready to observe the lesson.

---

## Case Study #4: Rigor

As Maria walks into the class, students have already begun reading the foreword to *The Bluest Eye*. Students mark up the passage in the first 10 minutes of class and jot a short response to the opening prompt, "What is Morrison conveying with the repetition of the Dick and Jane text?"

As Roger walks around, he notices that students have pretty superficial responses. He prompts them to go deeper in their analysis. He leans in with a few students and says, "But why do you think she removes the punctuation and then word spacing? Go deeper in answering that question." After seeing a pattern of this limited answer, he stops the class and repeats the prompt to go deeper and sends them back to work.

After 10 minutes, his timer goes off. "Ok, class. So, this is a pretty challenging text to analyze. Let's talk it through together. Turn and talk: What is Morrison conveying with the repetition of the Dick and Jane text?" Roger calls on Tim to start the conversation.

Tim says, "Morrison grew up during the same time in the 1940s, so maybe this is like what she remembers of learning how to read. She's referring to her own experience."

Roger nods, "Well, that's definitely part of it. Let's stick with part of your answer—learning how to read. Dick and Jane were common characters in a book series for young readers at that time. What do you all think about?"

Students stare at him blankly. After a lengthy silence, Roger calls on Ariana.

Ariana says, "They sound like old names, and we know the novel is happening in the past. Dick and Jane are young like Pecola (a central character). Maybe this is foreshadowing what Pecola will do in the book."

"Ok," Roger furrows his brow. "And what about their family?"

There is another long pause. A few students flip through the pages of the novel, looking for additional information that might help. Other students shoot quick glances at each other. Roger spends the next few minutes struggling to get students to pull a deeper meaning out of the foreword. After seeing them get frustrated, Roger leans in and gives them his own analysis: "What Morrison is doing is critiquing the vision for the American Dream. . . ."

Students take notes as he offers a deep analysis of the passage.

---

Use the Get Better Faster Scope and Sequence to decide on your action step.

## Stop and Jot: Case Study #4

Write down the bite-sized action steps you would give to Roger to improve his teaching:

Principles of Coaching  **47**

Roger is certainly doing many things right. Students are reading a challenging text, and his discourse question is a fruitful one. He is academically monitoring and prompting students to go deeper, and he sees the gaps in their analysis. He's trying to get them to do the thinking, but they are struggling. Where to focus?

The trouble lies in the preparation for the conversation. The students have no reference point for who Dick and Jane are—they don't have any image of the text nor understanding of their seminal role in reading in the 1940s. Without that knowledge, they cannot go deeper.

My colleague Art Worrell and I explore this idea at length in *Make History: A Practical Guide for Middle and High School History Instruction*.[4] Students in all content areas benefit when teachers strategically build knowledge. Analysis is not created in a vacuum; students need something substantive to think about in order to think more deeply.[5] Students simply cannot go further without more information!

The right knowledge at the right time is a powerful tool.

---

### Core Idea

The right knowledge at the right time is a powerful tool.

---

This leads us to the following action step:

### Case Study Action Step

**Activate Knowledge:** Prompt students to access their knowledge

- Point students to resources (word wall, notes, texts)
- "What do we know about __?"
- Use a knowledge organizer[6] (cheat sheet)—all key points on 1–2 pages
- Retrieve knowledge by applying it—give a simple task (e.g., organize events in chronological order, quick math fluency)
- "Drop" knowledge:
  - Give them knowledge in the middle of the lesson when it will unlock understanding (e.g., stating definition of a vocabulary word that cannot be understood with context)

Imagine if Roger had provided students with the following context before the discussion. How might it have changed the discussion?

> Dick and Jane are two siblings who are the main characters in an easy reader series about a family in the mid-1900s. This series represented the commonly held idea of the time of what a "perfect family" looked like: a cheerful white family with a mother and father, two kids, a pet dog, and a white picket fence. Children of all races growing up during that time often learned to read using these books. [Then show them pictures from the book so that they can see what Dick and Jane look like and their context.]

This is the power of activating knowledge—either planning for it in advance or "dropping knowledge" at the moment that you realize a knowledge gap. This additional context could have changed the game because it would have prepared students to read and talk about the text with more thoughtful analysis.

If you also identified Activate Knowledge as Roger's area of focus, kudos! You are well on your way to using the GBF Scope and Sequence to select the highest-leverage, bite-sized action step for your teachers. If you selected a different action step, look for potential gaps in your analysis. How could the waterfall method close those gaps?

## Conclusion

Just like teaching, coaching is also a set of skills that are built over time and with practice. Figuring out the right feedback to give at the right time is crucial to our success with teachers. Going bite-sized with our action steps can be a significant change if we are used to whole evaluation observations. Yet the smaller and more precise we go with our action step, the quicker the growth. And the most effective coaches take it a step further: they narrow their focus to the highest-leverage action step.

---

### Core Idea

The smaller and more precise the action step, the quicker the growth. The most effective coaches narrow their focus to the highest-leverage action step.

---

Principles of Coaching

### Findings from the Field: Use the GBF Sequence to Make It Clear

"It has taken me a while to realize that simpler and clearer is always better. Rather than try to wordsmith a very specific action step—and spending hours doing so—I just reach for my tool (The Get Better Faster Sequence of Action Steps). The 'how' of each action step clearly lays out how to do it. In using it, I create a more bite-sized action step, and even more valuable, a narrower focus for practice."
*—Scott Schuster, Principal, Brooklyn, NY*

There's no doubt that at first this change will feel like moving at a glacial pace. That was certainly the case with NASA's JWST: It took several months before the telescope sent back its first images. But somehow, what began with a slow start produces within months something extraordinary: a crystal-clear image of possibility.

Once you've identified the right action step, you've won half the battle. The second half is guiding a teacher to mastery of it. That's covered by the next principle.

### Final Reflection: Make It Bite-Sized

What are your biggest takeaways for identifying the right action step for a teacher?

_____

_____

_____

What action steps from the Scope and Sequence would most enhance your repertoire and make you better at giving feedback?

_____

_____

_____

Think of a new teacher you've worked with recently and an area in which that teacher struggled. What would be an effective series of action steps for that teacher?

_____

_____

_____

_____

## PRINCIPLE 2: PRACTICE WHAT YOU VALUE

My son Nico's greatest passion in high school was robotics. As a member of his school's robotics team, he and his teammates spent hours learning how to build and program robots. Their objective? To perform well in the FIRST (For Inspiration and Recognition of Science and Technology) Robotics Competition. The yearly competition draws more than 80,000 aspiring high school students from around the world and each year offers a unique challenge. Over the course of just a few months, each team builds a robot from scratch and programs it to meet the goals of the challenge. These hand-built robots are impressive: They can pick up and throw rings at high velocity to hit small targets, climb chains, and fend off opposing robots from doing the same. If you've never seen a FIRST competition, check them out—it is pretty inspiring!

But what's arguably most valuable about the experience is how often the robots break. The mechanical arm refuses to lower, or the motor that propels the robot forward fails. Hundreds and often thousands of pieces have to work properly for a robot to function—a single error can freeze it in its tracks.

The action step to fix it is seemingly simple: Take it apart, identify the problem, and try again. Nico quickly learned that each time the robot broke was an opportunity to perfect one more thing about it.

The real victory of every competitor was the work done outside the ring of competition. It was the practice of fixing, adjusting, and improving the robot that was the magic, much more than the moment of competition itself.

When you care about something as much as Nico cares about robotics, you practice it: diligently and consistently. If you love something, you'll spend hours in the pit. Sometimes you'll succeed; often you'll fail. And with every mistake, you learn a little more.

Principles of Coaching **51**

Nico spent hours fixing the robot because he valued it. And he became better at building robots because of how he spent his time. Just like a medical student learning to suture a wound, Nico made his practice specific. He diagnosed the problem. Corrected it. Then he tried again. That is the heart of meaningful practice: understanding what moves make the difference and practicing these repeatedly until you can't get them wrong. What we practice is what we value.

---

### Core Idea

What we practice is what we value.

---

In every field, the more effectively we practice, the better we perform. And what works for robotics engineers and doctors also works for teachers. In the case of teaching, the Get Better Faster Scope and Sequence provides the skills of getting better at teaching; practicing is the way to learn them faster.

The complexity of building a robot is clear. But what does it take to diagnose and develop a teacher?

When Jade walked into Jaz's office, he didn't know how to systematically look for the behaviors he wanted to see. When he walked out, he had practiced multiple times and was more prepared than ever to implement that skill in the classroom. Jaz built up his expertise outside the classroom, and that meant he had it ready to use when it counted most.

What Jaz and Jade proved—that teachers can grow dramatically by practicing outside the classroom—gets at the heart of transforming the dangerous myth that teachers cannot become great in any fewer than 10 years.[7] At the root of this myth is the assumption that teachers learn primarily—or even exclusively—from experience. And while experience is indeed a great teacher, we cannot afford to accept the premise that the process of becoming a master is impossible to accelerate. The new teachers of the most effective leaders didn't have to wait 10 years because their leaders lived by a simple mantra that has been repeated since the early 1900s: practice until you cannot get it wrong.[8]

---

### Core Idea

Contenders practice until they get it right;
champions practice until they cannot get it wrong.

---

So, what separates the practice of contenders from those of champions? There are a few basic principles Jaz used that made his practice effective. You can emulate them:

- **Define "perfect"**—name the what and the how of the skill.

- **Perfect your plan**—build an effective plan before you take it live.

- **Practice**—take it live.

- **Follow-up and repeat**—observe implementation to make sure the action is performed as flawlessly for the students as it is behind the scenes.

## Define "Perfect": Name the What

Imagine a swimming instructor who tells her students that today, they're going to learn how to do a basic flutter kick (the classic kick that accompanies front crawl strokes). She hands everyone a kickboard and stands at the edge of the pool. "Okay, kids," she says, with no further introduction. "Let's go! Show me your best kick!"

What followed would not truly be practice. It would get students into the water with their kickboards, but they wouldn't know what to do when they got there. There would be a lot of splashing in the pool but probably not much learning. That's the equivalent of assigning homework to students that they don't know how to do. They're just going to practice getting it wrong.

Now imagine that instead, the instructor has every child lie on their side outside the pool. "Bend your knees slightly," she might say, "like when you walk. Now separate your legs like scissors: one leg forward and the other leg back. Switch legs—the other one up and down. Now move them back and forth in quick strokes: keep cutting paper with your scissor legs. Kick hard when you kick down, and soft when you kick up!" She could walk around and correct the movements of students who are struggling. By the time the students actually get in the water, they've already improved their strokes and greatly increased their likelihood of success. The difference is night and day for many important reasons. One of the first reasons is that the coach knew exactly what she was looking for. Without a vision of the basic flutter kick, she could not have gotten her students to practice what mattered.

> ## Core Idea
> You can't make practice perfect until you define what "perfect" looks like.

Principles of Coaching    **53**

Think back to some of the action steps you read or designed in the previous section. When your action steps are observable and practice-able, high-leverage, bite-sized, they specify exactly what needs to be perfected—but the task of defining each component of "perfect" remains.

Defining "perfect" breaks down the action step to make it specific to the teacher's classroom. It paints the picture of success. Armed with a clear, shared vision, Jaz can target Jade's practice where it's most needed—on what keeps him from making the vision his own. Rather than asking teachers to practice anything (or everything), transformative coaches like Jaz use what teachers need to guide their decision making. The practice he selects solves for where they struggle.

> ### Core Idea
> Plan what teachers need, not what they already know.

Planning perfect works for both management and rigor—even if it's designing a lesson plan, the action step must always be practice-able. If not, teachers won't build the muscle memory. Think back to the earlier video where Erica leads a PD on bite-sized directions. How does Erica define perfect to make it practice-able?

 WATCH Clip 2: **What to Do Directions**
(Key Leadership Skill: See it)

Take a moment to practice this idea:

### Stop and Jot: Define "Perfect"

Choose one of the action steps you wrote or read earlier in this principle. Pick one of the teachers you will work with: imagine their classroom setting and context. What exactly would the teacher and their students have to be doing for this action step to be accomplished? Use the Scope and Sequence to define "perfect" for this action step.

Action Step:

_____

_____

_____

What would "perfect" look like? What is the teacher doing?

_____

_____

_____

What are the students doing?

_____

_____

_____

## Plan Before You Practice

Once you have a clear vision of what perfect looks like, the next step is to make sure your teacher has that same vision *before* starting to practice. It's easy to overlook this step, yet doing so is the number one factor that leads to ineffective practice.

Imagine that your 6th-grade math teacher is working on giving written feedback to student work (Phase 2—Academic Monitoring: Give written feedback to student work). You state the action step and then you say to your teacher, "Let's practice." The teacher stands before a row of desks with blank worksheets. She walks by each, stopping to scratch a quick check mark or question mark on each paper. Sounds effective, right?

Yet here is the problem: The hard part of monitoring is not writing down a piece of feedback. It's identifying what students got right, naming the missing knowledge or skill, and giving aligned feedback—all in fewer than 30 seconds. You can't practice a habit like that without having student work in hand.

Imagine that same teacher, and this time build a plan for practice. Review an upcoming set of problems together. Instead of speaking generally about types of feedback to provide, identify which problems teachers will review as they walk around.

Principles of Coaching    55

Think through the possible incorrect answers and the prompts to give at each moment for each type of error.

The problem set follows. Note the teacher's annotations.

## Sample Plan, Part 2: Academic Monitoring

Annotated student handout:

1) In Josie's garden, the ratio of zinnias to petunias is (5)(3). Which sentence correctly describes the ratio?   — wrong order   $5 + 3 = 8$ total
   a. For every 3 zinnias, there are 5 petunias.
   b. For every 8 petunias, there are 5 zinnias.
   c. For every 3 petunias, there are 8 zinnias.
   d.) For every 5 zinnias, there are 3 petunias.   Z : P   5 : 3 ✓

2) This table shows the number of books, by type, checked out from the school library on Monday.

   **Book Checkout**

   | Book Type | Number of Books |
   |---|---|
   | Mystery | 24 |
   | Nonfiction | 18 |
   | Adventure | 12 |
   | Humor | 16 |

   What is the ratio of mystery books checked out to nonfiction books checked out?
   M                      N
   a. 12 to 24          c. 12 to 16          M : N
   b. 24 to 12          d.) 24 to 18         24 : 18

3) Arnold's entire workout consisted of 10 minutes of warm-up exercises, 25 minutes of lifting weights, and 15 minutes on the treadmill. What was the ratio of the number of minutes he lifted weights to the total number of minutes of his entire workout?
   W                                                    L
                                     total    T
   a. 10:25:15
   b. 25:15
   c.) 25:50        L : total      10
   d. 50:10         25 : 50      + 25
                                 + 15
                                 ——
                                  50

Get Better Faster 2.0

The teacher drafts prompts to respond to students' conceptual errors.

## Sample Plan, Part 2: Academic Monitoring

**Key prompts to use while monitoring student work:**

| Anticipated Error | Prompts |
|---|---|
| Switches the order of the ratio | • Go back to the text and mark it up.<br>• What are the quantities in this scenario? Label them with an abbreviation.<br>• In what order should we write our ratio? |
| Does not add to find total | • What kind of ratio is this example asking for—a part to part or a part to total?<br>• What additional step should we take to find a part to total ratio? |
| When given more than two parts, chooses the wrong two quantities to represent a part-to-part ratio | • You have a lot of information in this problem.<br>• How many quantities are involved in this scenario?<br>• And how many quantities are you being asked for in the ratio you need to write?<br>• Choose carefully! Label your quantities with abbreviations to see if that helps you. |

What just happened? You dramatically accelerated the teacher's ability to respond to student errors in the moment *before* she entered the classroom.

By creating a plan, you created a vision for the teacher of what the class could look like before she even experiences it in practice. In doing so, you increase the odds of the teacher practicing—and teaching—successfully. To make practice meaningful, perfect the plan before you practice.

---

### Core Idea

Perfect the plan before you practice: You cannot practice well unless you know where you're headed.

---

Principles of Coaching    57

This process is no different than that of planning great lessons. Grant Wiggins and Jay McTighe are among the many pioneers who highlight the importance of "backward planning": starting with your objective (the what) for what students will be able to do at the end of the lesson, and working backward to plan a lesson that will get you there (the how).[9] Planning how to coach a teacher on a skill is similar.

---

### Findings from the Field: Don't Wing It—Perfect the Plan

"When I began filming myself leading feedback meetings with my teachers, I realized I talked too much and didn't ensure that the teacher left with a solidified plan they could implement. Now I tell myself (and all my leaders): Script, script, and script! Perfect your plan—as leaders we owe that to the principals and teachers we are privileged to coach! Just a few minutes spent planning during a coaching meeting offers hours of better learning. Invest in revising the plan for practicing, and it will pay great dividends—what you practice is what you value."
—Herminder Channa, Principal Supervisor, Birmingham, England, UK

---

Defining perfect is identifying your destination, and this next piece of the puzzle—planning how the teacher will practice it—is mapping the route there. Trennis Harvey does just that when working with his teacher on academic monitoring. Watch what he does to get his teacher ready to practice:

 WATCH Clip 3: **Academic Monitoring—Pen in Hand**
(Key Leadership Move: Do it)

Here are the most important keys that make Trennis's—and anyone's—planning effective:

- **Give time for it.** We most often skip planning because we don't think we have time for it. Yet there is no better time spent in a meeting than planning! Trennis knows this, so he makes sure the rest of the meeting is short enough to give time for it. Moreover, a fascinating thing happens with coaching: If you don't give time for planning, you spend double the time when practicing in fixing the errors. As counter-intuitive as it might seem, giving planning time ends up saving you time.

- **Spar rather than lecture.** During planning time (or ahead of time), write your own version of the plan. Then when the time is up, you and the teacher can put your plans side by side and pull the best from each. This keeps you from "lecturing" in giving feedback and puts the ratio wholly on the teacher to improve their plan.
- **Fix it before you practice.** Trennis knows that any new action step is hard, so he makes sure to lock in the revisions to the plan before practice. It also removes work from the teacher's plate and let's them walk out with a baked plan.

By locking in these elements before live practice, your teacher is so much more likely to succeed!

---

### Stop and Jot: Plan Before You Practice

Plan how you'd practice the skill for which you defined practice earlier, including challenges.

_____

_____

_____

## Practice: "Let's Take It Live"

Once you have your plan for success in place, it's time to take it live!

Na'Jee Carter and his elementary school teacher are working on an upcoming literacy plan. She has noticed that the class has a limited understanding of character motivation. After scripting a few targeted prompts using an upcoming text, Na'Jee cues her to practice:

 WATCH Clip 4: **Academic Monitoring—Gather Data** (Key Leadership Moves: Do it)

Principles of Coaching 59

Let's break down what Na'Jee does to make practice sessions effective.

- **Just do it.** The point bears repeating: For practice to be powerful, the teacher has to do what she will have to do during class. If the teacher being coached had played the part of the students, or if she and the coach had both just discussed what she would have to do instead of physically doing it, she would not have learned what she needed to learn. She might have been mentally prepared to implement the action step, but the precise goal of practice is for the teacher to build muscle memory: experiencing what it feels like to implement successfully.

- **Practice the gap.** All practice is powerful, but practicing where we want to get better is where the transformation occurs. Practicing the gap is just that—it addresses the most challenging barrier to doing it perfectly. Devote the bulk of time to practicing the specific moves that make the action step difficult for the teacher. In the second round of practice, Na'Jee prompted her to use a universal prompt, "What in the text makes you say that?" when students give a limited answer. Using a prompt like this, instead of asking a leading question or repeating the question, encourages the students to go back into the text to justify their response. This keeps the cognitive lift on the students and expands the types of support that she can now lend to her students. In doing so, Na'Jee tailored the practice to exactly what the teacher needs.

---

### Core Idea

Practice the gap to make practice permanent.

---

### Findings from the Field: Practice Perfect

"The quality of teaching changed in my school when we began to practice. We could work out the kinks prior to students being there. Just like actors rehearse before a show, practice jumpstarts a teacher's development. Let them see the model, and then let them do it—that's all it takes."

—*Ritu Pasricha, Principal, Pune, India*

- **Practice perfect—add complexity piece by piece.** Once a teachers have built a solid level of comfort with a new skill, deepen it with more complex practice. If the practice becomes imperfect, stop the teachers and have them began again. We want teachers to practice what to do the right way. Practice makes permanent.

- **Lock it in.** Whenever you finish practice, take a moment to reflect on what just happened. If you finally succeed with a new recipe that you've struggled with but don't write down what made the difference, you'll forget how you succeeded the next time. Take a moment to reflect on what made the teachers more successful and what to remember when they teach. There is a beautiful moment at the end of Na'Jee's debrief where the teacher reflects on her growth in this practice and how she will apply it to lessons moving forward. A simple moment like this solidifies the learning—locking it in—and making it more likely to translate to the classroom. It's this deep internalization that ultimately makes practice the game-changing tool it is.

Practice is powerful—and it can change the culture of your school and the trajectory of your teachers.

> ### Core Idea
> To make teaching effective, plan before you practice,
> and practice before you teach.

## Follow Up and Repeat: Lock in Success

To ensure the teacher effectively implements the plan you've made together, follow-up is essential. Simply look specifically for successful implementation of this skill the next time you observe the teacher, and let the teacher know what you've seen the next time you meet with them. Areas in which the teacher is successfully implementing the skill can become sources of precise praise; any spots that are still a challenge for the teacher can be practiced over again.

Let's revisit Trennis's feedback meeting again to note what happens at the close of his meeting.

 WATCH Clip 3: **Academic Monitoring—Pen in Hand**
(Key Leadership Move: Do it)

Principles of Coaching **61**

What makes this clip remarkable are the small, seemingly unremarkable things that lock in the learning. In just a few minutes at the end of the meeting, Trennis ensures greater likelihood of implementation:

- **Set dates.** Trennis's simple question of asking when he could observe his teacher's implementation sends a powerful message: He cares about her success, and he expects these actions to be implemented. Effective leaders choose the date to check in on completed materials and/or schedule the next observation. Have both coach and teacher write these down to ensure follow-up. I have seen school leaders take it even a step further with a teacher who is struggling with time and task management (as many of us do in the start of our teaching careers). Kelly Dowling, a school leader in Newark, NJ, has her teacher open up their Outlook and place the tasks in the prep periods that they have during the week. "This helps them see that it is doable," she says, "and also makes them more focused during their prep." (We discuss task lists and timelines in more detail in the Phase 2 Coaching Blueprint Section, "Set the Tone: The First Feedback Meeting.")

- **Plan for real-time feedback.** Agree on a pre-determined cue for the next observation. For Trennis, it was holding up one finger to signal to the teacher to gather and look at the student data. We'll explain additional cues in "Principle 3: Give Feedback Frequently" of the Principles of Coaching (next up!).

- **Lock in the tasks.** One of the hardest things for a newer teacher—or any educator for that matter!—is to remember all of the tasks that have to be accomplished. For a teacher who is still developing their time and task management skills, rather than leave this to chance, have the teacher write down the tasks right in their agenda or planner.

Follow-up is the natural segue into your next cycle of practice. Hold on to what the teacher did well and build upon that in practicing and mastering the next action step. The result is an ongoing cycle of growth, with each piece of the foundation you're building firmly in place before the next is cemented on top of it.

## Conclusion

When a challenge arises, the person you want on the scene to help is the person who's already been prepared to manage it. This is why the power of practice in PD cannot be overstated. Practicing relentlessly before you need to use your skills is the key to guaranteeing they'll be ready for you when you do need them. If you want to *hope* to overcome a massive challenge, trusting an unfamiliar miracle to see you through certainly works sometimes. But if you want to *guarantee* triumph, practicing to perfection leaves little to chance.

We've now covered two of the core coaching tools that leaders must harness to get teachers better faster: bite-sized action steps that give teachers clear knowledge of what to do and opportunities to practice those actions outside the classroom so that they can put them to work inside it. Now we move on to the third and last coaching technique we'll present in detail: giving feedback more frequently.

----

### Stop and Jot: Practice What You Value

Look back at your earlier Stop and Jots and select one of the action steps you designed.

Step 1 (Plan): What planning could you do with the teacher to set up the practice to be effective? Write out the script, task, and/or exemplar:

_____

_____

_____

Step 2 (Practice): What is the most important part of the practice with which the teacher will likely struggle?

_____

_____

_____

Step 3 (Follow-up): What are the key follow-up tasks you and the teacher should do to lock in the learning?

_____

_____

_____

## PRINCIPLE 3: GIVE FEEDBACK FREQUENTLY

Long before my wife Gabriela (Gaby for short) became the doctor she is today, she went through a residency in Internal Medicine. One of the things she learned during residency is how to insert a central line. This is a common medical procedure in which a thin tube is placed in a large vein in the upper body to deliver fluids, blood, or medication to a patient. Although it is a fairly common procedure, inserting a line is not without risk. Complications can trigger a medical emergency.

Gaby remembers vividly the first time she had to insert a central line. She was incredibly nervous. She didn't want to damage the vein in the patient's neck or bruise the surrounding area. Her attending physician stood nearby. Throughout the procedure, Gaby kept looking his way for guidance. "Am I doing it right?" she asked.

"Just go ahead," he answered, arms folded across his chest.

About a minute or so into the procedure, Gaby began to notice some bleeding. She kept looking to him for help, but the attending was silent. She soldiered on, heart thumping in her ears. The bleeding picked up, and the attendant abruptly stepped in to take over. As she walked out of the room, Gaby felt completely defeated.

A few days later when she had to do it again, she was a nervous wreck. But she had a different attending physician. "I'm really nervous," she said. "Don't worry," he said. "I'll walk you through it." Step-by-step, he talked her through the procedure and gave her small pieces of feedback to refine her technique: "Hold your elbow steady." "Enter at a higher angle." Gaby followed his advice, step-by-step, and placed the central line successfully. She was relieved and elated—and she knew exactly what to do for the next one.

Each case had similarly trained physician who were experts at their craft, yet Gaby had two vastly different outcomes. One destroyed her confidence and left her without improvement, and the other not only solidified the skill but bolstered her confidence. What made the difference? Real-time feedback. By stepping in and coaching in the moment, the second doctor gave Gaby the precise feedback she needed, and as a result, she got better faster.

---

### Core Idea

The more frequent the feedback, the quicker the growth.

---

So, I ask you: which doctor would you want training your general practitioner? And which resident would you want performing an operation on your loved one? And if that's what you want for your care, why wouldn't you want the same for your teachers? New teachers are not very different from hospital residents: They are green and yet immediately have to work with actual people. While the impacts in the classroom may not be as significant as the life-and-death circumstances of a doctor, the stakes are still high for our children, and more effective coaching can make the difference. To attest to this, Ross, Bennett, and others have shown that academic achievement increased for students whose teachers were coached more frequently.[10]

What would happen if we gave teachers feedback far more frequently, stepping in when needed with a new teacher, just like we expect doctors to do for residents? We would not only improve learning in the moment, but we would also accelerate a teacher's growth.[11]

---

### Core Idea

Follow the doctor's lead: accelerate learning with real-time feedback.

---

In today's education landscape, however, the frequent and real-time feedback that we assume is essential for surgeons is often missing or even taboo. Just prioritizing more frequent feedback is challenging (we address that further and in more detail in the Phase 2 Coaching Blueprint). More notably, there is an unspoken rule that when instruction is under way, a school leader's role should be that of a silent observer at most—that there's something untouchable, even sacred, about that moment when a teacher steps to the front of the classroom. The rule is rooted in a genuine risk: Real-time feedback done poorly can undermine the teacher's authority or reduce their sense of leadership within the classroom.

Real-time feedback done well, however, can take the best of medical practice and help teachers get better. This is essential precisely because there *is* something sacred about class time: the intellectual lives of the students. If we see something going wrong during a lesson that is hurting student learning, we do both those students and their teacher a disservice by not correcting it before the students lose valuable learning time. When we leave real-time feedback out of the picture, important learning moments are lost for students and teachers alike. Just as we would fear might happen with a surgeon, teachers who are never given real-time feedback runs a risk of not performing their job properly at a critical time—and repeating that mistake multiple times in the future. The person whose life has been entrusted to the teacher may suffer as a result. What begins

Principles of Coaching **65**

as well-intentioned respect for teachers' ownership of their own classrooms ends by deprioritizing the primary goal of education: students' learning.

The leaders who excel at quickly developing teachers prioritize student learning in the moment by improving teaching *as it happens*—and do so without undermining the teacher. Teachers can then incorporate those improvements into their practice for many hours to come, continuing to reach more students more effectively long after the leader who first delivered the feedback has left the room.

For a baseline idea of how real-time feedback can drive instruction to the next level without challenging the teacher's leadership, watch Art Worrell in action.

 WATCH Clip 5: **Stretch It—Sophisticate**
(Key Leadership Move: Real-time Feedback)

## Stop and Jot: Real-Time Feedback

What did Art do to model for the teacher as seamlessly as possible? Jot down the actions you saw him take.

_____

_____

_____

Art takes on the role of the teacher nonintrusively by first taking on the role of student. He follows all the same protocols his teacher's students have to follow when they wish to participate in class: He raises his hand and then asks permission. When the teacher affirms that Art could ask the class a question in that moment, Art explicitly addresses the students as a fellow participant, rather than giving the teacher directives in front of them. This means that for the entire time Art is modeling, the teacher retains control of his classroom.

Modeling has the added benefit of allowing teachers to see in the moment exactly what they could have done. Many of the new teachers we have interviewed have called this the best part of all their PD. Once they see a master teacher model for them with their own students, they start to believe more in what is possible for them to do. It may feel awkward at first, but the payoff of respectful modeling—both in the moment you do it and in the teacher's career for years to come—is immense. This is the power of real-time feedback: It facilitates the growth of students and teachers simultaneously. It puts the improvement process on fast-forward, making changes immediately that would otherwise take days or weeks for a teacher to implement.

To be sure, reaping the rich rewards of real-time feedback—especially when so many teachers are so unused to it—requires a careful touch. This section will cover every essential step of making real-time feedback not only effective but respectful to all within a school community. These steps are:

- **Prepare the surgical room—create a culture of real-time feedback.** In order for real-time feedback to work, leaders must be transparent about it—and teachers must anticipate it. Introduce the new culture, then give feedback regularly and consistently to bring it to life.

- **Pick the right moment.** Select the right time to deliver real-time feedback that will most leverage student and teacher development.

- **Deliver the feedback—with the least invasive approach.** Deliver real-time feedback quickly, clearly, and as non-invasively as possible (just like surgery!).

- **Close the loop.** Stick with it until they get it, debrief the moment of real-time feedback to identify what made the new teaching practice effective.

## Create a Culture

There are two major components of creating a culture of feedback:

1. Roll it out

2. Maintain consistency

Teachers who have never encountered real-time feedback before may find it off-putting at first—especially if they're not expecting it. The surest way to keep this from happening is to create a culture of feedback. The first step is simple: roll it out. At the beginning of the year, let them know that you regularly give real-time feedback while you observe lessons, and that real-time feedback is a typical piece of the coaching process that does not reflect badly on the teacher receiving it.

In *Dare to Lead*, researcher and social worker Brené Brown shares that the most successful teams are the transparent ones.[12] Clear is kind, she advises, and being unclear is unkind. In the world of work this looks like setting clear expectations for all members

Principles of Coaching **67**

of the team and giving well-evidenced, constructive feedback—no waffling or minimizing. Transparency about what real-time feedback means—and how every teacher can make the most of it—will go a long way toward making it a piece of your school's culture that teachers can expect and appreciate.

---

### Findings from the Field: Foster Culture and Connection with Feedback

"While it might seem counterintuitive at first, feedback and opportunities to practice are the behaviors that connect people. Both are essential to be a community that grows and improves. Without them, teachers are isolated and don't work together. You are not connecting humans to their humanity and desire to be seen and do better."

—*Becky Berry, Principal, Portland, OR*

---

To introduce teachers to real-time feedback, it is highly beneficial to launch the year with a short PD session on its power (which can be combined with the power of practice if that is also not a norm for teachers). See "Launch Real-Time Feedback—Opening PD" for a simple form for a PD you could deliver:

---

### Launch Real-Time Feedback—Opening PD

- **Show a video of real-time feedback being delivered in another profession.** Show how this feedback comes as an aid rather than an accusation and enables both the coach and the new teacher to make sure their job is done as well as it possibly can be. (You can look for videos of sports coaching, resident doctors, lawyers conferencing during a trial, pilots-in-training, and the like.)

- **Show a video of a leader giving real-time feedback to a teacher—and the teacher immediately implementing it.** Ideally, you would be the leader in this video, but if you're rolling out real-time feedback for the first time, you can use one of the videos in this book. Have teachers reflect on how the real-time feedback helps the teacher in the video to improve instruction.

- **Make the connection between the real-time feedback you'll be providing and the feedback your teachers give students every day.** "Imagine that you're teaching solving quadratic equations through factoring," you might say, "and a student makes an error. It would be a lot more powerful to coach her to fix it in the moment, rather than waiting to mark it wrong on that student's homework later. I give real-time feedback for the same reason. It gives you as the teacher a chance to learn something right away, and it ensures that your students get the most out of that lesson."

- **Model real-time feedback.** During the PD, have a teacher join you at the front of the room. Role-play a lesson observation in which this teacher plays the teacher, you play yourself, and some of the other teachers participating in the PD play the students. At some point, give the teachers real-time feedback and have them implement it in-the-moment. Then, as summer PD goes on, continue to occasionally give real-time feedback while teachers are rehearsing. Ideally, every new teacher would get to experience real-time feedback at least once in rehearsal before the first day of school.

- **Practice what you preach.** One of the fastest ways to win over your staff is to implement the same practices with yourself. Ask your own supervisor (a principal if you're a coach, or your principal supervisor if you're a principal) to give you real-time feedback while you are walking the school. When they see you getting and implementing real-time feedback, it will be the ultimate message that we all see its value.

*Note: In the online materials you'll find materials, like the Giving Effective Feedback one pager, that can help you implement this PD. Although these are written for instructional leaders, you can also adapt materials for your teachers.*

As the beginning of the Phase 1 section—the pre-teaching phase—we will describe in more detail the value of holding PD sessions before students arrive that prepare teachers for all they'll need to do in the earliest days of school. These sessions are the ideal time to introduce teachers to real-time feedback.

The one limitation of PD is that teachers don't actually know what will really happen until afterward. (Think about times when you've attended a workshop/meeting that announced a change. We don't really trust the message of a PD until we see if it has actually happening!) Trennis Harvey makes his culture clear by making it a normal part of the routine of his coaching meetings. If you watched the clip of Trennis Harvey in Principle 2, you might have noticed what he did in the final minute of the meeting. He previews the real-time feedback he will give prior to the observation.

Principles of Coaching **69**

REWATCH Clip 3: **Academic Monitoring—Pen in Hand** (Key Leadership Move: Do it)

This allows the teacher to know what is coming and to normalize this action. Trennis has converted something that could feel like a surprise (i.e., jumping in to give real-time feedback in the classroom) to something that feels helpful for a teacher's growth.

Once you've prepared teachers for real-time feedback, all that remains is to actually do it—and to do it consistently. Many leaders hesitate to roll out real-time feedback, preferring to wait until all staff members are on board. But you don't need unanimous buy-in to begin. Giving real-time feedback regularly creates the culture, and your consistency sustains it. The first time teachers receive feedback, they might be caught off guard. The second time, less so. Teachers anticipate it by the third and fourth time. With each passing visit, feedback becomes part of what the teaching culture looks like at that school. And staff buy-in grows organically as student learning improves.

## Pick the Moment

The most important determinant for picking the right moment for real-time feedback is whether it will help student learning and make the lesson go more smoothly. Imagine, for example, that a teacher you're observing begins teaching a lesson with a poor objective. Coaching the teacher to write stronger objectives would be an extremely valuable exercise, but real time isn't the time to do it. To do so would pull the rug out from under the lesson the teacher has planned, likely leaving them very uncertain as to how to proceed with the rest of the lesson. The students would lose more learning to a derailed lesson than to a lesson with an imperfect objective. In contrast, if one student is disengaged and you can get the teacher to change the student's behavior, you have increased student learning in that moment and in the future without a negative consequence.

The second determinant of whether it's the right moment for real-time feedback is whether the feedback is small enough to be implemented right away without practice. The first coaching principle, Make It Bite-Sized, focused on the power of making action steps as small and practice-able as possible, so that teachers can immediately implement them. When it comes to giving feedback in real time, going even more granular—that is, to deliver only feedback that's bite-sized enough for the teacher to implement it right then and there, with no practice whatsoever—becomes a necessity. If a teacher won't get it right in the moment, you will benefit from waiting until you can work on it more extensively in your feedback meeting.

> ### Keys to Picking the Right Moment For Real-Time Feedback
>
> 1. Keeps lesson on track and improves student learning.
> 2. Can be implemented immediately without practice.

When you've picked the right moment, your next task is to communicate the feedback to the teacher.

---

### Findings from the Field: Create Real-Time Shifts

"One of my teachers was struggling to work on fluency during guided reading. She was having students doing round-robin reading rather than giving each student a chance to focus in on the text and practice reading themselves. With a short, simple whisper prompt ('Have them all whisper read'), the teacher had all students whisper reading and truly engaging with the text rather than just waiting their turn. What my teachers love about real-time feedback is that they see and feel success immediately—and the students reap all the benefits. The small change the teacher makes sticks faster than it does when we practice in our coaching conversations, meaning the teacher can move on to their next action step more quickly."

—Tera Carr, Principal Supervisor, Boston, MA

---

## Deliver the Feedback

Just like the attending physician did with Gaby at the opening of this principle, leaders giving real-time feedback to teachers have to do so in the least-invasive way possible—that is, the way in which the teacher remains in control of as many of the actions as possible. Here are a series of techniques for delivering your real-time feedback, ranked in order of their invasiveness. The quickest, least-invasive ones are always the best to use; in more challenging situations, the more invasive ones may be necessary.

Principles of Coaching     71

### Quickest and Least Invasive: Silent Signals

The quickest real-time feedback doesn't require any words at all.

Watch in the following video what Ashley Anderson-Martin does when coaching her HS Math teacher.

 WATCH Clip 6: **Academic Monitoring—Gather Data**
(Key Leadership Move: Real-time Feedback)

Ashley simply makes the gesture of writing something down, and that is enough for the teacher to prompt the students to write down this key takeaway of the lesson. Because they are so non-invasive, silent signals are an incredibly powerful tool of real-time feedback. They can take many forms:

- A hand gesture—for example, touching forefingers to each other to indicate an opportunity to turn and talk or Ashley's writing gesture to jot notes.
- A visual cue—for example, holding up a red card to flag a particular error you've already set up with the teacher, such as when the teacher is doing more of the talking than should be the case.
- Another physical nonverbal cue—for example, exaggerating your own erect posture to indicate to a teacher to assume a confident stance.

Using a silent signal to deliver real-time feedback does require a bit of preparation as you need to let the teacher know what your signal will be and what it will mean. When you know in advance what you plan to coach teachers to do in real time, you can touch base with them before class about the signal you plan to use. Once you and the teacher have set these expectations, nonverbal real-time feedback moves at lightning speed. A quick gesture from the leader translates all but seamlessly into the teachers' performing an action that will have lasting positive impact in their classroom.

### Less Invasive: Whisper Prompt

Taro Shigenobu uses a different approach to achieve the same end. He watches his biology teacher facilitate classroom discourse on the structure and function of organelles (the microscopic organized structures inside cells) and sees an opportunity to push the conversation deeper. He waits for the right moment, and then he whispers.

WATCH Clip 7: **Guide Discourse 101—Stamp Understanding**
(Key Leadership Move: Real-time Feedback)

## Stop and Jot: Whisper Prompts

What did you see Taro do? Jot down the actions you saw him take.

___

___

___

Taro isn't just focusing on something like classroom management—he is paying attention to the quality of the learning. And by processing with the teacher what to do to respond to the student learning gaps, he is guaranteeing that learning happens. He doesn't wait until tomorrow; he and the teacher fix it today.

> ### Core Idea
> Don't wait for tomorrow: fix it today.

When carried out just right, a whisper prompt can be just as subtle as a nonverbal signal—even though it involves speaking out loud. You can communicate a message to the teacher without interrupting their teaching. Two keys will make whispering work:

1. Pick a moment when students are working.
2. Be quick: state the action and your rationale.

The best moments for whispering feedback are clear: during independent practice or small group work and turn and talks. This way, the students won't be distracted by the teacher-leader interaction; and with the students occupied, the teacher will be able to focus much more fully on what the leader is saying.

Principles of Coaching

All of this is valuable only if you are very concise in your feedback—saying probably no more than three sentences. Teachers can't devote their full attention to a leader for very long while class is going on. So, keep it simple: state the action step and the evidence/rationale. A surgeon will always choose the most efficient surgery; your words should be no different.

**More Invasive: Model**

Sometimes, words are not enough, and a teacher really needs to see it to understand. This is where modeling comes in. Modeling can be just as quick as the other two types of feedback, and it can be done without challenging the teacher's leadership. In Ashley's coaching of her Geometry teacher, she does just that.

 WATCH Clip 8: **Academic Monitoring—Gather Data** (Key Leadership Move: Real-time Feedback)

Students were missing a key understanding of the values of x and y, and her teacher wasn't seeing it. So, Ashley jumped in, modeling how to address it, and then debriefed with the teacher to make sure he noted the learning gap that prompted her modeling.

Modeling has the added benefit of allowing a teacher to see in the moment exactly what they could have done. Many of the new teachers we have interviewed have called this the best part of all of their PD. Once they see a master teacher model for them with their own students, they start to believe more in what is possible for them to do. It may feel awkward at first, but the payoff of respectful modeling—both in the moment you do it and in the teacher's career for years to come—is immense.

**Most Invasive: Extensive Model**

Sometimes, you need to model for longer than in the situation described previously in order to get the class on track. Simply continue leading the class for an extended period of time, probably getting students through a particular critical moment in the lesson that is proving challenging, before inviting the teacher back in. Be sure to debrief with the teacher later to ensure the teacher was able to identify why you did that and what was effective.

This list of real-time feedback moves is captured in the handout Real-Time Feedback—Making It Stick. For now, let's discuss what effective leaders do after the observation.

## Close the Loop

Real-time feedback is so effective because the teacher ends up putting it into practice right there in the moment. But make sure to close the loop: Stay with them until they get it right, and debrief it afterward. When you do that, the outcome is better student learning and faster teacher growth.

If you give real-time feedback and leave before they implement it, you don't know for certain if they understood or where their additional struggles might be. And you won't know where to target your next round of feedback. You can supercharge this learning even further by debriefing with the teacher after giving real-time feedback. You saw that in the Ashley clip. Even if you see the teacher implement the feedback during class without faltering, you also need to be sure the teacher knows *why* the feedback led to improvement, or it won't stick. The debrief may take place either during that same class period, or more easily, at the teacher's next feedback meeting. You might begin by saying something like, "When you were checking for understanding, I had you call on Leila first, and then on Daniel. How did that affect the way you taught the rest of the lesson?" This allows teachers to name the action and understand its impact, increasing the likelihood that they will continue that action in the future.

## Conclusion

Real-time feedback is a practice that puts professional development on fast-forward. It shortens the feedback loop with teachers, which means students learn more. It is also often the breakthrough moment for teachers' own reflection on their development.

When delivered effectively, real-time feedback adds a powerful tool to the repertoire of an instructional leader. Just like a resident starts to fly with real-time feedback from their attending physician, so too can teachers fly with your support.

The Get Better Faster Guide has recommended real-time feedback strategies aligned to each action step in the Get Better Faster Scope and Sequence. In addition to that, here is a summary guide for when and how to use real-time feedback.

Principles of Coaching    **75**

# Delivering Real-Time Feedback—Making it Stick

| Least Leader Presence to Most Leader Presence | Examples |
|---|---|
| **Silent Signals:**<br><br>• Pre-established signal/nonverbal cue<br><br> ○ Hand gesture<br> ○ Visual cue (whiteboard, color cards)<br> ○ Physical nonverbal cue (posture) | • Hand gesture:<br><br> ○ Write in the air: give the students an "everybody writes" task.<br> ○ Point at student from the back of the room: student off task.<br> ○ Crane your neck/Fingers point to eyes: look at students to see if they are engaged.<br> ○ Index fingers point to each other: turn and talk.<br><br>• Visual Cue: Cards/whiteboards with words: "Cold call," "Why" (ask why), "Eyes"<br>• Physical nonverbal cue: Exaggerate posture to indicate confident posture |
| **Whisper Prompt:**<br><br>• Right moment: when students are working or teacher is not in front<br><br> ○ Turn and talks or independent work<br><br>• What to do: state what to do, the evidence and the rationale, in fewer than 30 seconds | • Ratio (teacher is doing too much of the work):<br><br> ○ "When they come out of turn and talk, have four students share every time before you respond."<br> ○ "Tiana has a partially there answer and Ramon has one that's almost there. Call on Tiana then Ramon to share their answers with the class."<br><br>• Students are not engaged:<br><br> ○ "You have a handful of students who aren't engaged when you give directions. Stop, say 'eyes on me', and scan for eyes. Don't move on until those students are with you." |

76    Get Better Faster 2.0

| | |
|---|---|
| **Model:**<br><br>• **Step 1: Frame**<br>• "I'm about to model. Watch how I. . . ."<br>• **Step 2: Intervene + Exemplar Model**<br>• "Can I ask a question. . . ."<br>• "Mr. X, we don't have 100% of. . . ."<br>• Execute exemplar model of technique teacher will use to close gap.<br>• **Step 3: Debrief**<br>• "What did I do? What was the impact?"<br>• **Step 4: Monitor the Transfer**<br>• "I'm going stay a few more minutes to watch you do. . . ." | • Ask a question to the class:<br><br>  ○ "So, when you start writing, what are the important things Ms. X will be looking for?"<br>  ○ "What should I do if I finish my work early?"<br><br>• Right is right: prompt students for better answers<br><br>  ○ Writing task: "Scholars, nice job citing evidence from the text in your answers. My challenge to you is to revise your answer to explicitly connect your evidence to your argument."<br>  ○ "Scholars, eyes on me. I want to challenge you to use the language from the first paragraph as you are responding. I'm going to listen for the next few to see if you can do it."<br><br>• Model the skill:<br><br>  ○ "I want to ask a few break-it-down questions because I'm not sure everyone understands."<br>  ○ During independent work, conduct three conferences with scholars using universal prompts.<br>  ○ "I want to *Narrate the Positive* things I'm seeing in this room because I see [Student] [Praise]."<br>  ○ "Eyes on me." Model *See Your Students* and whisper to teacher. "Watch how I use *See Your Students* to monitor the students." |

*(Continued)*

Principles of Coaching   **77**

| Extensive Model: | Jump in by raising hand: |
|---|---|
| • Right moment: circumstances require you to lead the class for an extended period of time.<br>• Planned: select time beforehand to do model teaching for part or all of lesson. | ○ "Ms. B, you're making a key point. Would you mind if I added on to it?"<br>○ "I want to ask the next two questions. I want to make sure each answer is 'all the way right.'" |

## Stop and Jot: Delivering Real-Time Feedback

Think of a time when real-time feedback would have helped you coach a teacher you were working with. Of the four strategies described in the "Delivering Real-Time Feedback—Making It Stick" table, which would have been the most effective for delivering your feedback in that moment? Circle one:

- Silent Signal
- Whisper Prompt
- Model
- Extensive Model

Plan your next observation with real-time feedback. What will you say or do with this teacher?

_____

_____

_____

_____

Congratulations! Reaching the end of Principles of Coaching means you've learned the foundations for *how* to coach a teacher effectively. Now we'll examine more closely *what* skills that coaching must cover in each phase of a teacher's development.

Take a moment to evaluate where to go from here.

Recall from the Introduction that from this point forward, it's less crucial to read straight through the book from beginning to end. If you have time to do this, then by all means do so; but if you're in the midst of coaching a teacher and need to just dive right in, simply begin by reading over the Scope and Sequence itself and then jump to the part of the book that specifically addresses in greater detail what your teachers need the most.

Here's the best way to navigate this part of the book.

**If you are using the Scope and Sequence before the school year begins. . . .**

- **Read the Phase 1 Coaching Blueprint:** The Phase 1 Coaching Blueprint will help you prepare summer professional development sessions that train teachers in the skills they'll need most immediately from the first day of school onward.

- **Start from the top—the first Phase 1 action step:** A strong foundation is critical to beginning the year. Thus, start with the #1 action steps in Rigor (Develop Understanding of the Content) and Management (Routines and Procedures 101). Do not move forward until a teacher is proficient in these areas!

**If you are using the Scope and Sequence at any other point in the year. . . .**

- **Identify your teacher's action step:** Go to the Get Better Faster Scope and Sequence (first pages of the book; find a printable version online) and determine the highest-leverage action step for your teacher. Remember to think waterfall: Start from the top and stop as soon as you hit a problem area for the teacher.

- **Go to the appropriate Phase and read the Coaching Blueprint:** For example, if your teacher is struggling to model effectively, jump to Phase 3 and start with the Phase 3 Coaching Blueprint

- **In that same Phase, jump to the rigor or management section (depending on your action step), and go to the page that matches your teacher's struggle:** Use the quick reference guide that appears right before Phase 1 management/rigor to identify the challenges that the teacher is most struggling with, and skip to the corresponding section that presents the skills that will help them overcome those specific challenges. Since the challenges are organized in order of decreasing urgency, the first challenge you see on the list that you know is a major growth area for your teacher will be the right one to address with that teacher first.

Principles of Coaching   **79**

# START HERE QUICK REFERENCE GUIDE

Here's a cheat sheet that shows where to go from here.

## The Scope and Sequence Cheat Sheet: Where to Go to Meet Your Teachers' Needs[a]"

| If your teacher is struggling to. . . | . . .jump to: |
|---|---|
| Develop essential routines and procedures | **Phase 1 Management** |
| Build foundational content knowledge OR Design/internalize lesson plans | **Phase 1 Rigor** |

| If and once they have mastered all of Phase 1, and they are struggling to. . . | . . .jump to: |
|---|---|
| Roll out and monitor culture routines OR Build trust and rapport | **Phase 2 Management** |
| Roll out and monitor academic routines | **Phase 2 Rigor** |

| If and once they have mastered all of Phase 2, and they are struggling to. . . | . . .jump to: |
|---|---|
| Engage 100% of students | **Phase 3 Management** |
| Activate students' prior knowledge OR Model | **Phase 3 Rigor** |

| If and once they have mastered all of Phase 3, and they are struggling to. . . | . . .jump to: |
|---|---|
| Build and maintain classroom energy | **Phase 4 Management** |
| Deepen class discussion | **Phase 4 Rigor** |

[a]A more detailed guide with more specific challenges will appear at the beginning of each section.

80    Get Better Faster 2.0

Phase **1**

# Pre-teaching (Summer PD)

Take a moment and put yourself back in the seat of a new teacher before you start. Remember what it was like to walk into a school building as a teacher for the first time. The classrooms are empty but full of promise. You've done well in the past: graduating successfully from high school and college and accomplishing most things that you've set your mind to. But you are nervous: Teaching is a new challenge you've never tackled before. As you get closer to the first day of teaching, the more you realize what you don't know. The books you've studied have detailed the basics of teaching, yet you wonder what it feels like to do it confidently. You want to be ready for your first day with your students, but you don't quite know how. Some of us had good mentors to take us through the process, but others of us—like me—were left to fend for ourselves.

As leaders, how can we create a process for growth that can see each new teacher through this dramatic transition from learning to teach to actually teaching? How can we make sure they will earn students' respect? Keep them engaged? Get them to learn?

Principal Kelly Dowling takes these questions to heart. Her solution? Give the first day of school the Broadway treatment. In the weeks before school begins, Kelly will get her fellow teachers ready by rehearsing the school day as if it were a hotly anticipated new play: piece-by-piece, over and over, in the same amount of time and space as each teacher will have to do it when the show opens.

So, what does a dress rehearsal for teaching look like? Let's see how Kelly does it. In the video below, Kelly has her high school staff practice the call to attention that signals the end of breakfast. The seated teachers are playing students, while the standing staff play teachers:

 WATCH Clip 9: **Routines and Procedures 101—Practice Rollout** (Key Leadership Move: Do it)

## Stop and Jot

What actions does Kelly take to lead an effective dress rehearsal with staff?

_____
_____
_____

Kelly leaves nothing to chance: She explains and models an effective entry routine and then gives staff the opportunity to practice it—not once but multiple times.

Teaching and the performing arts share a critical similarity: both depend on *responsive performance*. They require professionals to do their most important work live, while simultaneously and appropriately modifying it based on the reactions of those watching. To deliver an excellent responsive performance—the kind that deserves a standing ovation—you need to master two sets of actions: the variations you'll make depending on audience response and the planned constants you'll do no matter what. Variations are challenging to prepare for and, because you can never anticipate all of them in advance, knowing they could appear at any time can make even highly experienced performers freeze up before the curtain rises (or the school doors open). But if you've rehearsed the constants so many times that you can get through them as automatically as you brew your morning coffee, you'll have what you need to gather your forces, emerge from backstage, and give your audience what they came for no matter what. Your muscle memory will see you through your stage fright, and the show will go on.

On the first day of school, that's exactly what we need from every teacher. Yet unlike an actor, singer, or dancer, a new teacher is all too likely to arrive at the head of a classroom without ever having physically rehearsed for the first day of school. These teachers have likely been exposed to the general demands of leading a classroom but have not prepared for the specific demands of leading their own. As Deborah Loewenberg Ball and Francesca M. Forzani put it in "Building a Common Core for Learning to Teach," it's common practice in the United States to focus more on hiring "better" teachers up front than on training teachers as they dive into their work. This practice, Ball and Forzani explain, is a "gamble," betting each teacher's actual success in the classroom on qualifications that don't necessarily make them a "better" teacher.[1]

Kelly refuses to gamble. Her summer rehearsal sessions lock in her teachers' success precisely because they require all teachers to perfect the precise teaching actions they'll need in the classroom, and to do so *before*, not after, they need them. That's why Phase 1 of the Get Better Faster Scope and Sequence takes place in the days before students arrive for the first day of school. Teachers need to master these skills before they even meet their students because the skills are the starter kit for a successful school year.

---

### Core Idea

A new teacher in the first days of school will freeze up.
Relentlessly rehearse to break the ice.

---

Let's take a look at the Phase 1 Coaching Blueprint to see what techniques will help you coach your teachers in these skills.

## PHASE 1 COACHING BLUEPRINT: LEAD PD

Recall the three essential coaching skills this book has already covered:

- Make It Bite-Sized
- Practice What You Value
- Give Feedback Frequently

How do those look before the school year begins? They are embedded in the professional development (PD) training you lead during that time. Because teachers don't yet have students in front of them, all the training occurs in workshop or simulated form. This training can culminate in a dress rehearsal of the first days of school that will let teachers put all those skills into action at once.

## Leading Professional Development

The best way to learn something is to live it. Adults learn new skills not by passively hearing or reading content but by putting the skills into action. This idea turns traditional PD on its head. The key to effective PD is not the delivery of the content but the quality of the practice.

> ### Core Idea
>
> The key to effective PD is not the delivery of the content but the quality of the practice.

In the simplest terms, effective PD gives participants a chance to see it, name it, and do it. Here, we provide a brief overview of the essential components of an effective Living the Learning PD. The highlights are also captured in the sample PD materials in the print-ready materials. For more information about leading PD, turn to *Leverage Leadership 2.0*, which includes a full-length chapter on this subject.[2]

1.  **See it.** Seeing is believing, and that is nowhere more apparent than in effective PD. Teachers need to see a model of what a skill looks like when it's done well, whether they see it by watching video of a master teacher in action or by reading an exemplar lesson plan. That model will be the basis for them to understand how to implement the skill.

2.  **Name it.** Seeing it is to believe it; naming it is to remember it. When participants are given the opportunity to share what they saw in the model and then given a common language to describe it, they internalize the model even more effectively. You also create a shared language that a school community can use to support each other in implementing a skill.

84  Get Better Faster 2.0

## Findings from the Field: Get Them to See It

"The culture of my building changed when I began to use the See It, Name It, Do It method to roll out routines and procedures. Teachers could clearly see the model, practice it in real-time, and receive on-the-spot feedback from peers and coaches. Once students were in the building, it was easy to see how these minute-by-minute culture routines gave teachers more time to teach."

—Marie Culihan, Principal, Albany, NY

The "see it, name it" combination is incredibly impactful in delivering PD. In clip 2, Erica Lim leads PD on how to give what-to-directions, a key Phase 2 Management skill. Look at how she uses the "see it, name it" methodology to help participants understand the core components of clear and concise directions.

REWATCH Clip 2: **What to Do Directions**
(Key Leadership Move: See it)

Rather than telling teachers to be less wordy with directions or giving them a boilerplate set of directions to use, Erica models the delivery of what-to-do-directions. She allows them to "see it" in action. After the model, they "name it": identifying the important components. Throughout this process, Erica is putting the thinking on the teachers understanding of the practices of effective teaching, which increases the likelihood of their retention of the information.

3. **Do it.** As we shared earlier in the Principles of Coaching, what you practice is what you value. So, a PD without practice is a PD with less value. Once teachers have seen a model, they need to get out of their chairs and practice. This is one of the most straightforward yet underutilized components of a great PD. It can't be said too many times: If teachers don't practice the skill during the PD, they will not learn it.

Pre-teaching (Summer PD)

## Findings from the Field: Practice Makes Everyone Better

"It takes every member of your staff to contribute to the success of routines and procedures at your school. If you're not consistent across classrooms and teachers, students will struggle to be consistent themselves. For that to happen, everyone needs to practice, not just the new teachers. This is not to devalue what experienced staff members bring to the table. Rather, you are practicing perfect the expectations that you have in your school. At my school every year we see the model, name the routine, and practice it with authentic feedback from one another even if we've been using the same routine for many years. Veteran teachers make new teachers stronger, and the consistency elevates student culture for everyone."

—Kim Tymkowych, Principal, Loveland, CO

In this clip, Annie Murphy and Ben Carman-Brown facilitate a practice PD session on positive narration. This is not a lecture-heavy PD: They keep the explanation and the model brief, concise, and purposeful. The bulk of the time is reserved for the most important aspect of their time together: the practice.

 WATCH Clip 10: **Narrate the Positive** (Key Leadership Move: Do it)

Leading PD sessions like these prior to teaching trains new teachers on every isolated skill in the Phase 1 (Pre-Teaching) Scope and Sequence. This form of PD also functions well because it introduces those skills incrementally, so that they can begin (for example) by scripting a routine, continue by scripting how they'll teach that routine, and ultimately role play teaching *and* executing the routine.

If you are overwhelmed by the thought of planning and developing PD sessions with this framework in mind, have no fear. There are outstanding resources available to you that have those PD sessions planned for you that can make this feasible. *Teach Like a Champion 3.0* and *Ten-Minute In-Service*[3] both have developed teacher-facing PD sessions with session plans and handouts. You can use these to jump-start your PDs and make it much easier to get up and running!

While this section of the book dives deeply into practice before school begins, developing teachers and other instructional leaders through practice is a year-long focus.

See the print-ready materials for guides to Instructional Leadership Team Meetings (for grade-level coaches, department chairs, and other members of your team) and Practice Clinics (for teachers).

But first, let's ready staff for day one.

## The Final PD Before School Starts: The Dress Rehearsal

After all the preparation, though, there's still something missing. New teachers still lack the experience of putting all the skills they're learning together as they'll need to do on the first day of school: leading routines, teaching lessons, and commanding student attention in real time, sustaining their best work over a period of six to eight hours. To fill that gap, Kelly Dowling and leaders like her take the Broadway mind-set a step further: They lead a dress rehearsal. Let's revisit Kelly's rehearsal, this time noting what she does to get teachers to succeed:

 WATCH Clip 11: **Routines and Procedures 101—Practice the Rollout** (Key Leadership Move: See it)

Clear models lead to clear success. Remember: If you don't know what it should look like, you won't be able to execute it.

> ### Core Idea
> Clear models lead to clear success.

This sort of rehearsal doesn't just work for high school; it works for any grade level. The following clip features Amy Gile, an elementary school leader, who has prioritized time for her teachers to practice recess routines.

 WATCH Clip 12: **Routines and Procedures 101—Practice the Rollout** (Key Leadership Move: Do it)

What's remarkable about this clip is that it takes place outside. Normally, when we think of preparation for Day One, we focus on students in classroom spaces. But the playground (for elementary) and other outside spaces (for all grades) are also areas where we want to be intentional about establishing routines and procedures. Amy coaches teachers on affirmative phrasing—telling students what to do, not what to stop doing, which is especially helpful for our youngest learners, who may not know many of the behaviors that we expect.

---

### Findings from the Field: Craft a Crystal-Clear Vision

"Make sure that you have developed a clear vision of what you want routines and procedures to look like in your building. Ensure that each step is so clearly articulated that anyone can envision it based on your steps. Once you've set the vision, practice it for yourself to make sure that no steps are missing, and you can clearly model what you expect in the building. Thinking through this process has helped my leaders share their vision for the building and change the culture of their schools."

—*Windy Dorsey-Carr, Principal Supervisor, Lumberton, NC*

---

The dress rehearsal gathers all staff two or three days before school begins to practice Day One from start to finish. Just as would happen if the teachers were actors, this dress rehearsal begins with everything in place—all materials set up, all staff in position—and plays out minute by minute exactly as it would if the students were there, too. Where possible, the presence of students can even be mimicked by teachers who play the role of students when they don't have other dress-rehearsal duties to perform; otherwise, every staff member can simply imagine that the students are in the building and proceed exactly as if this were the case.

The dress rehearsal is the bow on top of summer PD. It ties together all the other preparation new teachers have done and gives everyone a final chance to make sure every aspect of the school day—and of every lesson, every hallway transition, and every arrival and dismissal within it—will fit in its place. Then if any part of the plan is still rough around the edges—if any routines still need additional work, for example—teachers still have time to perfect them before opening night.

We have now thoroughly covered *how* leaders like Kelly train new teachers in key skill areas during Pre-Teaching. Now let's dive more deeply into *what* new teachers will learn in summer PD, starting with management skills and then moving on to rigor.

## Teaching Skills Overview

The core skills in Phase 1 correspond to the key areas to rehearse prior to beginning teaching. We narrow that focus to just three core skill areas to tackle during Phase 1: setting routines and procedures, establishing a strong presence in the classroom, and writing lesson plans. Following is the excerpt of the Get Better Faster Scope and Sequence that shows in more detail what these skill areas include.

### Phase 1 Action Step Sequence

| Management Trajectory | Rigor Trajectory |
|---|---|
| DEVELOP ESSENTIAL ROUTINES & PROCEDURES<br>1. **Routines & Procedures 101:** Design and Roll out<br> • Plan & practice critical routines and procedures moment by moment:<br>  ○ Explain what each routine means and what it will look like.<br>  ○ Write out what teacher and students do at each step, and what will happen with students who don't get it right at first.<br> • Plan & practice the roll out: How to introduce routine for the first time:<br>  ○ Plan the "I Do", i.e., how you will model the routine.<br>  ○ Plan the practice and what you will do when students don't get it right the first time. | DEVELOP CONTENT EXPERTISE & LESSON PLANS<br>1. **Develop Understanding of the Content:**<br> • Analyze end goal assessments: Identify the most rigorous end goal assessment (AP items, SAT, state test, etc.) and name what students need to know and show to complete the tasks.<br> • Develop/internalize unit plans: Sequence the big ideas of the content into a logical progression/story<br>  ○ Identify and name the key concepts/enduring understandings.<br>  ○ Describe the relationships between the concepts within the grade span and across preceding and upcoming grades. |

*(Continued)*

Pre-teaching (Summer PD)  **89**

2. **Confident Presence:** Stand and speak with purpose
   - Confident stance: When giving instructions, stop moving and strike a formal pose.
   - Warm-demander register: When giving instructions, use a warm but firm register, including tone and word choice.

*Note: Many other topics can be introduced during August training. What are listed above are the topics that should be addressed to reach proficiency. Other topics to introduce—even if the teachers will not yet master them—could be:*

- *What to Do.*
- *See your Students.*
- *Narrate the Positive.*
- *Individual Student Correction.*
- *Do It Again: have students do routines again if not done correctly.*

2. **Develop Effective Lesson Plans 101:** Build the foundation of an effective lesson rooted in what students need to learn:
   - Write precise learning objectives that are:
     - Data-driven (rooted in what students need to learn based on end-goal assessments & analysis of assessment results)
     - Centered on enduring understandings of the unit
   - Plan a launch: Use of Do Now, oral review, etc.
   - Create/identify key tasks for students that lead to the most important conceptual understanding of the lesson.
   - Plan the basic structure of the lesson (e.g., direction instruction, inquiry).
   - Design an exit ticket (brief end assessment) aligned to the objective.
3. **Internalize Existing Lesson Plans:** Make existing plans your own
   - Identify the moment of most productive struggle in the lesson—articulate what students need to know/be able to do to master it.
   - Internalize & rehearse key parts of the lesson.
   - Build time stamps into the lesson plan.
   - Adjust the lesson plan to target the knowledge/skills students need.

| | 4. **Write an Exemplar: Set the bar for excellence** |
|---|---|
| | • Script an ideal written response you want students to produce throughout the arc of the lesson. |
| |    ○  Humanities: includes key evidence, infer-ences, arguments |
| |    ○  STEM: If they get this right and you ask them why, what do you want them to say? |

# PHASE 1 MANAGEMENT—DEVELOP ESSENTIAL ROUTINES AND PROCEDURES

## Quick Reference Guide

| If your teacher is struggling to. . . | . . .jump to: |
|---|---|
| **Routines and Procedures 101** | |
| Establish clear routines for the classroom | Plan and practice critical routines and procedures moment by moment |
| Teach a routine that is new for the students | Plan and practice the rollout |
| **Confident Presence** | |
| Establish body language that communicates leadership | Confident presence |
| Speak with calm authority | Warm-demander register |

Pre-teaching (Summer PD)    **91**

## Phase 1 Scope and Sequence

| Management Trajectory | Rigor Trajectory |
|---|---|
| 1. **Routines & Procedures 101:** Plan and practice critical routines and procedures moment-by-moment<br>• Explain what each routine means and what it will look like.<br>• Write out what teacher and students do at each step and what will happen with students who don't get it right at first.<br>2. **Confident Presence:** Stand and speak with purpose<br>• Confident stance: When giving instructions, stop moving and strike a formal pose.<br>• Warm-demander register: When giving instructions, use a warm but firm register, including tone and word choice. | 1. **Develop Understanding of the Content:** Learn the content area deeply<br>• Analyze end goal assessment to name what students need to know and show to complete the tasks.<br>• Develop/internalize unit plans: Sequence the big ideas of the content into a logical progression/story.<br>2. **Develop Effective Lesson Plans 101:** Build the foundation of an effective lesson rooted in what students need to learn.<br>• Write precise learning objectives that are data-driven and centered on enduring understandings of the unit.<br>• Plan a launch: Use Do now, oral review, etc.<br>• Create/identify key tasks that lead to most important conceptual understanding of the lesson.<br>• Plan the basic structure of the lesson.<br>• Design an aligned exit ticket.<br>3. **Internalize Existing Lesson Plans:** Break down existing lesson plans to make them your own.<br>• Identify the moment of most productive struggle in the lesson.<br>• Internalize and rehearse key parts of the lesson.<br>• Build time stamps into the lesson plan.<br>• Adjust the lesson plan to target the knowledge/skills students need.<br>4. **Write an Exemplar:** Set the bar for excellence.<br>• Script an ideal written responses you want students to produce throughout the arc of the lesson. |

## Introduction to Phase 1 Management Skills:
## Develop Essential Routines and Procedures

Imagine you set a goal to run your first marathon. You download a three-month work-out plan. It details how often you run, the number of miles you run each day and week, and a series of tapering runs to prepare you for the big race day. For many of us, the first few training days come easy. Adrenaline and enthusiasm carry us forward. The difficulty arrives later, on the fourth run or the fifth. Perhaps you are tired, sore. Sleepy. That's where many of us drop the ball.

When we're trying to create a new routine, like running long distance consistently, how do we maintain it? Is success only for the grittiest? Or the most determined?

In his groundbreaking work, *Atomic Habits*, author James Clear says otherwise. What makes the difference is not your ambition or your desire. Success lies in the quality of your systems. And when Clear talks about systems, he means habits. As Clear eloquently states, "We don't rise to the level of our goals. We fall to the level of our systems."

---

### Core Idea

"We don't rise to the level of our goals. We fall to the level our systems."
—James Clear

---

I highly recommend you read the book and try out Clear's step-by-step guidance for yourself. Creating a routine that is easy to follow dramatically increases your likelihood of sticking to it. And if this rings true for adults, it's even more true for children. Think about all the routines we explicitly teach our children. How likely would they be to brush their teeth in the morning and evening without a routine? How about going to bed at the same time every day? Daily routines keep our children regulated and safe. What's true at home is also true in school.

A classroom is only a room—nothing more. But with the right routines in place, they become spaces designed to let our students' minds soar. Each predictable routine, from morning meeting to the transition from small group work to whole class, keeps students from spending precious energy on figuring out what to do now or what to do next. Instead, they can devote that same energy to thinking about what matters. Far from stifling cognition and creativity, the right routines and procedures nurture our students' greatest ideas, giving them the freedom to develop and flourish.

Pre-teaching (Summer PD)

> ## Core Idea
>
> The right routines don't stifle creativity—they enhance it.

What follows are the key skills a new teacher must master in Phase 1 to establish the right routines in the first weeks of the school year. These are the routines and procedures that make the classroom a space that nurtures learning, with a warm-demander[4] register that enables you to teach your students those routines. We'll break them down in a way that shows specifically how to prepare your teachers to make this vision a reality.

## Routines and Procedures 101

> ## Teacher Professional Development Goal
>
> **Routines and Procedures 101:** Solidify essential routines and procedures before Day One.

The number one glitch that leads to broken-down routines is insufficient planning. When a teacher doesn't know with absolute clarity, inside and out, what a routine should look like when the students are doing it properly, there's no way to get the real students to match the vision. That's why writing up and rehearsing the routine is the starting point for getting management right.

---

### Findings from the Field: Set the Gold Standard

"As leaders we are uniquely positioned to set the standard for our school routines and procedures. But it wasn't until I was clear with myself of what excellence in a routine looked like that I found I could confidently communicate it to my school community and coach it to 100%. And the only way for me to do this well was to give myself time to plan and codify. So, if you find yourself saying 'But there is no time!', as I once did, shift your thinking and instead consider, 'What impact will it have on kids if I spend the time now to get this routine right?' Great learning is built on the foundation of excellent culture; set the conditions early."
—*Yanela Cruz, Principal, Springfield, MA*

The work of planning applies to every sort of routine—from turn and talks to passing paper to moving around the classroom. For example, look at the precision with which Brittany Hollis and her co-teacher roll out and maintain a homework agenda routine with middle school students. Developing the habit of doing homework is so critical for the transition from elementary school to school, and one key tool that can help students create self-sufficiency is the use of a planner/agenda:

 WATCH Clip 13: **Routines and Procedures 101—Practice the Rollout**
(Teaching clip)

After giving clear what to do directions, she and her co-teacher circulate to check the quality of students' headings and the setup of their agendas. You solidify a routine by monitoring it until it is habit.

The following are the top challenges to implementing effective routines and procedures where new teachers will need coaching to overcome:

- The teacher does not have clear routines established for the classroom.
- The routine is new for students—either because it's the beginning of the year or because the teacher is changing the routine.

## Routines and Procedures 101: Plan Routines Critical Routines and Procedures Moment by Moment
## Coaching Tips

**Teacher Context**

**Challenge**

- The teacher does not have clear routines established for the classroom.

**Action Step**

- Plan and practice critical routines and procedures moment by moment:
    - Explain what each routine means and what it will look like
    - Write out what teachers and students do at each step and what will happen with students who don't follow the routine.

**Action Step Overview**

The best-planned classroom routines address these three questions:

1. What will the teacher say and do at every moment of the routine?

2. What will the students be doing?

3. What will the teacher say and do when a student does not follow the routine?

For new teachers, this might not be something they have thought about or planned for. Writing out exactly what this procedure will accomplish and what it will look like will bring this routine to life, scripting precisely what both the teacher and the students will do every step of the way.

The value of focusing on routines and procedures during summer PD is that it gives teachers a chance to script, script, and script their routines some more, leaving no foreseeable stone unturned. Giving new teachers time to do this is critical. By the time they're finished, they may have a 10- or 15-page document that captures each of their essential classroom routines in detail. If that sounds excessive, just imagine what you'd have given for a guide like that during your first year of teaching!

**Key Leadership Moves**

**See It**

- Show a model video of an exemplary classroom routine
  - If you can film the routine of one of the strongest teachers in your school, it will really help the teacher visualize it to bring it to life.

- Show an exemplar written routine/procedure:
  - Connect the written routine to the live model.
  - Prompt: "Why was the planning of the routine so important to rolling it out effectively?"

- Do a live model of an effective routine
  - The benefit of a live model is you can exaggerate your nonverbals (we'll talk about this even more with the action step "See your Students") and words to make the model really "pop."

- Fully unpack the model: Have the teacher break down all the steps of the model before moving to practice.

**Plan the Practice**

- Complete a template for the key routines in the teacher's classroom. (Most important: student entry and exit, transitions, materials distribution, and listening.) Plan each moment:
    - What will the teacher say and do?
    - What will the students be doing?
    - What will the teacher do when students don't follow the routine?

**Do It**

- Rehearse every routine in the classroom setting.
    - Round 1: Stick to the basics at first: focus on the specific words and actions the teacher will use, such as where they will look and stand, and key ways they could break the routine down into smaller steps for students.
    - Round 2: Add minor student misbehaviors or errors in following instructions (not too much: you want to build positive muscle memory!)

> **Tip from a Coach—Plan Critical Routines**
> "Have routines for everything! This helps ensure that you can focus on academics. It's an investment of time, but after you implement them, you only need to train new teachers and it becomes a part of the campus."
> —*Anabel Ruiz, Principal, Richardson, TX*

---

 REWATCH Clip 13: **Routines and Procedures 101—Practice the Rollout**
(Teaching clip)

---

## Findings from the Field: Don't Settle for "Good Enough"

"Mastering Routines and Procedures 101 lays the foundation for your professional development, coaching relationships, and student impact. It builds strong teaching habits that enhance learning. Without this mastery, your school and staff will struggle with weak habits that keep you in a cycle of classroom management rather than learning and growth."
—*Becky Berry, Principal, Portland, OR*

Pre-teaching (Summer PD)

## Strategies for Coaching Routines and Procedures 101

| Action Step | See It | Plan the Practice | Do It | Cues for Real-Time Feedback |
|---|---|---|---|---|
| **Plan and practice critical routines and procedures moment by moment** | • Show a model video of an exemplary classroom routine. If possible, use a video of one of your strongest teachers.<br>• Show an exemplar written routine/procedure:<br>  ○ Connect the written routine to the live model<br>  ○ Prompt: "Why was the planning of the routine so important to rolling it out effectively?"<br>• Do a live model of an effective routine: exaggerate your nonverbals and words.<br>• Fully unpack the model: have the teacher break down all the steps of the model before moving to practice. | • Complete a template for the key routines in the teacher's classroom (student entry and exit, transitions, materials distribution, and listening).<br>• Plan each moment:<br>• What will the teacher say and do?<br>• What will the students be doing?<br>• What will the teacher do when students don't follow the routine? | • Rehearse every routine in the classroom setting.<br>• Rd. 1: Stick to the basics at first: focus on the specific words and actions teachers will use, such as where they will look and stand, and key ways they could break down the routine into smaller steps for the students.<br>• Rd. 2: Add small moments where students struggle to follow the routine (not too much: you want to build positive muscle memory!) | N/A |
| **Plan and practice the roll out** | • Show a model video or do a live model of an effective routine.<br>• Make sure to unpack all the key components: hook, frame, model, practice. | • Focus on scripting the I Do and What to Do Break it down, pause, repeat piece by piece.<br>• Keep the language positive and enthusiastic, including a challenge. | • Rd 1: memorize the rollout speech, then stand up and practice (too much to do both at once!). If teachers are working on this action step in peer groups, have teachers take turns playing the students to make it more authentic.<br>• Rd. 2: Add small moments where students struggle to follow the routine. | If model is ineffective: "Mr. Smith, am I following your model effectively?" (then model the correct actions and narrate what you're doing). |

98   Get Better Faster 2.0

## Confident Presence

> ### Teacher Professional Development Goal
>
> **Confident Presence:** Attract students with your warmth; keep them with your authority.

Picture a highly successful coach of your favorite team striding up to a podium to deliver a speech. The coach you see before you can be present, past, or fictional—any person you envision will have the straight back, the steady shoulders, and the sure, even paces that declare, "I'm in charge here." You can probably even imagine what the speech will sound like when the coach begins to deliver it: You know that his words will be spare yet powerful, and delivered in a strong, even tone. Every pair of eyes within view of the podium is locked on the coach, and it's not just because of the position this person holds—it's also because coaches carry themselves presidentially. Stand and speak like a leader, and people will pay attention. Yet what gives leaders staying power is not just how well they speak, but how much they draw you in. There is a warmth to their high expectations that makes you believe you can succeed.

In *Teach Like A Champion*, Doug Lemov refers to this quality as "it"—a quality that usually seems intangible and elusive, possessed by some teachers and not by others. Teachers who have "it," Lemov says, "enter a room and are instantly in command. Students who moments before seemed beyond the appeal of reason suddenly take their seats to await instructions."[5]

However, Lemov goes on to say, "it" is in fact a concrete set of actions, ones that any teacher can put to use. You don't need a specific personality or experience level to command your students' attention just as surely as the president commands the citizens' attention. Instead, the teachers who lead their classrooms with confident strength do so through specific, concrete actions that Lemov lists in *Teach Like A Champion*, from keeping a calm tone to standing up straight.

We group those actions together in the skill area of Confident Presence. Naturally, during pre-teaching, new teachers must learn some of the most fundamental skills of Confident Presence, but there isn't enough time during this phase for them to master all of those skills at once. The 101-level techniques of Confident Presence we'll address here—striking a confident posture and speaking in a warm-demander register—will

Pre-teaching (Summer PD)

give a new and powerful jumpstart in the art of "it." These two deceptively small actions carry all the impact of a strong first handshake with a new colleague: They inspire immediate respect that paves the way to a fruitful partnership with the individuals in question. The descriptions that follow show how.

---

## Findings from the Field: Capture Students with Confidence

"A confident teacher captivates scholars' attention more effectively. This energy creates a more dynamic classroom atmosphere and encourages participation and interest. For teachers who are learning this skill, a confident presence helps them communicate more assertively and respond to classroom challenges, which boosts their sense of confidence."
—*Katie Harshman, Principal, Pueblo, CO*

---

The core challenge Confident Presence sets out to overcome is teacher body language or tone that comes across as lax, intimidated, or anxious. Specifically, Confident Presence will address weaknesses in the teacher's:

- Posture: teachers undermine their leadership presence by slouching, shifting foot to foot, or facing at an angle away from the students.
- Tone: teachers' vocal register are too casual/informal or too frenetic/shrill.

---

## Confident Presence: Confident Stance

## Coaching Tips

**Teacher Context**

**Challenge**

- Posture: Teachers undermine their leadership presence by slouching, shifting from foot to foot, or facing at an angle away from the students.

**Action Step**

- When giving instructions, stop moving and strike a formal pose.

100    Get Better Faster 2.0

## Action Step Overview

Early in their careers, teachers may not recognize the ways in which deceptively subtle body language undermines their ability to take charge of a classroom—such as slouching, shifting from foot to foot, or clasping an arm behind their back. What's more, they're likely not to be accustomed to receiving feedback on their posture or vocal register because the fields in which we typically give people feedback on their physical behavior are few and far between. Leaders usually need to be extremely specific and direct in order to get teachers to properly incorporate the two smallest, most powerful things they can do to get their students to listen to them: stop moving and stand up straight.

## Key Leadership Moves

### See It

- Watch model video:
  - If you are looking for a good video of this, *Teach Like a Champion 3.0* has a number of good videos from every gradespan!
- Model giving directions with a relaxed posture, then while squaring up and standing still.

### Do It

- Have new teachers practice delivering the opening routines for their earliest lessons while squaring up and standing still.
- Film the practice—or use a mirror—so that new teachers can see what they look like while delivering instructions. (Don't underestimate the power of seeing yourself to correct body language!)

 WATCH Clip 14: **Confident Presence**
(Key Leadership Move: Do it)

### Real-Time Feedback

- Nonverbal: model exaggerated posture and stance (e.g., make your posture more erect by pulling back your shoulders and standing up taller).

## Confident Presence: Warm-Demander Register
## Coaching Tips

**Teacher Context**

**Challenge**

- Tone: The teacher's vocal register is too low or lax or the directions the teacher delivers are wordy or overly casual. OR
- The tone is too frenetic or shrill and sounds like shouting all the time.

**Action Step**

- When giving instructions, use a warm-demander register, including tone and word choice.

**Action Step Overview**

The tone in which we speak, just like the way in which we carry ourselves, is something very difficult to self-identify. Yet it can be one of the first underminers of a teacher's authority. If teachers speak too casually, too softly, or too shrilly, they can lose the students in the first few minutes. Using many of the same techniques that work well for a warm-demander register; however, a leader can coach a teacher to the same levels of success in this aspect of their physical presentation as well.

### Key Leadership Moves

**See It**

- Watch a model video of a teacher with a warm-demander register
- Model giving directions with a warm-demander register
- Show an "anti-model"—what it doesn't look like
  - ○ Before or after your model, model the opposite:
  - ○ Speak too quickly and shrilly
  - ○ Speak with a monotone without breaking up your sentences/phrases so it all sounds the same.

**Do It**

- Select a scripted lesson on routines and procedures. Practice delivering the instructions in a warm-demander register.
- Practice maintaining a formal tone when delivering a lesson on routines and procedures. Note when the teacher is maintaining a formal register and when the teacher's register becomes too informal or casual.

102    Get Better Faster 2.0

- Record teachers during practice and review the footage so teachers can hear when they are maintaining a formal register, and when their register begins to become casual/informal.

**Real-Time Feedback**

- Nonverbal: Combine a Square up/Stand still gesture with pointing to your mouth to remind the teacher to speak in a formal register.

---

 WATCH Clip 14: **Confident Presence**
(Key Leadership Move: Do it)

---

## Findings from the Field: Build a Culture of Care with Confidence

"Being a warm demander is a key part of being a successful teacher. Teachers who exude confidence communicate to students that their time at school is valuable. At my school, coaching teachers to internalize what it means to be a warm demander with a confident presence has changed the overall climate of the classroom culture for the better. Scholars feel seen and challenged, and their trust in their teachers also allows for more productive student-teacher partnerships."

—Estrella de La Torre, Principal, Brooklyn, NY

---

## Strategies for Coaching: Confident Presence

| Action Step | See It | Plan the Practice | Do It | Cues for Real-Time Feedback |
|---|---|---|---|---|
| Confident Stance | • Watch a model video.<br>• Model giving directions with a relaxed posture, then while squaring up and standing still. | Have new teachers practice delivering the opening routines for the earliest lessons while squaring up and standing still. | Film the practice—or use a mirror—so that the new teacher can see what they look like while delivering instructions. | Nonverbal: Model exaggerated posture and stance—(e.g., make your posture more erect by pulling back your shoulders and standing up taller). |

*(Continued)*

Pre-teaching (Summer PD)    103

| Warm-Demander Register | • Watch a model video of a teacher with a warm-demander register. <br> • Model giving directions with a warm-demander register. <br> • Show an "anti-model" of what it doesn't look like: speak too quickly/shrilly, monotone. | Select a scripted lesson routines and procedures. Practice delivering the instructions in a warm-demander register. | • Record the teacher during practice, and review the footage during the check-in so the teacher can hear when they are maintaining a formal register, and when their register begins to become casual/informal. <br> • Practice maintaining a formal tone while delivering a lesson on routines and procedures. Note when the teacher is maintaining a formal register and when the teacher's register becomes too informal or casual. | Nonverbal: Combine Square up, Stand still gesture with pointing to your mouth to remind the teacher to speak in a formal register. |
| --- | --- | --- | --- | --- |

## Stop and Jot

What are the three top coaching ideas you plan to use to train your teachers in these Phase 1 Management skills? Jot them here.

# PHASE 1 RIGOR—DEVELOP CONTENT EXPERTISE AND LESSON PLANS

## Quick Reference Guide

| If your teacher is struggling to. . . | . . .jump to: |
|---|---|
| **Develop Understanding of the Content** | |
| Understand what students need to know and be able to do to master the content | Analyze end goal assessments |
| Understand how one concept leads to another throughout the course of a week/unit | Develop/internalize unit plans |
| **Develop Lesson Plans 101** | |
| Write lesson objectives that are data-driven, manageable and measurable | Write precise learning objectives |
| Engage students at the start of class | Plan a lesson launch (first 10 min) |
| Plan activities aligned to the objective | Create/identify key tasks for students |
| Have a meaningful structure or organization of the lesson | Plan basic structure of lesson (direct instruction or inquiry) |
| Gauge what students know at the end of class | Design an exit ticket |
| **Internalize Existing Lesson Plans** | |
| Know what matters most in a given lesson plan | Identify the moment of most productive struggle |
| Implement the basics of a given lesson plan (stumbles or gets lost during teaching) | Internalize and rehearse key parts of the lesson |
| Runs out of time, completing only part of the lesson plan | Build time stamps into the lesson plan |
| Identify the areas where students will struggle given their struggles in the previous lessons | Adjust the lesson plan to target the knowledge/skills that students need |

*(Continued)*

Pre-teaching (Summer PD)    105

| If your teacher is struggling to. . . | . . .jump to: |
|---|---|
| **Write an Exemplar** ||
| Know what it looks like when students "get it" | Script an ideal written response you want students to produce |

## Phase 1 Scope and Sequence

| Management Trajectory | Rigor Trajectory |
|---|---|
| 1. **Routines & Procedures 101:** Plan and practice critical routines and procedures moment by moment<br>• Explain what each routine means and what it will look like.<br>• Write out what teacher and students do at each step, and what will happen with students who don't get it right at first.<br>2. **Confident Presence:** Stand and speak with purpose.<br>• Confident stance: When giving instructions, stop moving and strike a formal pose.<br>• Warm-demander register: When giving instructions, use a warm but firm register, including tone and word choice. | 1. **Develop Understanding of the Content:** Learn the content area deeply<br>• Analyze end goal assessment to name what students need to know and show to complete the tasks.<br>• Develop/internalize unit plans: sequence the big ideas of the content into a logical progression/story<br>2. **Develop Effective Lesson Plans 101:** Build the foundation of an effective lesson rooted in what students need to learn<br>• Write precise learning objectives that are data-driven and centered on enduring understandings of the unit.<br>• Plan a launch: Use of Do now, oral review, etc.<br>• Create/identify key tasks that lead to most important conceptual understanding of the lesson.<br>• Plan the basic structure of the lesson.<br>• Design an aligned exit ticket.<br>3. **Internalize Existing Lesson Plans:** Break down existing lesson plans to make them your own.<br>• Identify the moment of most productive struggle in the lesson.<br>• Internalize and rehearse key parts of the lesson.<br>• Build time stamps into the lesson plan.<br>• Adjust the lesson plan to target the knowledge/skills students need. |

106    Get Better Faster 2.0

| | 4. **Write an Exemplar:** Set the bar for excellence. <br> • Script an ideal written response you want students to produce throughout the arc of the lesson. |
| --- | --- |

## Introduction to Phase 1 Rigor Skills: Develop Content Expertise and Lesson Plans

Most of us in the field of education have a shared experience when it comes to the transition from high school to college—even if we haven't lived it ourselves, some of our students likely have. Here's how it goes: You leave your high school with enough honors, awards, and glowing recommendations from your teachers to feel confident in your skills as an intellectual. Yet when you arrive in your first college lecture hall, you find yourself overwhelmed and underprepared. Despite the rigor of your high school education, college is a different ball game. The expectations under which your new classmates have been working, and those your new professors are setting, are far higher than what you're used to.

The core problem here is that it's not enough to say we have "high expectations" for our students. We have to define what we mean by high expectations, and we have to set our definitions in terms of concrete academic accomplishments, not abstract ideals. If we have high expectations already, we take them for granted—but high expectations are always made, not born. Who makes them? Teachers. If we're lucky enough to have teachers and coaches who have modeled high expectations for us, we may already have a reasonably good idea of what student achievements will reach the bar. But here's the good news for new teachers: Whether we were that fortunate or not, we can develop high expectations for our students at any time in our careers.

> ### Core Idea
> High expectations aren't born—they're made.
> And as teachers, we're the ones who get to make them.

In the classroom, the most critical time to define expectations is when designing the exemplar, the end-class measure of learning. Too often, teacher development programs focus first on delivery of instructions, modeling, and leading discussion; even though

Pre-teaching (Summer PD)

all of these are important, none of them drive students toward a clear destination unless we know where we want them to be by the end of class.

So, Phase 1 begins with knowledge building: not of students but of their teachers. Building foundational content knowledge is the first step to designing a rigorous exemplar. (It might take years to become a content expert, but that doesn't keep us from building the foundation right away!) After all, students can't learn what the teacher doesn't yet know. And the teacher can't set high expectations for the exemplar—what students can do independently—without knowing the intricacies of the content. The action steps in this section show how.

## Develop Understanding of the Content

> ### Teacher Professional Development Goal
>
> **Develop Understanding of the Content:** Develop foundational content knowledge to be able to guide the teacher when teaching the lesson.

One of the biggest challenges for a new teacher is to learn the content they are going to teach. On the surface, it seems like a nonissue. Given that a teacher went to college, shouldn't K-12 content be easy to master?

Yet there is a big difference between doing something automatically (like addition or subtraction, or reading a novel) and teaching someone else to do it. You have to learn the content from the perspective of someone who doesn't know it. And often you have to learn it conceptually even if you didn't explicitly understand that as a student yourself. (You might not articulate that multiplication is an array or the area of a shape, but this will be key to a student's understanding!). Similarly, for teachers of upper grades, you might have studied History, but it has been four years or more since you took a class on the period of History that you are asked to teach.

Over the course of many years, a teacher develops content knowledge through the art of teaching and learning through reading books on the content, curriculum resources, and professional development. Yet a new teacher doesn't have years before they start teaching. What is the most effective, efficient way to begin? By starting with the end game.

> ## Core Idea
>
> If you want to know where to start,
> know where to end.
> The end game gives a road map for your teaching.

When we know where we are headed—by looking at the end-goal assessments and the big ideas of the unit—we can create a road map for teachers. Suddenly the rationale for why they are teaching what they are teaching becomes clear, and they have a better sense of what to emphasize. This is essential both in a world where teachers are following existing curriculum/lesson plans and where they make their own. In either case, they end up missing what students most need.

Especially for new teachers, teaching what matters most makes sure that even when they are still learning to teach effectively, at least students are being exposed to the highest leverage content. By itself, that is more important than learning good teaching moves around low-rigor content. That sort of coaching runs the risk of putting process (how to teach) over output (whether students learn).

Here are common challenges that teachers encounter as they deepen content knowledge:

- The teacher doesn't understand what students need to know and be able to do to master the content.

- The teacher doesn't understand how the ideas of each lesson fit together to build toward larger understanding.

---

## Develop Understanding of the Content: Analyze End Goal Assessment

## Coaching Tips

**Teacher Context**

**Challenge:**

- Teacher is not sure what students need to know or do to show mastery.

**Action Step:**

- Analyze end goal assessments.

**Action Step Overview**

It's difficult for teachers to hit a target they can't see. *Driven by Data 2.0* drives this point home: standards are meaningless until we define how to assess them.[6] You can read every curriculum resource, but you won't have clarity of the bar to which you should teach until you view the end goal assessment. This is the road map for rigor and is the fastest way to determine what to teach. (For a more complete understanding of this rationale, read the Assessment chapter in *Driven by Data 2.0*. It provides exercises and key points that can help guide your coaching.)[7]

To begin this process, aim for the most rigorous end goal assessments available for their content area; these could be released AP items, SAT questions, or state tests. As teachers break down the key skills and knowledge that students need to reach mastery, the destination sharpens into view.

Key Leadership Moves

**See It**

- Show the teacher a set of different assessment items all aligned to the same standard but with different levels of rigor. You can use the examples in *Driven by Data 2.0*[8] or create your own. Guide the teacher to the conclusion that the curriculum itself doesn't teach you the rigor to which to teach until you define the end game.

- Show an example of a teacher's analysis of an assessment question.

  ○ Look at sample Know-Show charts or content resource guides: List what a student must know and be able to do to master the task.

**Do It**

- Look at assessment items from your end-goal assessment (i.e., state test, AP Exam, SAT, etc.) that are aligned to the standard the teacher is teaching that week. Unpack it:

  ○ What do students need to **know** and be able to **do** to demonstrate mastery?

  ○ Create a "Know-Show" chart (the knowledge/skills students need and how they need to solve the task/problem) to lock in the key things the teacher must focus on when teaching.

- Use a Know-Show chart or something similar.

Watch how Na'Jee Carter leverages assessments to develop his teacher's content knowledge:

 WATCH Clip 15: **Develop Understanding of Content—Analyze End Goals**
(Key Leadership Move: See it)

**Real-Time Feedback**

- (Action steps that are focused on planning—like this one—should not be coached in the moment of instruction. It could throw off the entire lesson.)

   **Tip from a Coach—Know the Content Yourself**
   "When coaching teachers around content, I need to go through the same process I am holding my teachers to. At Blanton Elementary, that means that as leaders, we do exemplars for all the future weekly assessments. After that, we are confident in our ability to understand what students will be learning and how to support teachers in it. It is also helpful to have resources that help you understand the standard at the student level so that you are able to unpack it, including the conceptual knowledge, the procedural steps, the likely misconceptions, and the academic vocabulary. Deepening our teachers' content knowledge has shifted what our teachers are able to accomplish with students, and it has dramatically accelerated their progress to become distinguished teachers."
   —*Alicia Iwasko, Principal, Dallas, TX*

## Develop Understanding of the Content: Develop/Internalize Unit Plans

## Coaching Tips

**Teacher Context**

**Challenge:**

- Teacher doesn't understand how one concept leads to another throughout the course of a week/unit—this can look like lessons that feel disconnected from the previous one or the upcoming one.
- Teacher doesn't understand how the big ideas of the content area fit together.

### Action Step

- Develop and internalize unit plans: Sequence the big ideas of the content into a logical progression/story:
  - Identify and name the key concepts/enduring understandings.
  - Describe the relationships between the concepts within the grade and across preceding and upcoming grades.

### Action Step Overview

When you first start teaching, everything is so overwhelming that often you just focus on teaching one lesson at a time without any idea of how they build on one another. You wake up each morning and start teaching, as if each day was in complete isolation from the next. The result? Students won't retain it. It will feel like disjointed, unconnected new information, which is the fastest way to make sure that students do **not** master the material. Thinking about how one lesson leads to another can unlock the bigger picture for the teacher. It becomes the glue that connects the learning of every lesson, which in turn helps students see themselves learning one concept that they can retain rather than 10 different ones. Teachers and students alike can start to see how this lesson is important for the next one, which makes it easier to pay attention to the importance of it. By building a deeper understanding of how the units are organized, teachers can see the overall picture better. They can zoom out to connect these big ideas across the grade span and previous and future grades.

### Key Leadership Moves

### See It

- Show an example of a unit map of another teacher: how they wrote out the connection between the big ideas of the unit and each individual lesson plan.
- Do a think aloud of how to work from a unit plan and see the purpose of each lesson. Key questions to emphasize in your think aloud:
  - Hmm. . . . What are the big ideas and key understandings of this unit?
  - Let me look at the first week: How do these lessons contribute to those understandings?
  - Why is each lesson important to getting to that understanding?
  - What is critical to learn in each lesson to be able to learn the next one?

### Do It

- Review unit-level plans to see how big ideas connect across the content.
  - Identify and name key concepts and enduring understandings.
  - Connect concepts across grade spans.

112   Get Better Faster 2.0

- Do this review independently and then spar with each other or with a resource; add on whatever is needed to enhance the understanding.

**Real-Time Feedback**

- **N/A**

Because content coaching looks different at various grade spans and content areas, we have provided three examples of coaching content—one of elementary school reading, one of middle school Math, and one of high school History:

**Elementary School Reading:** Na'Jee and his teacher break down the big ideas and skills in the text *Hermie the Crab*:

WATCH Clip 16: **Develop Understanding of Content—Internalize Unit Plans**
(Key Leadership Move: See it)

**Middle School Math:** Katie and her teacher are working on systems of equations:

WATCH Clip 17: **Develop Understanding of Content—Internalize Unit Plans**
(Key Leadership Move: See it)

**High School History:** Jesse and his teacher map out the arcs and patterns of history:

WATCH Clip 18: **Develop Understanding of Content—Internalize Unit Plans**
(Key Leadership Move: See it)

**Tip from a Coach: Make It Road Map, Not a Recipe**

"At the start of the year, we always remind teachers that while we have a set curriculum, that curriculum is a road map, not a strict recipe. Teachers must be the leaders of their classroom, thus they must own the role of curriculum writer. We spend time taking and annotating the end assessment for their course to develop a deep understanding of the end we have in mind for each course. Before the start of each quarter, we have teachers use the curriculum guides to create a curriculum map that will become their road map for the next 10 weeks. This is a living

document that they alter and adjust based on the weekly classroom data. Teachers also use exit ticket and classwork data to design reteach lessons and adjust future lesson plans to make sure they are providing the right practice for their students ahead of each assessment."
—*Syrena Burnam, Principal, Camden, NJ*

Deepening content knowledge is an ongoing practice (and adventure). Even the most experienced teachers continue to seek new approaches to and perspectives on a beloved content area. This foundation takes the first steps in that adventure.

## Strategies for Coaching: Developing Understanding of the Content

| Action Step | See It | Plan the Practice | Do It | Cues for Real-Time Feedback |
|---|---|---|---|---|
| Analyze end goal assessment | • Show the teacher a set of different assessment items all aligned to the standard but with different levels or rigor. Guide to the conclusion that the curriculum doesn't teach you the rigor to which to teach until you define the end game.<br>• Show an example of a teacher's analysis of an assessment question. | • Break down the key knowledge and skills of the end goal assessment.<br>• Use a Know-Show chart or something similar. | • Repeat the process for the teacher with multiple standards covered by the end goal assessment. | N/A (Action steps that are focused on planning—like this one—should not be coached in the moment of instruction. It could throw off the entire lesson.) |
| Develop/ internalize unit plans | • Show an example of a unit map of other teachers: how they wrote out the connection between the big ideas of the unit and each individual lesson plan.<br>• Do a think aloud of how to work from a unit plan and see the purpose of each lesson. Emphasize the big ideas and key understandings. | • Review unit-level plans to see how big ideas connect across the content.<br>• Identify and name key concepts and enduring understandings.<br>• Connect concepts across grade spans.<br>• Review independently and then spar with a colleague or with a resource; add whatever is needed to enhance the understanding. | • A continuation of the planning; Do it and Planning are the same with an action step like this. | N/A |

114    Get Better Faster 2.0

## Develop Effective Lesson Plans 101

### Teacher Professional Development Goal

**Develop Effective Lesson Plans:** Build the foundation of an effective lesson rooted in what students need to learn.

Steve Leinwand is Principal Research Analyst at American Institutes for Research in Arlington, a former president of the National Council of Supervisors of Mathematics and author of multiple books on teaching Math. I had a chance to ask him a question after we had just completed a school walkthrough together: "In your 25-year experience coaching Math teachers, what has been the most effective method to develop them?"

Without hesitation, Steve replied, "Plan a lesson together, teach it with others observing, collect the student work and analyze it, and then revise the lesson and reteach it that same day. You'd be amazed at what it does to unlock understanding and teacher skill."[9]

### Core Idea

Make lesson planning "pop":
Plan, practice, and plan again.

What is powerful about Steve's advice is it mirrors decades of research from education scholars Bradley A. Emerling and Genevieve Graff-Emerling about the Japanese practice of lesson plan study, they discovered a simple, logical shift in focus that made an enormous difference.[10] The instructors involved closely observed how students responded to an initial lesson, revising both that lesson and those that follow it to meet student needs better. This contrasts with the way many leaders evaluate teaching. As the Emerlings stated: "When asked to reflect and make revisions, our first instinct was to comment on whether the lesson went as planned and whether students were generally engaged." Shifting their method to more closely match that of their Japanese colleagues—using *data* to drive lesson planning, data collected not only through tests and quizzes but also by listening to what answers students generated in class—enabled them to write more effective lesson plans than they had ever developed before.

Pre-teaching (Summer PD)    115

In truth, it should come as no surprise that keying into student results in this way would lead to game-changing lesson planning. The planning process recommended in *Driven by Data* 2.0 is based on this same philosophy, and several other American educators—such as Jon Saphier in *The Skillful Teacher* —have also written extensively about data-based planning and the impact it could have on American classrooms. Knowing where students are and adjusting instruction to match their needs is the heart of great teaching.

## Findings from the Field: Build in "Halftime Meetings" to Adjust Lessons Same Day

"A year ago, we were struggling to get our teachers to improve student achievement and to see how their teaching and planning matter. So, we launched "Halftime meetings." I would observe the teacher's lesson in the morning, we'd then debrief with the exit tickets and revise the afternoon lesson with their second group of students to see if we could improve the learning. The results were immediate. Teachers could see that when they taught it differently in the afternoon, learning improved. This created a cycle of improvement in student learning that we previously hadn't seen. And it all centered around a few key questions we asked in every meeting:

1. What is the percent mastery?
2. What did you do to contribute to student successes?
3. What did you do or not do to contribute to student gaps?
4. What are you going to do about the student gaps?

These questions not only keep the thinking on the teachers in the meeting; they also empower teachers to see that their preparation and execution makes all the difference in student achievement. Teachers are often thrilled to see the increase in percent mastery as a result of their adjustments!"

—*Zach Roach, Instructional Leader, Camden, NJ*

The basic skills of great lesson planning will get a new teacher past the following challenges:

- The lesson objectives are not what students need: They are not data driven, are not manageable and measurable, or not centered around enduring understanding.

- The teacher stumbles or doesn't know how to plan the launch of the lesson.

- The teacher doesn't know what matters most in each lesson.

- The teacher doesn't have a sense of how to structure a lesson overall.

- The teacher doesn't have a way to assess whether students learned; the exit ticket doesn't align to the objective.

## Develop Effective Lesson Plans 101: Write Precise Learning Objectives

## Coaching Tips

### Teacher Context

### Challenge

- Teacher does not know how to create a solid lesson objective.

- The lesson objectives are not what students need: They are not data driven, are not manageable and measurable, or not centered around enduring understanding.

### Action Step

- Write precise learning objectives that are:
  - data driven (rooted in what students need to learn based on analysis of assessment results);
  - able to be accomplished in one lesson; and
  - connected to the key conceptual understandings of the unit.

### Action Step Overview
Let's unpack these criteria of an effective objective:

- **Data driven:** It addresses what students most urgently need to learn as demonstrated by assessment and analysis of data. The importance of this is thoroughly discussed in *Driven by Data* 2.0. Are we teaching what students need or what they already know?

- **Able to be accomplished in one lesson:** It calls out one piece from a bigger topic or skill set students need to master—a piece small enough that the students will be able to master it in one lesson and then move on to another small piece the following day. By the end of the lesson, there will be a clear way for the teacher to measure whether the students have learned the objective sufficiently.

- **Connected to the key conceptual understanding of the unit:** Students should have an opportunity to grapple with an aspect of the content that builds conceptual, long-lasting understanding of the topic.

Pre-teaching (Summer PD)   **117**

**Key Leadership Moves**

The first key to writing a great objective is to start with your end goal of what you want students to learn—the final assessment defines your objective. Once this is accomplished, the next most powerful way to help new teachers perfect the art of writing objectives is to have them complete an exercise in which they have to revise a too-broad objective to make it manageable in one lesson. After learning to write objectives that are end goal aligned, teachers' most common error is writing objectives that are too broad. Hold out for 100% quality objectives, because that will be the only way they can replicate them when they work independently.

**See It**

- Model a Think Aloud: Refine an existing objective to make it (1) data-driven, (2) manageable and measurable, and (3) centered around conceptual understanding.
  - "Hmm. . . . What must students know and be able to do to demonstrate mastery on the final assessment?"
  - "If I look at the previous lessons, what is the new part that students need to master in this lesson?"
  - "Let me step back: Can this objective be accomplished today? If not, how can I narrow my focus?"
  - "Ok. Now that I've narrowed my focus, is the objective still connected to the larger conceptual understanding of the unit?"

**Plan the Practice/Do It:**

- Pull out upcoming assessments and lesson plans for review.
  - Make sure you have all materials at hand during the meeting: upcoming lesson plans, curriculum/scope and sequence, interim assessment, final exam/state test released items, etc.
- Plan a full week of upcoming objectives together so that they have a solid beginning to their lesson planning.
  - Identify the right end goal from an upcoming assessment.
  - Break down too-broad objectives to make them manageable for individual lessons.
  - Rewrite lesson objectives to center them around the big ideas of the content.

**Real-Time Feedback**

- N/A

**118**   Get Better Faster 2.0

Watch how Katie Abrams gets to a precise learning objective with her teacher:

 **REWATCH Clip 17: Develop Understanding of Content—Internalize Unit Plans**
(Key Leadership Move: See it)

**Tip from a Coach—Zoom in on What Matters Most:**
"Diving into a deeper understanding of the lesson plan had a transformative impact and my school. Thinking through the most important information to convey during the lesson helped teachers build a visual of what should be seen during in the instructional block. Not only did it make teacher practice more meaningful, but it made lesson planning an accountability component for the teacher."
—Dr. Kristie Edwards, Principal, Washington, D.C.

## Develop Effective Lesson Plans 101: Plan a Launch
## Coaching Tips

**Teacher Context**

**Challenge:**

- Teacher stumbles or doesn't know how to engage students at the start of a lesson

**Action Step**

- Plan the launch that begins class.

**Action Step Overview**

Lesson launches are such an important part of any teacher's classroom but even more essential for a new teacher. The launch creates predictable routines that make it easy for students to settle into the learning after coming from a previous class, and it is also a moment to prime students for what they are about to learn. The key to coaching here is making the routine predictable and having a basic understanding of activating knowledge. (Note: Activating knowledge will be a bigger area of focus in Phase 3 where it is the first action step in that phase. Right now the teacher doesn't have to understand it or implement it perfectly but at least have the launch oriented toward this idea.)

Pre-teaching (Summer PD)

## Key Leadership Moves

### See It

- Present an exemplar lesson plan with a scripted launch and unpack the purpose of each part of the launch.
    - Why a teacher uses a Do Now activity (the value for getting students on-task **and** assessing what they have retained from previous lessons)
    - Why a teacher uses oral class review (e.g., "What do you already know about. . ..?" "What is the definition of area? etc.)
    - How a teacher hooks students at the start of a lesson to make it relevant while also being short and sweet
- Model a Think Aloud: Plan the activation of knowledge activities (do now, oral class review) for an upcoming lesson.
- Model—Think Aloud and Live Model: Script and deliver the introduction to the do-now or class oral review.

### Plan the Practice

- Select an upcoming lesson and plan an aligned do now or class oral review or hook.
- Script the introduction/routine for the do now or class oral review.

### Do It

- Deliver the introduction to the do now or class oral review.

### Real-Time Feedback

- Hold out your palm and point to it with the other hand to indicate to them to go back to their script and follow it.

---

# Develop Effective Lesson Plans 101: Create/Identify Key Tasks

# Coaching Tips

### Teacher Context

### Challenge

- Teacher doesn't know how to plan activities that are aligned to the objective of the lesson.

120     Get Better Faster 2.0

**Action Step**

- Create and identify the key tasks of each lesson that lead to the most important conceptual understanding of the lesson.

**Action Step Overview**

One of the first instincts of a teacher (new and veteran) can be to start thinking of engaging activities for the lesson. Engaging activities are essential, but when they aren't aligned to the objective, they become entertainment but not critical learning. The focus here is to work toward selecting and building activities that are aligned to the objectives of the lesson. If your school uses an established curriculum, coach the teacher to identify and/or adapt the key tasks that build conceptual understanding. If teachers are responsible for creating their own curriculum, give them feedback on the key unit tasks at the planning stage.

### Key Leadership Moves

**See It**

- Model a Think Aloud with an existing lesson plan/curriculum:
  - Review the tasks in an upcoming lesson plan and think aloud the process of figuring out which one is most important to the enduring understanding.
  - "Which of these activities is most important to students to master the lesson?"
  - "Is there any adjustment needed to align this activity more fully to the objective?"

- Model a Think Aloud when building a lesson plan from scratch:
  - "Let me look at my objective and my exit ticket and remind myself of the following: What are the most important things students must know and be able to do at the end of this lesson?"
  - "So, what task will allow them to practice that?"

**Do It:**

- Review existing curriculum or plan to identify the key tasks that students need to do to build conceptual understanding and master the objective.
- Build the key tasks for a new lesson plan that aligns to the objective.

This action step is particularly effective for literacy classrooms. Watch how Kelly Dowling unpacks the memoir *Warriors Don't Cry* to identify the key moments in the text that will be essential for students to get to the deeper understanding. (Note: Kelly mentions "NEZZ," which refers to a student's ability to (N) name the author's

Pre-teaching (Summer PD)    121

technique, (E) cite best evidence, and (ZZ) zoom in on the details of that evidence and zoom out to explain how it enhances the author's message):

 WATCH Clip 19: **Internalize Existing Lessons—ID Key Tasks** (Key Leadership Move: See it)

**Real-Time Feedback**

- N/A

## Develop Effective Lesson Plans 101: Plan Basic Lesson Structure Coaching Tips

**Teacher Context**

**Challenge**

- Lessons lack meaningful structure or organization.

**Action Step**

- Plan basic lesson structure (guided instruction or inquiry).

**Action Step Overview**

Lesson plans are a teacher's daily road map, and the lesson plan's basic structure creates the meaningful pathway toward the objective. Depending on the goal(s) of the lesson, this could look like direct instruction (modeling for students and then giving them opportunities to practice) or inquiry (guiding students to explore multiple avenues of thinking). Direct instruction is easier to plan first (which is why you'll see that modeling comes before discourse in the Get Better Faster sequence!) but encourage them to develop their skill sets in different lesson structures as they each have their own particular benefits for student learning.

### Key Leadership Moves

**See It**

- Do a Think Aloud for planning a model:

- Review tasks you have selected for the lesson: "So, if this is the task I want students to be able to do, what makes this challenging?"
- "So, when I model how to do this, what are the key questions I ask myself to solve this task?" (Tip: here are some universal thinking questions that can help)
  - "What is this question asking me to do?"
  - "What do I already know about this topic?"
  - "What information is available for me in the prompt/task?"
  - "What am I looking for as I read the text?"
  - "How could I summarize this passage?"
- Model a Think Aloud for inquiry:
  - Review tasks you have selected for the lesson: "So, if this is the task I want students to be able to do, what makes this challenging?"
  - "What prompts will I use when students are struggling?"
  - (Note: this is a pretty sophisticated task, so keep it pretty basic. The real full art of inquiry is addressed in Phase 4.)

**Plan the Practice/Do It:**

- Design the model or inquiry for the lesson.
- Draft the basic structure of the lesson around that moment.

**Real-Time Feedback**

- N/A

Chi Tschang helps his math teachers decide on the best lesson structure for an upcoming lesson:

 WATCH Clip 20: **Develop Effective Lesson Plans** (Key Leadership Move: Do it)

Pre-teaching (Summer PD) 123

# Develop Effective Lesson Plans 101: Design an Exit Ticket

## Coaching Tips

**Teacher Context**

**Challenge**

- The teacher cannot gauge what students know at the end of class.

**Action Step**

- Design an exit ticket (brief final mini-assessment) aligned to the objective.

**Action Step Overview**

A critical fact for new teachers to learn as early as possible is that an exit ticket—a written end-of-class assignment that requires students to put to use what they've learned in class—is the ultimate way to measure whether your teaching was successful. If you don't assess what matters, you don't really know what happened when your lesson was translated from plan to practice. Exit tickets solve this problem. They are directly aligned to the objective—so that the teacher can look at them and truly be able to answer the question: Did the students meet the objective? The following are keys to a good exit ticket:

- Keep them short to make them easy to check.
- Make sure they align to the upcoming interim assessment and the most important parts of the objective that you are trying to measure.

Here is an example from a high school physics class. Note how the exit ticket meets the criteria: It's easy to check, but also making sure they understand the concept:

---

**EXIT TICKET: Newton's Second Law**

1. **State Newton's Second Law:**
2. **A 5-kg object has the free body diagram shown below. Determine the net acceleration of the object. Show all work.**

---

3. **The graphs below are of net force versus acceleration for different objects. All graphs have the same scale for each respective axis. Rank the mass of the objects from greatest to least.**

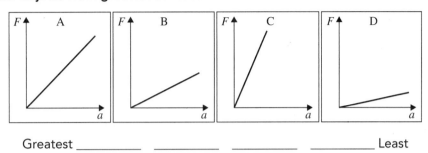

Greatest _____ _____ _____ _____ Least

## Key Leadership Moves

**See It**

- Model a Think Aloud: Review the upcoming objective and think aloud the process of creating an aligned exit ticket.
    - "Let me look back at the unit assessment/end goal assessment. What are the tasks that students need to be able to do?"
    - "In that context, what have they learned thus far up to this lesson? How can I create an exit ticket task aligned to the unit assessment, and what they've learned up to this point?"
    - "Let's check the task: Does it have the same complexity (of problem and/or text)?"
    - "Final check: does it align to what I taught this lesson? If it doesn't, what do I need to change about the lesson so students can master this?"
- Model a Think Aloud: Review an existing exit ticket against the objective and verify that it is aligned.
    - "Final check: Does it align to what I taught this lesson? If it doesn't, what do I need to change about the lesson so students can master this?"

**Plan the Practice/Do It:**

- Plan/revise a week's work of exit tickets. Have the upcoming interim/year-end assessment questions in hand to help set the rigor of the exit ticket.
- Look at previous exit tickets to see where students are struggling and what skills need to continue to be assessed.

**Real-Time Feedback**

- N/A

# Strategies for Coaching: Develop Effective Lesson Plans 101

| Action Step | See It | Plan the Practice | Do It | Cues for Real-Time Feedback |
|---|---|---|---|---|
| **Write precise learning objectives** | Model a Think Aloud: Refine an existing objective to make it (1) data-driven, (2) manageable and measurable, (3) center around conceptual understanding | • Pull out upcoming assessments to identify for review.<br>• Plan a full week of upcoming objectives together.<br>• Identify the right end goal from an upcoming assessment.<br>• Break down too-broad objectives to make them manageable for individual lessons.<br>• Rewrite lesson objectives to center them around the big ideas of the content. | • Plan and Do It are identical. | N/A |
| **Plan a Launch** | • Present an exemplar lesson plan with a scripted launch and unpack the purpose of each part of the launch.<br>• Model a Think Aloud: Plan the knowledge activation activities.<br>• Model-Think Aloud and Live Model of do now or class oral review. | • Select an upcoming lesson and plan an aligned do now or class oral review or hook.<br>• Script the introduction/routine for the do now or class oral review. | • Deliver the introduction to the Do Now or class oral review. | Hold out your palm and point to it with the other hand to indicate to them to go back to their script and follow it. |
| **Create/ Identify Key Tasks** | • Model a Think Aloud with an existing lesson plan/ curriculum.<br>• Model a Think Aloud when building a lesson plan from scratch. | • Review existing curriculum or plan to identify the key tasks that students need to do to build conceptual understanding and master the objective.<br>• Build the key tasks for a new lesson plan that align to the objective. | • Plan and Do It are identical. | N/A |
| **Plan the basic structure of the lesson** | • Do a Think Aloud for planning a model.<br>• Model a Think Aloud for inquiry. | • Design the model or inquiry for the lesson.<br>• Draft the basic structure of the lesson around that moment. | • Plan and Do It are identical. | N/A |

126    Get Better Faster 2.0

| Design an exit ticket aligned to the objective | • Model a Think Aloud: Review upcoming objective and think aloud the process of creating an aligned exit ticket.<br>• Model a Think Aloud: Review an existing exit ticket against the objective and verify that it is aligned. | • Plan/revise a week's work of exit tickets. Have the upcoming interim-/year-end assessment questions in hand to help set the rigor of the exit ticket.<br>• Look at previous exit tickets to see where students are struggling and what skills need to continue to be assessed. | • Plan and Do It are identical. | N/A |
|---|---|---|---|---|

## Internalize Existing Lesson Plans

> ### Teacher Professional Development Goal
>
> **Internalize Lesson Plans:** Update existing lesson plans to reflect the needs of your classroom.

My colleagues and I are huge advocates of sharing already-existing great lesson plans with new teachers. Teaching is so difficult and such a complex art that it's impossible to underestimate the power of filling in even one piece of the teaching puzzle for a new teacher just getting on their feet. When that piece is planning the lesson, it frees the teacher to get better at everything from perfecting tone to developing routines—the pieces you *can't* do for them—in hours that would otherwise have been spent developing a new lesson plan. In addition, if taken from a quality teacher, the already existing lesson plan will almost always be of better quality than what the new teacher would have developed on their own while also trying to prepare on all these other levels.

### Findings from the Field: Practice with Peers

"My teachers often collaborated to create lesson plans but there were many gaps between teachers at the time of the delivery on these same lessons. So, we started holding mini-planning clinics to help teachers internalize existing lesson plans. This was a game changer, particularly

Pre-teaching (Summer PD)

with my grade-level teams that had many first-year teachers! They spent less time spinning their wheels and more time perfecting a lesson."
—*Anabel Ruiz, Principal, Richardson, TX*

If you have access to quality lesson plans that you can share with a new teacher, the key is that the teacher must do more than just read through it. The action steps that follow will ensure new teachers can take full advantage of an existing lesson plan.

Here are a few challenges associated with adapting an existing lesson plan for use in one's own classroom:

- Teachers don't spend time on what matters most in the lesson (not because of pacing but because they don't realize what is most important).

- Teachers haven't internalized the lesson and may stumble when delivering it.

- Teachers run out of time, completing only part of the lesson plan and leaving large chunks untaught.

- Teachers don't anticipate areas where students will struggle given their struggles in previous lessons.

## Internalize Existing Lesson Plans: Identify the Productive Struggle in the Lesson

### Coaching Tips

**Teacher Context**

**Challenge**

- Lesson is unfocused or spends too much time in the wrong places.
- Teacher doesn't know what matters most in a given lesson.

**Action Step:**

- Identify the moment of most productive struggle in the lesson—what students need to know/be able to do to master the objective.

**Action Step Overview**
Recall the last time you learned something new, like a second language. A key concept in learning is trying to find what has been called the zone of proximal

development.[11] You cannot simply learn vocabulary lists and expect to master a new language. But you also cannot be thrown into an immersive environment without any foundation. How do we help students struggle? Make the struggle productive. You want students to be stretched but not so far that they are lost. What follows are ways to make sure students have productive struggle in every lesson.

> **Tip from a Coach—Pinpoint the struggle first:**
> "Always ensure that the potential gaps in learning or the academic struggles are identified in the teacher's lesson plans. This makes sure the rest of the lesson is built thinking about these gaps."
> —*Dr. Kenya Roberts, Principal, Shreveport, LA*

### Key Leadership Moves

**See It**

- Think aloud—review the lesson plan and identify the area of most productive struggle.
    - "Let's review the lesson plan. Which tasks are most important for them to master the objective but will also be a bit of a struggle for them?"
    - "Let me look back at yesterday's/last week's exit tickets: what gaps existed in their work that will likely appear again in this lesson?"
    - "Let me star that in my lesson plan—I have to focus here more than anywhere else when I'm teaching."

**Plan the Practice/Do It:**

- Review an upcoming lesson to determine the moment of most productive struggle.
    - Review past exit tickets to anticipate if students will struggle here.

**Real-Time Feedback**

- N/A

Zach Roach and Kelly Dowling coach their teachers to locate the most productive struggle for students in key sections of the memoirs *When I was Puerto Rican* and *Warriors Don't Cry*.

 WATCH Clip 21: **Internalize Lesson Plans—ID Productive Struggle**
(Key Leadership Move: Do it)

WATCH Clip 19: **Internalize Existing Lessons—ID Key Tasks**
(Key Leadership Move: See it)

## Internalize Existing Lesson Plans: Internalize Key Parts of Lesson

### Coaching Tips

**Teacher Context**

**Challenge**

- The teacher hasn't internalized the lesson and stumbles when delivering it.

**Action Step**

- Internalize and rehearse key parts of the lesson.

**Action Step Overview**

While the benefit of using an existing lesson plan is the teacher spends less time planning, an inherent risk is that they might not take the time to internalize it before teaching. The first most important area of focus for a new teacher is the delivery of the parts of the lesson where they do most of the talking: the I Do and all key instructions. Often, a new teacher will assume that these are the easy parts, and they won't practice them sufficiently. Memorizing these key parts can be a game-changer because, once that's done, the teacher is freed to focus on other parts of the lesson—the ones that can't be memorized in advance. Memorizing key parts of the lesson can be harder than it sounds: that's where your leadership is crucial.

### Key Leadership Moves

**See It**

- Think aloud the process of internalizing a section of the lesson:
    - "Ok, let me review my lesson routines. What are the key instructions I have to give at every part of the lesson? Have I mastered these, or would it be better to write them down?" (Model where you feel comfortable with one routine, but you write down the instructions for one where you are less comfortable.)
    - "Let me move to my model (if it exists.) What are the key questions I want to use in the model and what are the answers to each question?"

- (Tip: here are some universal thinking questions that can help)
- "What is this question asking me to do?"
- "What do I already know about this topic?"
- "What information is available for me in the prompt/task?"
- "What am I looking for as I read the text?"
- "How could I summarize this passage?"

**Plan the Practice**

- Build a lesson internalization routine: Determine when they will spend time each day memorizing key parts of the lesson, how they will practice, and who will be their practice partner (even if their "partner" is as basic as a mirror).
- Give the teacher a set time to learn a specific chunk of the lesson cold.

**Do It**

- Have teacher deliver a chunk of the lesson without reading straight off the lesson plan (but referring to it when needed).
- Practice one chunk of the lesson at a time. Once a teacher has it cold, put those chunks together until they have it completely internalized.

**Real-Time Feedback**

- When teacher is struggling with the lesson plan, intervene and cue students to turn and talk. Give teacher 30–60 seconds to skim the plan before jumping back into the lesson.

---

## Internalize Existing Lesson Plans: Build Time Stamps Into Lesson Coaching Tips

**Teacher Context**

**Challenge**

- The teacher runs out of time, completing only part of the lesson plan and leaving large chunks untaught.

**Action Step**

- Build time stamps into the lesson plan and follow them.

**Action Step Overview**

Every teacher constantly negotiates with time: "How can I fit as much learning as possible into the time I have for this lesson?" The challenge for new teachers is that it normally takes them far longer to teach the same material. Everything is slower: their instructions, their delivery, their class discussion, etc. One very simple strategy to help them is to put a time limit on every part of the lesson. If they know they should be done with homework review at 10:17 a.m., it helps give them urgency about moving forward. Time stamps are a teacher's best friend: They let them know immediately whether they are ahead of time or behind. It will be a while yet before teachers are necessarily able to meet all these time stamps—that's addressed further on in the Get Better Faster Scope and Sequence. For now, what's important is that they make it a habit to set realistic time management goals that will, when met, ensure that what's most important happens in each lesson.

## Key Leadership Moves

**See It**

- Model reviewing lesson plan and allotting time to each section.
  - "Let me start with the task of most productive struggle. How long do I want students to be able to spend on this?"
  - "Given that amount of time, how long can we spend on the launch?"
  - "If I'm running out of time, what can I cut without removing the productive struggle?"

**Plan the Practice**

- Write down specific time stamps in their lesson plan. Note which parts of the lesson could be trimmed or cut if teacher is running over.

**Do It**

- Rehearse the lesson with timer in hand. Cut unnecessary language that is slowing them down.

**Real-Time Feedback**

- Nonverbal: hold up fingers for how many more minutes to spend in that section the lesson.

- Jump in and cue students to turn and talk or work independently. Talk with the teacher for 30–60 seconds to decide what to cut from the lesson and how to adjust timing before jumping back in.

# Internalize Existing Lesson Plans: Adjust Lesson Plan to Target Student Needs

## Coaching Tips

**Teacher Context**

**Challenge**

The teacher doesn't anticipate areas where students will struggle given their struggles in previous lessons.

**Action Step**

Adjust the lesson plan to target the knowledge/skills that students need.

**Action Step Overview**

Teaching a lesson plan as is will rarely meet the needs of all students. Each class and students within the class have strengths and gaps when it comes to knowledge and skills. Knowing how to adapt lesson plans is not an intuitive skill. New teachers need support as they learn to adjust their lessons to meet student needs. As a leader, you can model using exit ticket data and other assessment data to target what students need to practice in a given lesson plan.

### Key Leadership Moves

**See It**

- Model Think Aloud:
  - Review last class's data: "Let's look at the last exit ticket: What did my students master and what are they struggling with? What are their gaps?"
  - Adjust the launch: "How can I adjust the opening 15 minutes to review/spiral concepts they are missing or give them knowledge they will need for the rest of the lesson?"
  - "Let me look at the moment of most productive struggle. Have I teed up the students to be able to access the task even if it will still be a struggle? Is there anything else that I need to do?"
  - (Note: We will dive even more deeply into this work in the section on Activating Knowledge in Phase 3.)

Pre-teaching (Summer PD)    133

**Plan the Practice/Do It:**

- Adapt the upcoming lesson plan to target the knowledge/skill that students need.

   **Tip from a Coach—Use the Menu as a Model:**
   "Many districts have preset curriculum and scripted lesson plans, yet teachers need to make these their own in order to teach effectively. I like to use the analogy of ordering from a menu to help teachers think through the lesson internalization process. When you visit a restaurant, you view the menu items, ingredients, side selections, and ultimately decide on what you want most. Lesson internalization follows the same process, save one small tweak—you make your decision based on what students need most."
   —Kimberly Ellis, Principal, Corpus Christi, TX

**Real-Time Feedback**

- N/A

Katie and her teacher refine his upcoming 8th grade math lesson:

 WATCH Clip 22: **Internalize Existing Lesson Plans—Adjust** (Key Leadership Move: Do it)

## Strategies for Coaching: Internalize Existing Lesson Plans

| Action Step | See It Questions | Plan the Practice | Do It | Cues for Real-Time Feedback |
|---|---|---|---|---|
| Identify the moment of most productive struggle | • Think aloud—review the lesson plan and identify the area of most productive struggle. | • Plan and Do It are identical: Review an upcoming lesson to determine the moment of most productive structure.<br>• Review past exit tickets to anticipate if students will struggle here. | • Plan and Do It are identical. | N/A |

134  Get Better Faster 2.0

| | | | |
|---|---|---|---|
| **Internalize and rehearse key parts of the lesson** | • Think aloud the process of internalizing a section of the lesson. | • Build a lesson internalization routine: Determine when they will spend time each day memorizing key parts of the lesson, how they will practice, and who will be their practice partner (even if their "partner" is as basic as a mirror).<br>• Give the teacher a set time to learn a specific chunk of the lesson cold. | • Have teacher deliver a chunk of the lesson without reading straight off the lesson plan (but referring to it when needed).<br>• Practice one chunk of the lesson at a time. Once a teacher has it cold, put those chunks together until they have it completely internalized. | • When the teacher is struggling with the lesson plan, intervene, and cue students to turn and talk. Give the teacher 30–60 seconds to skim the plan before jumping back into the lesson. |
| **Build time stamps into the lesson** | • Model reviewing lesson plan and allotting time to each section. | • Write down specific time stamps in their lesson plan. Note which parts of the lesson could be trimmed or cut if teacher is running over. | • Rehearse the lesson with timer in hand. Cut unnecessary language that is slowing them down. | • Nonverbal: Hold up fingers for how many more minutes to spend in that section of the lesson.<br>• Jump in and cue students to turn and talk or work independently. Talk with the teacher for 30–60 to decide what to cut from the lesson how to adjust timing before jumping back in. |
| **Adjust the lesson plan to target student needs** | • Model Think Aloud: Review upcoming lesson plan against recent student data.<br>• Model Think Aloud: Adjust the launch to review/ spiral concepts students are missing or need. | • Adapt the upcoming lesson plan to target the knowledge/skill that students need. | • Plan and Do It are identical. | N/A |

Pre-teaching (Summer PD)   **135**

**Write an Exemplar**

> ## Teacher Professional Development Goal
>
> **Write the Exemplar:** Script ideal student responses that show what it looks like when students "get" it.

Mark Twain famously wrote, "The difference between the right word and almost the right word is the difference between lightning and a lightning bug."[12] Doug Lemov makes the same distinction in the first edition of *Teach Like a Champion* cautioning, "The likelihood is strong that students will stop striving when they hear the word 'right,' so there's a real risk to naming as right that which is not truly and completely right."[13] Although a new teacher needn't perfect the basics of responding to an almost-right (or outright wrong) answer until Phase 3, *identifying* the right answers is a fundamental building block in this critical skill set that must be put in place during Phase 1.

Several years ago, my colleagues and I—along with countless other educators across the nation—faced the daunting task of raising the rigor of our writing instruction to match the demands of the Common Core. Together, we looked closely at exactly what our most successful teachers were doing to raise the bar for rigor higher than ever before while still meeting students at their level. The single biggest game-changer we discovered? The act of writing an exemplar. It's a practice that revolutionized how we taught not only English classes, but history, science, and even math.

The most successful teachers, we found, didn't stop at just writing a lesson objective—however precise and measurable—or even at defining how they would assess whether students had met that objective (both skills that were addressed in Phase 1 Rigor). They took it one step further and scripted *exactly what student responses would look like* when the students had learned what they needed to know. When teachers create a strong exemplar at the beginning of their lesson planning process, they don't just have an end goal for their lesson: they have an end goal in high definition.

> ## Core Idea
>
> When you create a strong exemplar, you don't just have an end goal for your lesson: You have an end goal in high definition.

136   Get Better Faster 2.0

They can then "backward-plan" with unparalleled clarity, creating exactly the lesson that will get students to be able to produce that exemplar themselves.

What does writing an exemplar look like? After you have designed an effective question, the teacher's next step is to answer the question as an adult—not a hypothetical student, the result of which would be a watered-down version of what the teacher thinks the students at the relevant grade level can accomplish. Too often, we prematurely lower our expectations for what students can do. Writing an adult exemplar prevents the teacher from falling into that trap. After doing so, teachers can unpack all the steps they took in order to write that response, considering, for example: "What were you thinking at each phase? How did you know to cite this evidence or write this transition?" The answers to these questions will get you into the mind-set of the students, and they will help you clarify what to look for and where the students will likely not have developed the same writing habits.

To be clear, when you look for student success in meeting your exemplar, you're not looking for a response that mimics the teacher's verbatim. On the contrary, you're looking for answers that reflect the analytical skill represented in your exemplar—so much the better if students are able to analyze texts with rigorous and independent thinking to reach, articulate, and support a rich array of valid conclusions. So, how's a teacher to tell the difference between a limited student response and a response that simply voices a different, yet equally valid interpretation than the one the teacher captured in the exemplar? By *sparring with your own exemplar*—just as you would want your students to intellectually spar with each other in an animated class discussion—in advance of the lesson. The teacher can accomplish this by reading the critics who have written about the text their students are reading or comparing notes with other educators who are teaching the same literature. Then they can enhance the exemplar to include any new findings, change it, or note what evidence students would have to cite to adequately support other conclusions. Then, when the teacher checks students' responses, they will have a sense of whether varying responses are coming way from way out in left field, or just giving the teacher another chance to spar with an alternate reading of the text.

---

### Core Idea

If you want to be exemplary, spar with an exemplar.

---

Pre-teaching (Summer PD)    **137**

Let's look at a couple of examples of the process of writing an exemplar. In the first, we'll build off of the example of Sonya, a high school English teacher, who is working with her students on Shakespeare's sonnet 65.

> Since brass, nor stone, nor earth, nor boundless sea,
> But sad mortality o'er-sways their power,
> How with this rage shall beauty hold a plea,
> Whose action is no stronger than a flower?
> O, how shall summer's honey breath hold out 5
> Against the wreckful siege of battering days,
> When rocks impregnable are not so stout,
> Nor gates of steel so strong, but Time decays?
> O fearful meditation! Where, alack,
> Shall Time's best jewel from Time's chest lie hid? 10
> Or what strong hand can hold his swift foot back?
> Or who his spoil of beauty can forbid?
> O, none, unless this miracle have might,
> That in black ink my love may still shine bright.

Sonya generated an exemplar response final writing task: how does Shakespeare's use of figurative language help convey the theme of his sonnet? After doing do, she compared her answer to that of the head of her English Department, Steve Chiger:

> Shakespeare's Sonnet 65 is, in many ways, a poem about the transcendent power of writing. Through his use of imagery and metaphor, Shakespeare is ultimately able to underscore his poem's theme: That his writing, despite the entropic processes of the natural world, is ultimately what will sustain beauty. Here, time plays the role of the aggressor, devastating all in its path. Shakespeare develops an extended metaphor in lines 5–8 to highlight this notion, worrying that "summer's honey breath" cannot hold out against Time's "wreckful siege" (5–6). The diction of this metaphor suggests that Time is a conquering army with the power to destroy "rocks impregnable" and "gates of steel." The writer's choice amplifies the power of Time to destroy even a powerfully fortified city. Interestingly, beauty is not described a fortified citadel but rather simply as "honey breath" (5). Clearly, it is not long for the

world. Shakespeare engineers a similar contrast during his first quatrain, where he offers up the concrete diction of "brass," "stone," and "boundless sea" only to remind the reader that they will be shuddered by time (1). When he compares beauty to a flower in line 4, the contrasting imagery signals that its doom is a foregone conclusion. With all of this in mind, it is perhaps the imagery at the poem's final couplet that is most compelling. When the speaker hopes the "miracle" of his writing "may still shine bright," his implied comparison to a star relies on a symbol that now outranks the earthly imagery used in the first two quatrains of his poem (13-14). That is, his writing is more powerful than an army, more powerful than a stone, more powerful than the earth itself. Time may be able to destroy Earth, but the speaker's poetry is of the heavens. By coding this hierarchy into the very level of his language, Shakespeare emphasizes the speaker's faith in the power of his writing.

She realized that she picked some different evidence (which was totally reasonable), but that Steve's depth of analysis of particular diction used by Shakespeare went beyond her own. As she unpacked the differences, she was able to start to identify the key areas where her students might overlook Shakespeare's power and where she should look when monitoring how students were doing during their writing.

Although math is a very different subject, generating exemplar responses to a complex word problem is just as valuable. Let's take a look at third-grade math, when students are learning to multiply. One of the core problems they will solve in class is as follows:

> Renee had 14 cups of juice. Each cup of juice had 3 tablespoons of sugar. How many tablespoons of sugar did Renee drink in all? Show all your work, write a number sentence, and explain your strategy.

On the surface, this is a basic question: 14 x 3 = 42. But for third graders who don't yet multiply numbers of this size with fluency or automaticity, there are a myriad of ways in which they might try to solve the problem. Moreover, the key is not just the answer, but their ability to articulate why: If they get this right and you ask them why, what do you want them to say?

Pre-teaching (Summer PD) **139**

> ### Core Idea
>
> When writing an exemplar, move beyond just the "what" to the "why":
> If they get this right and you ask them why, what do you want
> them to say?

When you ask this question to yourself, you start generating multiple plausible responses and the reasoning behind each one. You think about a student who could choose to add manually (14 + 14, then add 14 more), a student that will build a model, with tens and ones and another that knows how to multiply. So when asking the class why the answer is 42, the teacher is looking for a response like this one:

> I broke down 14 into 10 and 4, and then made 3 groups of each. Since I
> know that 10 x 3 = 30 and 4 x 3 equals 12, 14 x 3 must equal 42, because
> 30 + 12 = 42. This matches the problem because each of the 14 cups
> of sugar is an equal group of 3 tablespoons, and so if you split up the
> 10 equal groups and the 4 equal groups, you can more efficiently solve.

Is this the only way to answer the question? By no means. And it can help (time permitting) to draft a number of different plausible answers. Drafting these exemplars allows the teacher to look out for it while teaching, and it gives her clarity as to what additional strategies she will try to emphasize with students who are struggling. In short, it gives her a road map to rigor.

## Findings from the Field: Craft an Ideal Response to Understand the End Goal

"When we first started utilizing common assessments and exit tickets, we got teachers to think with the end goal in mind. But it wasn't until they drafted their own exemplar responses that they started thinking about what it would take to get there. They started thinking like a student, which helped them teach the students."

—*Lisa Hill, Principal Supervisor, Atlanta, GA*

Once you have an exemplar in hand, the implementation of independent practice can fly (more on independent practice in Phase 2).

What follows are the classroom challenges that a teacher will be able to meet most immediately by mastering the art of writing an exemplar:

- The teacher doesn't know what a rigorous student response looks like.

Let's take a closer look at the action step that will enable a teacher to meet these challenges, as well as starting them down the road to writing great exemplars.

## Write the Exemplar: Script an Ideal Response
## Coaching Tips

### Teacher Context

### Challenge

- The teacher doesn't know what a rigorous student response to a question looks like.

### Action Step

- Script the ideal written responses you want students to produce during independent practice.

### Action Step Overview

A new teacher's first step to working with an exemplar successfully is scripting the exemplar word for word. By doing this a teacher defines what "high expectations" means for every lesson. But scripting the exemplar also serves a secondary purpose: It subtly develops the teacher's own expertise. Writing and sparring with an exemplar serve to exponentially deepen the teacher's understanding of the topic they are teaching, because doing so forces them to think through what it really means to understand this topic.

### Key Leadership Moves

In working on exemplar responses with your new teacher, your See It will naturally blend into your planning and practice as everything will be centered around producing or revising the actual exemplar in your meeting.

### See It

- Model scripting out an ideal written response for an independent practice task, thinking aloud as you do the process.

Pre-teaching (Summer PD) **141**

- For STEM, consider generating multiple possibilities (e.g., solving graphically and algebraically).
- For Humanities, focus on the quality of your evidence and argument that you want students to match.

**Plan the Practice/Do It:**

- Write or revise exemplars for a written-response questions in upcoming lessons.
  - Make sure the teacher scripts the exact answer they are expecting. That way, the teacher will be able to recognize it when they hear it (or don't) from their students.
- Spar with another exemplar: either another teacher's exemplar, or the analysis of the experts in the field (for example, the analysis that Shakespearean experts have done of the same sonnet or play).
- Break down the exemplar and identify the key things the student will need to do to produce a response of the same quality. This will be critical for the execution of the rest of the teacher's lesson.

**Real-Time Feedback**

- N/A

Literacy:

 REWATCH Clip 21: **Internalize Leson Plans—ID Productive Struggle**
(Key Leadership Move: Do it)

Math:

 WATCH Clip 23: **Write the Exemplar**
(Key Leadership Move: Do it)

## Strategies for Coaching: Write an Exemplar

| Action Step | See It | Plan the Practice | Do It | Cues for Real-Time Feedback |
|---|---|---|---|---|
| **Script an Ideal Response** | Model scripting out an idea written response for an independent practice task, thinking aloud as you do the process. | • Write or revise exemplars for a written-response question in upcoming lessons.<br>• "Spar" with another exemplar: either another teacher's exemplar or experts in the field (e.g., Shakespearean critics).<br>• Break down the exemplar: ID key things the student will need to do to produce a response of the same quality. | • Plan and Do It are identical. | N/A |

## Stop and Jot

What are the three top coaching ideas you plan to use to train your teachers in these Phase 1 Rigor skills? Jot them here.

_____

_____

_____

_____

## CONCLUSION

As James Clear shares in *Atomic Habits,* solid systems transform new behaviors into established habits. Just as regular runs prepare runners for a marathon, summer rehearsals give teachers multiple opportunities to design and practice their essential routines and procedures. This muscle memory becomes engrained over time, making it possible for new teachers to start the year strong, confident that they know what they want their classroom to look like and how to get students there. Either by building routines (Management) or the systems for learning (Rigor), these run-throughs prepare teachers for showtime—the first day with students.

With the opening number complete, you can move on to Phase 2: Instant Immersion.

# Phase 2

# Instant Immersion

My first days of teaching began in Mexico City. When my wife Gaby and I first got married, we moved back to Mexico so she could complete medical school. While Gaby is completely bilingual, I was not even close when we first arrived. I still remember how at ease Gaby was in conversation with family, friends, and co-workers and how much I had to think before I could utter a coherent sentence. While Gaby was right in her element in Mexico, I was in a state of instant immersion.

I started working as an English teacher at a nearby school and taught there for six years. During that time, nearly all of my colleagues were Mexican and spoke only Spanish with me. The one exception was the English Department, which was largely made up of recently arrived native speakers like myself who were all struggling to communicate effectively in Spanish.

Over the course of the next several months, our small team began to divide. Some of us grew more proficient at a surprisingly rapid pace, while others never felt comfortable saying much more in Spanish than basic interactions and how they preferred their coffee. Even up to five years later, they struggled to communicate with their students' parents or follow local politics.

What made the difference? It wasn't a matter of which among us were more outgoing or even who had studied Spanish the longest before making the journey to Mexico. Instead, the teachers who were able to ride the waves of instant immersion—both functioning and learning as we went—had two key characteristics in common: They had learned a solid foundation of grammar and vocabulary to be able to string sentences together, and they took every opportunity to apply them each day.

I recall my own first days interacting with colleagues at my school. I listened intently to see what phrases they were using to describe certain things, and then I practiced. I didn't try to do it all at first (engaging in a dinner conversation was too difficult because of trying to keep up with the pace and all the different voices!) but focused on one-on-one conversations where I had more time to think and formulate my words. Because of my own language limitations, I was most successful at first with using as few words as possible. When I got a blank stare or look of confusion, I went back and revised my words or conjugation until I was understood. I would often formulate whole phrases in my head first before speaking to have a better chance at success. I observed, took mental notes, and practiced. Each time I fell flat on my face, I would get up and try again.

The process didn't feel quick—it felt agonizingly slow!—but those around me could see the difference much more than I could.

Learning to teach is the same as learning a foreign language: you need a solid foundation, but then you need to dive in with the basics. Phase 1 was all about the foundation. Phase 2 is about diving in: using the experience of instant immersion into teaching not as a drowning experience but an opportunity to tread water as you learn to swim.

> ### Core Idea
>
> Learning to teach is like learning a language.
>
> Phase 1 is about learning the rules.
> Phase 2 is about using them to communicate.

Of course, instant immersion is a challenge even with this level of support. (Treading water can be terrifying when first learning to swim!).

Phase 2 doesn't eliminate the stress and anxiety of a first-year teacher's experience (although it can definitely reduce it). When implemented well, Phase 2 allows a teacher to move toward swimming and away from drowning—and that makes all the difference.

## PHASE 2 COACHING BLUEPRINT: MAKE TIME FOR FEEDBACK

The number one thing you'll need to kickstart your year of delivering feedback is a schedule that ensures you have time to do it. Here, we'll show how to schedule time to engage the coaching principles presented in Make It Bite-Sized and Practice What You Value; we'll also provide materials to make your first feedback meeting with each of your new teachers a success.

### Make Time for Feedback

At a training I once led, I showed a video of a coach giving a teacher feedback and had asked participants to share their responses to the video. Many participants commented on the positive tone of the feedback or on how specific it was; but one school leader was distracted by one specific word the coach in the video had used: "today."

"The first thing she said was, 'When I observed you *today*,'" he remarked. "Not 'way back before Halloween,' but 'today.' That teacher is going to remember exactly the moment she's talking about and be able to do something about it tomorrow. What kind of scheduling makes it possible for a leader to have such fast turnaround on observation feedback?"

The answer takes up an entire chapter in *Leverage Leadership 2.0*—one that explains how to arrange your whole schedule around providing weekly observation and feedback to every teacher in your school. This section, however, will be more succinct, summing up just the most important steps to establishing a reliable observation and feedback schedule for all your new teachers. If you've already built a solid schedule that locks in observations of all your teachers, skip forward to next section. If not, read through the following three steps. For best results, pull out your calendar and build your schedule as you read!

Instant Immersion    **147**

### Block, Lock, and Backward-Plan: Four Steps to Scheduling Observation and Feedback

1. **Delegate—distribute your teachers among the members of your leadership team.** The first key is to make sure you have a reasonable load of teachers to observe. Our experiences with leaders across the country have shown that getting to a ratio of 30 teachers to one instructional leader meets the needs of 90 percent of school leaders. 30-to-1 allows for biweekly observations; 15-to-1 allows for weekly observations. For new (and most!) teachers, that is far more ideal!

2. **Block out time when you're likely to be interrupted.** The next key to making feedback meetings stick in your schedule is a simple one: Don't plan them for the times of day when you're likely to get interrupted. Meetings planned around breakfast, lunch, or after school usually become missed meetings because that's when principals most often need to speak with students or parents about specific, immediate challenges. Block out moments like this, as well as any other hours of the week you can't devote to teachers. The time that remains is what you have to work with in planning the feedback meetings.

3. **Lock in feedback meetings first.** Locking in your feedback meetings *before* you plan when you'll observe each teacher is an excellent accountability tool: If you've already arranged to meet teachers and you know they will be waiting in your office to receive your feedback, you have an added incentive to follow through. You also save yourself a ton of time because you remove long strings of email exchanges to try to find a time to meet. By pinning down regular check-ins with each teacher, you save time and create a solid structure around which teachers can plan.

4. **Plan your observation schedule.** The final step is obvious: Plan when to observe. Observing your teachers in action as soon as possible before your weekly feedback meeting with them will help you know firsthand what coaching the teacher most urgently needs that week—and the teacher will be able to implement it immediately. Plan a 20- or 30-minute slot—one that comes earlier in the week than the time you've planned to hold a feedback meeting with the new teacher—during which to observe them. (Like the feedback meetings, observations may be planned back to back to increase efficiency.)

Once you've done this, here's what your schedule might look like if you manage 15 teachers.[1]

| | Monday | Tuesday | Wednesday | Thursday | Friday |
|---|---|---|---|---|---|
| 6am | | | | | |
| :30 | | | | | |
| 7am | | | | | |
| :30 | | | | | |
| 8am | | | | | |
| :30 | | | | | |
| 9am | | Observe Myers, Thomas, Glassman | | Meet Lajon | Meet McClain |
| :30 | | | Observe Park, Lennox, Quintero | Observe McClain, Gomes, Bradford | Meet Gomes |
| 10am | Observe Woods, Leon, Adu | | | | Meet Bradford |
| :30 | | | | | |
| 11am | | | | Meet Quintero | |
| :30 | | | | Meet Lennox | |
| 12pm | | Observe Choudhury, Dennis, Lajon | | Meet Park | |
| :30 | | | | | |
| 1pm | Meet Leon | Meet Myers | Meet Dennis | | |
| :30 | Meet Woods | Meet Thomas | Meet Choudhury | | |
| 2pm | Meet Adu | Meet Glassman | | | |
| :30 | | | | | |
| 3pm | | | | | |
| :30 | | | | | |
| 4pm | | | | | |
| :30 | | | | | |
| 5pm | | | | | |
| :30 | | | | | |

Instant Immersion **149**

What have you accomplished when you set this schedule? You've committed to regularly completing the one step that will most fuel teacher growth: providing the specific coaching each teacher needs most urgently at all times. Building this coaching into your calendar is half the battle to making sure every teacher receives it.

> ## Core Idea
>
> When it comes to giving teachers feedback,
> setting up the schedule is half the battle.

Once you have a schedule and observe regularly, how do you keep from spending too much time in preparing to give your leaders feedback? If it takes hours to prepare each meeting, you will quickly find it unsustainable. In the next "Findings from the Field," Ritu Pasricha provides some helpful tips to save time and become more efficient in planning meetings:

### Findings from the Field: Tips to Save Time

"When I first started school leadership, I couldn't find time to prepare for meetings. Over time, I learned the following that changed my practice:

1. **Calendar prep time for yourself:** Block out time where other leaders can cover the school and you can hide away to prepare for your coaching meetings. (Leave your office: interruptions will always find you there!)

2. **Stay consistent by following your one-pagers*:** Use your guides for feedback meetings or data meetings. Even if you could find a better way to say it, it takes time, and that's what you have the least of as a leader.

3. **Use economy of language.** Trust me—it actually helps you as a leader to Get Better Faster at all that you do (professionally and in personal life too!)."

—Ritu Pasricha, Principal, Pune, India

*These one-pagers can be found in the print-ready materials.

(If you're interested in additional tools to help you monitor and maintain observation and feedback, *Leverage Leadership 2.0* includes a great deal more guidance and resources.)

## Set the Tone: The First Feedback Meeting

It's one thing to schedule your feedback meetings and another to know what to do when a teacher who's never received this kind of feedback before is sitting right in front of you. The "Coaching Principle 2: Practice What You Value" section of Principles of Coaching addressed the core areas of giving effective feedback as well as how to create a culture of feedback ("Principle 3: Give Feedback Frequently"). However, those alone don't change the reality that a first feedback meeting is daunting for anyone! Such a meeting comes more easily when you create a safe, productive meeting environment where teachers can thrive. Your first feedback meeting is critical for setting the tone for the year.

---

### Core Idea

You never get a second chance to make a first impression.
The quality of your first meeting sets the tone for the rest of the year.

---

What does it take to start on the right foot? The key is to focus on rolling out what feedback meetings will look like: make the routines visible. If this strikes you as similar to the emphasis on teachers setting up student routines which you worked on during Phase 1, you're correct—adults need these types of routines just as much as students do. Let's take a look at the most important ones that will drive the first feedback meeting.

What's the greatest challenge new teachers face in the earliest part of the year? Managing the sheer amount of work it takes to teach. Personal organization may not sound momentous, but it can be the single hardest part of setting up a successful classroom—as many of us recall all too well. "I was spending too much time on materials, and staying too late," one new teacher remembered of her first month in the classroom. "My morale was taking a hit, and it was hard to get little tasks done when all I could do was think about how much I had to do."

The solution? Provide teachers with tools for personal organization and use them with teachers to track their priorities throughout the year.

Instant Immersion    151

> **Core Idea**
>
> Save teachers hours in just a few minutes:
> Give them tools to track their time.

See the next "Findings from the Field" to consider the tools used by Nikki Bridges with teachers:

## Findings from the Field: Provide Tools for Personal Organization

"My first move at my first meeting with a new teacher is to give them a binder full of all the materials they will need to stay organized throughout the year. That includes:

- **Task Management Tracker**—The task management tracker establishes what each teachers' tasks are and the space to plan how they will complete them. Consolidating this information in one place is immensely helpful for a new teacher trying to remember so many different tasks at once.

- **Calendar**—Previewing a school calendar with a new teacher may seem like a mundane agenda item to include during a feedback meeting, but it's a critical one. Making sure the teacher has a calendar that shows important deadlines or upcoming school events—and has reviewed that calendar!—will go a long way toward ensuring the teacher plans their time effectively.

- **Weekly Meeting Notes**—To be sure the teacher is able to make use of what you cover during your feedback meeting, provide them with a space to take notes while you're working together. Just like an observation tracker for you, the weekly meeting note space will remind the teacher of what's most important to work on right now even in the midst of everything else going on during a busy school day.

- **Data-Driven Instructional Plan**—With so many daily tasks for a new teacher to accomplish, it's easy to lose track of the big picture: the learning goals for every student for the year. A copy of the current instructional plan serves as a reminder that all these smaller daily and weekly actions align with student learning needs— something that can help both to motivate the teacher and to build their understanding of the "why" behind each week's action step."

When a new teacher has all of these located in one binder, I remove a major obstacle that could keep them from being successful."

—*Nikki Bridges, Instructional Leader, San Antonio, TX*

152    Get Better Faster 2.0

It needn't take more than five minutes to present these tools in your first meeting with a teacher—and once you've done it with one teacher, you can do it with everyone else, too.

The meeting templates that follow, as well as the Sample Data-Driven Instructional Plan, are some samples you could use or adapt.

## Task Management Tracker

### Monday

| Time | | |
|---|---|---|
| 7:00-7:30 | | |
| 7:30-8:10 | | |
| 8:10-8:40 | | |
| 8:40-9:25 | | |
| 9:25-10:10 | | |
| 10:10-10:40 | | |
| 10:40-10:25 | | |
| 10:25-12:10 | | |
| 12:10-12:40 | | |
| 12:40-1:30 | | |
| 1:30-2:15 | | |
| 2:15-2:30 | | |
| 2:30-3:25 | | |
| 3:25-4:05 | | |
| After School | | |

| Before I leave | Prep 1 |
|---|---|
| At home | Prep 2 |

Instant Immersion  **153**

# Meetings Notes Template

**Weekly Meeting Notes Page**

| Date: | | Meeting Type:<br>(feedback, data, co-teacher) | |
|---|---|---|---|
| **My Strengths** | | | |
| ☐ | | | |
| ☐ | | | |

| My Action Steps | Timeline |
|---|---|
| ☐ | |
| ☐ | |

| **Notes for Planning & Practice** |
|---|
| |

| **Follow-up Steps** |
|---|
| |

## Sample Data-Driven Instructional Plan:

*Part III. 5-Week Re-Teach Plan—Next 3 Weeks – Dates: 11/14 through 1/22*

**Week 3 (11/26–11/30): SD, 2-2, Review of 10-1 Grammar IA, *The Piano Lesson* Act I, Quote Integration**
- Vocab: 2-1 and 2-2 Review
- Literature: *The Piano Lesson* Act I—(Symbol and Conflict)
- Writing: Focus on Thesis Statements
- Quiz: 2-1 and 2-2, Grammar Review

**Week 4 (12/3-12/7): SD, 2-3, Pronoun Antecedent Agreement, *The Piano Lesson* Act I and Act II,**
- Vocab: 2-3
- Grammar: Pronoun Antecedent Agreement Guided Practice
- Literature: *The Piano Lesson* Acts I and II (More Symbol and Conflict)
- Writing: Integrating Citations more Fluidly
- Quiz: 2-3, SD, Pronoun Antecedent Agreement

**Week 5 (12/10-12/14): ER, 2-4, Pronoun Reflective/Reciprocal, *The Piano Lesson* Act II,**
- Vocab: 2-4; Grammar: Pronoun Reflexive/Reciprocal Guided Practice
- Literature: *The Piano Lesson* Act II (Theme)
- Writing: Clinching Statements: So What?
- Quiz: 2-4, ER, Pronoun Reflexive/Reciprocal

---

## Stop and Jot: Tools for Personal Organization

Which of the tools shared here do you plan to use with your teachers? Which do you have already and which will you need to create?

Instant Immersion   155

Once you've set up the organization of your feedback meeting, it's time to set the tone with a preview of the format your meeting will follow. This is also the time to plant the roots of the relationship you intend to build with this teacher, one based on both professionalism and trust. Here's an overview of what to include and do:

- **Preview the format:** Walking through what you will do in the meeting reduces anxiety and allows teachers to focus on the current moment.

- **Create an emotional safe space:** Asking teachers how they are doing—and genuinely listening to their response—is a vital foundation for feedback.

- **Share the tools:** Task management, calendar, meeting templates.

- **Set PD goals:** Save the setting of professional goals until the end of the first meeting: a perfect segue into giving feedback. (Use your Get Better Faster sequence to guide you.)

- **Give feedback!** Refer to the Giving Effective Feedback guide in the print-ready materials to script this portion of the meeting. Many school leaders rely on this document to build their capacity to give precise, specific feedback. It is one of the most commonly used handouts in the Rainbow Guide.

These simple steps don't take much time, but they change outcomes. By acknowledging where teachers are emotionally and organizing their time, you free up mental space for them to focus on their teaching—that can make all the difference.

## Findings from the Field: End on a Strong Note

"When I plan my meetings with my staff, I make it a point to always end on a strong note:

1. Always close the feedback meeting with a plan for the next step (including the upcoming observation).

2. Plan to observe to close the loop on the feedback.

This way, my team knows that I care and that the substance of the meeting is important."

—*Siva Kotla, Principal Supervisor, Pune, India*

We're now ready to give Phase 2 feedback. Read on!

## Teaching Skills Overview

In Phase 1, we set the foundation—developing routines and lesson planning. Phase 2 takes that foundation and rolls it out: implementing the major routines— both for engagement and academic learning—that will transform classrooms into productive spaces for learning.

Structured, consistent routines maximize learning time. Instead of students spending precious time figuring out what happens next and what it looks like to do it well, they can instead focus on the demands of the academic tasks we set before them.

### Phase 2 Action Step Sequence

| Management Trajectory | Rigor Trajectory |
|---|---|
| **Roll Out and Monitor Routines**<br><br>3. **What to Do:** Use economy of language when giving directions:<br>• Make them bite-sized (e.g., 3–5 words) and observable.<br>• Chunk your directions: give them one by one in sequential order.<br>• Check for understanding on complex instructions.<br><br>4. **See your Students:** Know when students are engaged or unengaged<br>• Make eye contact: look at all students for on-task engagement:<br>    ○ Choose 3–4 focus areas (places where you have students who often get off task) to look toward consistently.<br>• Circulate the room with purpose (break the plane):<br>    ○ Move among the desks and around the perimeter. | **Roll Out Academic Routines**<br><br>5. **Independent Practice:** Set up daily routines that build opportunities for students to practice independently:<br>• Write first, talk second: give students writing tasks to complete prior to class discussion, so that every student answers independently before hearing their peers' contributions.<br>• Implement a daily entry prompt (Do Now) to either introduce the day's objective or review material from the previous day.<br>• Use an exit ticket (brief final task) to assess end-of-class mastery.<br><br>6. **Academic Monitoring 101:** Check students' independent work to determine whether they're learning and what feedback is needed |

*(Continued)*

Instant Immersion    **157**

| Management Trajectory | Rigor Trajectory |
|---|---|
| ○ Stand at the corners: identify three spots on perimeter of the room to which you can circulate to stand and monitor student work.<br>○ Move away from the student who is speaking to monitor the whole room.<br>5. **Routines and Procedures 201:** Revise and perfect them<br>• Revise any routine that needs more attention to detail or is inefficient, emphasizing what students and teachers are doing at each moment.<br>• Do It Again: have students do the routine again if initially incorrect.<br><br>**Build Trust and Rapport**<br>6. **Narrate the Positive**<br>• Warm welcome: make eye contact, smile, and greet students.<br>• Narrate what students do well, not what they do wrong:<br>○ "Table two is ready: their books are open and all are reading."<br>○ "I like how Javon has anticipated a counter-argument to strengthen his thesis."<br>• Praise intellect, not just behavior–reinforce students getting smarter:<br>○ Affirm the effort, not just the outcome: "Your diligence on revising your thesis really paid off here." | • Create and implement a monitoring pathway:<br>○ Name the lap: Announce what you will be looking for and how you will code work/give feedback as you circulate.<br>○ Monitor the fastest writers first to gather trends, then the students who need more support.<br>• "Pen in hand": Give written feedback to student work:<br>○ Compare answers to the exemplar: what are they missing?<br>○ Give quick feedback (star, circle, pre-established code).<br>○ Cue students to revise answers using minimal verbal intervention (affirm the effort, name error, ask to fix it).<br>• Gather data while monitoring and prepare to respond:<br>○ Track student responses: ideal, almost there, further off.<br>○ Determine how to respond: stop the class for a quick fix, activate knowledge, model or discourse.<br>7. **Guide Discourse 101:** Launch the discourse cycle around the productive struggle:<br>• Everybody writes or Show-call (post student work for students to analyze—exemplars, non-exemplars or both). |

158   Get Better Faster 2.0

| Management Trajectory | Rigor Trajectory |
|---|---|
| • While narrating the positive, look at student(s) who are off-task.<br>7. **Make authentic connections:**<br>  • Memorize student names and use them each time you call on them.<br>  • Make self-to-student connection when they share a struggle, interest or passion ("I struggled when. . ." or "I love that, too!")<br>  • Show genuine concern: keep a tracker of important details and dates for each student to follow up with them; check in with them after class when something is off. | • Turn and talk<br>• Cold call, then volleyball (multiple students speak before teacher)<br>• Prompt for and praise basic Habits of Discussion to strengthen conversation and listening skills (i.e., build, evaluate, agree/disagree, etc.)<br>• Stamp the key understanding: "What are the keys to remember?" |

## PHASE 2 MANAGEMENT—ROLL OUT AND MONITOR ROUTINES/BUILD TRUST AND RAPPORT

### Quick Reference Guide

| If your teacher is struggling to: | . . .jump to: |
|---|---|
| **What to Do** ||
| Give clear directions | Make them bite-sized and chunk them |
| Make sure students understand the directions | Check for understanding on complex instructions |
| **See your Students** ||
| Notice if students are paying attention | Make eye contact |
| Leave the front of the room or teacher desk | Circulate the room |

Instant Immersion   159

| Routines and Procedures 201 | |
| --- | --- |
| Fix an inefficient or ineffective routine | Revise any routine that needs more attention/detail |
| Get all students to follow a routine | Do it again |
| **Narrate the Positive** | |
| Start class on a positive note | Warm welcome |
| Name what's working well in the classroom | Narrate what students do well, not what they do wrong |
| Praise more than just student behavior | Praise intellect, not just behavior |
| Leverage praise to re-engage off-task students | While narrating the positive, look at student(s) who are disengaged |
| **Make Authentic Connections** | |
| Make students feel seen | Memorize student names and use them |
| Find commonalities with students | Make self-to-student connection |
| Show care in the classroom | Show genuine concern |

## Phase 2 Scope and Sequence

| Management Trajectory | Rigor Trajectory |
| --- | --- |
| **Roll Out and Monitor Routines**<br>3. **What to Do:** Use economy of language when giving directions:<br>• Make them bite-sized (e.g., 3–5 words) and observable.<br>• Chunk your directions: Give them one by one in sequential order.<br>• Check for understanding on complex instructions. | **Roll Out Academic Routines:**<br>5. **Independent Practice:** Set up daily routines that build opportunities for students to practice independently<br>• Write first, talk second: give students writing tasks to complete prior to class discussion, so that every student answers independently before hearing their peers' contributions. |

160   Get Better Faster 2.0

| Management Trajectory | Rigor Trajectory |
|---|---|
| 4. **See your Students:** Know when students are engaged or unengaged<br>• Make eye contact: look at all students for on-task engagement:<br>  ○ Choose 3–4 focus areas (places where you have students who often get off task) to look toward consistently.<br>• Circulate the room with purpose (break the plane):<br>  ○ Move among the desks and around the perimeter.<br>  ○ Stand at the corners: Identify 3 spots on perimeter of the room to which you can circulate to stand and monitor student work.<br>  ○ Move away from the student who is speaking to monitor the whole room.<br>5. **Routines and Procedures 201:** Revise and perfect them<br>• Revise any routine that needs more attention to detail or is inefficient, emphasizing what students and teachers are doing at each moment.<br>• Do It Again: have students do the routine again if initially incorrect.<br><br>**Build Trust and Rapport**<br>6. **Narrate the Positive**<br>• Warm welcome: make eye contact, smile, and greet students<br>• Narrate what students do well, not what they do wrong<br>  ○ "Table two is ready: their books are open and all are reading." | • Implement a daily entry prompt (Do Now) to either introduce the day's objective or review material from the previous day.<br>• Use an exit ticket (brief final task) to assess end-of-class mastery.<br>6. **Academic Monitoring 101:** Check students' independent work to determine whether they're learning and what feedback is needed<br>• Create and implement a monitoring pathway:<br>  ○ Name the lap: Announce what you will be looking for and how you will code work/give feedback as you circulate.<br>  ○ Monitor the fastest writers first to gather trends, then the students who need more support.<br>• "Pen in hand": Give written feedback to student work<br>  ○ Compare answers to the exemplar: what are they missing?<br>  ○ Give quick feedback (star, circle, pre-established code).<br>  ○ Cue students to revise answers using minimal verbal intervention (affirm the effort, name error, ask to fix it).<br>• Gather data while monitoring and prepare to respond:<br>  ○ Track student responses: ideal, almost there, further off.<br>  ○ Determine how to respond: stop the class for a quick fix, activate knowledge, model or discourse. |

*(Continued)*

Instant Immersion    **161**

| Management Trajectory | Rigor Trajectory |
|---|---|
| <ul><li>○ "I like how Javon has anticipated a counter-argument to strengthen his thesis."</li><li>• Praise intellect, not just behavior—reinforce students getting smarter:<ul><li>○ Affirm the effort, not just the outcome: "Your diligence on revising your thesis really paid off here."</li></ul></li><li>• While narrating the positive, look at student(s) who are off-task.</li></ul>7. **Make authentic connections:**<ul><li>• Memorize student names and use them each time you call on them</li><li>• Make self-to-student connection when they share a struggle, interest or passion ("I struggled when. . ." or "I love that, too!")</li><li>• Show genuine concern: keep a tracker of important details and dates for each student to follow up with them; check in with them after class when something is off.</li></ul> | 7. **Guide Discourse 101:** Launch the discourse cycle around the productive struggle:<ul><li>• Everybody writes or Show-call (post student work for students to analyze—exemplars, non-exemplars or both).</li><li>• Turn and talk</li><li>• Cold call, then volleyball (multiple students speak before teacher)</li><li>• Prompt for and praise basic Habits of Discussion to strengthen conversation and listening skills (i.e., build, evaluate, agree/disagree, etc.)</li><li>• Stamp the key understanding: "What are the keys to remember?"</li></ul> |

## Introduction to Phase 2 Management Skills

Roll Out and Monitor Routines and Build Trust and Rapport

Bill Walsh was a legendary figure and one of the most successful football coaches of all time. He was aptly nicknamed "The Genius" for all of the innovations he led that transformed the sport. While most football fans know him as the creator of the West Coast Offense, his impact on the coaching world went much further. One of his biggest contributions was his method for game planning.

When Walsh was an assistant coach for the Cincinnati Bengals working under Paul Brown in the 1970s, he began scripting a set of two to three plays to open the game. It worked so well that when he moved on to head coaching, he expanded his script.

He had 10–12 scripted plays to start the game while coaching the Chargers, then 20 plays at Stanford, and 25 plays while coaching the Forty-Niners—that is nearly half the game! At the time, coaches viewed this approach as ludicrous. How can you possibly plan all your plays in advance when you should be adjusting to the flow of the game? Walsh's response is telling:

> "Your ability to think concisely, your ability to make good judgments is much easier on Thursday night than during the heat of the game. So, we prefer to make our decisions related to the game almost clinically, before the game is ever played . . . . As the game is being played, to be honest with you, you are in a state of stress. Sometimes, you are in a state of desperation and you are asked to make very calculated decisions. Your decisions made during the week are the ones that make more sense."[2]

If this approach works for one of the most insightful minds in sports, it certainly works for a new teacher. When classes start, they are in the heat of the game and under great stress. Rather than try to make the best decisions in the moment, teachers thrive on a set number of plays that will carry them through most of their lesson—just like Walsh.

---

### Core Idea

Keep a cool head in the heat of the moment by having a plan:
the more we plan, the more we can be flexible.

---

Phase 2 Management is all about following Walsh's playbook. In the case of teaching, these "plays" are the moves teachers make at each part of the lesson: the words they say with each instruction and how they monitor and move around the classroom. Building and executing on these scripted plays can dramatically transform the classroom of a new teacher. Later, they'll need to know how to modify that plan based on unforeseeable factors. For now, their energy is best allocated to learning the moves they can know in advance by heart. If we lead this phase well, their classroom will be humming as well as Walsh's West Coast Offense.

Instant Immersion

## What to Do

> ### Teacher Professional Development Goal
>
> **What to Do:** Give directions that make something complicated feel simple.

One of the biggest impediments to great classroom management is a lack of precision in the quality of communication. Use too many words or too many unclear directions, and students will immediately start to check out.

The first step in building a classroom where all students are doing what they should be doing is having all students *know* what they should be doing. For this, you need a teacher who gives crystal-clear instructions, conveying even the most complex information in a way that leaves all students knowing what comes next.

---

### Findings from the Field: Clear and Concise Create Incredible Growth

"The number one action step I have used with my teachers going into their first three years of teaching is What to Do directions. Without these, nothing else functions. With a few coaching sessions, that all can change. I have seen the growth from the beginning of the school year up until now by pushing them to use economy of language (this is the hardest part!) and checking for understanding. With consistent practice of What to Do, my teachers start flying, and it has transformed their teaching."
—*Kendra Randle, Principal, Indianapolis, IN*

---

The following is the most common Phase 2 challenge that can typically be addressed by What to Do:

- Teacher's directions are too vague or confusing, often using too many words.

- The teacher gives out a ton of complex directions all at once, and students are overwhelmed by the flood of information.

- Teacher doesn't check to see if student understands a complex task before sending to practice. Despite the clarity of the directions, students struggle to hold onto all of them.

164   Get Better Faster 2.0

## What to Do: Make Them Bite-Sized and Chunk Them
## Coaching Tips

**Teacher Context**

**Challenge:**

- Teacher's directions are too vague or confusing, often using too many words.
- The teacher gives out a ton of complex directions all at once, and students are overwhelmed by the flood of information.

**Action Step**

- Make directions bite-sized and observable (e.g., 3–5 words)
- Chunk them: Give the directions one by one in sequential order

**Action Step Overview**

Teachers can give overly long and complicated directions for a variety of reasons:

- Their original plan did not have the words completely scripted.
- They get nervous and stumble over their script in the moment or they talk through them so quickly no one can follow along.
- They add more words without realizing it.

Scripting and practicing directions before the lessons enable a teacher to deliver clear directions on the spot without having to pause and consider what to say. Sufficiently detailed directions might look something like this: "Eyes on me. Books closed. Now turn to page 47." Pause until all students are on the same page. "Please finish problems one through three. You have 10 minutes. Begin."

What is the lesson here? The fewer the words the better, and chunking them makes them visible and digestible: if you pause after "Turn to page 47," you can make sure everyone is there before going on to the next direction.

### Key Leadership Moves

**See It**

- Video: Watch a clip of a teacher giving What to Do directions: bite-sized, observable and chunked for clarity.
  - Unpack the quality of each direction—how small and observable it is.
  - Unpack the pauses between each direction—how that enabled all students to keep pace and for the teacher to see if they were following along.

Instant Immersion    165

**Plan the Practice**

- Script bite-sized, observable directions for an upcoming lesson. Plan them out word by word—don't take shortcuts!
  - Be as specific as possible to make it clear with students what you want to see: "Open to Chapter 2, page 34" instead of "Begin reading."
  - Pause between each observable direction. This gives you time to check that the whole class is with for you each step. "Pencils down in 3-2.1. (Pause) Turn to page 2. (Pause). You have 15 minutes for this section."
- Provide feedback on clarity before practice: Most errors can be fixed before your practice.

**Do It**

- Rehearse key directions in the lesson.
- Focus on economy of language (not adding extra words beyond what was in their script) and the pregnant pause between each component of the instruction: Students often become confused when given too many directions at one.

**Real-Time Feedback**

- Model: giving concise directions using three to five words.
- Verbal: Could you name the steps for us again?
- Verbal: What should students be doing with their/the ___?
- Whisper prompt: "When you bring everyone back from this assignment, just say: "Pencils down. Eyes on me!" No extra words.

> **Tip from a Coach—Set Up Students for Success**
> "Training 100% of your teachers on giving crystal clear what-to-do directions is the most important do-not-pass-go competency for the start of the school year. If your teachers can consistently give students clear, bite-sized and sequential directions they and their students will be set up for a successful school year launch."
> —Toby Shepherd, Principal, Providence, RI

**Video Examples:**
One-on-one coaching meeting:

 WATCH Clip 24: **What to Do—Check for Understanding** (Key Leadership Skill: See it)

A practice clinic (short PD on What to Do directions):

 REWATCH Clip 2: **What to Do Directions**
(Key Leadership Skill: See it)

---

Once you've pared down your instructions and practiced chunking them, you can take one more step, particularly for complex directions: check for understanding.

## What to Do: Check for Understanding on Complex Instructions
## Coaching Tips

**Teacher Context**

**Challenge:**
- Teacher doesn't check to see if student understands a complex task before sending to practice. Despite the clarity of the directions, students struggle to hold onto all of them.

**Action Step**
- Check for understanding on complex instructions.

**Action Step Overview**
When instructions are relatively simple (like turning to the right page in a book), bite-sized, chunked directions normally suffice to get every student to understand. There are times, however, where directions are more complicated and require far more steps (like describing all the steps each small group will take when performing a science experiment). In this case, you can make each direction bite-sized and chunk it, but students still have a lot to remember. Checking for understanding is the additional step you can take to make sure that students are prepared to fully engage with their work. After scripting your chunked, bite-sized directions, insert a check for understanding question or ask students to restate the directions. Either method gives you quick feedback on what students understand, and you can quickly address any confusion before students begin working.

Instant Immersion

## Key Leadership Moves

**See It**

- Video: Watch a model video of a teacher checking for understanding.
- Live model: Model delivering directions with a check for understanding or a request for students to rephrase.

**Plan the Practice**

- Script a check for understanding or a student rephrase after a set of directions.
    - Cold call a student: "Jeremy, what are we about to do?"
    - For multistep directions, ask students to restate the steps in parts: "What is the first step of analyzing the poem?" "After we've read for claim, what do we do next?"

**Do It**

- Deliver your directions followed by a check for understanding question.
- Note: It is valuable to deliver all the directions and not just the check for understanding questions. This allows you to cumulatively build on the previously mastered skill and lock it in: You can never get too much practice of delivering clear directions!

**Real-Time Feedback**

- Verbal: "Ms. Smith, those directions are so important. Could you call on a student to see if everyone understands?"
- Whisper prompt: "Ask a student to restate the instructions to the class."

 REWATCH Clip 24: **What to Do—Check for Understanding** (Key Leadership Skill: See it)

# Strategies for Coaching What to Do

| Action Step | See It | Plan the Practice | Do It | Cues for Real-Time Feedback |
|---|---|---|---|---|
| **Make Them Bite-Sized and Chunk Them** | • Video: Watch a clip of a teacher giving What to Do Directions: bite-sized, observable and chunked for clarity.<br>• Unpack the quality of the direction and the pauses. | • Script bite-sized, observable directions for an upcoming lesson. Plan them out word by word.<br>• Provide feedback on clarity before practice: most errors can be fixed before practice. | • Rehearse key directions in the lesson.<br>• Focus on economy of language and the pause between each component of the instruction. | • Model: giving concise direction using 3–5 words.<br>• Verbal: Could you name the steps for us again?<br>• Verbal: What should students be doing with their/the ___?<br>• Whisper prompt: "When you bring everyone back from this assignment, just say: 'Pencils down. Eyes on me!' No extra words." |
| **Check for Understanding on Complex Instructions** | • Video: Watch a model video of a teacher checking for understanding.<br>• Live model: Model delivering directions with a check for understanding or a request for students to rephrase. | • Script a check for understanding or a student rephrase after a set of directions. | • Deliver your directions followed by a check for understanding question.<br>• Note: It is valuable to deliver all the directions and just check for understanding questions. You can never get too practice delivering clear directions. | • Verbal: "Ms. Smith, those directions are so important. Could you call on a student to see if everyone understands?"<br>• Whisper prompt: "Ask a student to restate the instructions to the class." |

Instant Immersion    169

**See Your Students**

> ## Teacher Professional Development Goal
>
> **See Your Students:** To make sure students are "with you", watch what they do as you teach.

My family and I once attended a party where a number of other families with young children were gathered. We adults were talking among ourselves while the kids played in the living room. All of a sudden, one mother bolted toward the couch. We only had a moment to wonder what she was doing before the couch began to topple over—with a two-year-old climbing on top of it. The mother caught the child just in time.

Every other adult in the room was astounded. It looked to us as if this woman had used X-ray vision or successfully predicted the future. But as we gaped at the scene of the narrowly averted disaster, we saw what had really happened: The mother had seen that the couch had no backing, and she predicted that as soon as the toddler clambered up on the headboard, it would tip. She was able to save him an injury not because she saw him falling but because she saw he was on unstable ground. Her mother's instinct was the instinct of prevention, of stopping the catastrophe before it happened by spotting the right warning signs the moment they appeared.

A teacher's instinct—or, as we'll call it, Seeing Your Students—is just the same. It often seems magical, even superhuman, to those who have never taught before; but in truth, Seeing Your Students comes from knowing how to spot the tipping couches of the classroom. Are students looking down at their independent writing assignments, or are their eyes casting about the room? Are their hands on their own pencils, or are they busy passing something to a neighbor? Just as the backless couch became a threat to the children playing in the living room, so these small actions can quickly become a threat to children trying to learn: staring out the window becomes not writing; or passing pencils becomes passing notes, which in turn becomes two students hitting each other. Seeing Your Student prevents those small behaviors from causing the well-managed classroom to figuratively topple over.

In the pages that follow, we'll unpack the actions that make Seeing Your Students look like magic, and show how to make them doable for a new teacher. Here are a few root causes of classroom management challenges that a new teacher can learn how to catch—thus preventing the chaos from actually occurring—with the action steps we'll summarize in this section:

- The teacher is not noticing the earliest actions of disengaged behavior.
- The teacher is not watching the students; students veer off task as a result.
- The teacher is stationary, and the lack of movement makes it easier for students to disengage.
- When one student is speaking, the teacher stands very close to them while listening and ignores other students, allowing them to become disengaged.

---

## See Your Students: Make Eye Contact
## Coaching Tips

### Teacher Context

### Challenge

- The teacher is not noticing the earliest actions of off-task behavior and may wait until challenges have escalated before they do anything.

### Action Step

- Make eye contact—look at all students for on-task engagement.
  - Choose three or four active areas (places where you have students who often get off task) to scan constantly.

### Action Step Overview

Every classroom management challenge has a beginning: a moment when one or two students go off track before the rest follow. Just like the tipping couch we described previously, though, this moment is very often predictable—which means it's preventable.

The first key to catching those first moments of disorder when they happen is to identify the places in the room where they usually spark—and to be seen looking. Often, all it takes for students to stay engaged is to know that you are paying attention to them. Without that, the one student who nearly always ends up whispering to peers when he or she shouldn't, for example, will do just that. Those hotter zones (seats of students whose off-task actions often escalate into major disruption) cool down when you pay attention to them and notice when that first student starts looking around the room.

Instant Immersion    **171**

Thus, this action really involves two parts—actually noticing off-task behavior and making sure students see that you are seeing it. Knowing where to target your looking helps you see your students more effectively. Making nonverbal movements to exaggerate the act of seeing is the second part.

### Key Leadership Moves

A move like Seeing Your Students is most effectively coached through real-time feedback because it depends so much on the teacher's immediate response to student actions. Outside-of-class practice serves mostly to exaggerate the act of scanning around the room and to prepare the teacher as much as possible for the real-time feedback. As a result, it's especially powerful when practicing this action step with a teacher to use video, so the teacher can watch what's happening and have a strong sense of how scanning for focus areas works before returning to class. From there, having someone in the room to point out right away any roadblocks the teacher is hitting is the best way to make sure the teacher will sharpen their ability to see student behaviors more clearly.

**See It**

- Model: Give instructions to the class and as you do exaggerate your body language to be monitoring the room—crane your neck, turn your body toward different parts of the room, use a finger to point to different groups/rows.

- Model: Have teacher (as student) exhibit off-task behavior. Make eye contact and redirect behavior.

**Plan the Practice**

- Video: Watch video of recent lesson. Debrief the moment when students begin to go off track. Point out the small-scale behaviors that preceded the larger disruption. Plan how to see those moments next time.

- Have the teacher identify areas in the classroom where students are off-task and the moments in the lesson plan to scan these areas.

**Do It**

- Role play student behavior you want the teacher to be able to catch and correct by scanning. Repeat until the teacher is consistently scanning and identifying off-task behavior.

- Have teacher practice maintaining eye contact long enough to note the behavior and see the student stop behavior before looking away.

- Start small: Begin with one off-task behavior, e.g., eyes not on teacher when giving directions. Once the teacher successfully notes this and redirects with eye contact, change the target off-task behavior.

172   Get Better Faster 2.0

**Real-Time Feedback**

- Nonverbal: Gesture toward the area where you want the teacher to notice and redirect off-task behavior.
- Nonverbal: Crane your neck to indicate that the teacher should look around the room.
- Model: Take over the routine and crane your neck/scan with your finger while scanning students.

**Video Example:**
Watch how Denarius Frazier enhances the teacher practice to include seeing all students. Notice the difference in the teacher's eye contact before and after Denarius's feedback. He pauses more deliberately to look across the room in the second round—this exaggerated, slow glance helps him pick up more disengaged behaviors.

 WATCH Clip 25: **See Your Students—Make Eye Contact** (Key Leadership Move: Do it)

## See Your Students: Circulate With Purpose

## Coaching Tips

**Teacher Context**

**Challenge**

- Teachers are stationary, and their lack of movement makes it easier for students to go off task.

**Action Step**

- Circulate the room with purpose (break the plane)
    - Move among the desks and around the perimeter.
    - Stand at the corners: Identify three spots on the perimeter of the room to which you can circulate to stand and monitor student work.
    - Move away from the student who is speaking to monitor the room.

Instant Immersion

**Action Step Overview**

Beginning teachers often get "frozen": They start near the board at the front of the room and never venture into the rest of the classroom. Yet breaking the plane (moving away from the front of the room or away from the projector) keeps students from checking out and allows the teacher to keep a more accurate pulse on what's going on in the classroom. A move like circulating the perimeter also helps a teacher to listen to the one student who is speaking while simultaneously reminding the rest of the students that they need to be listening, too.

### Key Leadership Moves

**See It**

- Video: Debrief a clip of a teacher circulating the classroom.
- Model: Walk purposefully around the room, moving toward groups of desks and individual students as you speak. Pause near these groups/students.

**Plan the Practice**

- Identify the areas in the room where off-task behaviors often occur.
- Create a set of key spots on the perimeter (often corners of the room) where you can circulate toward to monitor student work and plan a pathway to walk around the room.

**Do It**

- Simple practice: Practice moving along the pathway while teaching, stopping at areas when disengagement is higher and giving students a nonverbal redirect.
  - Avoid having your back to students as you circulate; this can encourage disengagement. Instead, angle your body so that you can still see all students. You can do this standing or squatting near a student's desk.
- Added complexity: Have the teacher call on imaginary students in different parts of the room and walk away from them, continuing to keep the rest of the class between the teacher and the speaker.
  - While the imaginary student is responding, you can be playing the part of another student in another part of the room who is off task. The teacher can then practice moving around to remind the other student to be listening.

**Real-Time Feedback**

- Nonverbal: Use two fingers to mime legs walking.
- Nonverbal: Point to a corner of the room where the teacher should stand.
- Nonverbal: cue the teacher to move away from the student who is speaking.

**Tip from a Coach: Don't Just Talk About it—Practice!**
"I encourage leaders to go beyond naming circulation as a key management move and shift toward practicing this in the meeting. Have teachers pre-identify the specific times in the lesson when they will circulate with purpose, and pre-determine the strategic places in the room to stop and scan the room for 100%. Since implementing this practice, I've noticed stronger attention to detail on the part of teachers and increased engagement from students."

—*Knick Dixon, Principal, Greensboro, NC*

  WATCH Clip 26: **See Your Students—Circulate** (Key Leadership Move: Do It)

## See Your Students: Move Away From the Student Who Is Speaking

## Coaching Tips

**Teacher Context**

**Challenge**

- The teacher is locked in on the single student who is speaking, and other students lose focus or engage in off-task behaviors.

**Action Step**

- Move away from the student who is speaking to monitor the whole room.
  - Move among the desks and around the perimeter.
  - Stand at the corners: Identify three spots on the perimeter of the room to which you can circulate to stand and monitor student work.

**Action Step Overview**

Most of us are used to looking at and standing near the person who is speaking to us—it's considered good manners. In the classroom, however, this combination of proximity and attention can make a teacher miss what's going with the rest of the students. Moving away from a speaking student may feel counterintuitive to facilitating good conversation, but it actually allows the teacher to take in the whole class at once and make sure that the other students are attending to what their peer is saying.

Instant Immersion

## Key Leadership Moves

**See It**

- Model: Have the teacher play the role of a responding student. Move away from the teacher as they speak to stand near different clusters of desks around the room.

**Plan the Practice**

- Identify a moment in an upcoming lesson where the teacher will call on a student. Plot three areas in the room where the teacher can move while the student responds.

**Do It**

- Have the teacher pretend to call on an imaginary student. Then, while the imaginary student is responding, you can be playing the part of another student in another part of the room who is off task. You can then practice moving around to remind the other student that he or she is still obligated to pay attention and, if necessary, to give a silent redirect.

**Real-Time Feedback**

- Nonverbal: cue the teacher to move away from the student who is speaking.

---

# Strategies for Coaching: See Your Students

| Action Step | See It | Plan the Practice | Do It | Cues for Real-Time Feedback |
|---|---|---|---|---|
| **Make Eye Contact** | • Model: Give instructions to the class and exaggerate your body language to be monitoring the room, e.g., crane neck, angle your body toward different areas of the room, use finger to point to groups/rows. | • Video: Watch recent lesson. Debrief the moment when students begin to go off track. Point out the initial small-scale behaviors. Plan how to see those moments next time. | • Practice: Role play student behavior you want the teacher to be able to catch and correct by scanning. Repeat until the teacher is consistently scanning and identifying off-task behavior. | • Nonverbal: gesture toward the area where you want the teacher to notice and redirect off-task behavior.<br>• Nonverbal: crane your neck to indicate that the teacher should look around the room. |

176    Get Better Faster 2.0

| Action Step | See It | Plan the Practice | Do It | Cues for Real-Time Feedback |
|---|---|---|---|---|
| | • Model: Have a teacher (as student) exhibit off-task behavior. Make eye contact and redirect behavior. | • Have the teacher identify areas in the classroom where student are off-task and the moments in the lesson plan to scan these areas. | • Have teacher practice maintaining eye contact long enough to note the behavior and see the student stop behavior before looking away.<br>• Start small: Begin with one off-task behavior. Once the teacher notes this and redirects with eye contact, change the target off-task behavior. | • Model: Take over the routine and crane your neck/scan with your finger while scanning students. |
| Circulate with Purpose—Move Around the Room | • Video: Debrief a clip of teacher circulating the classroom.<br>• Model: Walk purposefully around the room, moving toward groups of desks and individual students as you speak. Pause near these groups/students. | • Identify the areas in the room where off-task behaviors often occur.<br>• Create a set of key spots on the perimeter (think: corners where you can circulate toward to monitor student work and plan a pathway to walk around the room). | • Simple practice: Practice moving along the pathway while teaching, stopping at areas when disengagement is higher and giving students a nonverbal redirect.<br>• Added complexity: have the teacher call on imaginary students in different parts of the room and walk away from them, continuing to keep the rest of the class between the teacher and the speaker. | • Nonverbal: Use two fingers to mime legs walking.<br>• Nonverbal: Point to a corner of the room where the teacher should stand.<br>• Nonverbal: Cue the teacher to move away from the student who is speaking. |

*(Continued)*

Instant Immersion **177**

| Action Step | See It | Plan the Practice | Do It | Cues for Real-Time Feedback |
|---|---|---|---|---|
| Circulate with Purpose—Move Away from the Student Who is Speaking | • Model: Have the teacher play the role of a responding student. Move away from the teacher as he or she speaks to stand near different clusters of desks around the room. | • Identify a moment in an upcoming lesson where the teacher will call on a student. Plot three areas in the room where the teacher can move while the student responds. | Have the teacher pretend to call on an imaginary student. Then, while the imaginary student is responding, you can be playing the part of another student in another part of the room who is off task. The teacher can then practice moving around to remind the other student that they are still obligated to pay attention, and, if necessary, to give a silent redirect. | • Nonverbal: cue the teacher to move away from the student who is speaking. |

## Routines and Procedures 201

> ### Teacher Professional Development Goal
>
> **Routines and Procedures 201:** Revise routines to match student needs that emerge when the teacher rolls out the routine in the classroom.

Routines and Procedures 201 takes up where we left off in Phase 1. Although you and the teacher planned the opening routines as carefully as possible, you couldn't fully anticipate where the teacher or students would struggle in the implementation. The following are two challenges that new teachers most often encounter during the first week of school:

1. Students are following the routine correctly, but it is inefficient or ineffective.

2. The routine is effective, but students aren't following it.

178  Get Better Faster 2.0

Here are the action steps that will most effectively help new teachers meet those challenges.

## Routines and Procedures 201: Revise Routines
## Coaching Tips

**Teacher Context**

**Challenge**

- Students are following the routine correctly, but it is inefficient or ineffective.

**Action Step**

- Revise any routine that needs more attention to detail or is inefficient, with particular emphasis on what students and teachers are doing at each moment.

**Action Step Overview**

Often, no matter how much work you put into designing a routine, when you roll it out you realize that it doesn't work. A student who needs extra time to get moving is in the front, slowing down the routine when s/he could be at the end. Or a group of students gets bottlenecked coming to the guided reading table because you didn't realize how little space there was in that part of the room. When a routine fundamentally isn't working in one way or another, the teacher will need to rewrite it altogether, identifying where it breaks down and generally adding more detail. Opening routines and class transitions are particularly important for the teacher to revise during Phase 2, as they're the routines that will most set the tone of the classroom and increase time for learning.

> **Tip from a Coach—Walk the School**
> "I find that the best way to see if routines are working is to walk the school at key moments to look for the pattern: arrival, classroom entry, homework collection, after lunch, before dismissal. When you see teachers back-to-back, you can notice gaps in some teacher's routines or implementation, and that makes it so much easier to coach them. Looking for the pattern also helps you see which teachers could be the model for them to observe! It helps you set a vision for what you are looking for both students and teachers to be doing during this time."
> —*Kristen McCarthy, Principal Supervisor, Newark, NJ*

## Key Leadership Moves

### See It

- Live observation: Go down the hall and watch a teacher who is implementing this routine effectively (this is by far the highest leverage model if you have a teacher to see!)
- Video: watch and debrief an exemplary routine.

### Plan the Practice

- Draft a new routine and script directions for the rollout.
- Anticipate the challenges: "Where will this break down? How can we revise it so that every student call follow it more easily?"

### Do It

- Simple practice: Focus practice at the point where the routine has been going wrong. You'll notice when you observe and practice with the teacher that some parts of the routine have become natural and flow easily—don't keep practicing those! Instead, focus on the isolated part that's hard for the teacher. Conduct the role play with you playing the student and the teacher rolling out this routine.
- Round 2: Role play the student who struggles to follow the routine. Rehearse the first words to say to nonresponsive students
- What to look for during the practice:
  - Teacher positioning: stand in the ideal position to see as many students as clearly as possible
  - Confident Presence and What to Do: Keep incorporating all the previous actions they have work on! Remember: the waterfall is cumulative.

### Real-Time Feedback

- Model: "This is my favorite routine. I want to practice it with all of you. Can I jump in?"

# Routines and Procedures 201: Do It Again[3]

## Coaching Tips

**Teacher Context**

**Challenge**

- The routine is effective, but students aren't following it.

**Action Step**

- Do It Again: Have students do the routine again if not done correctly the first time.

**Action Step Overview**

Every time we allow a classroom routine to be performed incorrectly, we solidify imperfection. For this reason, the best response if students don't do the routine correctly is almost always to have them do it again until they get it exactly right. The following key sequence of instructions is what usually works most effectively for getting students to do it again and do it better.

- Confident Presence—Stop the routine at the moment of error.
- Name the error (for example, "Students, we're not moving quickly enough to our seats.").
- Give a challenge (for example, "I know you can do better. Let's try it again and see if we can beat our best time!").
- Give a signal—Go back to the beginning of the routine and signal to restart the routine.

In *Teach Like a Champion 3.0*, Doug Lemov describes in more detail what makes Do it Again such an effective teaching technique; in brief, besides getting students to practice excellence, it does so in an immediate way that ends on the positive note of success.

### Key Leadership Moves

**See It**

- Video: Watch and debrief video of a teacher cuing students to practice a routine again
- Model: Watch clip of teacher's lesson. Pause video at first moment of error in routine. Modeling directing students to redo routine.

**Plan the Practice**

- Plan each step of the Do it Again sequence

Instant Immersion 181

- Confident Stance (square up, stand still, use formal register)
- What to Do (name the error, name the correct action)
- Give a challenge to do better
- Give the signal to restart the routine

**Do It**

- Role play the revised routine: Make student errors and have the teacher practice pausing the routine, stating the change, and implementing the Do it Again until the routine looks flawless.
- Pay attention to past action steps: Confident Stance, Warm-Demander Register, What to Do.

**Real-Time Feedback**

- Nonverbal signal: Make a circle with your finger to cue teacher to have students redo routine.
- Verbal cue: "Ms. Smith, I know the students can do that better. Let's see how well they can do it."
- Model: "Can I show our students what we'd like them to do?" Whisper to the teacher what you are modeling.

> **Tip from a Coach: Aim for 100%**
> "When coaching your teachers, remember that consistency of the implementation is key. Don't be satisfied with them getting it basically there one time. Keep rehearsing until it is easy—even automatic—to be consistent. Don't settle for less than 100%!"
> —Lisa Hill, Principal Supervisor, Atlanta, GA

**Video Example:**
Ashley Martin uses real-time feedback and a post-observation debrief to improve the quality of her Math teacher's class discussion:

 WATCH Clip 27: **Routines and Procedures 201—Do It Again** (Key Leadership Move: Real-time Feedback)

# Strategies for Coaching: Routines and Procedures 201

| Action Step | See It | Plan the Practice | Do It | Cues for Real-Time Feedback |
|---|---|---|---|---|
| **Revise Routines** | • Live observation: Go down the hall and watch a teacher who is implementing this routine effectively.<br>• Video: watch and debrief an exemplary routine. | • Draft a new routine and script directions for the rollout.<br>• Anticipate the challenges: "Where will this break down? How can we revisit so that every student can follow it more easily?" | • Simple practice: Focus practice at the point where the routine has been going wrong. Conduct the role play with you playing the student and the teacher rolling out the routine.<br>• Round 2: Role play the student who struggles to follow the routine. Rehearse the first words to say to nonresponsive students.<br>• What to look for during practice: Teacher positioning, Confident Presence, and What to Do. | • Model: "This is my favorite routine. I want to practice it with all of you. Can I jump in?" |
| **Do it Again** | • Video: Watch and debrief video of a teacher cuing students to practice a routine again.<br>• Model: Watch clip of a teacher's lesson. Pause video at first moment of error in routine. Model directing students to redo routine. | • Plan each step of the Do it Again sequence.<br>• Confident Stance<br>• What to Do<br>• Give a challenge<br>• Give a signal to restart routine. | • Role-play the revised routine: make student errors and have the teacher practice pausing the routine, stating the change, and implementing the Do It Again until the routine looks flawless.<br>• Pay attention to past action steps: Confident Stance, Warm-Demander Register, What to Do. | • Nonverbal: make a circle with your finger to cue teacher to have students redo routine.<br>• Verbal cue: "Ms. Smith, I know the students can do that better. Let's see how well they can do it."<br>• Model: "Can I show our students what we'd like them to do?" Whisper to the teacher what you are modeling. |

Instant Immersion    **183**

## Build Trust and Rapport

> ### Teacher Professional Development Goal
>
> **Build Trust and Rapport:** Cultivate a safe, collaborative classroom environment with and for students.

Sometimes, the smallest action can make an outsized difference.

Danny Murray's high school English seminar students are discussing Junot Díaz's immigrant short story collection "Drown." In each tale, a Dominican-American narrator struggles to exist in a world that makes significant demands on his masculinity. Students have been discussing Diaz's use of symbolism, particularly of the idea of "drowning" and its connection to the central themes of the text. But Danny has noticed that five students haven't yet spoken. In the last quarter of class, he invites them to contribute. Start the clip at 1:12 and watch until the end to see how they respond.

 WATCH Clip 28: **Make Authentic Connections** (Teaching clip)

Rilwan immediately raises his hand to offer his theory once discourse restarts, while Jamaya is gently encouraged by her turn-and-talk partner and Danny to share her analysis. Although she initially balks, she eventually offers her take on the symbolism of drowning in Yunior's life. Denise closes out the discourse with a recap of the conversation.

There are classrooms where a request like Danny's would have felt like an attack—a teacher calling out disengaged students. Yet the ways students respond show that he has built a different space. One student jumps right in and two more follow. They feel safe taking the risk.

In a classroom, we talked about the importance of routines and the sense of safety that predictable structures give students. When we combine that with a commitment to building trust and rapport, we have a powerful combination to propel students academically. Schools that focus on rapport at the expense of structure feel chaotic and unsafe. Those that emphasize structure without rapport feel cold and unloving. Students need both routine and relationship to excel.

> ### Core Idea
>
> Schools that focus on rapport at the expense of structure feel chaotic and unsafe.
> Those that emphasize structure without rapport feel cold and unloving.
> Students need both routine and relationship to excel.

Seemingly simple, this action step can be really hard for a new teacher, especially one who has just graduated from being a student. New teachers can often go to two extremes: acting too distant/nervous/cold or acting too much like a peer rather than an adult. Some wish to be so closely connected to students that they create a dynamic that looks more like friendship than that of a teacher and student.

Jamey Verrilli, Managing Director of the Relay Graduate School of Education, counsels teachers like these to, "Be the coach, not the captain." In other words, what students need to succeed is a classroom leader who sees what they are capable of and a road map to achieve it, not another classmate. And teachers who value being friends with students over being their teachers undermine their own instruction in the long run.

Successful athletic coaches show us what's possible when we build effective, positive relationships with students. Consider a strong coach of a youth soccer team. She will be a strong presence that can get the students to be fully on task in every part of practice. She will raise her voice when needed to make a point and correct a player. But the best coaches also know when to lower their voice to build up a player's confidence. They know what works for one player might be different than another, but they never lower the bar of their expectations. With the right coach, students will opt into the drills and the long runs not out of fear but because they believe that the coach has their—and the team's—best interest at heart. Engaging in the practice and listening to the feedback is how they commit to getting better, and they feel valued as they work hard because they know the coach always expects the best out of them. That's what students need in a teacher.

So, how do you create a relationship with students that gives them adult role models to follow? Read the following section for more on how teachers can begin to build positive, lasting relationships with students.

Instant Immersion 185

---

### Findings from the Field: Create a Culture of Belonging

"Foster an inclusive and positive student culture by prioritizing building a culture where scholars feel valued, respected, and connected. This involves actively listening to their voices, celebrating diversity, and creating opportunities for collaboration. When scholars feel safe and included, they're more engaged in their learning, which ultimately leads to better outcomes."

—*Katie Harshman, Principal, Pueblo, CO*

---

## Narrate the Positive[4]

In contrast to the common misconceptions that maintaining a well-managed classroom will eliminate joy from the classroom, narrating the positive reveals that keeping students on task can be a joyful action in itself. Narrating the positive is an extremely powerful step toward making joy something that great management doesn't deplete, but rather reinforces.

> ### Teacher Professional Development Goal
>
> **Narrate the Positive:** Name what students do right, not what they do wrong.

Two great benefits result from narrating the positive. The joy it will bring to the classroom is the first. The second is that you're positively reinforcing the actions that you want to see in the classroom. Praising students for doing something well stacks the odds significantly in favor of their doing it again next time. Thus, by narrating the positive, you create the classroom of your dreams both in the tone you strike and in the practical actions that are accomplished each day.

## Findings from the Field: Highlight the Good

"Don't underestimate the power of positive narration, both for adults and students in the building. When you highlight the good, the good happens more often. It is a virtuous cycle that feeds itself. Plan for opportunities to point out what's going right in every routine and procedure and in every moment where students have an "aha" and your classroom will soar."

—*Sue Brennan, Principal, Columbus, OH*

Here are a few common challenges that a teacher can mitigate by narrating the positive:

- Teacher jumps into instruction without welcoming students into the space.
- The teacher turns negative by narrating what is going wrong ("you aren't reading the text right now") and getting frustrated/overly negative.
- The teacher tries to narrate the positive but some students don't hear it and stay disengaged.
- Teacher tends to praise behavior rather than academic effort or achievement.

## Narrate the Positive: Warm Welcome
## Coaching Tips

**Teacher Context**

**Challenge**

- Teacher jumps into instruction without welcoming students into the space.
- Teacher's affect is flat and distant.

**Action Step**

- Give students a warm welcome: make eye contact, smile, and greet students.

**Action Step Overview**

When time is of the essence (as it often is for teachers), it can be easy to trim elements of class routines that seem less important. Skipping a warm welcome at the

Instant Immersion 187

door could mean more time for the Do Now or a longer lesson launch, but it also means students don't feel seen at the start of class. Greeting students warmly at the door is part of the instruction; it sets the tone for the learning that will follow. Seeing and welcoming students as they enter the space shows them that their daily presence matters to the teacher, and that they are seen as valuable members of the community.

Key Leadership Moves

### See It

- Watch video of warm classroom door greeting.
- Model: Warm greeting at the threshold with the teacher playing the role of student.

### Plan the Practice

- Plan the steps of an exemplar classroom entry.

### Do It

- Practice: Classroom entry routine. Focus on the eye contact, smile, and warmth of the greeting.
  - Integrate Seeing your Students: Make sure that the teacher is positioned to be able to see the full line of students in the hallways as well as being able to glance inside the classroom toward students who have already entered.

### Real-Time Feedback

- Nonverbal: Mime a big smile, point to both eyes and then point to students.

---

## Narrate the Positive: Narrate What Students Do Well

## Coaching Tips

### Teacher Context

### Challenge

- The teacher turns negative by narrating what is going wrong ("you aren't reading the text right now") and getting frustrated/overly negative.

### Action Step

- Narrate what students do well, not what they're doing wrong:
  - "I like how Javon has anticipated a counter-argument to strengthen his thesis."
  - "The second table is ready to go, and their books are open and all are reading."

**Action Step Overview**

Positive narration requires a mindset shift. Instead of naming what is going wrong in the classroom, positive narration reinforces what is going right. It is also an opportunity for students to hear directions repeated in the context of on task behaviors. This can be especially helpful for students who process more slowly or who missed a portion of the directions the first time.

**Key Leadership Moves**

**See It**

- Video: Watch an exemplary video of a teacher narrating the positive.

- Model narrative the positive: use actual student names from the teacher's classroom.

**Plan the Practice**

- Watch a clip of teacher's lesson. Notice the positive, observable actions of students that the teacher could name publicly.

- Re-write teacher's most frequent negative comments into positive statements.

- Script positive narration after each set of directions in an upcoming lesson plan.

**Do It**

- Role play keeping students on track through positive narration.

- While practicing, focus not only on the words but also the positive tone in which the teacher delivers them. Practice the tone until it feels authentic: not over-exaggeratedly positive nor too flat/negative.

**Real-Time Feedback**

- Nonverbal: index card with a plus sign written on it or sign that says "narrate the positive"

- Whisper prompt: "Narrate the positive."

**Narrate the Positive: Praise Intellect**

**Coaching Tips**

**Teacher Context**

**Challenge**

- The teacher tends to praise behavior rather than academic effort or achievement.

Instant Immersion **189**

### Action Step

- Praise intellect, not just behavior—reinforce students getting smarter:
  - Affirm the effort, not just the outcome: "Your diligence on revising your thesis really paid off here."

### Action Step Overview

Narrating the positive with classroom routine can reinforce behavioral expectations, but you can enhance its power even more by praising intellect. The lifelong learner is not the person who knows the right answer, but the person who knows *how to find* the right answer. So many of the best academic habits we strive to teach students, from showing your work in math class to citing your evidence in English, reflect this. For this reason, it is essential to praise students for their intellectual habits more than the answers they deliver. This reinforces the idea that you aren't born smart, you "get" smart—by your effort. By rewarding this part of their learning, we incentive and build the habits of grit and perseverance in the face of any challenge.

### Key Leadership Moves

### See It

- Video: Watch a video of a teacher giving precise academic praise.
- Video: Watch clip of teacher's instruction. Model where the teacher could have potentially added precise academic praise in recognition of student work or contribution.

### Plan the Practice

- With an upcoming lesson plan, script moments when the teacher could give precise academic praise that would reinforce students' effort.
  - Praise process: "Renee is using her knowledge organizer to help her outline her response."
  - Praise effort: "I see you've used two different strategies to solve the equation."
  - Praise innovation: "That's an interesting analysis of the poem. Tell me more about how you came to this conclusion."

### Do It

- Be the student and have the teacher give precise praise.
- Role play a questioning sequence in which the teacher specifically praises student thinking.

190   Get Better Faster 2.0

**Real-Time Feedback**

- Model: Jump in and praise student thinking. "Ms. Smith, can I jump in here? I just love what Ezekiel just said. . . ."
- Whisper to the teacher to give precise praise after another positive academic behavior.

---

# Narrate the Positive: Look at Students Who Are Disengaged

## Coaching Tips

### Teacher Context

### Challenge

- Disengaged students don't respond to positive narration.

### Action Step

- While narrating the positive and/or while looking at students during a redirect, look at the student(s) who are off task.

### Action Step Overview

Narrating the positive publicly isn't just for the student doing the action—it's to encourage other students to do the same. Some students may not realize right away this is a behavior they could emulate because they don't think the teacher is focused on them in the moment. Often as not, however, all it will take to correct this is a firm look at the student or students who are disengaged while narrating what other students are doing correctly.

## Key Leadership Moves

### See It

- Video: Watch a video of a teacher who uses narration while looking at off-task student.
- Model: Have the teacher be an off-task student. Narrate the positive while looking at teacher/student.

Instant Immersion **191**

**Plan the Practice**

- Script positive narration after a set of directions in an upcoming lesson plan. Note to look at off-task students.

  - Consider standing near disengaged students while narrating the positive. Proximity often gets students back on task more quickly, and this can be easily paired with a look.

**Do It**

- Role-play: You play the role of a student and model off-task behavior while the teacher looks at you and narrates the positive actions of another (imaginary) student.

**Real-Time Feedback**

- Whisper prompt: "Look at off-task students while narrating positive."

## Strategies for Coaching: Narrate the Positive

| Action Step | See It | Plan the Practice | Do It | Cues for Real-Time Feedback |
|---|---|---|---|---|
| **Warm Welcome** | • Watch video of warm classroom door greeting.<br>• Model: Warm greeting at the threshold with the teacher playing the role of the student. | • Plan the steps of an exemplar classroom entry. | • Practice: Doorway entry routine. Focus on the eye contact, smile, and warmth of the greeting.<br>• Integrate Seeing Your Students: Make sure the teacher can see the full line of entering students as well as the student already in the classroom. | • Nonverbal: mime big smile, point to both eyes and then point to students. |
| **Narrate What Students Do Well** | • Video: watch an exemplary video of a teacher narrating the positive. | • Watch a clip of teacher's lesson. Notice the positive, observable actions of students that the teacher could name publicly. | • Role play keeping students on track through positive narration. | • Nonverbal: index card with a plus sign written on it or sign that says "narrate the positive." |

192    Get Better Faster 2.0

| Action Step | See It | Plan the Practice | Do It | Cues for Real-Time Feedback |
|---|---|---|---|---|
| | • Model narrate the positive: Use actual student names from the teacher's classroom. | • Re-write teacher's most frequent negative comments into positive comments.<br>• Script positive narrations after each set of directions in an upcoming lesson plan. | • While practicing, focus not only on the words but also the positive tone in which the teacher delivers. Practice tone until it feels authentic. | • Whisper prompt: "Narrate the positive." |
| **Praise Intellect, Not Just Behavior** | • Video: Watch a video of teacher giving precise academic praise.<br>• Video: Watch clip of teacher's instruction. Model where the teacher could have potentially added precise academic praise in recognition of student work or contribution. | • With an upcoming lesson plan, script moments when the teacher could give precise academic praise that would reinforce student's effort:<br>• Praise process<br>• Praise effort<br>• Praise innovation | • Be the student and have the teacher give precise praise.<br>• Role play a questioning sequence in which the teacher specifically praises student thinking. | • Model: jump in and praise student thinking. "Ms. Smith, can I jump in here? I love what Ezekiel just said. . . ."<br>• Whisper prompt after another positive academic behavior: "Give precise praise." |
| **While Narrating the Positive, Look At Students Who Are Disengaged** | • Video: Watch a video of teacher who uses narration while looking at off-task student.<br>• Model: Have the teacher be an off-task. Narrate the positive while looking at teacher/student. | • Script positive narration after a set of directions in an upcoming lesson plan. Note to look at off-task students.<br>• Consider standing near disengaged while narrating the positive. Proximity often gets student back on task more quickly and can be paired with a look. | • Role-play: you play the role of a student and model off-task behavior while the teacher looks at you and narrates the positive actions of another (imaginary) student. | • Whisper prompt: "Look at off-task students while narrating positive." |

Instant Immersion    **193**

## Make Authentic Connections

> **Teacher Professional Development Goal**
>
> **Make Authentic Connections:** Forge positive adult-child relationships with students to support their academic growth.

Let's return to Danny's high school English seminar. Earlier, I recommended you watch the latter half of the clip to see the beauty of his classroom culture. Now we'll look at what he did to build that sense of safety and trust. The clip begins when students are a few minutes away from the start of a discussion of Junot Díaz's immigrant short story collection "Drown." To prepare students to grapple with the themes, Danny gives them the following prompt to answer:

- "What does Díaz argue through the relationship between the culture of silence and the machismo culture?"

As he walks around, he pays particular attention to Amelia. She's been hesitant to participate in past seminars. He pauses to scan the initial write of her argument. On her paper, she's written: *Diaz argues that silence is acceptable if the situation you are silent about goes against the machismo culture.* As he's reading, she looks up at him tentatively and says, "I don't think this is right." Danny finishes reading and turns toward her, "There are no wrong answers. It looks like you're on the right track. Where do you need help?"

 REWATCH Clip 28: **Make Authentic Connections** (Teaching clip)

Amelia's check-in might seem small, but it wasn't insignificant. Danny implemented the previous action step of narrating the positive (praising intellectual effort: "It looks like you're on the right track."), but he also did something more. He spends a moment with Amelia offering this help. How does that improve learning? Danny uses what he's learned about his students to nudge them along. He might not be able to get to every student every day, but when he knows Amelia is tentative, he can zoom in on her at just the right time. Pay attention to who your students are, and you can reach them more easily.

> ## Core Idea
>
> Pay attention to who your students are, and you can reach them more easily.

This section covers getting to know your student as individuals so that these micro-moments can reap big rewards for learning. Read on for techniques to build a class-room space that welcomes all students.

The most common barriers to making authentic connections are:

- Teacher does not take the time to get know student names or personalities.

- Teacher appears cold or distant because s/he never makes connections to the content.

- Teacher doesn't follow up after class when a student is off.

## Make Authentic Connections: Memorize Student Names

## Coaching Tips

### Teacher Context

### Challenge

- Teacher cannot call students by name.

### Action Step

- Memorize student names.

### Action Step Overview

Learning student names is a small but critical part of building welcoming learning spaces. If I don't know your name, how can I know you? Students nearly always respond more positively to adults who know them, and one of the easiest ways we start to learn about someone is by knowing their name. Typically, most teachers focus their energy on learning names at the start of the school year or semester. Yet it's the daily use that makes the difference. Every time you mention students' names in class, they sit up a little straighter and pay attention a little more (as adults, the same

Instant Immersion 195

thing happens to us when we are called by name in a PD or conference!). Encourage teachers to call students by name in academic and non-academic contexts (e.g., cold call, informal conversations).

## Key Leadership Moves

### See It

- Model: Use student names at the end of a comment or question.

### Plan the Practice

- Review roster to memorize names.
- If you have a seating chart, memorize the names in the context of where they sit—makes it easier to access.
- If teacher is still struggling to memorize names, create name tents for every student to reinforce the memorization.

### Do It

- Practice: Deliver part of the lesson and ask teacher to routinely call on different students by name.
- Practice: Point to different seats in the classroom and have teacher call on a student. Then check the seating chart and see if that was accurate.

### Real-Time Feedback

- Model using student name, "Thank you for sharing your opinion, Carlos."

---

# Make Authentic Connections: Make Self-to-Student Connection
## Coaching Tips

### Teacher Context

### Challenge

- Teacher rarely or does not share relevant information about self with students.

### Action Step

- Make self-to-student connection.

**Action Step Overview**

Students enjoy getting to know their teachers as people, and teachers can share personal stories (as appropriate) to build connection. Topics that are most likely to foster connection are those that connect to a shared student struggle, interest, or passion.

Tip and Caveat: The key to a self-to-student connection that promotes learning is to keep it short most of the time. If not, the teacher can spend more time describing themselves than having students learn!

### Key Leadership Moves

**See It**

- Video: Show exemplar video of teacher making self-to-student connection.

**Plan the Practice**

- Teacher looks at upcoming lessons and identifies moments to make a self-to-student connection. Script them to ensure economy of language.

**Do It**

- Practice: Teacher practices them, preserving economy of language:
  - I heard you like/I also enjoy/am a big fan of_____.
  - I struggled with _____ too. Something that helped me get through it was___.
  - Good luck at tryouts today! I played sports all throughout high school. It's great that you have something you're so passionate about.

**Real-Time Feedback**

- N/A

> **Tip from a Coach—Actively Build Connection**
>
> "A student's success is tied to a sense of belonging and being connected to the adults at school. As a leader, I have to model building these connections for teachers. I start with learning kids' names alongside my team. In addition, I encourage my team to be selectively vulnerable. Tell about a time you've failed—it makes failure normal for kids. Talk about your favorite book during a reading lesson. You hear a student is going on vacation; ask them how it was when they return. I do this at lunch. I do this in the halls. I do this when observing in classrooms. I have found that building these connections especially at the start of the year, and in places where other kids can see (class, lunch, hallway) leads the watchers to feel connected as well. We know that when the adults show care and make intentional connections, then kids are more willing to be academically pushed!"
>
> —*Michael Scott, Jr., Principal, Brooklyn, NY*

## Make Authentic Connections: Show Genuine Concern
## Coaching Tips

**Teacher Context**

**Challenge**

- Teacher doesn't follow up after class when a student is off.
- OR Teacher will see students who are off and spend 5–10 minutes trying to coax them back to engagement, which distracts the rest of the class and doesn't keep them learning.

**Action Step**

- Show genuine concern:
  - Keep a tracker of important details/dates for each student to follow up with them.
  - Check in with a student after class when something is off.

**Action Step Overview**

Showing genuine concern is something most of us aspire toward, but it is easier said than done in the time-sensitive nature of a classroom setting. You rarely have a few moments of one-on-one time with a student when managing all the rest. That's why often showing genuine concern starts outside the classroom and then spills into it.

The highest achieving teachers that I have observed know that most of the time the predictable routine of the classroom is a safe space and a way to help deal with whatever challenge is occurring outside of it (when we face unanticipated challenges, structures and routines help us cope rather than hurt us). But that only works if after class they follow up with them at a break, in between classes, and understand what's going on. The combination of these actions allows the student to feel seen and helps them view classroom as a place to keep learning.

Some teachers may struggle to show the care that they feel for students. Simple moves like checking in with students during class or remembering important details about their lives go a long way toward building a trusting relationship. Many teachers have found success using trackers to record important student information, like birthdays, that they can use throughout the school year.

### Key Leadership Moves

**See It**

- Video: Show exemplar video of teacher-student interaction.

198    Get Better Faster 2.0

**Plan the Practice**

- Draft survey to collect important information about students.

- Administer survey and record details in a tracker.

- Plan when a teacher can mention details at appropriate times.

- Plan when a teacher will find a student outside class and plan the conversation they will have with the student.

**Do It**

- Role play talking with the student whose normal affect is off:

  o You seem off today. Is something going on?

  o That sounds tough. Tell me more.

  o Is there something I can do to help?

**Real-Time Feedback**

- Whisper prompt: "Julia seems off today. Have you touched base with her?" (If not:) "Why don't you track her down at lunch to see what's up?"

> **Tip from a Coach—Leverage Whole School Moments to Connect**
>
> "Think about the moments in your day when you can truly connect with students and take full advantage of them. I am an introvert, but at school, I have learned the power of embracing the role of the extroverted principal. I coach all teachers to leverage breakfast, lunch and dismissal as key times to see our students. We (1) provide a warm greeting, (2) make eye contact, (3) smile and keep a calm open face, (4) ask questions that lead to a deeper understanding of who the student is (e.g., Do you have siblings? Are you a good brother/sister? Why?). Starting with a closed question and then building with more open-ended questions allows students to have an easy entry point into the conversation. Students (especially in high school) are always wondering if the teachers like them. We want to show them that we care about them inside and out of the classroom. Modeling and encouraging my teachers to make authentic connections has been a key step to school growth. When students feel seen, you can build trust with them and then, they will allow you to push their growth both academically and personally."
>
> —*Syrena Burnam, Principal, Camden, NJ*

# Strategies for Coaching: Make Authentic Connections

| Action Step | See It | Plan the Practice | Do It | Cues for Real-Time Feedback |
|---|---|---|---|---|
| **Memorize Student Names** | • Model: Use student names at the end of a comment or question. | • Review roster to memorize names.<br>• If you have a seating chart, memorize the names in the context of where they sit.<br>• If teacher is still struggling to memorize names, create name tents for every student to reinforce the memorization. | • Practice: Deliver part of the lesson and ask teacher to routinely call on different students by name.<br>• Practice: Point to different seats in the classroom and have teacher call on student. Then check the seating chart and see if that was accurate. | • Model using student name, "Thank you for sharing your opinion, Carlos." |
| **Make Self-to-Student Connection** | • Video: Show exemplar video of teacher making self-to-student connection. | • Teacher looks at upcoming lessons and identifies moments to make a self-to-student connection. Script to ensure economy of language. | • Practice: Teacher responds to a student comment with a shared struggle, interest, or passion. | N/A |
| **Show Genuine Concern** | • Video: Show exemplar video of teacher-student interaction. | • Plan: Teacher drafts survey to collect important information about students.<br>• Teacher administers survey and record details in a tracker.<br>• Plan: Teacher mentions details at appropriate times. | • Practice: Teacher asks about the wellbeing of a student whose normal affect is off. | • Whisper prompt: "Julia seems off today. Have you touched base with her?" (If not:) "Why don't you track her down at lunch to see what's up?" |

## Phase 2 Rigor—Roll Out Academic Routines

### Quick Reference Guide

| If your teacher is struggling to: | . . .jump to: |
| --- | --- |
| **Independent Practice** | |
| Prepare students to share in discussion | Write First, Talk Second |
| Get students working meaningfully at the start of class | Daily Do Now or Review |
| Gauge what students know at the end of class | Use an exit ticket |
| **Academic Monitoring 101** | |
| Work with more than a few students during independent practice | Create a monitoring pathway |
| Give feedback to student work during independent practice | Pen in Hand |
| Identify student confusion/misconception during independent practice | Gather data and respond |
| **Guide Discourse 101** | |
| Have students launch the discourse rather than the teacher | Everybody Writes or Show Call |
| Get more students talking | Turn-and-Talk |
| Hear from a wide range of students | Cold call and volleyball |
| Have students speak and listen to each other | Prompt for Habits of Discussion |
| Nail down the most important ideas at the end of the discourse | Stamp the key understanding |

Instant Immersion     201

## Phase 2 Scope and Sequence

| Management Trajectory | Rigor Trajectory |
|---|---|
| **Roll Out and Monitor Routines** | **Roll Out Academic Routines:** |

**Roll Out and Monitor Routines**

3. **What to Do:** Use economy of language when giving directions:
   - Make them bite-sized (e.g., 3–5 words) and observable.
   - Chunk your directions: give them one by one in sequential order.
   - Check for understanding on complex instructions.
4. **See your Students:** Know when students are engaged or unengaged
   - Make eye contact: look at all students for on-task engagement:
     - Choose 3–4 focus areas (places where you have students who often get off task) to look toward consistently.
   - Circulate the room with purpose (break the plane):
     - Move among the desks and around the perimeter.
     - Stand at the corners: Identify three spots on perimeter of the room to which you can circulate to stand and monitor student work.
     - Move away from the student who is speaking to monitor the whole room.
5. **Routines and Procedures 201:** Revise and perfect them
   - Revise any routine that needs more attention to detail or is inefficient, emphasizing what students and teachers are doing at each moment.

**Roll Out Academic Routines:**

5. **Independent Practice:** Set up daily routines that build opportunities for students to practice independently
   - Write first, talk second: Give students writing tasks to complete prior to class discussion, so that every student answers independently before hearing their peers' contributions.
   - Implement a daily entry prompt (Do Now) to either introduce the day's objective or review material from the previous day.
   - Use an exit ticket (brief final task) to assess end-of-class mastery.
6. **Academic Monitoring 101:** Check students' independent work to determine whether they're learning and what feedback is needed
   - Create and implement a monitoring pathway:
     - Name the lap: Announce what you will be looking for and how you will code work/give feedback as you circulate
     - Monitor the fastest writers first to gather trends, then the students who need more support.
   - "Pen in hand": Give written feedback to student work
     - Compare answers to the exemplar: what are they missing?
     - Give quick feedback (star, circle, pre-established code).

202   Get Better Faster 2.0

| Management Trajectory | Rigor Trajectory |
|---|---|
| • Do It Again: have students do the routine again if initially incorrect.<br><br>**Build Trust and Rapport**<br>6. **Narrate the Positive**<br>• Warm welcome: make eye contact, smile, and greet students<br>• Narrate what students do well, not what they do wrong<br>  o "Table two is ready: their books are open and all are reading."<br>  o "I like how Javon has anticipated a counter-argument to strengthen his thesis."<br>• Praise intellect, not just behavior—reinforce students getting smarter:<br>  o Affirm the effort, not just the outcome: "Your diligence on revising your thesis really paid off here."<br>• While narrating the positive, look at student(s) who are off-task.<br>7. **Make authentic connections:**<br>• Memorize student names and use them each time you call on them.<br>Make self-to-student connection when they share a struggle, interest or passion ("I struggled when. . . ." or "I love that, too!")<br>Show genuine concern: keep a tracker of important details and dates for each student to follow up with them; check in with them after class when something is off. |   o Cue students to revise answers using minimal verbal intervention (affirm the effort, name error, ask to fix it).<br>• Gather data while monitoring and prepare to respond:<br>  o Track student responses: ideal, almost there, further off.<br>  o Determine how to respond: stop the class for a quick fix, activate knowledge, model or discourse.<br>7. **Guide Discourse 101:** Launch the discourse cycle around the productive struggle:<br>• Everybody writes or Show-call (post student work for students to analyze—exemplars, non-exemplars or both).<br>• Turn and talk<br>• Cold call, then volleyball (multiple students speak before teacher).<br>• Prompt for and praise basic Habits of Discussion to strengthen conversation and listening skills (i.e., build, evaluate, agree/disagree, etc.)<br>• Stamp the key understanding: "What are the keys to remember?" |

Instant Immersion    **203**

## Introduction to Phase 2 Rigor Skills: Roll Out Academic Routines

In the introduction to Phase 1 rigor, we spoke to how high expectations are made—first with the teachers themselves. In Phase 2, we start to apply those to the students.

Think back to your own journey from kindergarten to college. For most of us, school starts as something that doesn't require much work outside of school, and over time, even as the homework increases, we can handle it without much thought. But there often comes a time (in middle school, high school, college or even when work starts!) when our organic habits for learning/studying no longer work. We are overwhelmed by the magnitude and complexity of a new task, whether it be a mountain of homework, a 12-page research paper, or an exam that requires more extended study than we have done before. In these moments, our old systems for learning fall short, and we are pushed to create new ones. When we succeed, we call them study habits.

Academic habits are no different than classroom management habits: As we noted earlier from James Clear, they depend on systems. Either we leave students to their own devices, or we can build systems in our classrooms that cultivate those habits. Academic habits start at school, not at home. Make them stick by making them visible and repeatable.

---

### Core Idea

Academic habits start at school, not at home.
Make them stick by making them visible and repeatable.

---

The starting place for the sort of habits we want all students to have is in our routines for independent practice and for discussion. These are the foundations for what will happen outside of school—learning how to work independently but also in groups. When implemented repeatedly and predictably, they help students practice and develop their thinking. They also provide valuable data that we can use to guide instruction. (We'll talk more about what that looks like in the Weekly Data Meeting in Phase 3).

The next section explores the following academic routines in detail:

- Building **independent practice** into every lesson

- **Monitoring academically** when students do independent work, so that the teacher knows exactly where students are
- Creating routines to **guide discourse**

Let's take a detailed look at each of these—and why they come first.

## Independent Practice

> **Teacher Professional Development Goal**
>
> **Independent Practice:** Prioritize independent time on task every lesson.

There are four key learning moments that make up a lesson (in whatever order you put them): times when the teacher is presenting information; times when the whole class is interacting with that information; small group work time; and independent practice. Many leaders instinctively focus first on helping teachers perfect either the first or second of these categories—probably because they're the ones that are most visible when they're not going smoothly. Yet managing large and small group discussion is one of the most complex arts of teaching. In contrast, ensuring that independent practice is happening—that 100% of students are having the chance to work and learn—is the fastest way to increasing the learning time of each student.

Watch how middle school English teacher Vy Graham prepares her students to speak in discourse by having them write first:

 WATCH Clip 29: **Independent Practice: Write First, Talk Second** (Teaching clip)

Starting with independent practice is valuable not only because it is easier. Independent practice is also the single one of these four moments when 100% of the class can engage in the heaviest work of learning. In Vy's case, that means 100% of the students had the chance to think about how Frederick Douglass's rhetorical moves evoke particular feelings in his audience. Before they listen to what others say in class discussion, they've formulated their own ideas.

Instant Immersion 205

Even during whole class discussion, when a skillful teacher can get to 90 percent engagement, still only one student can speak at a time. Independent practice is the time when all students are at work on a task that requires learning. Therefore, making time for it every day is the fastest way to kickstart learning for the greatest number of students.

---

## Findings from the Field: Prioritize Independent Practice to Prioritize Student Thinking

"Academic Monitoring and Independent Practice were instrumental in pushing our teachers toward responsive, data-driven instruction that prioritizes student thinking. Early on, we struggled with pushing teachers past the 'sage on the stage' model of instruction—they focused more on what they would say and less on what students would do. As a result, there was little time for students to think by doing. Now, by prioritizing time for independent practice and giving concrete action steps around the sequence of instruction (insisting that students work first and talk second), teachers are developing skills they need to get students to do the work that will make learning happen."

—*Sue Brennan, Principal, Columbus, OH*

---

Here, we'll look at several opportunities teachers can make throughout the lesson for students to engage in independent work. These are a few challenges that may arise in a classroom if a new teacher is not providing sufficient opportunities for students to practice independently:

- Class discussion begins without students having the opportunity to write first.
- Class begins with a teacher presentation before students have had a chance to write/work independently.
- Class ends without a measure of end-of-class learning.

Let's take a look at the action steps that can address each of these.

# Independent Practice: Write First, Talk Second

## Coaching Tips

**Teacher Context**

**Challenge**

- Students are not prepared to share in discussion and are tentative (only eager students raise their hands).

**Action Steps**

- Write first, talk second: give students writing tasks to complete prior to class discussion, so that every student answers independently before hearing their peers' contributions.

**Action Step Overview**

Few single actions can increase the rigor of the classroom more than having students respond in writing to key prompts before discussing those same prompts as a class: write first, talk second. During a discussion, you can never know for sure that the students who aren't speaking are doing the same heavy intellectual work as the ones who are actively speaking; if you have students answer related prompts in writing after that discussion, you can't know whether they would have been able to respond as they did without listening to their peers' insights beforehand. When students respond in writing first, on the other hand, you have documented evidence of the thinking they were able to do independently, and you can target the remainder of the lesson to their needs accordingly. Additionally, reluctant students or slower processers of information will often be more willing to participate in discussion when they've had the chance to generate a response.

## Key Leadership Moves

**See It**

- Show a video of a teacher launching discourse with having everyone write first.
- Live model giving a writing task prior to discourse.

**Plan the Practice**

- Take out an upcoming lesson plan and ID key moments where students can write before discourse. Script the language to launch the writing task right into the lesson plan.
- Do this same task for the remaining lessons of the week by making a quick annotation of "Everybody Writes" in each lesson plan.

Instant Immersion   207

**Do It**

- Role-play practice is minimal: It is a matter of simply practicing the launch of the writing task and bringing students back to discussion afterward. Focus on integrating the previous action steps around What to Do and See your Students.

**Real-Time Feedback**

- Raise your hand during class discussion to jump in: "Ms. Smith, I think that is a great prompt. Everyone, before we talk further, grab your pen and let's take two minutes to jot down our initial response. (Repeat the teacher's prompt). You have two minutes. Ready? Go."

**Video Example—Teaching Clip:**
Middle School English teacher Vy Graham

 REWATCH Clip 29: **Independent Practice: Write First, Talk Second** (Teaching clip)

---

## Independent Practice: Implement a Daily Entry Prompt
## Coaching Tips

**Teacher Context**

**Challenge**

- Teacher begins class without students having a chance to work independently and get ready to learn.

**Action Step**

- Implement a daily entry prompt (or Do Now) to either introduce the day's objective or review material from the previous day.

**Action Step Overview**
Many educators are aware of the immense advantages of having students begin each day's lesson with a writing prompt, or Do Now, that engages either the content they're about to learn, or that they learned the previous day. Some of the benefits

of Do Nows are related to management: getting students into the right mind-set for learning, giving them clear directions from the door, and so on. But the more valuable rewards are rigor rewards, and they're reaped by students and teacher alike. The students begin their day with the challenge of independent practice; the teacher gains an instant means of checking student comprehension, which can then be used to inform the rest of the lesson (although, in the case of new teachers, it will be later in the year that they develop the skill of using the data from the Do Now to alter lesson plans).

Key Leadership Moves

### See It

- Video: Watch a clip of a teaching getting students right to work on the Do Now.
- Model: Greet class and give directions to complete the Do Now.

### Plan the Practice

- Write Do Now questions for upcoming lessons: short (3–5 minutes to complete), easy to monitor (can check student work), and aligned to objective.
  - Have teacher start by reviewing the objectives of this lesson and previous lessons.
  - Vet each question according to the previous criteria (short, easy to check, aligned to the lesson objective).
- Note: Eventually teachers will get so proficient at this skill that they will convert the Do Now into highly effective activation of knowledge (See Phase 3 Rigor). While you can prompt them about this, they might not yet be fully proficient in doing so at this stage and you can simply add on to their task.

### Do It

- Rehearse a start-of-class greeting that will prompt the students to begin working on the Do Now.

### Real-Time Feedback

- N/A

Instant Immersion 209

# Independent Practice: Use an Exit Ticket[5]

# Coaching Tips

**Teacher Context**

**Challenge**

- Lessons end without a measure of student learning.

**Action Step**

- Implement and review a longer independent practice and/or a daily exit ticket (brief final mini-assessment aligned to your objective) to see how many students mastered the concept.

**Action Step Overview**

Practicing independently is essential for students to get better. Increasing the amount of independent practice in the lesson becomes the first step, via activities during the midst of the lesson and/or an exit ticket (an assignment that students complete and hand back to you at the very end of class that checks their understanding of the lesson objective). Exit tickets came up in Phase 1 when we looked at early lesson planning skills because they're so crucial that they should have been a daily lesson practice from the beginning. By this point in Phase 2, however, it may be necessary to ensure that exit tickets have been implemented properly and that new teachers are reviewing, as well as assigning, exit tickets.

Often what undermines the amount of time spent in independent practice is a teacher's pacing; that will be addressed more directly in Phase 3 Management.

## Key Leadership Moves

**See It**

- Model: Do a think aloud of how to check alignment among the exit ticket, the objective, and the other moments of independent practice in the lesson.

- Model the implementation of an exit ticket (mostly focused on exaggerating your model of What to Do directions and See your Students).

**Plan the Practice**

Planning and practice will depend on where teachers are struggling. If they just don't have quality independent practice/exit tickets, then most of the time can be spent in the design. If they are struggling to execute, then you can spend

210   Get Better Faster 2.0

time on the instructions they give to students during the time and implementing their management action steps. Here are some possible activities depending on your focus:

- If the challenge is the quality of the exit tickets, write exit tickets that confirm student mastery. Look at the objective, the remaining independent practice and the exit ticket side-by-side to make sure they align in level of rigor.
- If the challenge is the delivery of the exit ticket part of the lesson, spend time on the instructions they give to students during the times, integrating management action: Confident Stance, What to Do, Make Eye Contact.

**Do It**

- Delivery: Spend time on the instructions they give to students during these times, integrating management action.

**Real Time Feedback**

- N/A

## Strategies for Coaching: Independent Practice

| Action Step | See It | Plan the Practice | Do It | Cues for Real-Time Feedback |
|---|---|---|---|---|
| Write First, Talk Second | • Show a video of a teacher launching discourse with having everyone write first.<br>• Live model giving a writing task prior to discourse. | • Take out an upcoming lesson plan and ID key moments where students can write before discourse. Script the language to launch the writing task right into the lesson plan.<br>• Do this same task for the remaining lessons of the week by making a quick annotation of "Everybody Writes" in each lesson plan. | • Role-play practice is minimal: it is a matter of simply practicing the launch of the writing task and bringing students back to discussion afterwards. Focus on integrating the previous action steps around What to Do and See your Students. | Raise your hand during class discussion to jump in: "Ms. Smith, I think that is a great prompt. Everyone, before we talk further, grab your pen and let's take two minutes to jot down our initial response. (Repeat the teacher's prompt). You have two minutes. Ready? Go." |

Instant Immersion    211

| Action Step | See It | Plan the Practice | Do It | Cues for Real-Time Feedback |
|---|---|---|---|---|
| **Implement a Daily Entry Prompt** | • Video: Watch a clip of a teacher getting students right to work on the do now.<br>• Model: Greet class and give directions to complete the Do Now. | • Write Do Now questions for upcoming lessons: short (three to five minutes to complete), easy to monitor (the teacher can check student work) and aligned to objective. | • Rehearse a start-of-class greeting that will prompt the students to begin working on the Do Now. | N/A |
| **Use an Exit Ticket** | • Model: Do a think aloud of how to check alignment among the exit ticket, the objective, and the other moments of independent practice in the lesson.<br>• Model the implementation of an exit ticket (mostly focused on exaggerating your model of What to Do directions and See your Students). | Planning and practice will depend on where the teacher is struggling.<br>• If the challenge is the quality of the exit tickets, write exit tickets that confirm student mastery. Look at the objective, the remaining independent practice and the exit ticket side-by-side to make sure they align in level of rigor.<br>• If the challenge is the delivery of the exit ticket part of the lesson, spend time on the instructions they give to students during the times, integrating management action: Confident Stance, What to Do, Make Eye Contact. | • Delivery: spend time on the instructions they give to students during the times, integrating management action. | N/A |

## Academic Monitoring

> ### Teacher Professional Development Goal
>
> **Monitor Academically:** Review students' independent work as they complete it to check understanding and give immediate feedback.

212    Get Better Faster 2.0

The third principle of Coaching, "Give Feedback Frequently," showed dramatically how much more quickly teachers improve when they receive frequent feedback in-the-moment, particularly as contrasted with annual or semi-annual performance reviews. The same is true for our students: Five hours of grading papers in the evening may help them learn, but it won't do so nearly as quickly as with a few seconds of feedback delivered while students are in the act of writing. As with teachers, so with students: The more frequent the feedback, the quicker the growth.

---

### Core Idea

The more frequent the feedback, the quicker the growth.

---

Think back to your own experience in English/Literature classes during your K-12 school years. How often did you receive feedback on the quality of your writing? For most of us, the answer is rarely, perhaps three weeks or so after submitting a paper. The feedback that we received wasn't designed to be implemented immediately; the teacher expected to see it in some future essay, weeks or months away. As such, steady improvement wasn't guaranteed. We were just as likely to forget the guidance in the weeks that followed or struggle to apply it to the next assignment.

But it doesn't have to be that way. Teachers have a prime opportunity to give students valuable feedback on a consistent basis: during independent practice. While the previous section explored the benefits of the practice, there wasn't much detail about what the teacher does during this time. For many, the image of independent practice that most easily comes to mind is of a teacher standing at the front of the classroom, scanning simply to make sure students are quiet and focused. But the limitation of this model is that it doesn't really show you whether students are doing quality work. Shift the teacher's actions to academic monitoring, and independent practice becomes the rare opportunity to give students high quality feedback in a large-group setting.

The keys to successful academic monitoring are the following:

1. Create a monitoring pathway that enables you to get to as many students as possible during independent work (which means delivering feedback more swiftly).

2. Track student answers so that you can use them to inform your next teaching moves.

3. Give students immediate feedback.

Instant Immersion    213

If you have never seen effective monitoring in action, it can be difficult to visualize. To that end, we've included two brief teaching clips. Watch how Christina Fritz monitors student work during a math lesson on area:

 WATCH Clip 30: **Academic Monitoring—Pathway** (Teaching clip)

On the surface, this looks similar to any class. Beneath the surface, however, a number of extraordinary things are happening. In the brief minutes of the clip, Christina checks student work, marks it correct or incorrect, prompts students to fix areas of growth (without giving them the answer!), and even has time for a few high fives! As importantly, the monitoring sends a great message to the students: I am watching your work, and I'm really happy to see your effort. That sends such a powerful message of valuing learning that makes students even more on task during independent practice.

If you think this only applies to young students, think again. In the following clip, Brittany Hollis is working with her middle school students on volume. Watch how she uses the same principles to greatly enhance the amount and quality of feedback that each student receives:

 WATCH Clip 31: **Academic Monitoring—Pen in Hand** (Teaching clip)

Replicating what Christina and Brittany do is very doable, but you must avoid some challenges a teacher may run into if academic monitoring isn't occurring:

- The teacher is monitoring only a handful of students—or none at all—during each round of independent practice.
- The teacher monitors only the work of the students who are struggling the most.
- The teacher is not giving explicit feedback during independent practice to more than a handful of students, if any.
- The teacher does not see patterns in student answers and thus doesn't know how to adjust teaching in response.

Let's examine the actions that will address these challenges.

## Academic Monitoring: Create and Implement a Monitoring Pathway

## Coaching Tips

**Teacher Context**

**Challenge**

- The teacher is monitoring only a handful of students—or none at all—during each round of independent practice.

- Teacher only monitors the work of the students who are struggling the most.

**Action Step**

- Create and implement a monitoring pathway.

- Create a seating chart to monitor students most effectively.

- Monitor the fastest writers first, then the students who need more support.

**Action Step Overview**

One of the biggest differences between a teacher with strong results and one without (assuming both are starting with a quality lesson plan) is what the teacher does during independent practice.

Imagine attending a cooking class at your local community center. Would you prefer the chef to be walking around to see how you're doing or just standing in front as you try out the recipe? The traditional model of standing in the front of the room monitoring only for behavioral responsiveness is extremely limited in value. Monitoring student to student and delivering feedback changes the game.

Here are the steps that the highest-achieving teachers take to create an effective monitoring pathway.

- **Choose the two or three students you will support first (hint: the fastest writers).** When monitoring independent work, most teachers go straight to the students who tend to have the most trouble with the content. But if the goal is to give *all* students powerful feedback, a better approach is to go first to the fastest writers, regardless of their learning level. Why? Because they'll have something for you to give them feedback on when you get to them. Then, by the time you get to the slower writers, they'll have something written down as well. Identifying those two or three first quick writers to coach and going straight to them when independent work time begins enables teachers to get to far more students than they could otherwise in the same amount of time. And giving as many students individual attention as possible maximizes both the

Instant Immersion  **215**

instructional impact of the teacher's monitoring *and* the teacher's ability to keep everyone on task.

- **Create a seating chart that will make getting to all students as easy as possible.** By creating a data-driven seating chart that places the students in an order that mirrors the order in which you need to reach students when you monitor, you can save yourself valuable steps and time when you need them the most. Here's a sample image that reflects how you might cluster the students you need to reach first. The students are numbered according to their achievement (1 is the highest achieving on the latest assessment; 30 is the lowest):

| 11 | 16 | 15 | 12 | 14 | 13 |
|----|----|----|----|----|----|
| 10 | 17 | 18 | 9 | 19 | 8 |
| 5 | 22 | 21 | 6 | 20 | 7 |
| 4 | 23 | 24 | 3 | 28 | 27 |
| 1 | 26 | 25 | 2 | 30 | 29 |

You could organize your students in any way you'd like. This particular arrangement pairs up the highest achievers with the most struggling students when they do pair work, and it puts those struggling students up front where the teacher can teach them most easily. Just as importantly, the teacher can quickly scan the first and fourth rows and see how the highest-achieving students are doing and quickly scan the right corner to see how the lowest-achieving students are doing. This makes it easier to identify patterns in student responses.

- **Position yourself so you can still scan the remainder of the room for responsiveness.** From the right spot in the room, a teacher can tell whether all students are writing even at the same time as they give in-depth feedback to an individual student. The key is for the teacher to position himself or herself around the perimeter of the room as much as possible to make sure he or she is facing most of the students. This way, at any moment the teacher can poke his or her head up, see most of the students right away, and redirect any who aren't focused on the assignment.

216    Get Better Faster 2.0

## Key Leadership Moves

**See It**

- Video: Watch clip of a teacher monitoring independent practice (use one of the ones included in this book!).
- Sample seating chart of another teacher with students seated to maximize a pathway to reach all of them efficiently.

**Plan the Practice**

- Pull out seating charts from other teachers to use as guides and build a seating chart for this teacher's class with data in hand. Then, plan the monitoring pathway, starting with the fastest writers and then moving to the ones who need more time. Test out the seating chart and rearrange it if necessary. You'll need to have everyone seated in a way that doesn't disrupt classroom management (for example, by not putting multiple students who are often off-task near each other).

**Do It**

- Practice: Test out the seating chart by walking around. Revise for anticipated management/off-task behavior.

**Real-Time Feedback**

- Nonverbal or whisper prompt: cue teacher to use the pre-planned monitoring pathway.

 REWATCH Clip 3: **Academic Monitoring—Pen in Hand** (Key Leadership Move: Do it)

---

# Pen in Hand—Mark Up Student Work
## Coaching Tips

### Teacher Context

### Challenge

- The teacher is not giving explicit feedback during independent practice to more than a handful of students, if any.

Instant Immersion 217

**Action Step**

- Pen in hand: Mark up student work as you circulate:
  - Compare answers to the exemplar: what are they missing?
  - Use a coding system to affirm correct answer.
  - Cue students to revise, using minimal verbal intervention (name the error, ask them to fix it, tell them you'll follow up).

**Action Step Overview**

Once teachers start monitoring, the number one error is fixating on one or two students and spending most of their time with them. That might be good for those two students, but the rest of the class doesn't benefit from the teacher's feedback. Annotating student work takes feedback to the next level: It hugely increases the speed at which you can deliver valuable feedback to students doing independent work, and, therefore, the number of students who will get that type of feedback while independent work time is still occurring. Moreover, it's something teachers can do even at this early phase of this school year, when they likely have yet to master other ways of coaching students (such as responding to spoken student error during class discussion).

The act of swiftly checking over students' writing while they are working is greatly enhanced by the presence of an exemplar: This allows you to know what you are looking for. There are two other steps that will increase a teachers' awareness of which students are struggling:

- **Annotate the exemplar for the key pieces to monitor.** The best way to use an exemplar while monitoring is to flag in advance specifically what you're going to look for as you circulate: key evidence, a thesis statement, an isolated variable, and so on. You cannot monitor all of students' work in five to 10 minutes, but you can look for key pieces. Annotating your exemplar in advance allows you to do that.

- **Create a coding system for your feedback** (see more below)

Because teachers are pressed for time, they cannot do the elaborate kind of feedback/annotating you might associate with grading papers: You need a much quicker and simpler system. An easy solution is simply to assign symbols to the most important feedback they could give students during independent writing time. A writing teacher could mark A if the argument is flawed, an E if the evidence is missing or incorrect, and so on. A math teacher could write a check mark for correct answers and circle points of error or write E to explain/justify the answer.

To understand why this is so powerful, think back to that cooking class analogy of the previous action step. Would you prefer the head chef to simply look at your attempt to master the cooking or give you brief feedback on how to improve? Clearly the latter. Annotating independent practice allows you to provide equally manageable feedback for content. If all that teachers need to do is write that single

218    Get Better Faster 2.0

letter on a student's paper, they can get to 10 students in a minute during which you might previously have only reached one or two.

Because giving feedback on literary analysis is one of the harder things to do briefly, we offer two examples of systems teachers can use to annotate student writing in literacy:

- Elementary school: R-A-C-C-E:
  - <u>R</u>estate answer
  - <u>A</u>nswer question with a complete inference
  - <u>C</u>ite evidence
  - Give <u>C</u>ontext for that evidence
  - <u>E</u>xplain the new insight and its relevance to your argument.
- Middle and high School: ANEZZ:
  - State your <u>A</u>rgument
  - <u>N</u>ame the technique the author uses to establish that argument
  - <u>E</u>xplain the use of the technique and <u>E</u>vidence
  - <u>Z</u>oom in on particular words of the evidence and what they mean
  - <u>Z</u>oom out on the greater meaning (how this evidence/technique enhances the author's purpose).
- Simple coding for most other scenarios
  - Checkmark for correct answers
  - Circle if incorrect.

### Key Leadership Moves

### See It

- Watch a video of a teacher marking up student work. When debriefing, make sure to highlight:
  - How little time is spent with each student
  - How the teacher is prompting in an efficient, precise way
- Live model: Do a think aloud while modeling academic monitoring:
  - Before monitoring: "Hmm. Let me remind myself: what code can I use while monitoring to give quick feedback. Ah, yes. (State your code.)
  - During: "Hmm. Let me look back at my exemplar. What is this student missing? Yes. (State the gap). So which prompt that I planned can I use? That one (state prompt to the student.)

Instant Immersion    **219**

**Plan the Practice**

- Create a feedback code: Use simple cues teachers can write on student work to spur self-correction.

**Do It**

Make sure to make the practice real—use actual student work! If not, you will be going through the motions and not doing the hard part, which is assessing what students are missing in the moment:

- Put out a class set of student work on all the desks in the teacher's classroom (the best plan is to use that day's exit tickets to keep it fresh).
- Have the teacher try to monitor the room as quickly as possible and write feedback codes on as many papers as possible.
- Debrief what was challenging about the immediate feedback. Identify ways to speed up and try again.
- While practicing, make sure the teacher integrates the previous action steps:
    - Follow a clear monitoring pathway and collecting data
    - Use the teacher's response tracker template

**Real-Time Feedback**

- Walk alongside the teachers as they monitor and debrief as you go:
    - "What are the students missing?" "What prompt could you use?"
    - Jump in to prompt if the student doesn't understand.

> **Tip from a Coach—Model it and Coach it Live**
> "To coach this action step well, teachers need it modeled, and they need live coaching to get it right. Plan to be in the classroom with your teachers, walking and monitoring with them; plan to interrupt and prompt teachers to "send it to the crowd" before starting the discussion."
> —Sue Brennan, Principal, Columbus, OH

 WATCH Clip 32: **Academic Monitoring: Pen in Hand** (Key Leadership Move: See it)

 WATCH Clip 33: **Academic Monitoring—Pen in Hand** (Key Leadership Move: Real-time Feedback)

REWATCH Clip 30: **Academic Monitoring—Pathway** (Teaching clip)

## Academic Monitoring: Gather Data While Monitoring and Prepare to Respond

## Coaching Tips

**Teacher Context**

**Challenge**

- The teacher does not see patterns in student answers or adjust teaching in response.

**Action Step**

- Monitor the quality of student work:
  - Track correct and incorrect answers to class questions.
- Determine how to respond:
  - Stop the class for a quick fix, activate knowledge, model or discourse.

**Action Step Overview**

Once a teacher has started giving students targeted feedback (as in the previous action step of marking up student work), the next priority is looking for the pattern to determine how the class is doing as a whole. Are the students struggling more with question 1 or with question 4? Why?

From this level of awareness comes the ability to address the class as a whole during the remainder of the lesson, dramatically increasing the likelihood that, by the end of it, those students will comprehend.

Here are a few different means to track student responses:

- **Use your exemplar and student initials:** The simplest way to track responses is to use your exemplar. Whenever a student is missing a key part (e.g., correct evidence), write their initials next to that part of the exemplar. When you have rounded the class, wherever you see lots of initials is the pattern of error of the group. For example, four students might have a weak argument, but 15 lack strong evidence. You will immediately see more initials next to the right evidence, and you will also know which students in particular to target for that gap!

Instant Immersion

- **A simple, right/wrong tracker:** You can create a simple t-chart where you tick off every student for either having the correct or incorrect response. You can simply write this t-chart right on a student packet or your exemplar responses:

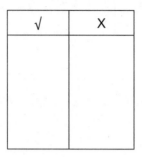

- **Use a multi-day, multi-standard tracker:** Remembering which students are struggling comes far more easily and reliably to a teacher of any experience level if they use a formal tool to note incorrect responses. The teacher can use the a "response tracker" to note when students answer incorrectly both during written work and class discussion, or when their responses improve over the course of the lesson. Figure 6 shows one example.

## 3rd Grade

| | Monday | Tuesday | Wed | Thursday | Friday |
|---|---|---|---|---|---|
| NYU | 88% | 87% | 94% | 76% | 100% |
| Tyla | 50% | 100% | 83% | 83% | 100% |
| Ani | 83% | 100% | 100% | 67% | 100% |
| Brian | 100% | 83% | 83% | 50% | 100% |
| Lanessa | 100% | 33% | 83% | 67% | 100% |
| Andrew | 67% | 100% | 67% | 100% | 100% |
| Orlando | 100% | 67% | 100% | 83% | 100% |
| Jessica | 100% | 83% | 100% | 50% | 100% |
| Isaiah | 100% | 100% | 100% | 100% | 100% |
| Marcus | 67% | 67% | 100% | 83% | 100% |
| Jada | 83% | 100% | 100% | 67% | 100% |
| Alexander | 83% | 100% | 100% | 100% | 100% |
| Frederick | 100% | 83% | 100% | 83% | 100% |
| Isabella | 100% | 100% | 100% | 100% | 100% |
| Chelsea | 100% | 83% | 83% | 67% | 100% |
| Kevin | 100% | 83% | 100% | 100% | 100% |
| Samiyah | 100% | 67% | 100% | 67% | 100% |
| Makahja | 33% | 67% | 67% | 33% | 100% |
| Chioma | 100% | 100% | 100% | 100% | 100% |
| Demarcus | 100% | 67% | 100% | 67% | 100% |
| Jacob | 83% | 83% | 100% | 50% | 100% |
| Nichelle | 67% | 100% | 100% | 83% | 100% |
| Trinity | 100% | 100% | 100% | 100% | 100% |
| Mikeria | 100% | 100% | 100% | 50% | 100% |
| Adeyemi | 100% | 100% | 100% | 100% | 100% |
| Ezekial | 100% | 100% | 100% | 83% | 100% |
| Chairf | 83% | 83% | 83% | 50% | 100% |

| | MONDAY | | | | | | TUESDAY | | | |
|---|---|---|---|---|---|---|---|---|---|---|
| | Q1:3.OA3 | Q2:3ND.7 | Q3:3NBT2 | Q4:3.OA3 | Q5:3MD.7 | Q1:3.OA3 | Q2:3MD.7 | Q3:3NBT2 | Q4:3.OA3 | Q5:3MD.7 |
| NYU | | | | | | | | | | |
| Tyla | | x | | x | | | | | | |
| Ani | x | | | | | | | | | |
| Brian | | | | | x | | x | | | |
| Lanessa | | | | | x | | x | x | x | x |
| Andrew | | x | | x | | | | | | |
| Orlando | | | | | | x | | | | x |
| Jessica | | | | | | | | | x | |
| Isaiah | | | | | | | | | | |
| Marcus | x | | x | x | | x | | x | | |
| Jada | x | | | | | | | | | |
| Alexander | x | | | | | | | | | |
| Frederick | | | | | | | | x | | |
| Isabella | | | | | | | | | | |
| Chelsea | | | | | | x | | | | |
| Kevin | | | | | | x | | | | |
| Samiyah | | | | | | x | | | x | |
| Makahja | | x | | x | | | | x | x | |
| Chioma | | | | | | | | x | x | |
| Demarcus | | | | | | | | x | x | |
| Jacob | | | | | | | | | | |
| Nichelle | | x | | | | | | | | |
| Trinity | | | | | | | | | | |
| Mikeria | | | | | | | | | | |
| Adeyemi | | | | | | | | | | |
| Ezekial | | | | | | | | | | |
| Chairf | x | | | | | | | | | |
| | 2 | 5 | 3 | 4 | 0 | 5 | 2 | 7 | 5 | 2 |
| | 92% | 81% | 88% | 85% | 100% | 81% | 92% | 73% | 81% | 92% |

Instant Immersion **223**

**Key Leadership Moves**

### See It

- Show the teacher an annotated lesson plan/exemplar where the teacher has added trackers for students.

- Live model: Do a think aloud while modeling academic monitoring:

  - After monitoring: "Hmm. What is the key gap that the students have as a whole? Let me look at my tracker. The struggle is largest with question four. I'm going to focus our efforts there."

### Plan the Practice

- Have the teacher take out the exemplar and annotate for the keys to look for. In the Humanities, that will often include the argument or thesis, evidence, or a writing technique. In STEM subjects, that will often be a certain formula or critical step in answering a problem.

- Create the tracker to use and insert it right into the exemplar/lesson plan.

### Do It

- Build off of the previous "Do it" (Pen in Hand) and monitor student work (ideally work from a recent class). Set out papers with students writing on them on desks and give the teacher a set amount of time to fill in note-taking template and note the patterns in student responses—just as they will need to during independent practice in an upcoming lesson.

- Evaluate the quality of their identification of the gap and give them feedback on how to identify the gap more easily.

### Real-Time Feedback

- Start on your own as the instructional leader: Walk the room and determine the pattern in student responses yourself.

- Whisper prompt:

  - "What are you seeing in student work?"

  - "What is the pattern/gap?"

  - If they have incorrect responses, tell them the gap and how you determined it. Then send them back to monitor.

**Tip from a Coach—What Does the Data Say?**
""What does the data say?" Often times, when we asked teachers how their lessons had gone, they'd say "great!" Yet when we changed the question to "What does the data say about how the lesson went?" they were often caught off guard. We began establishing a culture of letting the data do the talking, and in order to have data to discuss, you have to monitor intentionally"

—*Anabel Ruiz, Principal, Richardson, TX*

 WATCH Clip 34: **Academic Monitoring—Gather Data** (Key Leadership Move: Do it)

 WATCH Clip 33: **Academic Monitoring—Pen in Hand** (Key Leadership Move: Real-time Feedback)

 REWATCH Clip 4: **Academic Monitoring—Gather Data** (Key Leadership Move: Do it)

 REWATCH Clip 30: **Academic Monitoring—Pathway** (Teaching clip)

Instant Immersion

# Strategies for Coaching: Academic Monitoring 101

| Action Step | See It | Plan the Practice | Do It | Cues for Real-Time Feedback |
|---|---|---|---|---|
| **Create and Implement Monitoring Pathway** | • Video: watch clip of a teacher monitoring independent practice. (Use one of the ones included in this book!)<br>• Sample seating chart of another teacher with students seated to maximize a pathway to reach all of them efficiently. | • Pull out seating charts from other teachers to use as guides and build a seating chart for this teacher's class with data in hand and plan the monitoring pathway: Start with fastest writers and then move to the ones who need more time. | • Practice: Test out the seating chart walking around. Revise for anticipated management/off-task behavior. | • Nonverbal or whisper prompt: cue teacher to use the pre-planned monitoring pathway. |
| **Pen in Hand—Mark Up Student Work** | • Watch a video of a teacher marking up student work. During debrief, highlight how little time is spent with each student and how the teacher prompts in an efficient, precise way.<br>• Live model: Do a think aloud while modeling academic monitoring. | • Create a feedback code: simple cues to write on student work to spur self-correction. | • Practice: Put out a class set of student work on all the desks. Have the teacher monitor the room and write feedback codes on as many papers as possible.<br>• Round 2: identify ways to go faster.<br>• Integrate previous actions: Follow a clear monitoring pathway, collecting data. | • Walk alongside teachers as they monitor and debrief as you go:<br>• "What are the students missing?" "What prompt could you use?"<br>• Jump in to prompt if the student doesn't understand. |

226    Get Better Faster 2.0

| Action Step | See It | Plan the Practice | Do It | Cues for Real-Time Feedback |
|---|---|---|---|---|
| Gather Data While Monitoring and Prepare to Respond | • Show the teacher an annotated lesson plan/ exemplar where the teacher has added trackers for students.<br>• Live model: Do a think aloud while modeling academic monitoring: ID the key gap from the tracker. | • Planning: Have the teacher take out the exemplar and annotate for the keys to look for:<br>  ○ Humanities: the argument/thesis, evidence, or a writing technique<br>  ○ STEM: a certain formula or critical step in answering a problem<br>• Create a tracker for monitoring and insert into exemplar/ lesson plan. | • Monitor student work (ideally work from a recent class). Set out papers with student writing on them on desks to monitor and note the patterns in student response.<br>• Evaluate the quality of their identification of the gap and give them feedback on how to identify the gap more easily. | • Start on your own as instructional leader: Walk the room and determine the pattern in student responses yourself.<br>• Whisper prompt:<br>  ○ "What are you seeing in student work?"<br>  ○ "What is the pattern/gap?"<br>  ○ If they have incorrect responses, tell them the gap and how you determined it. Then send them back to monitor. |

The first two action steps of Phase 2 Rigor (Independent Practice and Academic Monitoring) create effective routines for when students work on their own. The next academic routine, Discourse 101, starts getting them working well together.

## Guide Discourse 101

> ### Teacher Professional Development Goal
>
> **Guide Discourse 101:** Teach students the basic habits of conversation that will form the foundation for rigorous discourse.

Instant Immersion     227

Many of us recognize the word "gumbo"—the classic New Orleans stew of okra and seafood or sausage served over rice. Some may have even tasted it. Yet a related phrase "gumbo yaya" likely leaves you puzzled even though you've experienced it countless times throughout your life.

In Louisiana Bayou country, "gumbo yaya" roughly translates to "everyone talking all at once." Big or surprising events are made for gumbo yaya: a wedding announcement, the final touchdown in the big game, or a shocking reveal. The classroom, however, is not. Yet it is all too easy for classroom discussions to slide into gumbo yaya if they're not well-managed or for the opposite to happen—a painful silence punctuated by one or two voices. How do teachers create a space where all students know how to contribute appropriately to classroom conversations? Habits of discussion.

Actions like listening attentively during a Turn-and-talk and disagreeing respectfully create a shared groundwork for participation. Students know that they can safely share "first drafts" of their arguments before the more intimidating stage of large group discussion. The teacher actively reinforces the culture as facilitator, asking students to respond directly to one another and requesting specific habits, like rephrasing a peer's statement, to elevate the conversation. Altogether, these moves form what we call a Discourse Cycle, a predictable cycle of moves that prepares students for whole group discussion. The steps follow:

- Independent Practice—Everybody writes or Show-call[6]
  - For Show-Call: Post student work for students to analyze—exemplars, non-exemplars or both
- Turn and talk
- Cold call, then volleyball (multiple students speak before teacher)
- Prompt for and praise basic Habits of Discussion to strengthen conversation and listening skills (i.e., build, evaluate, agree/disagree, etc.)
- Stamp the key understanding: "What are the keys to remember?"

The power of a predictable cycle is that students get comfortable with discourse more quickly, and the class can fly higher. The discourse cycle is the perfect example of the sum being greater than the parts. Although each component of the cycle has a unique benefit, its full potential can't be unlocked unless they work together.

## Findings from the Field: Take It Step-By-Step

"Guided Discourse transformed my school and it allowed us to ensure that student discourse was taking part during the most rigorous part of the lesson. Because teachers were planning around the productive struggle, it increased the complexity of the tasks and the cognitive lift was shifted to students.

To do so, take it step-by-step. Start with lesson planning (Phase 1), then academic monitoring (Phase 2) then doing a Show-Call (Discourse 101). Waking around the school and seeing Show-Calls throughout the building was the clear evidence that our shift was raising the bar for our students."

—*Jessica Mullins, Principal, Denver, CO*

When the cycle rolls steadily along, discourse can be fruitful and generative. The most common challenges are the following:

- The teacher spends a lot of time talking before launching the discourse because students don't have anything to react or respond to.

- Only a limited number of students participate in whole group conversations, or the teacher calls only on students who raise their hands.

- Teacher has a lot of "ping pong:" One student responds, teacher gives lengthy response, and only then calls on another student.

- Students are not actively speaking or listening to each other during discourse.

- Discourse ends without students recording key takeaways.

Instant Immersion 229

# Guide Discourse 101: Everybody Writes or Show Call Coaching Tips

**Teacher Context**

**Challenge**

- The teacher spends a lot of time talking before launching the discourse because students don't have anything to react or respond to.

**Action Step**

- Use Everybody Writes or Show-Call to launch discourse

**Action Step Overview**

The heart of using student work is to allow students to diagnose their own errors or the effective strategies their peers are using to help their own practice. There are two keys to Show-Call, aptly divided by the name itself: the "Show" and the "Call". "Show" is picking the right piece of student work to show to the class (it all depends on your focus). "Call" is asking the right questions and calling on the appropriate student to start the conversation. James Cavanaugh uses a Show-Call for a lesson on determining the area of a circle.

 WATCH Clip 35: **Guide Discourse 101—Show Call** (Teaching clip)

Note how he selects a single student's work and calls on multiple students to explain the strategy for solving, which reinforces the newly introduced strategy. Although James uses one piece of work, it's also common to share two pieces of student work and ask the class to compare and analyze. (See coaching clips below for those examples!)

**Key Leadership Moves**

**See It**

- Watch a video on Show-Call. Prompt on the value of using student work to launch discourse.
- Live model: Incorporate a think aloud by integrating the previous action step on Academic Monitoring (Phase 2):
    - "Hmm. . . . So what is the pattern of error for the students? Yes, it is around question 3."

- "So, which pieces of student work could I Show-Call to help them see the gap? Hmm. I could use Malakai's as an exemplar response, and Juan's as an incorrect response. Let me gather those now to put up on the board."
- Then launch the routine of a Show-Call: "All eyes on the board! We have two responses here. Evaluate them: Do you agree with one of them, both of them or neither?"

**Plan the Practice**

- Look at a set of student work from the previous class and determine what could be the best pieces of student work. Give them the choices and determine which is best for this setting:
    - One exemplar and one non-exemplar response (when there is one trending error)
    - Two correct responses that utilize different strategies/representations (to push for the conceptual understanding of how those responses are connected)
    - One exemplar response (to highlight key moves that could be pulled from that example)

**Do It**

- Practice the What to Do directions when using a Show-Call to launch discourse.

**Real-Time Feedback**

- Walk around the classroom and look for representative student samples that could be used for a Show Call.
- Prompt the teacher: "What are you seeing?" "What is the gap?" "Which pieces of student work could you Show-Call to close the gap?" If they struggle to identify good work samples, point them to the student that you saw yourself.

 WATCH Clip 36: **Guide Discourse 101**
(Key Leadership Move: Real-time Feedback)

 WATCH Clip 37: **Guide Discourse—Show Call**
(Key Leadership Move: Real-time Feedback)

Instant Immersion

WATCH Clip 46: **Weekly Data Meetings—Practice** (Key Leadership Move: Do it)

## Guide Discourse 101: Turn and Talk

## Coaching Tips

**Teacher Context**

**Challenge**

- Discourse is only whole group, so only a few students have the opportunity to talk in each discussion.

**Action Step**

- Use a turn and talk to encourage students to talk to one another.

**Action Step Overview**

Many teachers love to facilitate whole class discourse. It's a great opportunity to hear from a variety of students. But it also has a serious limitation—only one student can share their thinking at a time. Turn-and-talks—having every student turn toward another to answer the prompt—directly solve this problem. The benefits are boundless:

(1)  They get more students talking (50% of the class at a time).

(2)  Students can strengthen their thinking in conversation.

(3)  Students who are less likely to share out in the whole group (due to tentativeness or being a slow processor) can practice sharing in a low-stakes environment, thus giving them more courage to share large group.

On the surface, the act of asking students to talk to each other is pretty easy. Yet you have two challenges: one is breaking the bad habit of a teacher who never uses them. The other is making sure students actually talk to each other when you prompt them. Read on for the Key Leadership Moves to address this.

**Key Leadership Moves**

**See It**

- Model think aloud: Identify multiple opportunities in an upcoming lesson for turn and talks.

- Model the clear bright lines of launching a turn and talk: setting up, releasing, and bringing students back from a turn and talk:
  - "Turn your shoulders toward the person you will talk to so that you can easily make eye contact."
  - Scan the room to notice any students who don't have a partner or are in trios. "Julia, Mark can be your partner. You two can turn toward each other."
  - "The person closest to the windows will share first."
  - "Evaluate these two pieces of student work—which one do you agree with and why? Ready? Turn and talk."
  - Scan the room to notice which partners don't immediately speak: Give them a nonverbal to turn and talk. Prompt out loud if that doesn't work: "Chassity, share your answer with your partner."
  - Once all groups have started, lean in to listen to student responses.
  - Raise hand (or a hand clap) to call students back together. Narrate the positive and wait for all students to be quiet (utilize nonverbals or prompts for those who don't get quiet).

**Plan the Practice**

- Identify moments in upcoming lesson to do a quick turn and talk.

- Script your directions for the turn and talk.

**Do It**

- Simple practice: Deliver the instructions for the turn and talk.

- Round 2 of practice: Deliver the instructions and redirect off-task students.

**Real-Time Feedback**

- Nonverbal: Point your index fingers toward each other to indicate doing a turn and talk.

- Verbal: "Ms. Smith, can students share their responses with the person next to them before sharing out whole group?"

# Guide Discourse 101: Cold Call, Then Volleyball
## Coaching Tips

**Teacher Context**

**Challenge**

- Teacher calls mostly or entirely on raised hands.
- Teacher tends to comment after every student comment, creating a "Ping Pong" environment that limits the time for student voice.

**Action Step**

- Cold call, then volleyball

**Action Step Overview**

Discourse at its best is a generative conversation between students. At its worst, it's a ping-ponging conversation between the teacher and a few students, often only those with raised hands. One of the most effective ways to change that is by first cold calling (avoiding those raised hands, who likely already know the answers) and then immediately calling on additional students before responding as the teacher. This is what we call volleyball: Multiple students keep the volleyball of discourse aloft before you enter.

### Key Leadership Moves

**See It**

- Model: Cold call student to launch discourse and call on 3–4 students in a row before responding.

**Plan the Practice**

- Plan: Script names to cold call in lesson plan.

**Do It**

- Practice cold call and volleyball.

**Real-Time Feedback**

- Whisper: "Cold call students."
- Nonverbal: Point to another student that teacher should call on after a student responds.

234   Get Better Faster 2.0

# Habits of Discussion

> **Teacher Professional Development Goal**
>
> **Habits of Discussion:** Teach and model for students the habits that strengthen class conversation.

In schools throughout the country, the area in which students are graded least meaningfully is class discussion. Far too often, educators presume that simply "participating" in a discussion by speaking at all is sufficient for a satisfactory grade despite the discussion being redundant or anemic. One student may follow another's comment with a comment that essentially repeats what the first student said; others might bring up an insightful or relevant comment but not one which indicates they heard or comprehended what the previous student said; and the conversation never goes further because the students lack the skills to push each other.

How can teachers ensure that students contribute rather than merely participate? By training students in the habits of discussion. That's the name my colleagues and I use to describe skills that come naturally in high-level dialogue and discourse: agreeing with someone meaningfully, disagreeing with someone respectfully; pushing an academic conversation to a deeper level. All of these are teaching skills that even our youngest students can master.

I described the rollout of habits of discourse in depth in Love and Literacy (see pg. 251). Here's the condensed framework: Hook, Frame, Model, Practice.

For the hook, provide a compelling reason for students to learn a particular habit of discussion. Next, give context to the model they are about to see. After that, have students debrief the model, pulling out the key actions that you want to know how to do. After that, lead students through multiple rounds of practice so that they get a sense of what it sounds and feels like to use a habit of discussion. Finally, monitor this habit over time to keep it tight. If the habit weakens over time, remember action step 5—Routines and Procedures 201—to reset it.

Here's a teacher example of a habits of discussion rollout.

 WATCH Clip 38: **Guide Discourse 101—Habits of Discussion** (Teaching clip)

Instant Immersion

# Guide Discourse 101: Prompt for and Praise Basic Habits

## Coaching Tips

**Teacher Context**

**Challenge**

- Student answers are disconnected from each other.
- Students look to teacher to facilitate conversation.
- Students mostly talk to teacher, not to each other.

**Action Step**

- Prompt for and praise basic habits of discussion.

**Action Step Overview**

Students often talk past each other before they learn to talk to each other. Prompting for the basic habits of discussion focuses their attention on their peers' contribution. As students build off and agree and disagree with each other, they more actively engage with all the ideas in the room, not just their own.

Here is a scope and sequence of Habits of Discourse that can serve as a resource of what to teach your students. Choose a habit that you want to introduce from this list:

| LEARNING TO CONTRIBUTE *(CCSS SL 8.1)* | | |
|---|---|---|
| **HABIT** | **IDEAL STUDENT ACTION** | **TEACHER PROMPTS** |
| **Project** | • Speak audibly in a professional tone, and shift body to make eye contact with classmates. | • Put hand to ear or move to opposite side of the room.<br>• "Project!" or "Strong voice!"<br>• "Speak in a professional tone."<br>• "Speak to your peers." |
| **Share In Turn** | • Speak in turn. | • "Give her a chance to finish her point."<br>• "One voice at a time." |
| **Speak as a Professional** | • Use classmates' names. | • "With whom do you agree?" |
| | • Use complete sentences. | • "Speak in complete sentences." |
| | • Address question succinctly. | • Point to timer.<br>• "Complete your point and give a peer the floor in 15 seconds." |

236    Get Better Faster 2.0

| | | |
|---|---|---|
| **Listen as a Professional** | • Track speaker with hands down.<br>• Nod or snap professionally. | • Gesture at students to track speaker and/or hands down.<br>• Model appropriate snapping/ stop inappropriate snapping. |
| | • Turn to page if speaker references.<br>• Pause to give time to turn to page and scan to confirm class is ready. | • Model turning to page/line (ex: use document camera).<br>• "Destiny, give the class a moment to find the page and confirm that everyone is with you." |
| **Take Notes as a Professional** | **Observer (during discussion):**<br>• Copy down key information.<br>• Annotate diagrams. | • Model or select strong student to model strong note-taking.<br>• "If you are not currently participating in the discussion, you should be taking notes." |
| | **Participant (after discussion):**<br>• Write down/summarize key information. | • Provide time at the end for key takeaways to be recorded.<br>• Show-call / cold call for a strong summary/key info.<br>• "Students in the discussion should be engaging completely with their peers; prioritize speaking, not note-taking." |
| **LEARNING TO BUILD (*CCSS SL 9.1 and 9.4*)** | | |
| **CORE HABIT** | **IDEAL STUDENT ACTION** | **TEACHER PROMPTS** |
| **Argue from Evidence** | • Utilize textual or numerical evidence to justify claim. | • "Support that" or "Prove that" or "Justify."<br>• "What evidence backs up your argument?" |
| | • Connect textual evidence to the argument. | • "How does that quote support your argument?"<br>• Gesture for student to keep going. |
| | • Show your work/explain your thinking. | • "Can you show us what you did to determine that?"<br>• Put work on the document camera. |

*(Continued)*

Instant Immersion    **237**

| | | |
|---|---|---|
| **Acknowledge** | • "That's an interesting point about ____." <br> • "I like Destiny's thinking about _____" | • "Acknowledge what Destiny said." <br> • "What about Destiny's point do you find interesting?" |
| **Go Deeper** | • Support peer's ideas with evidence. <br> • "If we look at p. 141. . . . this supports what Destiny is saying _____" <br> • "I agree with Destiny's thinking about. . .as on p. 12 Poe writes _____." | • "We should probably explore Destiny's thinking more. Can anyone provide evidence to support what she said?" <br> • "What evidence can we use to develop Destiny's comment? "From where in the text did Destiny get that idea?" <br> • "How does it connect to Destiny's thinking?" |
| | • "I want to zoom in on Destiny's evidence; I think it's interesting that Poe uses 'slaughtered' instead of 'killed' because _____." <br> • "I'd like to zoom in on 'red' because I think it connotes violence ____." | • "There is juicy diction in Destiny's quote. Let's zoom in." <br> • "What are the connotations of that word? <br> • "Why would Poe use 'slaughtered' instead of 'killed'?" <br> • "Why did Destiny use the word "hopeful" in her comment?" |
| **Critique** | • Agree with parts of ideas but not all. <br> • "I agree that. . .but ____." <br> • "While Destiny's point is right, I'm not sure it will get us to the best answer." <br> • "Actually, there is evidence in the text that refutes that view." | • "How are Destiny's and Amir's thoughts similar/different?" <br> • "What specifically do you agree with and disagree with?" <br> • "It seems we have a debate between Amir's position and Destiny's position. With whom do you agree?" <br> • "Is there evidence to refute Destiny's thinking?" |
| | • Examine evidence in a different way. <br> • "I actually viewed that text differently." | • "Who looked at that evidence differently?" |

# Key Leadership Moves

**See It**

- Live Model: Role play a conversation. Use the teacher previous prompts to encourage habits of discussion.
- Live Model: Role play rolling out a habit of discussion for the students to encourage them to use it. Leverage Leadership 2.0 can give more detail on effective rollouts, but here is a summary:
  - Hook: explain why this habit is valuable (1 min or less)
  - Frame: tell the students what to look for while you model it
  - Model: Model the habit ("I agree with this part of what you are saying, Ana, but I disagree with _____")
  - Practice: prompt the students to use the habit in the upcoming conversation

**Plan the Practice**

- Script points in an upcoming lesson to prompt for habits of discussion.

**Do It**

- Practice prompting students when they are not using the habits of discussion using the previous guide.

**Real-Time Feedback**

- Verbal: "Camila, how does your comment connect to Eddie's? Do you agree or disagree?"
  Coaching Clip—Watch Na'Jee model the teacher rollout of Press for Reasoning.

 WATCH Clip 39: **Guide Discourse—Habits of Discussion** (Key Leadership Move: See it)

Teaching Clips:

 REWATCH Clip 38: **Guide Discourse—Habits of Discussion** (Teaching clip)

Instant Immersion  239

WATCH Clip 40: **Stretch It—Sophisticate**
(Teaching clip)

# Guide Discourse 101: Stamp Key Understanding Coaching Tips

**Teacher Context**

**Challenge**

- Teacher ends the class discussion without nailing down the most important ideas.

**Action Step**

- Stamp the key understanding.

**Action Step Overview**

Discourse is a beautiful moment when students can generate a deeper understanding of what they are learning. However, the power of discourse—letting students grapple with their understanding and trying out multiple answers before landing on a plausible one—is also the risk: Students may walk away not knowing which ideas are the most important to hold onto. Once discourse has occurred, the key is to nail down the key understanding you want to pull from the students: we call that "stamping." After that is done, give them time to practice: It's that simple!

### Key Leadership Moves

**See It**

- Model Think Aloud: Identify the key takeaways in a lesson plan.
    - "What are the key understandings I will be listening for during the discourse?"
    - Model stamping the key takeaway. "Let's stamp that. What are the key things we want to remember from this discourse?"
    - If students are struggling to stamp it, call on a student who had the deep understanding and build off of their answer if necessary.

**Plan the Practice**

- Plan: Teacher revises lesson plans to include a stamp at the end.
    - Remember: The stamp should be the major takeaways from the whole lesson, not just what was discussed at the end of the lesson.

**Do It**
- Practice:
  - Role play discourse, giving a variety of answers. Once key understandings have surfaced, teacher asks students to recap and write down the key points of the lesson.

**Real-Time Feedback**
Verbal: "What should we remember about X? Let's write that down."
Coaching Examples:

 WATCH Clip 41: **Guide Discourse—Stamp Understanding** (Key Leadership Move: Do it)

 REWATCH Clip 7: **Guide Discourse—Stamp Understanding** (Key Leadership Move: Real-time Feedback)

Teaching Examples:

 WATCH Clip 42: **Guide Discourse** (Teaching clip)

Instant Immersion 241

# Strategies for Coaching: Guide Discourse 101

| Action Step | See It | Plan the Practice | Do It | Cues for Real-Time Feedback |
|---|---|---|---|---|
| **Everybody Writes** | • Watch a video on Show-Call.<br>• Live model think aloud: ID the pattern of error, determine which pieces of student work to Show-Call<br>• Live model: launch the routine of a Show-Call. | • Look at a set of student work and determine what could be the best pieces of student work to show-call (exemplar vs, non-exemplar, two different strategies, or just exemplar response). | • Practice the What to Do directions when using a Show-Call to launch discourse. | • Walk around the classroom and look for representative student samples that could be used for a Show-Call.<br>• Prompt the teacher: "What are you seeing?" "What is the gap?" "Which pieces of student work could you Show-Call to close the gap?" |
| **Turn and Talk** | • Model think aloud: Identify multiple opportunities in an upcoming lesson for turn and talks.<br>• Model the clear bright lines of launching a turn and talk: Setting up, releasing, and bringing students back from a turn and talk. | • Identify moments in upcoming lesson to do a quick turn and talk.<br>• Script directions for the turn and talk. | • Simple practice: Deliver the instructions for the turn and talk.<br>• Round 2 of practice: Deliver the instructions and redirect off-task students. | • Nonverbal: Point your index fingers towards each other to indicate doing a turn and talk.<br>• Verbal: "Ms. Smith, can students share their responses with the person next to them before sharing out whole group?" |
| **Cold Call, then Volleyball** | • Model: Cold call students to launch discourse and call on 3–4 students in a row before responding. | • Plan: Script names to cold call in lesson plan. | • Practice cold call and volleyball. | • Whisper: "Cold call students."<br>• Nonverbal: Point to another student that teacher should call on after a student responds. |

242    Get Better Faster 2.0

| Action Step | See It | Plan the Practice | Do It | Cues for Real-Time Feedback |
|---|---|---|---|---|
| **Prompt for and Praise Basic Habits of Discussion** | • Live Model: Role play a conversation, prompting to encourage habits of discussion.<br>• Live Model: Role play rolling out a habit of discussion for the students to encourage them to use it.<br>  ○ Hook: Explain why this habit is valuable.<br>  ○ Frame: Tell the students what to look for.<br>  ○ Model: Model the habit.<br>  ○ Practice | • Script points in an upcoming lesson to prompt for habits of discussion. | • Practice prompting students when they are not using the habits of discussion using the guide above. | • Verbal: "Camila, how does your comment connect to Eddie's? Do you agree or disagree?" |
| **Stamp the Key Understanding** | • Model Think Aloud: Identify the key takeaways in a lesson plan.<br>  ○ "What are the key understandings to listen for?"<br>  ○ Model: "Let's stamp that. What are the key things to remember?" | • Plan: Teacher revises lesson plans to include a stamp at the end. | • Practice: Role play discourse, giving a variety of answers. Once key understandings have surfaced, teacher asks students to recap and write down the key points of the lesson. | • Verbal: What should we remember about X? Let's write that down. |

Instant Immersion    243

---

## Stop and Jot

What are the three top coaching ideas you plan to use to train your teachers in these Phase 2 Rigor skills? Jot them here.

_____

_____

_____

_____

## CONCLUSION

The very term *instant immersion* calls to mind the feeling of having leaped into deep waters. Whether you're surrounded by water, by voices speaking in a new language, or by 25 students with distinct learning needs, a time of instant immersion is a time of being surrounded by something unfamiliar, often disarming. Sometimes, it may be a time of anxiety: Are you really going to be able to keep your head above the water? But at its best, instant immersion also leads to something incredibly empowering: the experience of learning to stay afloat.

For a new teacher, this is an especially profound moment because it's not just about treading water himself or herself. Rather, the new teacher who can navigate deeper waters is the teacher who's operating a seaworthy craft, gradually exploring deeper and deeper waters with every student on board. As we move on to Phase 3, we'll see what new teachers become capable of once teaching becomes not just about avoiding sinking but about sailing away on the learning adventure everyone is there to embark upon.

# Phase 3

# Cleared For Takeoff

Air travel remains one of the safest modes of transportation—in 2022, the Federal Aviation Administration safely managed an astounding 16,000,000 flights.[1] In the United States alone, an average of 45,000 flights take off daily, each one managed by the Federal Aviation Administration.[2] The sheer number of aircraft traveling at any given time makes the potential for a mid-air mishap seem likely. But the statistics prove otherwise. The last mid-flight collision between two commercial aircraft occurred in 1960, and no comparable incidents since.[3] What makes such a remarkable safety record possible? The quality of the air traffic controllers.

The basic training to become an FAA air traffic controller is relatively straightforward: Pass the required introductory classes and spend several months training onsite at the FAA training academy in Oklahoma City. From there, graduates are placed in facilities around the United States. But they're not yet ready to direct traffic in the skies. The real work begins once these aspiring air traffic controllers reach their first facility where they will undergo one to three years of additional training to become certified professional controllers.

Apprentices arrive with a solid foundation, yet no amount of preparation can prepare them for everything they will encounter in the flight tower. A sea of rapidly changing

245

information surrounds them, and changing weather conditions, engine troubles, and updated flight plans all have real world consequences. Part of what apprentices learn on the job is how to see this information for what it is: data that they can use to make decisions. But not all data are created equally. Apprentices must separate the signal from the noise, responding to the factors that matter most in a given situation. Once they have chosen the important points of data, they consider these within the context of their training to make informed decisions. And what they decide and ultimately communicate to pilots is what keeps us all safe when we fly.

Phase 3 of teaching is the apprenticeship phase. Teachers have studied all the foundations and implemented them; now it's time to deal with the unexpected—responding to real-time data. This stage is not only about seeing the data (whether it be students' on-task behavior or the pattern in student work) but acting on it—making changes to give students what they need. When teachers can do that, they are cleared for takeoff.

> ### Core Idea
>
> Teachers are cleared for takeoff
> when they can make real-time changes to respond to what students need.

Let's take a look at the leadership actions that entails.

## PHASE 3 COACHING BLUEPRINT: LOOK AT STUDENT WORK

At this stage, you've now seen the three essential coaching skills play out in professional development settings and in feedback meetings: Make It Bite-Sized, Practice What You Value, and Give Feedback Frequently.

How do these appear in your next phase of coaching? Precisely in the way you use student work to help your teacher grow.

### Weekly Data Meetings: Putting Student Learning First

Apprentice air traffic controllers levels up when they can look at and respond to multiple points of data. The same is true for teachers. The focus shifts from setting up the classroom environment to looking at what students are doing. Yet learning can't take off without clear methods in place to see it. Academic monitoring, introduced in Phase 2,

246    Get Better Faster 2.0

allows teachers to easily see what students get and what they don't. Phase 3 focuses on what to do when teachers notice a gap, and the Weekly Data Meeting (WDM) is the place where teachers discuss it. During this time, teachers ask and answer the question: What did students learn? And if they didn't learn it, what do we do about it?

---

### Core Idea

The key questions for teaching:
What did students learn?
And when they didn't, what do we do about it?

---

The weekly data meeting is known by many names: a professional learning community (when focused on student work), a student work meeting, short-cycle analysis, and so forth. Whatever you may call them, the impact of these meetings for a new teacher is enormous. Multiple leading authors in education, including the pioneering Richard DuFuor, have demonstrated the impact of data-driven groups of teachers looking at student work.[4]

Data meetings are one of the biggest drivers of student achievement. In *Driven By Data 2.0* and *Leverage Leadership 2.0*, I detail their transformative impact at numerous high-achieving schools worldwide. Weekly data meetings give new teachers (and all teachers) clarity on how to monitor the learning in their classroom and they also give them the chance to interpret data themselves, building on the strength of their leaders and their peers. Teachers develop the short-term ability to meet their students where they are and build the strength to do so as a matter of second nature in the long run.

---

### Findings from the Field: Progress Changes Mindsets

"Data-driven instruction becomes a part of the culture when you practice it consistently with teachers/leaders. A teacher's mind set changes when they see the progress students make on their formative or common assessments. When they look at student work, and then see that their re-teach plan makes a difference, something clicks—they see the power of their ability to teach."
—*Charles Newborn, Principal Supervisor, Memphis, TN*

---

Cleared For Takeoff    247

An effective data meeting follows a similar structure to that of a regular feedback meeting: Leaders prepare for the meeting by identifying the most urgent problem to solve (this time a student learning need rather than a teacher move), identify the gap, and plan/practice how to reach it to improve student learning. These key components follow the same See It, Name It, Do It structure as the feedback action steps.

- **See It: Start with the Exemplar:** Look to the teacher exemplar and top student exemplar to identify what students need to do to be successful.
- **Name It: Identify the Gaps:** Find the most noteworthy ways in which students at varying achievement levels are struggling to create exemplar responses.
- **Do It: Plan and Practice the Re-teach:** Pin down a strategy for re-teaching the material and closing the gaps you identified.

Let's look at each of these in more detail, one by one.

### See It—Start with the Exemplar

In Phase 1, we discussed starting from an end goal (an exemplar). After all, without knowing where you're headed, it's hard to decide what to teach. The same holds true when it comes to student learning. You can't figure out where the problem lies until you remind yourself where you're headed. Let's take a look at how Jaz Grant uses the exemplar to launch a weekly data meeting:

 WATCH Clip 43: **Weekly Data Meetings—See Exemplar** (Key Leadership Move: See it)

### Stop and Jot

What actions did Jaz take to start his data meeting?

_____
_____
_____
_____

Get Better Faster 2.0

So, what's the value of going back to the exemplar when looking at student work? Unpacking the exemplar keeps the end game in mind, so you can keep your focus when looking at student work.

> ## Core Idea
>
> Anchor your analysis in the end game:
> identify where you want to go and how far away you are.

This simple move also deepens the teacher's understanding. With a clear target in mind, Jaz's teacher will more easily be able to identify gaps. Jaz did this by looking at the exemplar response alongside unpacking the standard. The latter provides valuable academic language to describe the student thinking needed to answer the question. It also grounds the exemplar in the specific knowledge or skills that students need to show evidence of to achieve mastery.

At the heart of this work is that key idea that a standard without an assessment is undefined. And without a standard, teachers run the risk of choosing a procedural solution to a conceptual problem.

> ## Core Idea
>
> A standard without an assessment is undefined.
> An assessment without standards can prioritize procedures over concepts.

When unpacking the teacher's exemplar, the following prompts may be helpful for completing these tasks effectively:

- "What were the keys to an ideal answer?"
- "How does this (part of the exemplar) align with the standard?"
- "Is there anything you would add to our chart of the unpacked standard?"

Once the teacher-created exemplar has been unpacked, Jaz has the teacher pull out the best student answer—which we'll call the "student exemplar." As counterintuitive as it might sound, starting with the top response allows teachers to make sure their instruction is high enough for every student, and it allows them to identify the gaps for even the strongest students in the class. When unpacking the student exemplar, prompts include the following:

- "How does your student exemplar compare to the teacher exemplar? Is there a gap?"
- "Do students have different paths/evidence to demonstrate mastery of the standard?"
- "Does the student exemplar offer something that your exemplar does not (sometimes student answers are even better than our own!)?"

## Identify the Gaps

Once the teachers have a clear vision of the specific student response they're aiming for, they can focus on uncovering the gap, as Na'Jee Carter does here:

 **WATCH Clip 44: Weekly Data Meetings—See Gaps**
(Key Leadership Move: See it)

### Stop and Jot

What does Na'Jee say and do to identify the learning gaps in student work?
_____
_____
_____

Here we see the power of unpacking the exemplar: The teachers can use it as a reference to identify the gaps in the rest of the student work. During this process, teachers focused on naming as precisely as possible the trending error(s) that the students were making, including the conceptual misunderstanding that the error reflected. From there, they can plan how to clarify the confusion.

- "What are the key gaps between the rest of the student work and the exemplar?"
- "Look back at our chart: using the language of the standard and exemplar, what are the key misconceptions for our students?"

Whether done in a team or one-on-one, Weekly Data Meetings are powerful way to push student learning.

---

## A Word on Struggling Students

One of the most frequent questions I get asked during workshops on data-driven instruction is how this applies to special education and English language learner (ELL) students. Too often we think special needs students don't benefit from this approach. I cannot emphasize how wrong that assertion is! In reality, special educators/ELL teachers can repeat the same process focusing in on their students. In my experience interacting with high-achieving special educators across the country, they repeatedly tell me the same thing: data-driven instruction is at the heart of good teaching for students with special needs. The teaching techniques might end up being different (because these students have different learning needs) but rooting one's teaching in responding to student work is the foundation for differentiated instruction and for good special education instruction.

---

## Findings from the Field: Make It Easy to Collect

"One thing that can make it easier to lead weekly data meetings is to make the collection of student work easier. If a teacher has to bring 75 exit tickets to their weekly data meetings, you'll spend half the meeting simply sorting through it all. We used to make it even worse with complicated spreadsheets and reports on student learning. But now we have learned: make it easy by keeping it simple. Have a designated place for teachers to turn in student work (whether it be a mailbox outside the principal's office or an online Google folder) and only collect what you will actually analyze. There is nothing more frustrating for a teacher than to collect something that never gets reviewed! Your tools are only as helpful as the outcomes they produce."

—*Kristen McCarthy, Principal Supervisor, Newark, NJ*

## Plan and Practice the Re-teach

Gap analysis is important, but only effective re-teaching will change outcomes. This step is often overlooked in some meetings that look at student work. Jaz avoids this error:

 WATCH Clip 45: **Weekly Data Meetings—Plan**
(Key Leadership Move: Do it)

Yet Jaz doesn't stop with a plan for reteaching—he puts it into practice. By practicing "perfect" (trying it until it becomes naturally effective), Jaz increases the likelihood that his teacher's reteach lesson will be effective:

 WATCH Clip 46: **Weekly Data Meetings—Practice**
(Key Leadership Move: Do it)

Julia Dutcher believes in the same work for literacy. Here, she refines her middle school teacher's practice with a simple tweak: directing questions toward specific students or groups of students (we'll dive into this skill more in Phase 4: Strategic Calling):

 WATCH Clip 47: **Weekly Data Meetings—Practice**
(Key Leadership Move: Do it)

## Stop and Jot

What key actions do Jaz and Julia take to prepare their teachers to reteach?

When you want to change results, you have to teach differently. Follow the protocol coaches like Julia use, and you're prepared to bring a whole cohort of teachers—and, by extension, their students—up into high gear for learning.

## Findings from the Field: Follow the One-Pager

"When you lead these data meetings, make it easier by using the tools. The consistency of using the materials to guide your work makes it simpler and more efficient. You spend less time thinking about how to move from one part of the meeting to the next and more time on the nature of the gap and reteach lesson itself. As you use the materials, you get better each time—you use fewer words and become more efficient as well!—and your grasp of the materials becomes more natural and like second nature."

—*Charles Newborn, Principal Supervisor, Memphis, TN*

This following one-pager sums up the components of a successful data meeting looking at student work:

## Weekly/Daily Data Meetings Leading Teacher Teams to Analyze Student Daily Work

| Prepare Before the meeting | Prepare |
|---|---|
| | • **Student work ready:** Student exemplar and representative sample of work that meets the standard is almost there and further off (including from students with disabilities and English Language learners) |
| | • **Lesson materials ready:** Upcoming lesson plan(s), pertinent prompting guides, reteaching one-pager |
| | • **Prime the pump:** unpack standard, ID the gap(s) in student understanding; script the reteach plan(s) |
| | • **Lock in participants:** core teachers that teach/support (general education, special education and ELL) |
| | • **Preview protocol with teachers:** assign roles, novice teachers speak first, veteran teachers add on and clarify, leader provides additional clarity at end, chart, preview the need for concision from more verbose team members, use of a timer, creation of note taking template |

*(Continued)*

Cleared For Takeoff    **253**

| See It 12 min | See Past Success, See the Exemplar, and See and Analyze the Gap |
|---|---|

**See Past Success (1 min):**

- "Last week we planned to reteach _____ and we went from ___ % proficient to ___%. Nice job!"
- "What actions did you take to reach this goal?"

**See an Exemplar (8 min):**

- Narrow the focus: "Today, I want to dive into (specific standard) and the following assessment item."
- Unpack the standard/text:
  - Humanities: Analyze the text and task
  - STEM: Interpret the standard(s)
  - "Take 1 minute: in your own words, what do students need to know/and be able to do to master this task and text?"
  - Chart it: Know and Show (OR use a previous know/show chart)
  - Go last: add anything that is missing
- Unpack the teacher's written exemplar:
  - "Take 1–2 minute to review the exemplar: What were the keys to an ideal answer?"
  - "How does this (part of the exemplar) align with the standard?"
  - "Is there anything you would add to our chart of the unpacked standard?"
- Analyze a student exemplar:
  - "Take 1 minute: How does your student exemplar compare to the teacher exemplar? Is there a gap?"
  - "Do students have different paths/evidence to demonstrate mastery of the standard?"
  - "Does the student exemplar offer something that your exemplar does not?"

**See the Gap (5 min):**

- Look at a representative sample of un-mastered student work:
  - "Take 2 minutes: What are the key gaps between the rest of our student work and the exemplar?"
  - "Look back at our chart: using the language of the standard and exemplar, what are the key misconceptions for our students?"
  - (When multiple teachers present) Each teacher determines the gap for their set of student work.

254    Get Better Faster 2.0

| Name It 2 min | **Stamp the key conceptual ("know") and procedural ("show") misunderstanding** |
|---|---|
| | **Punch it—Stamp the Conceptual and Procedural Understanding:**<br>• "So our key area to reteach is:<br>  ○ the conceptual understanding (the "know"): "If they get this right and you ask them why, what do you want them to say?"<br>  ○ the procedural gap (the "show"): e.g., annotating text, showing work, line-by-line computation.<br>• Highlight the key parts of your Know/Show chart or write down the highest leverage action for students. |
| | **Plan the Reteach, Practice, and Follow Up** |
| Do It 2 min | **Plan the Reteach for the Trending Gap (8–10 min):**<br>• Select the re-teach structure:<br>  ○ "Should we use modeling or guided discourse?" "Why?"<br>    • Prompt to use the reteaching one-pager if they need guidance.<br>• Select upcoming task and needed knowledge, and identify exemplar response:<br>  ○ Select materials: task, text, student work to show-call, what to chart.<br>  ○ Activate/drop knowledge: "Is there any knowledge we need to activate or teach that will help them understand the model/discourse?"<br>  ○ "What is the ideal answer we want to see that will show we've closed the gap?"<br>  ○ (If needed—follow-up question): "What is the 'why' that students should be able to articulate?"<br>• Plan the re-teach:<br>  ○ "Take _____ min and write your script. I will do the same so we can spar."<br>    • **If a model**: write the think aloud and questions<br>    • **If guided discourse:** select student work for show-call, write prompts<br>    • Plan what knowledge needs to be activated or given<br>  ○ Spar: "Let's compare our reteach plans. What do you notice? What can we pull from each to make the strongest plan?" (Revise the plan)<br>• Plan the independent practice:<br>  ○ "What will you monitor to see if they are doing this correctly? What laps will you name?" |

*(Continued)*

Cleared For Takeoff    **255**

**Practice the Gap (remaining time):**

- "Let's practice."
  - **If a model:** practice modeling the thinking, precision of language, and checking for understanding
  - **If guided discourse:** practice Show-Call, prompting students, and stamping the understanding
  - **If monitoring:** practice the laps, annotations, and prompts when students are stuck
- (If a struggle) "I'm going to model the teaching for you. (Teach.) What do you notice?"
- Repeat until the practice is successful. CFU: "What made this more effective?"
- Lock it in: "How did our practice meet or enhance what we planned for the reteach?"

**Follow Up (last 2 min):**

- Set the follow-up plan: when to teach, when to re-assess, when to revisit this data
  - (When multiple reteach plans) Finalize which students will get which reteach plans.
  - Observe implementation within 24 hours; teacher sends re-assessment data to leader.
  - Spiral: Identify multiple moments when teacher can continue to assess and track mastery: Do Now questions, homework, modified independent practice.
- Move to the lowest scoring work:
  - "What students do we need to pull for tutoring? What do we need to remediate?"
  - "How can we adjust our monitoring plan to meet the needs of these students?"

## Teaching Skills Overview

Phase 3 marks a shift from thinking about the teaching to thinking about the learning. Here's the segment of the Scope and Sequence that covers Phase 3 of the school year.

## Phase 3 Action Step Sequence

| Management Trajectory | Rigor Trajectory |
|---|---|
| **Engage Every Student:**<br>8. **Whole-Class Reset**<br> • Implement a planned whole class reset to re-establish student expectations when a class routine has slowly weakened over previous classes:<br>   ○ "I've noticed that only 40% of us are writing end notes. These are important because they demonstrate your understanding of the text as a whole. Today I'll be looking for end-notes in all your annotations."<br> • Implement an "in-the-moment reset" when a class veers off task during the class period:<br>   ○ Example: Stop teaching. Confident stance. Clear What to Do: "Pencils down. Eyes on me in 3-2-1. Thank you: that's what Harvard looks like." Pick up tone and energy again.<br>9. **Engage All Students:** Make sure all students participate:<br> • Cold Call: record which students participate in each class; cold call those who don't to ensure everyone participates.<br> • Pre-call/warm call: Let a student who needs more time know you're calling them next.<br> • Turn and talk: Implement briefly (15–60 seconds) and frequently. | **Activate Knowledge and Model:**<br>8. **Activate Knowledge:** Prompt students to access their knowledge<br> • Point students to resources (word wall, notes, texts).<br> • "What do we know about __?"<br> • Use a knowledge organizer (cheat sheet)—all key points on 1–2 pages.<br> • Retrieve knowledge by applying it—give a simple task (e.g., organize events in chronological order, quick math fluency)<br> • "Drop" knowledge:<br>   ○ Give them knowledge in the middle of the lesson when it will unlock understanding (e.g., stating definition of a vocab word that cannot be understood with context).<br>9. **Model:** Model for students the thinking behind the doing<br> • Narrow the focus to the thinking students are struggling with.<br> • Give students a clear listening/note-taking task that fosters active listening.<br> • Model the thinking, not just the procedure:<br>   ○ Model replicable thinking steps that students can follow (e.g., "Hmm . . . . so what is this prompt asking me to do?" OR "So what do I already know about this time period?") |

*(Continued)*

Cleared For Takeoff    **257**

| Management Trajectory | Rigor Trajectory |
|---|---|
| • Intentionally alternate among multiple methods in class discussion: cold calling, all hands, and turn and talks.<br>• Provide supports to students with pre-identified needs:<br>  ○ Executive functioning (e.g., checklist, written steps, timer)<br>  ○ Social supports (e.g., communication strategies, strategies for resolving conflict )<br>  ○ Stress (e.g., strategies for naming and managing)<br>10. **Individual Student Corrections**<br>• Anticipate unengaged student behavior and rehearse the next two things you will do when that behavior occurs. Redirect students using the least invasive intervention necessary:<br>  ○ Proximity<br>  ○ Eye contact<br>  ○ Use a nonverbal<br>  ○ Say student's name quickly<br>  ○ Small consequence<br>• Engage in "close the loop" conversations with students to process what happened and improve for next time. | ○ Vary your tone and cadence from the normal teacher voice to highlight the thinking skills.<br>○ Make your thinking visible (anchor chart, annotations)<br>• Check for understanding after the model:<br>  ○ Debrief the model by asking students to identify the thinking skills.<br>  ○ Stamp the key points/steps to make sure you draw out the aspects you students to focus on.<br>  ○ Give students additional "at-bats" to practice independently. |

## PHASE 3 MANAGEMENT—ENGAGE EVERY STUDENT

### Quick Reference Guide

| If your teacher is struggling to: | . . .jump to: |
|---|---|
| **Whole Class Reset** | |
| Re-establish expectations for an ineffective class routine (weakens over days) | Planned whole class reset |
| Re-establish expectations for an ineffective class routine (weakens within the period) | In-the-moment reset |
| **Engage All Students** | |
| Keep all students engaged during class discussion | Cold Call |
| Encourage quieter students to participate | Pre-call/Warm Call |
| Prevent student restlessness during class discussion or get reluctant students to participate more | Turn and talk |
| Maintain the energy in the classroom | Multiple methods of class Discussion |
| Meet the needs of certain students | Provide support for students with identified needs |
| **Individual Student Corrections** | |
| Redirect disengaged students | Use least invasive correction |
| Repair after a correction | Close the loop conversations |

Cleared For Takeoff

# Phase 3 Action Step Sequence

| Management Trajectory | Rigor Trajectory |
|---|---|
| **Engage Every Student:**<br>8. **Whole-Class Reset**<br>• Implement a planned whole class reset to re-establish student expectations when a class routine has slowly weakened over previous classes:<br>  ○ "I've noticed that only 40% of us are writing end notes. These are important because they demonstrate your understanding of the text as a whole. Today I'll be looking for end-notes in all your annotations."<br>• Implement an "in-the-moment reset" when a class veers off task during the class period:<br>  ○ Example: Stop teaching. Confident stance. Clear What to Do: "Pencils down. Eyes on me in 3-2-1. Thank you: that's what Harvard looks like." Pick up tone and energy again.<br>9. **Engage All Students:** Make sure all students participate:<br>• Cold Call: Record which students participate in each class; cold call those who don't to ensure everyone participates.<br>• Pre-call/warm call: Let a student who needs more time know you're calling them next.<br>• Turn and talk: Implement briefly (15–60 seconds) and frequently. | **Activate Knowledge and Model:**<br>8. **Activate Knowledge:** Prompt students to access their knowledge<br>• Point students to resources (word wall, notes, texts).<br>• "What do we know about __?"<br>• Use a knowledge organizer (cheat sheet)—all key points on 1–2 pages.<br>• Retrieve knowledge by applying it—give a simple task (e.g., organize events in chronological order, quick math fluency).<br>• "Drop" knowledge:<br>  ○ Give them knowledge in the middle of the lesson when it will unlock understanding (e.g., stating definition of a vocab word that cannot be understood with context).<br>9. **Model:** Model for students the thinking behind the doing:<br>• Narrow the focus to the thinking students are struggling with.<br>• Give students a clear listening/note-taking task that fosters active listening.<br>• Model the thinking, not just the procedure:<br>  ○ Model replicable thinking steps that students can follow (e.g., "Hmm. . ..so what is this prompt asking me to do?" OR "So what do I already know about this time period?") |

260   Get Better Faster 2.0

| Management Trajectory | Rigor Trajectory |
|---|---|
| • Intentionally alternate among multiple methods in class discussion: cold calling, all hands, and turn and talks.<br>• Provide supports to students with pre-identified needs:<br>  ○ Executive functioning (e.g., checklist, written steps, timer)<br>  ○ Social supports (e.g., communication strategies, strategies for resolving conflict)<br>  ○ Stress (e.g., strategies for naming and managing)<br>10. **Individual Student Corrections**<br>• Anticipate unengaged student behavior and rehearse the next two things you will do when that behavior occurs. Redirect students using the least invasive intervention necessary:<br>  ○ Proximity<br>  ○ Eye contact<br>  ○ Use a nonverbal<br>  ○ Say student's name quickly<br>  ○ Small consequence<br>• Engage in "close the loop" conversations with students to process what happened and improve for next time. | ○ Vary your tone and cadence from the normal teacher voice to highlight the thinking skills.<br>○ Make your thinking visible (anchor chart, annotations).<br>• Check for understanding after the model:<br>  ○ Debrief the model by asking students to identify the thinking skills.<br>  ○ Stamp the key points/steps to make sure you draw out the aspects you students to focus on.<br>  ○ Give students additional "at-bats" to practice independently. |

## Introduction to Phase 3 Management Skills: Everybody on Board

What are students doing in an ideal classroom? The picture-perfect image likely varies by teacher. Some are energized by the hustle and bustle of an active classroom. Others might see an oasis of quiet concentration. No matter the visualization, a common thread unites them all: engaged, focused students.

The guiding belief behind each course of action we've recommended teachers take within the first 90 days of the school year is that *every* student can and must be learning on target at all times throughout the year. The groundwork laid in Phases 1 and 2 got us most of the way there. Phase 3 is about getting us the rest of the way through whole class moves and individual corrections.

## Whole-Class Reset

> ### Teacher Professional Development Goal
>
> **Whole-Class Reset:** Stop and restart the class any time students begin to veer off task.

Do It Again (see Phase 2: Routines and Procedures 201) described how a new teacher can have students redo a routine when it's not done well. Sometimes, however, student nonresponsiveness doesn't begin with a broken routine, but rather is a small building wave of student misbehavior. One student whispering turns into two, then a slow murmur arises, then loud talking throughout the room. In another case, the routine has been slightly weakening over the course of a few days. In each case, you don't need to revise the routine but reset the class, just as you might refresh a website that has frozen during a Google search. A whole-class reset re-establishes teacher expectations for student behavior in that moment.

---

### Findings from the Field: Bring Order to Disorder

"A whole-class reset can often have outsized impact. One of our new teachers had difficulty with classroom management. After meeting with her several times, it appeared that she needed a full reset. The reset also included her scholars helping to create classroom expectations. After setting clear expectations everyone agreed upon, they practiced until they got it right. Now I see this class as one of the most well behaved in the school. I'm confident that this reset has helped move achievement in her classroom because more time can now be spent on learning."
—*Leslie Bonner, Principal, St. Louis, MO*

---

The following are the most common challenges of Phase 2 that can be solved with a whole-class reset:

- A class has slid into low engagement over a few days *or* within the same class period without the teacher realizing it:
    - Small talk is occurring during specific moments in the lesson.
    - Students are not on task during independent practice.
    - Turn and talks are off task.

Although the two action steps that can both resolve these challenges are very similar, we address each of them separately below.

## Whole-Class Reset: Planned Whole-Class Reset
## Coaching Tips

### Teacher Context

### Challenge

- A class has slid into low engagement *over a few days* without the teacher realizing it:
    - Routines no longer function efficiently.
    - Small talk is occurring during specific moments in the lesson.
    - Students are not on task during independent practice.
    - Turn and talks are off task.

### Action Step

- Implement a whole-class reset to re-establish student behavioral expectations when a routine weakens or becomes ineffective within a class period or over a series of days.

### Action Step Overview

If students aren't following a routine, the teacher must reset, or reteach, that routine. The most reliably effective way the teacher can do this is to script a plan for the reset ahead of time.

> **Tip From a Coach: Block Out Time for Culture Resets**
> "Repeat! Repeat! Repeat! Plan whole school resets after school breaks and spend the week on those cultural actions. Make sure these resets

Cleared For Takeoff  **263**

reach every area of the building and leverage your leadership team to give real-time feedback to staff. A strong school culture prevents chaos and gives you more time to focus on instruction."

—*Melissa St. Joy, Principal, Atlanta, GA*

### Key Leadership Moves

#### See It

- Show video of a teacher resetting a class.
- Live model a whole class reset.

#### Plan the Practice

- Script the reset word by word. Keep the script to language as minimal as possible. Sample scripts could include best practices such as:
  - Pause.
  - "Eyes on me."
  - Narrate the problem.
  - Give direction.
  - Scan/see.
  - Wait for 100%. If not there, give a second direction to students not on task.
  - Narrate the positive.
  - Continue the lesson.

#### Do It

- When practicing, really focus on incorporating all previous action steps, particularly:
  - Confidence Presence (posture and register)
  - What to Do (using as few words as possible)
  - Make eye contact (scan to make sure students are complying)
- Add complexity as you go:
  - Round 1: All students "comply" right away.
  - Round 2: A few students still don't comply, and teacher has to get them on target.

#### Real-Time Feedback

- If reset is ineffective, jump in and help lead the reset. Be sure to cede control back to the teacher and affirm their leadership as you do so.

## Whole-Class Reset: Implement an In-the-moment Reset

## Coaching Tips

**Teacher Context**

**Challenge**

- A class has slid into low engagement *within the same class period* without the teacher realizing it:
  - Small talk is occurring during specific moments in the lesson.
  - A basic routine is sloppier/less efficient than normal.
  - Students are not on task during independent practice.
  - Turn and talks are off task.

**Action Step**

- Implement an in-the-moment reset when a class veers off task during the class period.
  - Example: Stop teaching. Square up. Give a clear What to Do: "Pencils down. Eyes on me. Hands folded in 3-2-1. Thank you: That's what Harvard looks like." Pick up tone and energy again.

**Action Step Overview**

When you script a planned reset as described in the previous section, you're planning to use that reset in your next class no matter what—you already know the problem that will occur. The in-the-moment reset is somewhat different: It can still be scripted in advance, but you'll only need to use it only when students are having an "off" day, getting something wrong that typically they get right. What makes this type of reset such an effective way to redirect a class is that it works across a broad range of in-the-moment challenges. If the teacher has prepared a stock response like the one in the previous example, rehearsing it diligently until both the words and the tone come automatically, most management challenges will result in only temporary, not permanent, disruption. In time, the students' improved behavior will come as quickly and naturally as the teacher's reset does.

### Key Leadership Moves

Most of the same leadership moves in the planned reset work for the in-the-moment reset as well. The key difference will be helping the teacher identify the moments when they need it.

Cleared For Takeoff  **265**

**See It**

- Show a model video of teacher doing an in-the-moment reset.

**Plan the Practice**

- Ideally, watch video of the teacher's classroom, and have teacher identify when the engagement is starting to drop and the signs that indicate the lower engagement.

- Coach the teacher through the process of scripting a generic in-the-moment reset that could be used in every situation.
  - Pause.
  - "Eyes on me."
  - Narrate the problem.
  - Give direction.
  - Scan.
  - Wait for 100%. If not there, give a second direction to students not on task.
  - Narrative the positive.
  - Continue the lesson.

**Do It**

- Just as with planned resets, when practicing, really focus on incorporating all previous action steps, particularly:
  - Confident Presence (posture and register)
  - What to Do (using as few words as possible)
  - See Your Students (scan to make sure students are complying)

- Just as with planned resets, add complexity as you go:
  - First role play: all students "comply" right away.
  - Second role play: a few students still don't comply and teacher has to get them on target.

**Real-Time Feedback**

- Nonverbal: Create a cue for "reset" or show a sign.

- Model: "Students, we need to reset ourselves right now." Model a reset for the teacher.

266    Get Better Faster 2.0

## Strategies for Coaching Whole-Class Reset

| Action Step | See It | Plan the Practice | Do It | Cues for Real-Time Feedback |
|---|---|---|---|---|
| **Plan a whole class reset** | • Show of video of a teacher resetting a class.<br>• Live model a whole class reset. | Script the reset word-by-word:<br>• Pause. "Eyes on me."<br>• Narrate the problem and give a direction.<br>• Scan. Wait for 100%. Redirect off-task students.<br>• Narrate the positive.<br>• Continue the lesson. | • Practice reset:<br>  ○ Confident presence<br>  ○ What to Do<br>  ○ Make eye contact<br>• Add complexity:<br>  ○ Rd 1: all students "comply" right away.<br>  ○ Rd 2: a few students still don't comply. | • If reset is ineffective, jump in and help lead the reset. Be sure to cede control back to the teacher and affirm their leadership as you do so. |
| **Implement an in-the-moment reset** | • Show a model video of teacher doing an in-the-moment reset. | • Ideally, watch video of the teacher's classroom and have teacher identify when the engagement is starting to drop and the signs that indicate the lower engagement.<br>• Coach the teacher through the process of scripting a generic in-the-moment reset that could be used in every situation. | • Practice reset:<br>  ○ Confident Presence<br>  ○ What to Do<br>  ○ Make eye contact<br>• Add complexity:<br>  ○ Rd 1: all students "comply" right away.<br>  ○ Rd 2: a few students still don't comply. | • Nonverbal: Create a cue for "reset" or show a sign.<br>• Model: "Students, we need to reset ourselves right now." Model a reset for the teacher. |

Cleared For Takeoff    267

## Stop and Jot

What are the three top coaching ideas you plan to use to train your teachers in these Phase 3 Management skills? Jot them here.

_____

_____

_____

_____

---

## Teacher Professional Development Goal

**Engage All Students:** Keep every student dialed in—even when you're calling on just one at a time.

---

## Engage All Students

For many new teachers, having most of the class with them seems good enough: Almost everyone is learning. But almost isn't all. Without 100 percent of students with us, we don't have a full picture of the understanding in the room. We can't know what students get or don't get if they're not trying. And when we allow students to check out, we miss their academic struggles.

## Findings from the Field: Engage the Disengaged

"When we find how to engage the disengaged, we give them an entry point to participate in the work. Scholars want to engage and do what they are asked; sometimes they just don't know how."
—Katie Harshman, Principal, Pueblo, CO

Getting all students on board goes beyond a whole class reset. The second part includes knowing what to do when most of the class is with you and just a few are not. The following sections show how to pull in the rest.

268  Get Better Faster 2.0

These actions steps for engaging all students will overcome the following specific challenges:

- Some students disengage when the teacher asks a question.

- The teacher tends to call on the same few students over and over.

- Teacher only uses cold-calling or raised hands.

- Students become restless during a lengthy I Do or other teacher presentation of material.

- Students become restless during a lengthy class discussion.

- The teacher over-relies on just one technique for engaging all students.

- Students with pre-identified needs struggle to participate in the class.

## Engage All Students: Cold Call[5]

## Coaching Tips

### Teacher Context

### Challenge

- Some students disengage when the teacher asks a question, assuming that if they don't raise their hands, they won't have to answer.

- The teacher tends to call on the same few students over and over.

### Action Step

- Cold-call students.

### Action Step Overview

In some cases, it makes sense for a teacher to choose which student to call on from among those who have volunteered to answer the question—but not always. To limit yourself to calling only on students with their hands raised is to give some students the ability to opt out of participation. That cedes control of who engages and who doesn't to the students rather than the teacher. One solution is cold calling, a practice whose many powerful benefits Doug Lemov discusses in detail in *Teach Like a Champion 3.0*: By letting students know that they could be called on at any moment, the teacher holds students accountable for their learning at all times, improving both management and rigor.

Cleared For Takeoff    **269**

**Key Leadership Moves**

### See It

- Quick model from the lesson plan: Follow a scripted question sequence and cold call from the teacher's roster.

### Plan the Practice

- Choose students to cold call in advance.

### Do It

- Rehearse a questioning sequence from an upcoming lesson, with the leader playing the part of various students and the teacher strategically cold calling these students.

### Real-Time Feedback

- Nonverbal: Point at the ideal student for the teacher to cold call.

---

## Engage All Students: Pre-Call/Warm Call

## Coaching Tips

### Teacher Context

### Challenge

- Teacher doesn't know how to get more reluctant participants to share in large-group discussion.

### Action Step

- Pre-call (or warm call) students to add more voices to the conversation.

### Action Step Overview

Some students may be less likely to participate in whole-group discussion for a variety of reasons. Encourage their participation with a pre-call—letting them know that you'll call on them next in your questioning sequence. This gives a shy student a chance to prepare their response and lowers their anxiety about speaking out in large group settings.

**Key Leadership Moves**

### See It

- Model think aloud: Ask yourself which students are less likely to participate, and jot this list as the students to warm call.

270   Get Better Faster 2.0

- Model: Give a task/turn and talk to the students and then discreetly confer with students and ask that they share their response/thought with the class. Call on that student during the questioning sequence.

**Plan the Practice**

- Plan: Choose students for pre-call/warm-call in advance.

**Do It**

- Practice: Discreetly let a student know you would like them to participate, run through a questioning sequence and call on that student.

**Real-Time Feedback**

- Whisper: "Daniel has a strong response. Let him know that you'd like him to share with the class."

---

## Findings from the Field: Use the GBF Sequence to Spot What's Missing

"Use the GBF Sequence to Spot What's Missing: When I observe and it is clear the engagement in the classroom is lagging, I compare the Engage All Students strategies against the teacher's moves and think, "Which strategy is missing?" or "Which strategy would best be paired for the stage of development of this teacher?" This method helps me quickly identify the most impactful action step for the teacher."

—*Scott Schuster, Principal, Brooklyn, NY*

---

## Engage All Students: Turn and Talk

## Coaching Tips

**Teacher Context**

**Challenge**

- Students become restless during a lengthy I Do, other teacher presentations of material, or lengthy class discussions.
- Only a few students participate in each large group class discussion.

Cleared For Takeoff 271

**Action Step**

- Implement brief (15-to 60-second) turn and talks.

**Action Step Overview**

Turn and talk is the only action step that is listed twice in the Get Better Faster Sequence—as part of Guided Discourse 101 (Phase 2) and here. The reason for that is that turn and talk offers so much value to multiple parts of the lesson. Phase 2 discussed using it to launch discourse; here, turn and talk is used to keep students engaged throughout the rest of the lesson. It can provide a short break/check-for-understanding in the midst of a teacher model, a moment to unscramble confusion, or to break up a reading passage. The practices are largely the same as what was listed in Phase 2—the only difference is deciding when to use it.

HS science teacher Emelia Pelliccio's lesson launch features two turn-and-talks. Watch the clip to see how they support the day's essential question.

 WATCH Clip 48: **Activate Knowledge—What Do We Know About?**
(Teaching clip)

**Key Leadership Moves**

**See It**

- Model think aloud: Identify opportunities in an upcoming lesson for a turn and talk.
- Model the clear bright lines of launching a turn and talk: Setting up, releasing, and bringing students back from a turn and talk:
  - "Turn your shoulders toward the person you will talk to so that you can easily make eye contact."
  - Scan the room to notice any students who don't have a partner or are in trios. "Julia, Mark can be your partner. You two can turn toward each other."
  - "The person closest to the windows will share first."
  - "Evaluate these two pieces of student work—which one do you agree with and why? Ready? Turn and talk."
  - Scan the room to notice which partners don't immediately speak: Give them a nonverbal to turn and talk. Prompt out loud if that doesn't work: "Chassity, share your answer with your partner."
  - Once all groups have started, lean in to listen to student responses.
  - Raise hand (or a hand clap) to call students back together. Narrate the positive and wait for all students to be quiet (utilize nonverbals or prompts for those who don't).

**Plan the Practice**

- Identify moments in upcoming lesson to do a quick turn and talk.

- Script your directions for the turn and talk.

**Do It**

- Simple practice: Deliver the instructions for the turn and talk.

- Round 2 of practice: Deliver the instructions and redirect off-task students.

**Real-Time Feedback**

- Nonverbal: Turn forefingers toward each other.

- Model: Lead a turn and talk and then explain rationale to teacher during the turn and talk.

---

# Engage All Students: Use Multiple Methods to Call on Students

## Coaching Tips

**Teacher Context**

**Challenge**

- The teacher over-relies on just one technique for engaging all students.

**Action Step**

- Intentionally alternate between multiple methods in class discussion: cold calling, choral response, all hands (having all students raise their hands when it is a question where everyone should know the answer) and turn and talks.

**Action Step Overview**

Once new teachers learn certain techniques for calling on students, they have the tendency to over-rely on them. They will always cold call—and no students raise their hands—or they will always call on one student at a time—and students will figure out that they won't be called on again for a long time. To engage all students to the fullest possible extent, teachers are best served by not only being mindful of which student would be best to call on, but to mix it up: Vary the methods to keep the energy. There's no one-size-fits-all here: the magic is in the variation.

Cleared For Takeoff    273

**Key Leadership Moves**

**See It**

- Deliver a segment of the lesson with multiple question techniques.

**Plan the Practice**

- Plan a whole-group discussion: Note which questions are best suited for cold call, all hands, choral response or turn and talk.

**Do It**

- Role-play the discussion following the script the teacher created.
  - Cold calling, choral response, all hands, and turn and talks

**Real-Time Feedback**

- Nonverbal: Create/Use cue for cold call, turn and talk, choral response or all hands.

- Whisper prompt: "When you call the group back together, start with a choral response followed by a cold call."

> **Tip from a Coach—Engage All Minds**
> "Implementing and coaching around "engage all students" completely transformed the way my school promoted a culture of "all minds on." Strategically using a variety of engagement techniques created a sense of all-in, community-based learning. As this became the norm, students began to take more academic risks and participate in discourse. Engaging all students was the breakthrough step we needed to move from compliance to invested learning."
> —*Yanela Cruz, Principal, Springfield, MA*

# Engage All Students: Equip Pre-Identified Students With Tools
## Coaching Tips

**Teacher Context**

**Challenge**

- Students with pre-identified needs struggle to participate in the class.

**Action Step**

- Provide supports to students with pre-identified needs:
  - Executive functioning (e.g., checklist, written steps, timer)
  - Social supports (e.g., communication strategies, strategies for resolving conflict)
  - Stress (e.g., strategies for naming and managing)

**Action Step Overview**

Knowing what students need goes beyond academic strengths and gaps. Certain students may require additional supports to be successful in class. These could look like checklists (for executive function), communication strategies (for social supports), or stress management techniques. While teachers can give reminders to use these techniques in-the-moment, these strategies are most successful when planned or considered in advance.

Middle school teacher Jessica Rabinowitz coaches a student to use a math resource to check her thinking.

  WATCH Clip 49: **Engage All Students**
(Teaching clip)

**Key Leadership Moves**

**See It**

- Show a lesson plan from another teacher with annotations about how to reach students with pre-identified needs.
- Do a think aloud on what adjustments to make for students needing more executive functioning or social support.

**Plan the Practice**

- Annotate upcoming lesson plans with supports for students with pre-identified needs.

**Do It**

- Practice reinforcing executive function: referring students to their resource (e.g., timer, checklist).
- Practice encouraging social supports: reminding students of communication strategies, strategies to resolve conflict, name/manage stress.

Cleared For Takeoff

**Real-Time Feedback**

- If aware of a pre-identified need that can be addressed in the moment, whisper to teacher.

## Strategies for Coaching: Engage All Students

| Action Step | See It | Plan the Practice | Do It | Cues for Real-Time Feedback |
|---|---|---|---|---|
| **Cold Call** | • Model from the lesson plan: Follow a scripted question sequence and cold call from the teacher's roster. | • Choose students to cold-call in advance. | • Practice: Run through a questioning sequence from an upcoming lesson. Leader plays the part of various students. Teacher strategically cold calls. | • Nonverbal: Point at the ideal student for the teacher to cold call. |
| **Pre-call/ Warm Call** | • Model think aloud: Ask which students are less likely to participate, jot this list as the students to warm call.<br>• Model: Give a task/turn and talk to the students. Discreetly confer with student and ask that they share their response/thought with the class. Call on student during questioning sequence. | • Choose students for pre-call/warm-call in advance. | • Practice: Discreetly let a student know you would like them to participate, run through a questioning sequence and call on that student. | • Whisper: "X has a strong response. Let him know that you'd like him to share with the class." |
| **Turn and Talk** | • Model think aloud: Identify opportunities in an upcoming lesson for a turn and talk.<br>• Model the clear bright lines of launching a turn and talk: Setting up, releasing, and bringing students back from a turn and talk. | • ID moments in upcoming lesson to do a quick turn and talk.<br>• Script your directions for the turn and talk. | • Simple practice: Deliver the instructions for the turn and talk.<br>• Round 2 of practice: Deliver the instructions and redirect off-task students. | • Nonverbal: Forefingers turn toward each other.<br>• Model: Lead a turn and talk and then explain rationale to teacher during the turn and talk. |

276　Get Better Faster 2.0

| Action Step | See It | Plan the Practice | Do It | Cues for Real-Time Feedback |
|---|---|---|---|---|
| Use Multiple Methods to Call on Students | • Deliver a segment of the lesson with multiple question techniques. | • Plan a whole group discussion: note which questions are best suited for cold call, hands, choral response, or turn and talk. | • Role play the discussion following the script the teacher created.<br>• Cold calling, choral response, all hands, turn and talks. | • Nonverbal: Create/Use cue for cold calling, turn and talk, choral response, and all hands.<br>• Whisper prompt: "When you call the group back together, start with a choral response followed by a cold call." |
| Provide Supports to Students with Pre-identified Needs | • Show a lesson plan from another teacher with annotations about how to reach students with pre-identified needs.<br>• Do a think aloud on what adjustments to make for students needing more executive functioning or social support. | • Annotate upcoming lesson plans with supports for students with pre-identified needs. | • Practice reinforcing executive function (e.g., timer, checklist).<br>• Practice encouraging social supports: communication strategies, resolve conflict, manage stress. | • If aware of a pre-identified need that can be addressed in the moment, whisper to teacher. |

## Individual Student Corrections

> ## Teacher Professional Development Goal
>
> **Individual Student Corrections:** Redirect off-task individual students, not the entire class.

At this stage, the teacher has gotten 90% of the way there: What remains are the handful of students that are still not responding. You cold call and receive a blank stare in return. You cue these students to turn and talk and their partner chats away while they

Cleared For Takeoff    277

remain silent. The disruptions are individual and don't impact enough students to warrant a whole class reset, but they could become an issue if not addressed. This is where individual student corrections come in.

These redirections are designed to get students back on task: They are lightning quick, unobtrusive, and respectful.

Initial challenges of correcting individual students may include the following:

- The teacher sees the problem, but the basic strategies of What to Do and Narrate the Positive aren't working for a few students.
- Teacher does not consistently or effectively provide consequences when students show minor misbehaviors.
- The teacher uses corrections that draw more attention than necessary to the student who has been off task.
- Students consistently exhibit certain off-task behaviors that teacher struggles to manage.
- Teacher does not follow up with student after redirection.

## Individual Student Corrections: Least Invasive Intervention Coaching Tips

### Teacher Context

### Challenge

- The teacher sees the problem, but the basic strategies of What to Do and Narrate the Positive aren't working for a few students.
- Teacher does not consistently or effectively provide consequences when students show minor misbehaviors.
- The teacher uses corrections that draw more attention than necessary to the student who has been off task.
- Students consistently exhibit certain off-task behaviors that teacher struggles to manage.

278    Get Better Faster 2.0

**Action Step**

- Redirect students using the least invasive intervention necessary:
  - Proximity
  - Eye contact
  - Use a nonverbal
  - Say a student's name quickly
  - Small consequence

**Action Step Overview**

Off-task behaviors are a signal that students are not actively learning. Getting them back on track with a subtle redirection minimizes lost learning time. Nevertheless, new teachers often struggle to know how or when to use less invasive techniques, and in their desire to get all students back on task, they may use a technique that calls more attention than necessary to the off-task student or behavior, e.g., stopping a lesson to tell a student or students what to do. Learning how to use less invasive techniques helps teachers maintain the flow of their instruction and provides predictable consequences to students (maintaining the structure of the behavior management system).

## Key Leadership Moves

**See It**

- Model: Play the role of teacher. Have the teachers play an off-task student and respond to their behavior with a less invasive technique. Then ask the teachers to remain off-task so that you have to use each of the possible individual corrections in order.

**Plan the Practice**

- Choose a common off-task behavior from the classroom. Plan each of the individual corrections and script them on the front of the lesson plan.

**Do It**

- Play the role of the off-task student.
  - Round 1: Have the teacher redirect the off-task behavior using proximity, eye contact, and a nonverbal. In this round, the student responds positively to these corrections.
  - Round 2: Repeat the practice, but in this case the student remains off task. Have the teacher respond to the off task-behavior using the student's name and then a small consequence.

Cleared For Takeoff **279**

- Round 3: Role play multiple students off-task, some requiring only the least-invasive correction and others requiring more. Focus feedback on making sure the teacher doesn't jump to a consequence before trying every other action.

**Real-Time Feedback**

- Model: Use a Confident Stance near off-task students.
- Nonverbal: Point to your eyes and then point at an off-task student or students.
- Nonverbal: Mime two legs walking and point to an off-task student or students.
- Whisper Prompt: "The back table is off task. Use proximity."
- Whisper Prompt: "Angelica is off task again. Give a small consequence."

 **WATCH Clip 50: Individual Student Correction**
(Key Leadership Move: See it)

 **WATCH Clip 51: Individual Student Correction**
(Key Leadership Move: Do it)

## Individual Student Corrections: Close the Loop Conversations Coaching Tips

**Teacher Context**

**Challenge**

- Teacher redirects without checking in with student at a later time.

**Action Step**

- Close the loop conversations.

**Action Step Overview**

Most students respond positively to individual student corrections and get themselves back on track. However, some students will get upset and might sulk or disengage after a correction. In these cases, teachers will reconnect with students in what we call a "close the loop" conversation: The teacher and the student process what happened and name the steps for improvement. This is best done outside of class or during extended independent practice so as not to detract from the learning.

### Key Leadership Moves

### See It

- Model a "close the loop" follow up conversation with a student.

### Plan the Practice

- Script follow up conversation with sample student.

### Do It

- Practice the follow up conversation.

### Real-Time Feedback

- Whisper prompt: "Check in with Robert at the end of the lesson."

## Strategies for Coaching: Individual Student Corrections

| Action Step | See It | Plan the Practice | Do It | Cues for Real-Time Feedback |
|---|---|---|---|---|
| Least-Invasive Intervention | • Model: Play the role of teacher. Have the teacher play off-task students and respond to their behavior with a less invasive technique. Then ask the teacher to remain off-task so that you have to use each of the possible individual corrections in order. | • Choose a common off-task behavior from the classroom. Plan each of the individual corrections and script them on the front of the lesson plan. | • Round 1: Have the teacher redirect the off-task behavior using proximity, eye contact, and a nonverbal.<br>• Round 2: Repeat the practice, but in this case the student remains off task. Use student's name and then a small consequence.<br>• Round 3: Role play multiple students off-task, some requiring only the least-invasive correction and others requiring more. | • Model: Use a Confident Stance near off-task students.<br>• Nonverbal: Point to your eyes and then point at an off-task student or students.<br>• Nonverbal: Mime two legs walking and point to an off-task student or students.<br>• Whisper Prompt: "The back table is off task. Use proximity."<br>• Whisper Prompt: "Samuel is off task again. Give a small consequence." |

*(Continued)*

Cleared For Takeoff    281

| Action Step | See It | Plan the Practice | Do It | Cues for Real-Time Feedback |
|---|---|---|---|---|
| **Close the Loop Conversations** | • Model a "close the loop" follow up conversation with a student. | • Script follow up conversation with sample student. | • Practice the follow up conversation. | • Whisper prompt: "Check in with Robert at the end of the lesson." |

---

## Stop and Jot

What are the three top coaching ideas you plan to use to train your teachers in these Phase 3 Management skills? Jot them here.

_____

_____

_____

# PHASE 3 RIGOR—ACTIVATE KNOWLEDGE AND MODEL

## Quick Reference Guide

| If your teacher is struggling to: | . . .jump to: |
|---|---|
| **Activate Knowledge** | |
| Get students to access resources prior to asking teacher a question | Point students to resources (word wall, notes, texts, etc.) |
| Get students to remember prior lessons | Prompt students "What do you know about?" |
| Get students to retain key information | Use a knowledge organizer (cheatsheet) |
| Get student to use prior knowledge in new contexts | Apply your knowledge |

282    Get Better Faster 2.0

| | |
|---|---|
| Respond to content gaps mid-lesson that cause students to be stuck | Drop knowledge |
| **Model** | |
| Make the model simple or don't target what students need | Narrow the focus to the thinking students are struggling with |
| Keep student attention during the model | Give students a clear listening/ note taking task |
| Go beyond procedural steps or explanations | Model the thinking, not the procedure |
| Know if students understand the thinking behind the model | Check for understanding after the model |

## Phase 3 Action Step Sequence

| Management Trajectory | Rigor Trajectory |
|---|---|
| **Engage Every Student:**<br>8. **Whole-Class Reset**<br>• Implement a planned whole class reset to re-establish student expectations when a class routine has slowly weakened over previous classes.<br>  ○ "I've noticed that only 40% of us are writing end notes. These are important because they demonstrate your understanding of the text as a whole. Today I'll be looking for endnotes in all your annotations."<br>• Implement an "in-the-moment reset" when a class veers off task during the class period:<br>  ○ Example: Stop teaching. Confident stance. Clear What to Do: "Pencils down. Eyes on me in 3-2-1. Thank you: that's what Harvard looks like." Pick up tone and energy again. | **Activate Knowledge and Model:**<br>8. **Activate Knowledge:** Prompt students to access their knowledge<br>• Point students to resources (word wall, notes, texts).<br>• "What do we know about __?"<br>• Use a knowledge organizer (cheat sheet)—all key points on 1–2 pages.<br>• Retrieve knowledge by applying it—give a simple task (e.g., organize events in chronological order, quick math fluency).<br>• "Drop" knowledge:<br>  ○ Give them knowledge in the middle of the lesson when it will unlock understanding (e.g., stating definition of a vocab word that cannot be understood with context). |

*(Continued)*

Cleared For Takeoff    **283**

| Management Trajectory | Rigor Trajectory |
|---|---|
| 9. **Engage All Students:** Make sure all students participate:<br>• Cold Call: Record which students participate in each class; cold call those who don't to ensure everyone participates.<br>• Pre-call/warm call: let a student who needs more time know you're calling them next.<br>• Turn and talk: implement briefly (15–60 seconds) and frequently<br>• Intentionally alternate among multiple methods in class discussion: cold calling, all hands, and turn and talks<br>• Provide supports to students with pre-identified needs:<br>  ○ Executive functioning (e.g., checklist, written steps, timer)<br>  ○ Social supports (e.g., communication strategies, strategies for resolving conflict )<br>  ○ Stress (e.g., strategies for naming and managing)<br>10. **Individual Student Corrections**<br>• Anticipate unengaged student behavior and rehearse the next two things you will do when that behavior occurs. Redirect students using the least invasive intervention necessary:<br>  ○ Proximity<br>  ○ Eye contact<br>  ○ Use a nonverbal<br>  ○ Say student's name quickly<br>  ○ Small consequence<br>• Engage in "close the loop" conversations with students to process what happened and improve for next time. | 9. **Model:** Model for students the thinking behind the doing<br>• Narrow the focus to the thinking students are struggling with.<br>• Give students a clear listening/note-taking task that fosters active listening.<br>• Model the thinking, not just the procedure:<br>  ○ Model replicable thinking steps that students can follow (e.g., "Hmm. . ..so what is this prompt asking me to do?" OR "So what do I already know about this time period?")<br>  ○ Vary your tone and cadence from the normal teacher voice to highlight the thinking skills.<br>  ○ Make your thinking visible (anchor chart, annotations).<br>• Check for understanding after the model:<br>  ○ Debrief the model by asking students to identify the thinking skills.<br>  ○ Stamp the key points/steps to make sure you draw out the aspects you students to focus on.<br>  ○ Give students additional "at-bats" to practice independently. |

## Introduction to Phase 3 Rigor Skills: Adjust the Flight Pattern

When ready to act, air traffic controllers know how to adjust the flight pattern based on having all the necessary tools at their disposal—effective models from their mentors and guidebooks on what to do. Effective teaching requires the same.

Over the course of my career, I've had the privilege to see thousands of hours of great teaching. But occasionally, I get to enjoy the reverse: a student leading teachers in instruction. A striking example of this happened at a HS Student Talent Showcase in 2024. Carlos, a high school student, stood before an audience of teachers and school leaders. In his hand, he held a camera. Our crash course in portrait photography was about to begin.

"Today, you're going to learn how to avoid one of the biggest challenges when it comes to taking pictures of a subject." He scanned the audience, and then asked for a volunteer who wore glasses. A woman stepped up to sit on the stool. She smiled tentatively as Carlos snapped a few photos, which appeared moments later on the computer monitor. White squares of light hid parts of her eyes in all three photos. "That's the biggest challenge," Carlos said. "Getting rid of glare."

Over the next 10 minutes, I was struck by the quality of what he did to teach us. He showed us how to make adjustments to the model (tilt the head down or adjust the stem of the glasses up) and to the light source (move it to 10 o'clock or 2 o'clock). With each adjustment, he took a new photo and had us search it for glare. Once all the glare was removed, he handed the camera over to us. "Now it's your turn. Remember what to do!" One of the teachers in the audience stepped up and prepared the new model/person with glasses to be the model. Sure enough, the glare was dramatically reduced by each teacher photographer and in many cases totally eliminated.

Although I don't consider myself a skilled photographer, Carlos's lesson made me a better one. The next time I took a picture of someone with glasses, I knew I could capture their full face and didn't need to worry about the flash. Carlos primed us for learning with a move I've seen countless successful teachers do: modeling. Along the way, he took us from passive observers to active learners—the same dream we have for our students.

Yet all too often, when our students don't learn, we think it's on them. The first question to ask is this: Have we given them all the tools to master the content? For teachers who are hungry to see what students know and can do, Phase 3 is an exciting time. This phase of the rigor trajectory is all about giving students what they need. Sometimes, it is a model; sometimes it's activating knowledge.

> ## Core Idea
>
> To prepare students for learning, adjust the flight pattern:
> Activate knowledge and model.

Let's take a look at both.

## Activate Knowledge

> ## Teacher Professional Development Goal
>
> **Activate Knowledge:** Guide students to use what they already know to unlock new content.

In our book *Make History: A Practical Guide for Middle and High School History Instruction*, my colleague Art Worrell and I cited the work of Sam Wineburg who was fundamental in helping us understand the power of activation of knowledge. He shared the case study of analyzing the purpose of President Harrison officially establishing Columbus Day in 1892:

> I, Benjamin Harrison, President of the United States of America, do hereby appoint Friday, October 21, 1892, the four hundredth anniversary of the discovery of America by Columbus, as a general holiday for the people of the United States. On that day let the people so far as possible cease from toil and devote themselves to such exercises as may best express honor to the discoverer and their appreciation of the great achievements of the four completed centuries of American life. (*New York Times*, July 22, 1892, p 8)

The topic is a great one to stir controversy in a MS/HS classroom, but it also illuminates a larger point.

On the surface, Harrison's declaration is a simple appeal to the values of American life, championing progress and enlightenment. A layer deeper, students might critique the purpose. Some of the middle school students in Art's school replied with answers like "Harrison is trying to unite the country around a White/European hero, insisting on the 'discovery' of America without mention of indigenous history."[6]

But something changed when we gave the students key historical context about that time period at the end of the 19th century:[7]

- The United States was in a rapid state of change as the nineteenth century drew to a close.
  - Between 1880 and 1910, 18 million new immigrants came to the United States.
  - This created a population boom.
- This new wave of immigrants, primarily from Southern and Eastern Europe, were different from previous immigrant groups.
  - They looked differently than previous immigrants and spoke different languages.
  - They worshipped differently as well. They tended to be Catholic rather than Protestant.
- As an example, consider Italian Americans:
  - In the early 1880s, there were approximately 300,000 Italians in the United States.
  - That number doubled by 1890.
  - By 1910, there were 2 million Italians in the United States—making up 10% of all immigrants.
  - They practiced Catholicism and settled in cities, along with Poles and Portuguese—forming a new block of immigrants—"the urban Catholic."
  - This was in opposition to the goal of many politicians to create a "melting pot."
- This new group of immigrants presented new challenges.
  - There was a growing sense of nativism as they assimilated slower than previous groups of immigrants and were more easily identified as "other."
- Politicians were working to gain support from these new groups in the population.

Armed with this new information, students' answers changed to highlight Harrison's desire to get re-elected and to win over the immigrant vote. In that context, choosing Columbus was choosing an immigrant more than a traditional hero! When you look at the evolution of the responses, the impact is pretty stunning: analysis without knowledge is not only superficial but inaccurate.

Cleared For Takeoff    **287**

> ### Core Idea
>
> Analysis without knowledge is not only superficial but inaccurate.

Higher-order thinking is considered the goal of many of our classrooms—the ability to analyze, synthesize, evaluate, and more. Yet students need background knowledge to get there. Cognitive science describes this process as knowledge retrieval, and it is essential to learning.

"All new learning requires a foundation of prior knowledge," declare Brown, Roediger, and McDaniel in *Make It Stick: The Science of Successful Learning*.[8] Familiar class routines like Do Nows or class oral reviews activate the brain's long-term storage system (home of established information), refreshing that material to better connect it to content that will enter working memory (home of easily forgotten new information).[9]

Over the past several decades, leading cognitive scientists like Daniel Willingham have built a strong case for centering background knowledge in the classroom.[10] As Willingham eloquently states in *Why Don't Students Like School*:

> Data from the last thirty years lead to a conclusion that is not scientifically challengeable: thinking well requires knowing facts, and that is not true simply because you need something to think about. The very processes that teachers care about most—critical thinking processes such as reasoning and problem solving—are intimately entwined with factual knowledge that is stored in long-term memory (not just found in the environment)[11].

In other words, to think well, we need something substantive to think about, and that's where background knowledge comes in. The more that students know about a topic, the more deeply they can think about it.

> ### Core Idea
>
> The more students know about a topic, the more deeply they can think about it.

288  Get Better Faster 2.0

### Findings from the Field: Get Student Thinking in Gear

"Paul once shared with me that one thing he always considers when observing a class is what the class would sound like if you removed all of the teacher talk. If only student voices remained, how rigorous, insightful and precise would the discourse be? That question became a guiding principle to my work as a teacher and instructional leader. How could I push students, in as few words as possible, to articulate the most detailed and elaborate ideas as possible each day? The answer lies in everything you do before you ever ask students the question in the first place: it starts with arming them with quality resources and building a foundation of comprehensive knowledge/schema through retrieval practices. Then they are set up for success when being pushed to stretch their responses. With the foundation laid, few questions are more powerful questions than "why?", "how?" or "where do you see evidence of this?"
—*Art Worrell, Co-author of* Make History *and Instructional Leader, Newark, NJ*

(For more resources on retrieval practice strategies, please see the end notes.[12]) The actions steps collected here address common strategies to activate knowledge:

- Students fall into a learned helplessness, constantly asking the teacher for help when they have (or could have) resources available to them that could help.

- Students are not making connections between what they're previously learned and what they are about to learn.

- Students are not remembering the information they've learned in previous classes.

- Students are stuck on something that they won't be able to figure out without background knowledge.

## Activate Knowledge: Prompt Students to Use Resources
## Coaching Tips

**Teacher Context**

**Challenge**

- Students are not recalling knowledge learned in previous lessons.
- Students are asking teachers questions when they are confused, even when they have resources at their disposal that could help them answer the question.
- Students don't have resources to help them answer questions, creating a dependency on the teacher during independent practice.

**Action Step**

- Point students to resources (notes, posted concepts and content, handouts).
- Ask them to recall: "What do we know about _____ (content students learned in previous classes)?"

**Action Step Overview**

One of the quickest ways to develop students' problem-solving abilities and independent work habits is to provide them with resources that they can access while completing a task. These could take many forms: a Word Wall with key academic terms or vocabulary, a notebook with notes from previous lessons (a game-changer for high school when used well!), textbooks, and more.

As one example, watch how Danny Murray elevates his HS English class discussion with the use of their in-class notes and Emelia her HS Physics classroom with previous knowledge:

 WATCH Clip 52: **Activate Knowledge—Resource**
(Teaching clip)

 WATCH Clip 48: **Activate Knowledge—What Do We Know About?**
(Teaching clip)

Here is a written example of an exemplar note-taking page for Math classrooms from Patricia Griffin—and a guide for how to create such notes from Michelle Marquez:

## Geometry

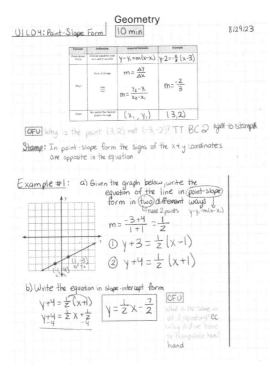

## AP Calculus AB - Limits of Hierarchy of Dominance - Notebook Page

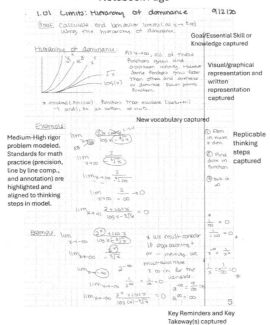

- Goal/Essential Skill or Knowledge captured
- Visual/graphical representation and written representation captured
- New vocabulary captured
- Medium-High rigor problem modeled. Standards for math practice (precision, line by line comp., and annotation) are highlighted and aligned to thinking steps in model.
- Replicable thinking steps captured
- Key Reminders and Key Takeaway(s) captured

Cleared For Takeoff

When teachers devote time at the beginning of a unit to share these resources with students, they can simply prompt students to use them at any point in the lesson:

- "Look at your resource (notes, content posted on walls, handout). What are _____ (whatever core content they should know)?"
- "What do we know about _____ (content students learned in previous classes)?"
- "What do we need to remember when solving these sorts of problems?"

### Key Leadership Moves

**See It**

- Watch a video of a teacher leveraging classroom resources to activate knowledge.
- Show a picture of a teacher's wall that has excellent visual anchors for the students.
- Show an exemplar note-taking page from a student notebook, highlighting how it could be used as a study tool/resource when solving other problems.
- Model utilizing simple prompts to direct students to their resources.

**Plan the Practice**

- Look at upcoming lessons and identify where students would benefit from a knowledge resource. Add prompts to the lesson plan where students could benefit from accessing those tools.
- Develop a knowledge tool for the classroom.
   - Chart of key terms posted in the room (key understanding itself, or previously solved problem that highlights use of the skill)
   - Handout in the students' folder/binders
   - Previous notes taken on the topic in the students' binder

**Do It**

- Rehearse the part of the lesson where students could get stuck and have the teacher use their prompts to point them to a resource.

**Real-Time Feedback**

- Nonverbal: Point to the resources in the room.
- Whisper prompt: "Ask them to use their knowledge organizer/resources in the room to answer the question."

---

 **WATCH Clip 53: Activate Knowledge—Resource**
(Key Leadership Move: See it)

# Activate Knowledge: Use a Knowledge Organizer
## Coaching Tips

**Teacher Context**

**Challenge**

- Students don't have a tool to help hold onto all the information of a larger unit/novel of study.

**Action Step**

- Use a knowledge organizer (cheatsheet)—all key points on 1–2 pages.

**Action Step Overview**

A cheatsheet (or knowledge organizer) has been a proven study tool for years. More recently, the field of cognitive science has verified its value: Putting all key information in a condensed, small location makes it easier for the brain to retain it.[13]

Having students use a knowledge organizer can change the quality of what they learn. Here is an example from *Make History*:[14]

### AP World History Reference Sheet—Unit 1:

| Key Terms | |
|---|---|
| **Navigational Technology** *adapted from Asian, Islamic and Classical civilizations* | |
| 1. astrolabe | origins in Classical Greece, this tool allows navigators to use the sun to measure the latitude of their ship at sea |
| 2. astronomical charts | star map - by developing better maps of the night sky, Europeans were able to better navigate using constellations as guides |
| 3. cartography | map-making - through the sponsorship of Ptg. Prince Henry the Navigator, Ptg. (then more broadly European) knowledge of map-making and geography ↑ |
| 4. compass | crucial navigational tool that originated in China, uses magnetism to tell the cardinal direction the user is facing (North-East-South-West) |
| 5. lateen triangular sails | common feature of Euro ships (origin S. Asian dhow ship), effective b/c allows sailors to tack "against the wind" → easier to sail regardless of wind direction |
| 6. Prince Henry the Navigator | Portuguese initiator of "Age of Discovery" thru sponsorship of innovations in navigational tech, exploration W. coast of Africa (searching for gold + Prester John) |
| 7. volta do mar | in Ptg. "turn of the sea," navigational technique perfected by Ptg. sailors allowing them to understand trade winds and currents (like I.O. monsoon winds) |
| **European Innovations in ship design** | |
| 8. caravel | small, highly maneuverable sailing ship developed by Portuguese in 15th c.to explore W. Africa coast (ex. La Niña used on Columbus's journey to the Americas) |
| 9. carrack | replaced the caravel, this is a 3 or 4-mast ship, larger cargo area allowed for greater profit and longer voyages; replaced in 17th c. by larger Spanish **galleons** |
| 10. fluyt | 17th c. Dutch sailing vessel designed for efficient transoceanic voyages; had ample cargo space, only needed small crew; ↓ Dutch cost of transportation (VOC) |
| **Motives** | |
| 11. Christopher Columbus | Italian explorer sent by Spanish monarchs Ferdinand & Isabel to find maritime route to Asia → landed in Caribbean → initiated European colonization of Ams. |
| 12. commodity | a raw material or agricultural product that can be bought and sold (i.e. cotton, tea, coffee, silk, etc.) |
| 13. demand | the amount of consumer desire for a certain commodity (the higher the demand, usually the higher the price that can be charged if the supply is low) |
| 14. Italian city-states | Venice, Milan, Florence, Genoa etc. were crucial trade links btw. Europe & Asia in Post-Classical→ Early Modern; Venice had monopoly on spice trade via Arabs |
| 15. Ottoman conquest of Constantinople | 1453: Islamic gunpowder empire conquered capital of Byzantine (Christian) Emp, turning point prompting ↑ Euro search for maritime route to Asia |
| 16. Reconquista | 700-year war fought by Christians in Iberian Peninsula to overthrow Muslim rule (Al-Andalus), ended w/ Chr. victory in 1492 and expulsion of Jews & Muslims |
| 17. spice trade | cloves, cinnamon, pepper, nutmeg etc. originated SE Asia; high demand in Afro-Eurasia since Classical, traded Silk Rds. & I.O. → motivated Euro. maritime trade |

Knowledge Organizers can also be active teaching tools as we see in this classroom clip of high school history teacher Rachel Blake.

 **WATCH Clip 54: Activate Knowledge—Organizer** (Teaching clip)

Cleared For Takeoff 293

**Key Leadership Moves**

### See It

- Review a sample knowledge organizer (*Make History* has a number of them you could use).
- Recall the cheatsheets the teacher used in college to study—unpack what made them effective.

### Plan the Practice

- Build a knowledge organizer for the unit.
- Script activities to review the knowledge organizer in the first 15 minutes of class. For example:
  - Give students two minutes to review their knowledge organizer.
  - Turn the knowledge organizer face down and do oral recall: Cold call students to answer questions from the knowledge organizer. If they struggle, they can turn over their knowledge organizer to get the answer.

### Do It

- Role play the use of the knowledge organizer to set up the class.

### Real-Time Feedback

- Nonverbal: Point to the knowledge organizer.
- Whisper prompt: "Ask them to use their knowledge organizer to answer the question."

---

# Activate Knowledge: Retrieve Knowledge By Applying It
## Coaching Tips

### Teacher Context

### Challenge

- Students are not using prior knowledge in new contexts.

### Action Step

- Retrieve knowledge by applying it—give a simple task (e.g., organize events in chronological order, quick math fluency).

294    Get Better Faster 2.0

**Action Step Overview**

Students solidify their knowledge the more times they are asked to recall it and they make it more flexible by using it in differing contexts.[15] New teachers can keep prior knowledge "fresh" with knowledge retrieval activities that ask students to apply prior knowledge in a variety of ways and contexts.

These activities can be more creative and valuable than you might think. Look at how these Math, English, and Social Studies teachers use various strategies to elevate the learning with applying to tasks:

MS Math:

**WATCH Clip 55: Activate Knowledge—Apply It**
(Teaching clip)

HS English:

**WATCH Clip 56: Activate Knowledge—Apply It**
(Teaching clip)

MS Social Studies

**WATCH Clip 57: Activate Knowledge—Apply It**
(Teaching clip)

## Key Leadership Moves

**See It**

- Model: Revise lesson plan to add application-based knowledge retrieval activities.

**Plan the Practice/Do It**

- Plan: Revise lesson plans to include opportunities for students to apply prior knowledge in new contexts.
    - History: List the following Enlightenment revolutions in chronological order: Haitian Revolution, French Revolution, American Revolution, Latin-American Revolutions.

Cleared For Takeoff

- Math: Find the x-intercept of the pictured parabola. How many x-intercepts are there?
- Science: Define an electron carrier and provide an example.
- Literature: What are the features of iambic pentameter in poetry?

**Real-Time Feedback**

- N/A

 WATCH Clip 58: Activate Knowledge—What Do We Know About?
(Key Leadership Move: See it)

## Activate Knowledge: Drop Knowledge
## Coaching Tips

**Teacher Context**

**Challenge**

- Student analysis is stalled mid-lesson by missing knowledge.

**Action Step**

- Drop knowledge.

**Action Step Overview**

Student's ability to puzzle out a challenge is dependent on what they already know. A missing piece of knowledge, in that case, can quickly become a roadblock that brings thinking to a halt. In those unanticipated moments, teachers can "drop" knowledge—providing the necessary and missing piece of information helps students reengage with the problem without giving away the answer.

Literature class abounds with moments like this. For example, Steve Chiger and I highlighted an example from *The Great Gatsby* in our book *Love and Literacy*.[16] F. Scott Fitzgerald talks about uncut books in the famous scene describing Gatsby's library, and you need to know that, in 1920, books were printed on large sheets of paper that were folded several times to make pages. To read a book, one needed to cut the pages apart by cutting the fold that ran along the top. If students don't know what uncut books are, they cannot fully analyze the superficial nature of Gatsby's library.

Dropping knowledge can also be as simple as giving the students the definition of a word that cannot be inferred from context clues, thus allowing students to continue reading. As long as you make sure not to drop knowledge that students could figure out on their own, this is a very effective strategy to keep students intellectually engaged.

Watch how a small piece of new information adds complexity to students' initial analysis of Jay Gatsby (of *The Great Gatsby*) in Sarah Schrag's HS English class.

 **WATCH Clip 59: Activate Knowledge—Drop Knowledge** (Teaching clip)

## Key Leadership Moves

**See It**

- Model think aloud: Analyze lesson plan for the key knowledge students need to engage in critical thinking. Note where you can drop this knowledge if student analysis stalls.

**Plan the Practice**

- Plan—Identify in lesson plan where students will become stuck if they don't have the necessary knowledge. Select the knowledge to provide in this instance.
    - Think: If students don't get ___, they won't get ____.
    - "Let me give you additional context about ____. How does that affect your thinking?"

**Do It**

- Practice—Drop a missing piece of knowledge when student problem solving falters.

**Real-Time Feedback**

- Verbal: "Students are missing ___ information. Drop knowledge so that they can keep doing the deeper thinking."

Cleared For Takeoff

# Strategies for Coaching: Activate Knowledge

| Action Step | See It | Plan the Practice | Do It | Cues for Real-Time Feedback |
|---|---|---|---|---|
| **Prompt students to access previously learned knowledge** | • Watch a video of a teacher leveraging classroom resources to activate knowledge.<br>• Show a picture of a teacher wall with visual anchors.<br>• Show an exemplar note-taking page from a student notebook.<br>• Model utilizing simple prompts to direct students to their resources. | • ID in lesson plan where students would benefit from a knowledge resource. Add prompts to the lesson plan.<br>• Develop a knowledge tool for the classroom (chart, handout, word wall, etc.). | • Rehearse the part of the lesson where students could get stuck and have the teacher use their prompts to point them to a resource. | • Nonverbal: Point to the resources in the room.<br>• Whisper prompt: "Ask them to use their knowledge organizer/resources to answer the question." |
| **Use a knowledge organizer (cheatsheet)—all key points on 1–2 pages** | • Review a sample knowledge organizer.<br>• Recall the cheatsheets the teacher used in college to study: unpack what made them effective. | • Build a knowledge organizer for the unit.<br>• Script activities to review the knowledge organizer in the first 15 minutes of class. | • Role play the use of the knowledge organizer to set up the class. | • Nonverbal: Point to the knowledge organizer.<br>• Whisper prompt: "Ask them to use their knowledge organizer to answer the question." |
| **Retrieve knowledge by applying it** | • Model: Revise lesson plan to add application-based knowledge retrieval activities. | • Revise lesson plans to include opportunities for students to apply prior knowledge in new contexts. | • Plan and practice are identical. | N/A |
| **Drop knowledge** | • Think aloud Model: Analyze lesson plan for the key knowledge students need to engage in critical thinking. Note where you can drop this knowledge if student analysis stalls. | • Identify in lesson plan where students will become stuck if they don't have the necessary knowledge. Select the knowledge to provide in this instance. | • Practice: Drop missing piece of knowledge when student problemsolving falters. | • Verbal: "Students are missing ____ information. Drop knowledge so that they can keep doing the deeper thinking." |

298   Get Better Faster 2.0

## Model

> ### Teacher Professional Development Goal
>
> **Modeling:** Model the thinking for students, not just the procedure, to answer a question or perform a task effectively.

The heart of great instruction is teaching (and re-teaching) something when students struggle (and then giving them a chance to try it again). Although there are many ways to teach, two of the most frequent types are modeling—teacher models for the student what to do—and guided discourse—the teacher guides the students to figure it out through their discussion. Guided discourse will be addressed more deeply in Phase 4 and is the hallmark of great teachers. Modeling comes first because it is slightly easier but still highly effective when done well.

Here are some common challenges new teachers may run into as they try to model for students how to accomplish a task/write an essay/solve a problem:

- The teacher model is too large (includes too many steps or details) and/or doesn't target what students need.
- The teacher gives a clear model, but the students don't have a task to do while listening to the model.
- The teacher presents the model as a list of steps but doesn't unpack the thinking or conceptual understanding that helped them arrive at that procedure.
- The teacher doesn't check for understanding after modeling.
- The teacher gives a clear model, but the students don't have the opportunity to try to replicate it after the model is done.

Cleared For Takeoff **299**

## Model: Narrow the Focus

## Coaching Tips

**Teacher Context**

**Challenge**

- The teacher's model is too large (includes too many steps or details).

- The model doesn't target what students need most to be able to do the skill/problem.

**Action Step**

- Narrow the focus to the thinking students are struggling with.

**Action Step Overview**

A model with too many steps or details can quickly overwhelm students. They may become bogged down in the details and lose their way after the first few steps. It also can turn into a set of steps to memorize without understanding why. Less is often more when it comes to modeling. Studies have shown the human brain can remember between 3–5 steps well, so try to pare down a model to that number of steps whenever possible.[17]

   Look at what students have learned up to this point and identify the key thinking they are struggling to master. Then narrow the model to those thinking processes.

### Key Leadership Moves

**See It**

- Video: See an exemplary clip of teacher modeling a related or same procedure.

- Model: Do a think aloud to simplify an overly comprehensive model from an upcoming lesson plan. Make the resulting model 3–5 steps.

**Plan the Practice**

- Plan a streamlined model for an upcoming lesson. Reduce the model to 3–5 steps.

**Do It**

- By itself, this is really just a planning task. Integrate with the upcoming action step "Model the Thinking, not the Procedure" to practice delivering the model

**Real-Time Feedback**

- N/A: If the model is too confusing or long, you will likely need to fix that in the next coaching meeting rather than in the moment.

300   Get Better Faster 2.0

WATCH Clip 60: **Modeling—Narrow the Focus**
(Key Leadership Move: Do it)

## Model: Give Students a Clear Listening Task
## Coaching Tips

**Teacher Context**

**Challenge**

- The teacher gives a clear model, but the students don't have a task to do while listening to the model.

**Action Step**

- Give students a clear listening/note-taking task that fosters active listening to the model, and then debrief the model:
    - What did I do in my model?
    - What are the key things to remember when you are doing the same in your own work?

**Action Step Overview**

Before teachers' models can have impact, they need to make sure students are actively listening.

By giving them a listening and note-taking task, the teacher makes them more active learners or more likely to be able to retain what the teacher models.

### Key Leadership Moves

**See It**

- Watch a video like the previous one: Video should feature an intentional listening or writing task
- Live model: Explain to students what they should be thinking about and doing during the model, including taking notes. Check for student understanding.

**Plan the Practice**

- This action is dependent on already developing the model and the key skills that students need to see. Once that is complete, identify the note-taking/

Cleared For Takeoff   **301**

listening task that will get students thinking and not just copying. Then check for understanding.

**Do It**

- Practice delivery.

**Real-Time Feedback**

- Verbal Prompt: "Ms. Smith, before you begin your model, I want to make sure the students have their notebooks out to take notes: this is too valuable not to write anything down!"

---

# Model: Model the Thinking, Not the Procedure
## Coaching Tips

**Teacher Context**

**Challenge**

- The teacher's model is blurry, blending right in with everything else the teacher says (for example, delivered in a monotone or without emphasis on key points), making it difficult for students to know which parts are most important.
- The teacher tells them a process or procedure but doesn't unpack the thinking and conceptual understanding that helped them arrive at that procedure.

**Action Step**

- Model the thinking, not just a procedure:
  - Narrow the focus to the thinking students are struggling with.
  - Model replicable thinking steps that students can follow.
  - Model how to activate one's own content knowledge and skills that have been learned in previous lessons.
  - Vary the think aloud in tone and cadence from the normal "teacher" voice to highlight the thinking skills.
  - Make your thinking visible (anchor chart, annotations).

**Action Step Overview**
When students struggle to master something the first time, an effective teacher will try a way of teaching it differently. Modeling their own thinking for the students—often called a think aloud—is one of those core teaching and re-teaching strategies.

302   Get Better Faster 2.0

Many people confuse a model with listing a set of steps—but that is often more aptly named a lecture. You are simply given information. A model that will change student understanding will model the thinking itself. The easiest way to cue that for a teacher is to ask, "What are the questions you have to ask yourself to answer this problem?" That will move you away from a list of steps to a list of questions than can model the thinking involved.

Watch this clip of Susan Hernandez leading her elementary grade level team to script a strong model for a lesson on nonfiction text features. Notice how she emphasizes the inclusion of what she calls the "look fors," the key thinking steps that students should use.

 WATCH Clip 61: **Model—Model The Thinking**
(Key Leadership Move: Do it)

While implementing a model, the first step is as simple as the intonation of their voice. What makes a think aloud effective is the change in the teacher's tone at key points: The teachers' "think aloud" voice is different than their "teacher" voice, giving student a bright line as to when the thinking is being modeled. (If this sounds like the bright lines in pacing, you are absolutely right!).

### Key Leadership Moves

**See It**

- Watch a model video: Chosen teacher should clearly exaggerate between teaching voice and think aloud voice.
- Live Model: Deliver a concise model that is targeted at student errors. The think aloud should be targeted toward building a greater conceptual understanding.
- Model: Emphasize the key points by varying tone and cadence.
- Model: Make your thinking visible with an anchor chart or annotations.

**Plan the Practice**

- Unpack the errors students have made in recent classes and anticipate what will be challenging with this content. Refer to the key steps listed in the Phase 3 Coaching Blueprint for Data Meetings:
  - Start with the exemplar: Look to the teacher exemplar and top student exemplar to identify what students must do to be successful.
  - Identify the gaps: Find the key ways in which students at varying achievement levels are struggling to create exemplar responses.

- Then draft the thinking questions you will ask yourself when modeling. Here are some universal thinking questions that can help the model:
  - "Hmm. . . . What is this question asking me to do?"
  - "What do I already know that can help me answer this question?"
  - "What can I recall from my resources (notebook, knowledge organizer) that will help unpack this question?"
  - "What do I look for to find (a characteristic of the text, e.g., a change in tone)?"
  - "How can I check to make sure this answer is correct?"
- Make sure to have the knowledge resource available (anchor chart, annotations, etc.).

**Do It**

- Practice delivery
  - Vary tone and cadence of think aloud/model to emphasize key points and be as clear as possible. Look up and raise your register when asking a question; look back at the class and lower your register when answering the question.

**Real-Time Feedback**

- Verbal Prompt: "Ms. Smith, that was very interesting. Can you tell me again what you were thinking when you took that step? I want to make sure I understand."
- Model: do a think aloud yourself.

> **Tip from a Coach—Narrate Your Internal Monologue**
> "One key piece of advice is to ensure that teachers understand that "model the thinking" goes beyond simply demonstrating steps to solve a problem. It involves making the internal thought process visible to students. Many teachers misinterpret this strategy as just "showing how," but the real impact comes from modeling why and how you think. This looks like shifting from modeling "To solve this equation, my first step will be to. . ." to "Mmm. . . I remember from last class that Ms. X told that the first thing to do when facing an equation is to. . ."
> —Paula Gomez, Instructional Leader, Santiago, Chile

 WATCH Clip 61: **Model—Model the Thinking**
(Key Leadership Move: Do it)

## Model: Check for Understanding After the Model
## Coaching Tips

**Teacher Context**

**Challenge**

- The teacher gives a clear model but doesn't check to see if students get it.
- The teacher gives a clear model, but the students don't have the opportunity to try to replicate it after the model is done.

**Action Step**

- Check for understanding after the model.

**Action Step Overview**

Once a teacher models effectively and students have listened (see previous action steps), the key is to make sure students understand the thinking behind the model. Without that, the students won't understand the "why" behind the procedural steps. Stamp the key points as you check for understanding. This is where you want students to focus their attention. Lastly, make sure that students have multiple "at-bats" to practice independently.

HS math teacher Anushae Syed uses multiple engagement techniques (turn and talks, cold calling, and hypothetical questions) to check for student understanding of her math model.

 WATCH Clip 62: **Model the Thinking—Check for Understanding**
(Teaching clip)

### Key Leadership Moves

**See It**

- Video: Show a clip of teacher checking for understanding after the model.
- Model asking students to identify the thinking skills used in the model.

**Plan the Practice**

- Add a check for understanding question after the model. Make sure that the question or task addressed the key points or steps that you want students to remember.
- Give students multiple opportunities for independent practice in that lesson and/or upcoming lesson.

**Do It**

- Practice delivery (Note: This should be pretty simple and could be easily incorporated with other action steps around modeling).

**Real-Time Feedback**

- Verbal: "Could someone explain to me how we X?"
- Verbal: "Students, what do we have to remember when we X?"

## Strategies for Coaching: Model

| Action Step | See It | Plan the Practice | Do It | Cues for Real-Time Feedback |
|---|---|---|---|---|
| **Narrow the focus** | • Video: See an exemplary clip of teacher modeling a related or same procedure.<br>• Model: Do a think aloud to simplify an overly comprehensive model from an upcoming lesson plan. Make the resulting model 3–5 steps. | • Plan a streamlined model for an upcoming lesson. Reduce the model to 3–5 steps. | • By itself, this is really just a planning task. Integrate with the upcoming action step "Model the thinking, not the procedure" to practice delivering the model. | N/A |
| **Give students a clear listening task** | • Watch a video with an intentional listening or writing task<br>• Live model: Explain to students what they should be thinking about and doing. Check for student understanding. | • This action is dependent on already developing the model and the key skills that students need to see. Once that is complete, identify the note-taking/ listening task that will get students thinking and not just copying, Then check for understanding. | • Practice delivery. | • Verbal Prompt: "Ms. Smith, before you begin your model, I want to make sure the students have their notebooks out to take notes: this is too valuable not to write anything down!" |

306 Get Better Faster 2.0

| Action Step | See It | Plan the Practice | Do It | Cues for Real-Time Feedback |
|---|---|---|---|---|
| **Model the thinking, not the procedure** | • Watch a model video: Chosen teacher should clearly exaggerate between teaching voice and think aloud voice.<br>• Live Model: Deliver a concise model that is targeted at student errors. The think aloud should be targeted toward building a greater conceptual understanding.<br>• Model: Emphasize the key points by varying tone and cadence.<br>• Model: Make your thinking visible with an anchor chart or annotations | • Unpack the errors students have made in recent classes and anticipate what will be challenging with this content.<br>• Then draft the thinking questions you will ask yourself when modeling.<br>• Make sure to have the knowledge resource available (chart, annotation, etc.). | • Practice: Vary tone and cadence of think aloud or model to emphasize key points and be as clear as possible. | • Verbal prompt: "Ms. Smith, that was very interesting. Can you tell me again what you were thinking when you took that step? I want to make sure I understand."<br>• Model: do a think aloud yourself. |
| **Check for understanding after the model** | • Video: Show clip of teacher checking for understanding after the model.<br>• Model asking students to identify the thinking skills used in the model. | • Add a check for understanding question after the model. Make sure that the question or task addressed the key points or steps that you want students to remember.<br>• Give students multiple opportunities for independent practice in that lesson and/or upcoming lesson. | • Practice delivery | • Verbal: "Could someone explain to me how we __ ?"<br>• Verbal: "Students, what do we have to remember when we___?" |

Cleared For Takeoff    **307**

## CONCLUSION

Congratulations! You have just taken a major step forward in your teacher's development—your teacher is cleared for takeoff!

Completing Phase 3 is a major milestone, as the teacher has not only mastered the most basic skills of teaching but has started to think strategically about how to shift more of the thinking onto students. What comes next starts to enter the terrain of a truly strong teacher. Onward!

# Phase 4

# Go Deeper

As legend has it, the original eureka moment took place in an incredibly private space: the bathtub of the renowned mathematician Archimedes. Sinking into the bath after a long day of work, Archimedes thought he was about to take a break from the problems that had been puzzling him. Instead, he noticed the way the water rose when he sank into the water, and instead of relaxing, was struck by inspiration. Supposedly, Archimedes was so excited by his discovery that he cried "Eureka," the Greek for "I have found it!" It was in this way that Archimedes became the first to articulate the law of motion that explains why some objects float in water and others sink.

This story is so ingrained in our culture that we often describe the moment when inspiration strikes as a eureka moment. We have a tendency to think of that moment when inspiration strikes as an incredibly individual experience, forged by solitude and deep thinking.

Yet contemporary research has begun to debunk this theory of creativity. Two thinkers in the field are Kevin Dunbar and Steven Johnson, the latter the author of *Where Good Ideas Come From: The Natural History of Innovation*. In Johnson's study of people who are considered great innovators—from the time of the Enlightenment to modern-day science laboratories—he discovered that the real innovations happened

309

when groups of people came together, sharing their ideas and the errors, and putting previous ideas together in new ways. While one person was often credited for the innovation, the network of people and ideas made the difference. In Johnson's own words, "Innovation didn't happen alone at the lab in front of the microscope, but at the conference table during the weekly lab meeting."[1] In other words, eureka moments are not "I have found it!" but "*We* have found it!"

Nowhere does this play out more in the classroom than in class discussion and small group work. Now that a teacher has established clear classroom routines and procedures and processing for managing independent practice and teacher-centered parts of the lesson, you can start to work on some of the real "magic" of great instruction: high quality intellectual discussion where students grapple with difficult tasks.

> ## Core Idea
>
> Student thinking sharpens faster on the whetstone of peer-to-peer discourse.

How do you guide your teacher to create an environment where class discussion isn't off-track banter but intellectual discourse? The next steps reveal how.

## PHASE 4 COACHING BLUEPRINT: RESPOND TO IN-THE-MOMENT DATA

The Phase 4 Coaching Blueprint builds perfectly on the blueprint from Phase 3. Where Phase 3 focuses on weekly data meetings and responding to student gaps with modeling and activating knowledge, Phase 4 goes deeper. It focuses on leveraging discourse to respond to student learning needs.

A masterful coach becomes a coparticipant in analyzing student learning with the teacher while observing. Let's look at two ways a leader can accomplish this: monitoring the learning in the classroom and targeting real-time feedback toward rigor.

### Monitor for Learning While Observing

After a certain point, you can't give a teacher feedback for rigor unless you're making in-the-moment observations about what their students are learning. Just like the teacher, you shift your focus from checking whether students are behaving well to whether they're mastering the material.

HS principal Taro Shigenobu keeps student learning top of mind. If you recall his video from the section on real-time feedback, Taro observes with student learning in mind:

 REWATCH Clip 7: **Guide Discourse 101—Stamp Understanding**
(Key Leadership Move: Real-time Feedback)

Taro doesn't jot down feedback to save for the next meeting. Instead, he confers with the teacher about what she can do to respond to the trend. The action is both small and powerful: Rather than let students' needs go unmet, Taro coaches the learning while he observes.

> ### Core Idea
> Coach the learning while you observe.

Everything we have worked on thus far in *Get Better Faster 2.0* has one purpose—to improve the quality of learning. But that won't happen unless we look for it and are prepared to see it.

It all starts with a basic premise: Students first. Teacher second. Look at student work to determine the gap. Then look at the teaching to find the actions that are contributing to it.

> ### Core Idea
> Students first.
> Teachers second.
> Start from the student work, and then look at the teacher actions contributing to it.

Go Deeper

Taro's philosophy boils down to simple logic: If her in the room, student learning should improve. Guiding the teacher to sophisticate her prompting has two benefits: (1) students connect previously unconnected facts and (2) the teacher improves while maintaining her authority in the classroom. Weekly observations mean that not only does a teacher get an action step per week, but they can improve the learning while getting better. This is why real-time feedback increases student achievement so quickly.

To be able to do so, Taro prioritizes his preparation. He reviews the lesson plan to see what is the most important thing students need to know (in this case, naming the specific ways in which an organelle's structure enables it to perform a particular function). That laser-like focus on the end goal then allows Taro to use the Get Better Faster sequence to choose the action step that will help students close the gap for themselves.

Teachers of all skill levels benefit from real-time feedback. Kristen McCarthy does the same in her elementary Math classrooms:

 REWATCH Clip 33: **Academic Monitoring—Pen in Hand**
(Key Leadership Move: Real-time Feedback)

Paying attention to both the students and the teacher can be challenging at first. To help her, Kristen follows a simple, repeatable protocol. It's included here and in the print-ready materials for your convenience (the print-ready version also includes the prompts you can use with a teacher or coach to guide them through this protocol).

### Monitoring the Learning

1. **Start from the end goal:**
   - What is the most important thing for the students to learn today?
   - Where is the productive struggle in this lesson?
2. **See the student gap:** Monitor student work to see the misunderstanding
   - Do they have habits of completion? (pen to paper, notebooks)

- Do they have habits of learning? (using notebooks, annotating text, line-by-line computation, etc.)
- Do they have correct/plausible answers? (key misunderstandings, errors)

3. **See the teacher gap:** Monitor the teaching to see what is contributing to the student gap
   - What in the teacher's actions is causing this level of student work?
   - Reference your Get Better Faster Scope and Sequence—What is highest leverage to move the learning?

4. **Improve the learning and develop the teacher:**
   - RTF:
     - What will fix the learning in this moment?
     - What can you coach and what do you need to teach?
   - Next Coaching Meeting:
     - How can I debrief my real-time feedback to lock in understanding of the teacher action step?
     - How can I model this teacher action step at the moment of the lesson that has the most important content?

---

Phase 4 is all about making sure the learning improves. Starting with student work while observing is the heart of that process.

## Teaching Skills Overview

In Phase 4, management transitions from classroom management to increasing the energy of the classroom. Rigor takes center stage by focusing completely on leading quality discourse—much harder than it seems! Teachers will learn to leverage their monitoring of student work to target the discussion on what will most push forward the learning, and then they will learn universal prompts to keep the conversation going. These are then solidified even further by leveraging habits of discussion and strategic calling so that students can take even more control of the quality and rigor of the discourse.

Go Deeper **313**

This section of the Get Better Faster Scope and Sequence shows the skills teachers will develop during Phase 4:

## Phase 4 Action Steps Sequence

| Management Trajectory | Rigor Trajectory |
|---|---|
| INCREASE THE ENERGY OF THE CLASSROOM:<br>11. **Build the Momentum:**<br>• Give the students a simple challenge to complete a task:<br>  ○ Example: "Now I know you're only 4th graders, but I have a 5th grade problem that I bet you could master!"<br>• Warm energy: speak faster, walk faster, vary your voice, & smile<br>12. **Pacing:** Create the illusion of speed so students feel constantly engaged:<br>• Use a hand-held timer to stick to the time stamps in the lesson and give students an audio cue that it's time to move on.<br>• Increase rate of questioning: no more than 2 seconds between when a student responds and a teacher picks back up instruction.<br>• Use countdowns to work the clock ("do that in 5..4..3..2..1").<br>• Use Call and Response for key words.<br>13. **Engaged Small Group Work:** Maximize the learning for every student during group work:<br>• Deliver explicit step-by-step instructions for group work:<br>  ○ Make the group tasks visible/easily observable (e.g., a handout to fill in, notes to take, product to build). | DEEPEN DISCOURSE:<br>10. **Universal Prompts:** Push the thinking back on the students through universal prompts that can be used at any point:<br>• Revoice: Prompt students to paraphrase others' reasoning:<br>  ○ "If I hear you correctly, you seem to say X. Is that right?"<br>  ○ "Are you really saying [paraphrase or re-work their argument to see if they still defend it]?"<br>• Press for reasoning: Prompt students to elaborate or justify their answer with evidence:<br>  ○ "Tell me more." "Why/why not?"<br>  ○ "How do you know?" "Prove it." "Why is that important?"<br>11. **Strategically Call on Students Based on Learning Needs:**<br>• Create a sequence of students to call on based on the rigor of each prompt and a review of student work (e.g., first ask a student who is struggling, then one who is partially there, then almost there).<br>• Launch discourse by calling on a student with a limited answer.<br>• Call on students whose responses are closer to the exemplar when the class is struggling.<br>• Call on student with originally limited response to stamp new understanding. |

314    Get Better Faster 2.0

- Create a role for every person (with each group no larger than the number of roles needed to accomplish the tasks at hand).
  - Give timed instructions, with benchmarks for where the group should be after each time window.
- Monitor the visual evidence of group progress:
  - Check in on each group every 5–10 minutes to monitor progress.
- Verbally enforce individual & group accountability:
  - "You are five minutes behind; get back on track."
  - "Lorena: focus."

12. **Stretch it:** Prompt to push for depth and conceptual understanding:
   - Problematize: Create tension
     - Name the debate: "Some of you say X. Some of you say Y. What do you think?"
     - Provoke debate: "[Name] would say [counter-argument]. How would you respond?"
     - Play devil's advocate: "I disagree. I actually think. . ." or "Who can play devil's advocate?"
     - Feign Ignorance: "I don't understand. I was thinking. . ."
   - Sophisticate: Add complexity:
     - Apply within different or new context/perspective: "Consider $2x + 5y = 4$. Does our rule still apply?"
     - Give a hypothetical: "What if. . ."
     - Consider alternatives: "What's another way to interpret this?"
     - Generalize: "So what's the emerging rule we could apply to all problems like this one?

# PHASE 4 MANAGEMENT—INCREASE CLASSROOM ENERGY

## Quick Reference Guide

| If your teacher is struggling to: | . . .jump to: |
| --- | --- |
| **Build the Momentum** | |
| Present content in a way that grabs student attention and motivates them | Give students a challenge |
| Bring high energy to the teaching | Warm energy: speak/walk faster, vary your voice and smile |

*(Continued)*

Go Deeper   **315**

| Pacing | |
|---|---|
| Get to the later portions of the lesson | Use a timer |
| Keep up the pace of instructions when asking students questions | Increase rate of questioning |
| Get students to move quickly during whole-class transitions | Use countdowns |
| Keep student attention while modeling or talking | Use Call and Response |
| **Engaged Small Group Work** | |
| Get students started effectively with small group work | Deliver step-by-step instructions for group work |
| Know the progress of a group project | Monitor the visual evidence |
| Keep student groups on task despite clear instructions | Verbally enforce individual/ group accountability |

## Phase 4 Action Steps Sequence

| Management Trajectory | Rigor Trajectory |
|---|---|
| **Increase the Energy of the Classroom:**<br>11. **Build the Momentum:**<br>  • Give the students a simple challenge to complete a task:<br>    ○ Example: "Now I know you're only 4th graders, but I have a 5th grade problem that I bet you could master!"<br>  • Warm energy: speak faster, walk faster, vary your voice, and smile.<br>12. **Pacing:** Create the illusion of speed so students feel constantly engaged:<br>  • Use a hand-held timer to stick to the time stamps in the lesson & give students an audio cue that it's time to move on. | **Deepen Discourse:**<br>10. **Universal Prompts:** Push the thinking back on the students through universal prompts that can be used at any point:<br>  • Revoice: Prompt students to paraphrase others' reasoning:<br>    ○ "If I hear you correctly, you seem to say X. Is that right?"<br>    ○ "Are you really saying [paraphrase or re-work their argument to see if they still defend it]?"<br>  • Press for reasoning: Prompt students to elaborate or justify their answer with evidence:<br>    ○ "Tell me more." "Why/why not?"<br>    ○ "How do you know?" "Prove it." "Why is that important?" |

- Increase rate of questioning: no more than two seconds between when a student responds and a teacher picks back up instruction.
- Use countdowns to work the clock ("do that in 5..4..3..2..1").
- Use Call and Response for key words.

13. **Engaged Small Group Work:** Maximize the learning for every student during group work:
   - Deliver explicit step-by-step instructions for group work:
     - Make the group tasks visible/easily observable (e.g., a handout to fill in, notes to take, product to build).
     - Create a role for every person (with each group no larger than the number of roles needed to accomplish the tasks at hand).
     - Give timed instructions, with benchmarks for where the group should be after each time window.
   - Monitor the visual evidence of group progress:
     - Check in on each group every 5–10 minutes to monitor progress
   - Verbally enforce individual & group accountability:
     - "You are five minutes behind; get back on track."
     - "Lorena: focus."

11. **Strategically Call on Students Based on Learning Needs:**
   - Create a sequence of students to call on based on the rigor of each prompt and a review of student work (e.g., first ask a student who is struggling, then one who is partially there, then almost there).
   - Launch discourse by calling on a student with a limited answer.
   - Call on students whose responses are closer to the exemplar when the class is struggling.
   - Call on student with originally limited response to stamp new understanding.

12. **Stretch it:** Prompt to push for depth and conceptual understanding:
   - Problematize: Create tension:
     - Name the debate: "Some of you say X. Some of you say Y. What do you think?"
     - Provoke debate: "[Name] would say [counter-argument]. How would you respond?"
     - Play devil's advocate: "I disagree. I actually think. . ." or "Who can play devil's advocate?"
     - Feign Ignorance: "I don't understand. I was thinking. . ."
   - Sophisticate: Add complexity:
     - Apply within different or new context/perspective: "Consider $2x + 5y = 4$. Does our rule still apply?"
     - Give a hypothetical: "What if. . ."
     - Consider alternatives: "What's another way to interpret this?"
     - Generalize: "So what's the emerging rule we could apply to all problems like this one?

Go Deeper     317

## Introduction to Phase 4 Management Skills: Increase Classroom Energy

What makes a two-hour action movie seem to fly by more quickly than a painstaking 20-minute silent film? Why is it possible to feel like you're driving at a normal speed in a sports car going 80 miles per hour on a six-lane highway, whereas you fear for your life in a taxi driving 45 miles per hour on a narrow side street? Why does an airplane ride seem interminable, whereas a roller-coaster ride gives you an incredible rush of adrenaline?

The answer comes down to one principle: the illusion of speed. What makes us feel like we are going fast or slow are markers in the environment around us: buildings, sound, perspective, and sudden motion to name a few. When we are on a highway and buildings are at least one hundred yards away on either side, we lose a sense of our distance from those buildings—they seem to be moving past so slowly that we feel we must not be moving very quickly. In the taxi on a narrow street, in contrast, the buildings are only 15 feet away, and everything feels as if it's moving faster. Sound is the same: An elegant sports car hums softly at 80 miles an hour, creating the sense that everything is happening at a steady, comfortable pace, while the engine of an old Volkswagen bug will scream for its life at sixty. All of these factors can transform our sense of speed. They have the power to make potentially ho-hum experiences into wild rides so exciting we can't believe our watches when they're over.

As anyone who's ever attended either an extraordinarily poor or an exceptionally good class or workshop can attest, the same concept applies to the classroom. A poor speaker can make one hour of listening and learning feel like three, while a skilled one engages the audience so fully that a two-day workshop doesn't seem long enough. It's not about going faster, but *appearing* to go faster: creating the illusion of speed.

When it comes to our children's education in the modern era, the illusion of speed is a powerful tool. Students' time in the classroom is too precious for them to spend it checked out. Phase 4 Management looks at the techniques a teacher can use to draw them in. Some of them, such as teaching with a timer in hand, are specific to the teaching profession; others, like physically moving and speaking quickly and loudly, aren't so different from the tricks of the action movie trade. All of them, though, when deployed properly, can make a lesson as riveting as a high-speed car chase.

> ## Core Idea
>
> Students stall when it feels slow.
> Draw them in with the illusion of speed.

In this section, we'll focus on increasing engagement for every child in three key ways: picking up the pace of the lesson without sacrificing students' thinking time; increasing the teacher's (and thus the students') enthusiasm; and getting individual off-task students involved in the class. Let's dive in.

## Build the Momentum

> ### Teacher Professional Development Goal
>
> **Build the Momentum:** Transform tasks into challenges that bring students to the edges of their seats.

Teachers often make statements like "This is a little boring, but. . ." or "This next part is going to be pretty hard, so. . ." The intention behind such disclaimers is usually to prepare students for what's coming and remind them that the challenge they're about to take on will reap long-term rewards. Unfortunately, however, the real impact of these words is usually to undermine the lesson. In short, they increase drag.

The trick to creating momentum where a lesson might otherwise drag is to re-frame challenges so that they are exciting, not dull. Change "This is going to be pretty hard" to "Okay, 4th graders, here's a 6th grade problem I bet you can solve!" and you transform your classroom from a place of drudgery to a place of motivation. Students will treat the challenge with enthusiasm if you do, becoming eager to show how prepared they are to meet the challenge. Building the momentum doesn't just make students engaged: it makes them riveted.

Building the momentum will help a new teacher overcome the following core challenges:

- The teacher states or acknowledges the boring/hard nature of the content he or she is teaching.

- Teacher's tone is flat: it doesn't convey joy and excitement for the lesson.

Go Deeper  **319**

# Build the Momentum: Create a Challenge

## Coaching Tips

**Teacher Context**

**Challenge**

- The teacher states or acknowledges the boring/hard nature of the content he or she is teaching.

**Action Step**

- Give the students a simple challenge to complete a task, e.g.: "Now I know you're only 4th graders, but I have a 5th grade problem that I bet you could master!"

**Action Step Overview**

If you've ever struggled to keep students focused in the classroom, you may have felt a twinge of frustration on noticing the same students rush as one enthusiastic mass into a ball game during P.E. or recess a few moments later. But here's the good news, teachers: Any teacher can channel the same qualities that make handball and basketball so exciting. A huge part of the appeal of playground games is that they set up something for students to beat, making students eager to show they can do it. There's no reason a math problem or close reading exercise can't be framed as a suspenseful game—and the difference in student engagement when a teacher does so is stunning.

### Key Leadership Moves

**See It**

- Watch video of creating a challenge.
- Live model 2–3 ways to pose a challenge, using the teacher's own lesson plan to demonstrate where it could happen.

**Plan the Practice**

- Have teacher script challenges into lesson plan.

**Do It**

- Practice delivering challenges to the students. Once you have a good challenge scripted, focus on the delivery:
  - Drop the tone of your voice to create a sense of hushed excitement.
  - Look at the key students who need to hear the challenge the most.
  - If a student perks up when hearing the challenge: "Mark looks like he's up for the challenge."

**Real-Time Feedback**

- Whisper prompt to add a challenge.

- Intervene: "Ms. Smith, that's a pretty nice challenge—normally only 6th graders can accomplish this. Class, are you up to the challenge?"

---

## Build the Momentum: Warm Energy

## Coaching Tips

### Teacher Context

### Challenge

- Teacher's tone is flat: It doesn't convey joy and excitement for the lesson.

### Action Step

- Speak faster, walk faster, vary your voice, and smile (sparkle)!

### Action Step Overview

Think of a classic storyteller, one whose energy is contagious and who can entrance you completely with words alone. Just by speaking animatedly, smiling, and varying the tone and energy of one's delivery (lowering the voice to build suspense or increase tension, for example, can be just as powerful as speaking more loudly to emphasize a climax), any speaker can accomplish this. For a teacher, this is incredibly valuable: it makes your students not just engaged but riveted on the lesson. Some of my colleagues call this deceptively simple technique "sparkle."

### Key Leadership Moves

### See It

- Show model video.

- Do a live model of a part of the teacher's lesson, highlight the greater speed, voice variation, and nonverbals.

### Plan the Practice

- Review the upcoming lesson plan to see how to incorporate warm energy.

Go Deeper **321**

**Do It**

- Teach part of upcoming lesson while speaking faster, varying voice, and smiling.
  - ○ Real-time feedback: Stop teachers and repeat what they have just said while smiling and speaking more quickly.
  - ○ Real-time feedback: Have the teachers vary their voice, dropping lower to create tension rather than always remaining at high or low volume.
- Your feedback will be critical here: Modulating the voice is very hard for teachers to develop on their own. In some case, you'll be changing the way they've spoken for years! Make sure you create a safe space where they don't get discouraged while they practice.

**Real-Time Feedback**

- Nonverbal: Point to corners of your mouth to remind teacher to smile, or gesture with your hand to remind them to speak more quickly.
- Whisper Prompt: "Sparkle! Smile! Jump back into teaching!"

## Strategies for Coaching: Build the Momentum

| Action Step | See It | Plan the Practice | Do It | Cues for Real-Time Feedback |
|---|---|---|---|---|
| **Create a Challenge/ Build Momentum** | • Watch model video of creating a challenge.<br>• Live model 2–3 ways to pose a challenge, using the teacher's own lesson plan to demonstrate where it could happen. | • Script challenges into lesson plan. | • Practice delivery. | • Whisper prompt to add a challenge.<br>• Intervene: "Ms. Smith, that's a pretty nice challenge—normally only 6th graders can accomplish this. Class, are you up to the challenge?" |
| **Warm Energy: Speak faster, walk faster, vary your voice, and smile (sparkle)!** | • Show model video.<br>• Do a live model of a part of the teacher's lesson, highlight the greater speed, voice variation, and nonverbals. | • Review the upcoming lesson plan to see how to incorporate warm energy. | • Teach part of upcoming lesson while speaking faster, varying voice, and smiling. | • Nonverbal: Point to corners of your mouth to remind teacher to smile, or gesture with your hand to remind him or her to speak more quickly.<br>• Whisper Prompt: "Sparkle! Smile! Jump back into teaching!" |

322   Get Better Faster 2.0

## Pacing[2]

> ### Teacher Professional Development Goal
>
> Pacing: Create the illusion of speed to keep students constantly engaged.

In *Teach Like a Champion 3.0*, Doug Lemov describes the pace of the lesson as "students' perception of progress as you teach, that is, the illusion of speed."[3] Rushing through your presentation of a new math concept, for example, won't help students learn it better; it may do just the opposite. But if you dive into that concept with great gusto, building suspense and energy, students can process vital information at a reasonable pace—all while feeling like they're flying at lightning speed that will keep them at the edge of their seats.

Here are challenges that pacing can typically address during this phase:

- The teacher falls way behind the planned pacing of their lesson plan. (For example, thirty minutes into the lesson, the class is still reviewing the Do Now.)

- The teacher pauses too long between questions, resulting in losing the students' engagement.

- Students are slow to get started with shifting from one part of the lesson to the next: whole-group discussion to pair-share to independent practice, and so on.

- Students lose focus and engagement while teacher is modeling or talking.

---

### Pacing: Time Yourself

### Coaching Tips

**Teacher Context**

**Challenge**

- The teachers fall way behind the planned pacing of their lesson plan (for example, 30 minutes into the lesson, the class is still reviewing the Do Now).

**Action Step**

- Use a hand-held timer to stick to the time stamps in the lesson and give students an audio cue that it's time to move on.

Go Deeper

### Action Step Overview

If the teacher's lesson doesn't keep to its time stamps, students are probably running out of time for end-of-lesson independent work—the most important step in their learning. To keep the lesson moving as planned and to keep students attentive and eager to learn, have the teacher use a timer to make sure that an activity that ought to last for only, say, 15 minutes, really does conclude after 15 minutes.

### Key Leadership Moves

**See It**

- Live model—deliver a portion of the lesson while keeping track of progress using a timer. Set off timer early and model segueing into the next section of the lesson.

**Plan the Practice**

- With lesson plan in hand, have the teacher look at the time stamps for each part of the lesson. Plan together what to do when the timer goes off and the teacher hasn't finished that section. Make decisions of what can be cut from that part of the lesson and the language the teacher can use to transition to the next section.
- Plan ahead where teacher can cut certain questions or small-group work when falling behind to make sure the core parts of the lesson are protected.

**Do It**

- Have the teacher practice teaching the parts of the lesson with a timer set. Practice what to do when the timer goes off and teacher isn't finished with that section.

**Real-Time Feedback**

- Nonverbal: Point at watch/wrist when time to move on.
- Nonverbal: Give a hand signal of how many more minutes to stay on this activity.

**Coaching Example:**
Watch how Owen Losse reinforces the use of time as a teaching tool while observing middle school classrooms:

 WATCH **Clip 63: Pacing—Give Time Stamps**
(Key Leadership Move: Real-time Feedback)

# Pacing: Increase Rate of Questioning

## Coaching Tips

**Teacher Context**

**Challenge**

- The teacher pauses too long between questions during class discussion, resulting in losing the students' engagement.

**Action Step**

- Increase the rate of questioning: no more than two seconds between when a student responds and when a teacher picks back up instruction.

**Action Step Overview**

In casual conversation, the occasional pause between one person speaking and the other responding isn't necessarily awkward or harmful. But in the classroom, too many long pauses can drag down the pace of instruction. A teacher can avoid this by intentionally waiting no more than two seconds after a student finishes speaking before continuing instruction.

### Key Leadership Moves

The heart of increasing the response time for a teacher is knowing what to do next after a student responds. They can pick up instruction with the pre-written questions or instructions that they have in their lesson plan. Thus, much of mastering this skill is internalizing the lesson plan.

**See It**

- Model: Deliver a questioning sequence with a consistent, brisk rate.

**Plan the Practice**

- Review the questions in an upcoming lesson plan. Plan how many students to call on after each question and when to move onto the next.

**Do It**

- Role-play a questioning sequence from an upcoming lesson, keeping track of the rate of questioning.
  - Real-time feedback: Prompt the teacher to pick up the pace whenever the rate slows due to pauses in between questions.

Go Deeper

- Key teacher actions to look for: knowing the questions cold and knowing which student to call on.

**Real-Time Feedback**

- Model: model the questioning pace for the teacher.

---

# Pacing: Work the Clock

## Coaching Tips

**Teacher Context**

**Challenge**

- Students are slow to get started with shifting from one part of the lesson to the next: whole-group discussion to pair-share to independent practice, and so on.

**Action Step**

- Use countdowns to work the clock ("Do that in 5. . . 4. . .3. . .2. . . 1").

**Action Step Overview**
When the teacher has gotten the hang of using the timer to keep the lesson moving, the next step is to bring the students on board. Teachers can accomplish this by making the students aware of the time stamps they are trying to stick to. Activities can begin with a statement like "You have five minutes to complete your Do Now," be punctuated by reminders like, "We're halfway done" and "30 seconds to go," and end with a final countdown. Work that students once approached listlessly becomes an exciting challenge that they focus on intently and complete as quickly as possible.

### Key Leadership Moves

**See It**

- Watch model video.

- Live model using a countdown and/or Bright Lines to transition in a lesson or between lessons.

**Plan the Practice**

- Script and practice Bright Lines—cues to signal a significant shift from one activity to the next: claps, hand gestures, and so on.

Get Better Faster 2.0

**Do It**

- Play the part of students and have teacher transition from one activity to the next using a countdown to work the clock.

**Real-Time Feedback**

- Nonverbal: signal "5-4-3-2-1" with your fingers when it's time for a countdown.

---

## Pacing: Call and Response

## Coaching Tips

**Teacher Context**

**Challenge**

- Students lose focus and engagement while teacher is modeling or talking.

**Action Step**

- Use Call and Response for key words.

**Action Step Overview**

Asking students to answer questions in unison reaps untold benefits. Students pay close attention, knowing they might be asked to speak up at any moment, and the teacher is automatically checking the understanding of everyone in the room.

### Key Leadership Moves

**See It**

- Live model engaging students in a call and response. Imagine students respond with low energy and have them Do It Again.

**Planning and Practice**

- Identify moments when it would be most useful to implement a choral response. Script how you will launch the choral response for those moments.

**Do It**

- Role-play that part of the lesson while you, in the role of student, provide the choral responses.

Go Deeper     327

- Provide occasional lackluster responses so teacher can practice having students Do it Again for choral response.

**Real-Time Feedback**

- Nonverbal: create/use a cue for choral response.

## Strategies for Coaching: Pacing

| Action Step | See It | Plan the Practice | Do It | Cues for Real-Time Feedback |
|---|---|---|---|---|
| **Time Yourself** | • Live model: Deliver a portion of the lesson while keeping track of progress using a timer. Set off timer early and model segueing into the next section of the lesson. | • Review time stamps for each part of the lesson. Script how to move on when the timer goes off and the teacher hasn't finished that section.<br>• Plan where to cut from lesson if falling behind on time. | • Practice lesson with a timer. Rehearse what to do when timer goes off and the teacher isn't finished with that section. | • Nonverbal: point at watch/wrist when time to move on.<br>• Nonverbal: give a hand signal of how many more minutes to stay on this activity. |
| **Increase the rate of questioning** | • Deliver a questioning sequence with a consistent, brisk rate. | • Review the questions in an upcoming lesson plan. Plan how many students to call on after each question and when to move onto the next. | • Role-play a questioning sequence from an upcoming lesson, keeping track of the rate of questioning. Use real-time feedback. | • Model: Model the questioning pace for the teacher. |
| **Use countdowns to work the clock** | • Watch model video.<br>• Live model using a countdown and/or Bright Lines to transition in a lesson or between lessons. | • Script and practice Bright Lines—cues to signal switching between activities: claps, hand gestures, and so on. | • Play the part of students and have teacher transition from one activity to the next using a countdown to work the clock. | • Nonverbal: Signal "5-4-3-2-1" with your fingers when it's time for a countdown. |

| Call and Response | • Live model engaging students in a call and response. Imagine students respond with low energy and have them Do It Again. | • In upcoming lesson plan, identify moments when it would be most useful to implement a choral response. | • Role-play the choral response.<br>• Provide occasional lackluster responses so teacher can practice having students Do it Again for choral response. | • Nonverbal: Create/Use a cue for choral response. |

## Engaged Small Group Work

---

### Teacher Professional Development

**Engaged Small Group Work**: Give every student a task to maximize the learning.

---

Managing small-group work and whole-class discussion can be challenging even for the most experienced teacher. The whole nature of group work implies that students will be working simultaneously on all sorts of different projects. When this work is not managed well, the outcomes are mixed. Certain groups will work very well together and produce high-quality work; other groups will be largely off task, or one team member will carry the weight of all the others. The same can happen in whole-class discussion: a few students are actively learning and the rest are passively observing or totally checked out. Thus whole-class discussions can create great learning experiences for some at the expense of wasted learning time for the rest.

---

### Core Idea

Great small group work must be time well spent for *all* students—not active learning time for a few and wasted learning time for the rest.

---

The heart of maximizing the learning time is to design solid routines that create clear expectations for each individual so that everyone benefits from the networking of

Go Deeper    **329**

ideas. When we build these routines, the collective eureka moments have every possible second to sprout, take root, and blossom.

The power of small-group work is similar to Turn and Talks: More students are able to directly engage in learning at the same time than in a whole-class discussion. The challenge? Creating routines that make small-group work time productive. Small-group work is the most difficult type of classroom activity to manage because of how challenging it is to move from group to group and discover whether each discussion is going well—more difficult than either monitoring individual students or directing a whole-class discussion.

Here are difficulties that many teachers encounter along the way to making the most of small-group work:

- Groups are off task because they're confused about what to do or because not every student has something to do.

- The teacher doesn't know how much work students have done.

- Some groups or individuals are off task despite clear instructions.

---

## Engaged Small-Group Work: Deliver Explicit Instructions
## Coaching Tips

**Teacher Context**

**Challenge**

- Groups are off task because they're confused about what to do or because not every student has something to do.

**Action Step**

- Create explicit step-by-step instructions for group work:
  - Make the group tasks visible and easily observable (a handout to fill in, notes to take, product to build, and the like).
  - Create a role for every person (with each group no larger than the number of roles needed to accomplish the tasks at hand).
  - Give timed instructions, with benchmarks for where the group should be after each time window.

330  Get Better Faster 2.0

**Action Step Overview**

When students split off into small-group work, what they should be doing needs to be clearer than ever, so that they both can and will do it even without constant teacher supervision (and so that the teacher can see the trouble quickly if they don't). The best way to ensure this is through explicit step-by-step instructions for group work: they will make it easier for students to follow them and for the teacher to monitor whether or not they're on track.

Middle school English teacher Julia Dutcher gets small group discussion underway with What-To-Do directions.

 WATCH **Clip 64: Engaged Small Group Work—Directions** (Teaching Clip)

Julie's directions are a masterclass in clarity and concision. Students efficiently rearrange the classroom after the first set of directions, and dive into discussion (with a clear idea of the expectations) after the second set. Her What-to-directions took students fewer than three minutes to follow—saving the majority of the practice time for rigorous peer-to-peer discussion.

### Key Leadership Moves

**See It**

- Model delivering explicit directions for group work. Each student should have a job to do.

**Plan the Practice**

- Guide the teacher through the process of scripting out explicit directions for group work. Make sure to consider all the needed components:
  - What materials they will need (e.g., pen, notebook)
  - What knowledge resources they will use (e.g., word wall, reference sheet, lab instructions)
  - Where they will make their work visible so you can easily check their progress (e.g., charting it, writing it on a handout, using a whiteboard).
  - Chunk the directions:
    - ☐ First, have them gather the needed materials.
    - ☐ Then, have them move to the location of their small group.
    - ☐ Once all are settled and quiet, deliver the instructions.

Go Deeper

☐ End with the amount of time they have and a bright line: "You have 10 minutes for this task. Ready? You may begin."

**Do It**

- Have the teacher practice delivery. Focus on the cycle of What to Do directions:
  - ○ Deliver the directions one at a time. Scan to make sure everyone has completed them. Raise hand for silence. Then continue with the next direction and repeat.

**Real-Time Feedback**

- Model: Re-establish the small-group work instructions.

---

## Engaged Small Group Work: Monitor Group Progress

## Coaching Tips

**Teacher Context**

**Challenge**

- The teacher doesn't know how much work students have done.

**Action Step**

- Monitor the visual evidence of group progress.

- Check in on each group every 5 to 10 minutes to monitor progress.

**Action Step Overview**

Sometimes, small groups of students will go off task despite clear instructions. The first step is to have the radar to notice it: that is accomplished by the visual evidence in the previous action step. This can be a handout, whiteboard/chalkboard, chart paper or any other visual tool. The second step is to actually monitor that evidence and pull groups/students back on track. The key in coaching is to develop in the teacher the habit of checking in on all groups every five minutes (not get stuck too long in helping one group).

### Key Leadership Moves

**See It**

- Model Think Aloud: Set up student work at classroom desks. Circulate through the space and look for visual evidence of student work. Ask yourself this: Which

332    Get Better Faster 2.0

groups are on track and which aren't? Where do I need to jump in to get them on task or push them further?

**Plan the Practice**

- Plan out the visual evidence—exactly what the teacher will want to see on chart paper, in student notebooks, and/or work product—at each stage of the class period. Determine by which time groups should reach each stage.

**Do It**

- Minimal.

- Combine with the next action step (Verbally enforce accountability) to practice redirecting groups who are off track (see below).

**Real-Time Feedback**

- Whisper prompt: look at student work. "What are you noticing? Are they on task and on track?"

---

## Engaged Small Group Work: Verbally Enforce Accountability

## Coaching Tips

**Teacher Context**

**Challenge**

- Individual students or groups don't know how much time they have for task or are off task.

**Action Step**

- Verbally enforce individual and group accountability:
  - "You are five minutes behind; get on track."
  - "Brandon: focus."

**Action Step Overview**

Quick verbal interventions can keep groups on task. Use these moments to reinforce expectations ("You have 10 minutes for Part 2") and to redirect individuals or whole groups. These moves underscore the importance of the task and the teacher's belief that all students can rise to the occasion.

Go Deeper    **333**

## Key Leadership Moves

**See It**

- Watch model video.

- Model announcing time checks to groups and redirecting off-task students or groups.

- Think aloud what you are looking for when monitoring the groups:
  - Lack of evidence charted/written.
  - Pairs that appear to be laughing or talking about something else (even if you cannot be certain from afar).
  - Nonverbal body language that suggests off-task behavior.

**Plan the Practice**

- Script time checks into lesson plan for when the teacher will make an announcement to groups.

- Script the language for an effective reset or individual correction. The teacher is likely to have already mastered this and just needs to be prompted to utilize those skills for small-group work. Incorporate all the keys from those action steps:
  - Practice: Monitor group work and practice individual student corrections and whole-class reset.

**Do It**

- Practice announcing time stamps to groups and verbally redirecting students or groups who are not on-task.

**Real-Time Feedback**

- Whisper Prompt: Let students know how much time they have left.

- Whisper: "Student/Group X is off task."

# Strategies for Coaching: Engaged Small Group Work

| Action Step | See It | Plan the Practice | Do It | Cues for Real-Time Feedback |
|---|---|---|---|---|
| **Deliver explicit instructions for group work** | • Model delivering explicit directions for group work. Each student should have a job to do. | Script explicit directions for group work. Make sure to consider all the needed components:<br><br>• materials they will need<br>• knowledge resources they will need<br>• where they will make their work visible<br>• chunk the directions | • Practice delivery. | • Model: Re-establish the small-group work instructions. |
| **Monitor group progress** | • Model Think Aloud: Set up student work at classroom desks. Circulate through the space and look for visual evidence of student work. Ask yourself: which groups are on track and which aren't? Where do I need to jump in to get them on task or push them further? | • Plan out the visual evidence—exactly what the teacher will want to see on chart paper, in student notebooks, and/or work product—at each stage of the class period. Determine by which time groups should reach each stage. | • Minimal. Combine with next steps (verbally enforce accountability) to practice redirecting off-track groups. | • Whisper prompt: Look at student work. "What are you noticing? Are they on task and on track?" |
| **Verbally enforce accountability** | • Watch model video.<br>• Model announcing time checks to groups and redirecting off-tasks students or groups.<br>• Think aloud what you are looking for when monitoring the groups:<br>  ○ Lack of evidence charted/written<br>  ○ Pairs that appear to be laughing or talking about something else (even if you cannot be certain from afar)<br>  ○ Nonverbal body language that suggests off-task behavior | • Script time checks into the group work section of lesson plans.<br>• Script the language for an effective reset or individual correction. Incorporate all the keys from previous action steps. | • Practice announcing time stamps to groups and verbally redirecting students or groups who are not on-task. | • Whisper Prompt: Let students know how much time they have left.<br>• Whisper: "Student/Group X is off task." |

Go Deeper    335

---

### Stop and Jot

What are the three top coaching ideas you plan to use to train your teachers in these Phase 4 Management skills? Jot them here.

_____

_____

_____

_____

## PHASE 4 RIGOR—DEEPEN DISCOURSE

### Quick Reference Guide

| If your teacher is struggling to: | . . .jump to: |
|---|---|
| **Universal Prompts** | |
| Get students to listen to what other students are saying | Revoice |
| Get students to defend their thinking | Press for reasoning |
| **Strategically Call on Students** | |
| Call on students other than those who already know the answer, thus reducing the rigor and value for the rest of the class | Create a sequence of students to call on based on what students need |
| Start discourse at a "just-right" entry point for all students | Launch discourse with a student with a limited answer |
| Get the discourse "unstuck" when it stalls because students are confused. | Call on students whose responses are close to exemplar when the whole class is struggling |
| Make sure that previously struggling students now get it | Call on student with originally limited response to stamp new understanding |

336    Get Better Faster 2.0

| Stretch It | |
|---|---|
| Push for deeper, more conceptual understanding or for alternative arguments | Problematize: Create tension |
| Get students to add nuance to overly simple analysis | Sophisticate: add complexity |

## Phase 4 Action Steps Sequence

| Management Trajectory | Rigor Trajectory |
|---|---|
| **Increase the Energy of the Classroom:**<br>11. **Build the Momentum**<br>   • Give the students a simple challenge to complete a task:<br>     ○ Example: "Now I know you're only 4th graders, but I have a 5th grade problem that I bet you could master!"<br>   • Warm energy: speak faster, walk faster, vary your voice, and smile.<br>12. **Pacing:** Create the illusion of speed so students feel constantly engaged.<br>   • Use a hand-held timer to stick to the time stamps in the lesson and give students an audio cue that it's time to move on.<br>   • Increase rate of questioning: no more than two seconds between when a student responds and a teacher picks back up instruction.<br>   • Use countdowns to work the clock ("do that in 5..4..3..2..1").<br>   • Use Call and Response for key words.<br>13. **Engaged Small Group Work:** Maximize the learning for every student during group work:<br>   • Deliver explicit step-by-step instructions for group work:<br>     ○ Make the group tasks visible/easily observable (e.g., a handout to fill in, notes to take, product to build). | **Deepen Discourse:**<br>10. **Universal Prompts:** Push the thinking back on the students through universal prompts that can be used at any point:<br>   • Revoice: Prompt students to paraphrase others' reasoning:<br>     ○ "If I hear you correctly, you seem to say X. Is that right?"<br>     ○ "Are you really saying (paraphrase or re-work their argument to see if they still defend it)?"<br>   • Press for reasoning: Prompt students to elaborate or justify their answer with evidence:<br>     ○ "Tell me more." "Why/why not?"<br>     ○ "How do you know?" "Prove it." "Why is that important?"<br>11. **Strategically Call on Students Based on Learning Needs:**<br>   • Create a sequence of students to call on based on the rigor of each prompt and a review of student work (e.g., first ask a student who is struggling, then one who is partially there, then almost there).<br>   • Launch discourse by calling on a student with a limited answer.<br>   • Call on students whose responses are closer to the exemplar when the class is struggling.<br>   • Call on student with originally limited response to stamp new understanding. |

*(Continued)*

| Management Trajectory | Rigor Trajectory |
|---|---|
| ○ Create a role for every person (with each group no larger than the number of roles needed to accomplish the tasks at hand).<br>○ Give timed instructions, with benchmarks for where the group should be after each time window.<br>• Monitor the visual evidence of group progress:<br>○ Check in on each group every 5–10 minutes to monitor progress.<br>• Verbally enforce individual & group accountability:<br>○ "You are five minutes behind; get back on track."<br>○ "Lorena: focus." | 12. **Stretch it:** Prompt to push for depth and conceptual understanding:<br>• Problematize: Create tension:<br>○ Name the debate: "Some of you say X. Some of you say Y. What do you think?"<br>○ Provoke debate: "[Name] would say [counterargument]. How would you respond?"<br>○ Play devil's advocate: "I disagree. I actually think. . . ." or "Who can play devil's advocate?"<br>○ Feign Ignorance: "I don't understand. I was thinking. . . ."<br>• Sophisticate: add complexity<br>○ Apply within different or new context/perspective: "Consider 2x +5y = 4. Does our rule still apply?"<br>○ Give a hypothetical: "What if. . . ."<br>○ Consider alternatives: "What's another way to interpret this?"<br>○ Generalize: "So what's the emerging rule we could apply to all problems like this one?" |

## Introduction to Phase 4 Rigor Skills: Deepen Discourse

The students in Art's 11th grade AP History class have revolution on their minds. We join them as they discuss Reconstruction (1865–1877), the name given to the period immediately following the American Civil War. These years were marked by several significant changes, like the passing of the 13–15th amendments and the Reconstruction Act of 1867, that promised to reshape foundational ideas of the country. These changes were in many ways so radical to what came before that American historian Eric Foner described Reconstruction as a second founding of America, one free from enslavement. Art wants his students to think deeply about these changes as he poses this question to his students:

• "To what extent did the developments between 1860 and 1877 constitute a social and/or constitutional revolution?"

Take a moment to listen in. What do you notice about how students discuss the question?

REWATCH Clip 40: **Stretch It—Sophisticate**
(Teaching clip)

Students listen thoughtfully as peers share their arguments. Engagement is high: Every student is taking notes, referring to resources, listening, or contributing. No one is checked out. When one student speaks up, confused, about how nationalism could be considered revolutionary in spite of previous periods of nationalism, students don't look to Art for answers. They use their own historical knowledge and analysis to answer her question. Even though Art is present, he doesn't drive the conversation—students do. He only steps in to push thinking or clarify; the conversation belongs to them. (See *Make History* and *Love and Literacy* for more on how to use discourse to drive sense-making in the content areas.[4])

While some teachers try to make time for class discussion, teachers like Art make time for discourse. What's the difference? Discourse is talk designed to change and challenge thinking. And if you change the way students talk, you change the way they think. Unlike classroom conversations that restate basic information or debates that seek a clear "winner" or "loser", discourse improves the thinking of every person in the room.

> ### Core Idea
> Change the way students talk, and you change the way they think.
> The quality of student discourse is measured by the caliber of what students—not teachers—say.

In Phase 4 Rigor teachers become skilled facilitators of discourse. By starting our students on discourse at a young age, we give them the lifelong ability to question, to listen, and to analyze the world with a balance of thoughtfulness and independence.

The next section includes three techniques to increase the quality of student thinking in discourse: universal prompts, strategic calling, and stretch it prompts.

## Universal Prompts

> ### Teacher Professional Development Goal
>
> **Universal Prompts:** Push the thinking back on the students with multiuse prompts.

In any society, there are certain social graces that its citizens know so automatically that they become collective habits. Saying "please" and "thank you," shaking hands, waiting to begin a meal until everyone has been served—we repeat all of these actions without a second thought. By having these habits, we can focus more on the quality of the interaction and conversation and don't need to spend mental energy on how to behave. (If you have been in a setting where you don't know the proper etiquette, think about how difficult it was to track the conversation because of simply trying not to mess up!)

Universal prompts are the "please" and "thank you" of facilitating quality discourse. They are habits teachers can build to give them time to diagnose what is going on in the conversation. After the students master these habits, the teacher can move on to more sophisticated prompting (see the discussion of strategic prompting in the Stretch It section). Yet it's nothing short of miraculous how far the most basic prompts can take you, and you'll keep using them no matter how far you advance. The prompts described in this section are powerful in any subject area, and they continue to be so even for teachers who are also able to prompt much more specifically within their particular subject.

---

### Findings from the Field: Use Back Pocket Prompts

"There is rarely enough time for a teacher, especially a more novice teacher, to prepare the exact right, specific question at every moment. Luckily, pushing the thinking on to students more often than not can be made through a universal prompt. If every teacher has these prompts in their back pocket, you will more quickly see rigor increase across your organization. Invest teachers in the power here, give them time to mark up their plans, and real-time feedback of when and how to use them."

—*Megan Murphy, Principal, Indianapolis, IN*

Universal prompts address the following challenges during class discussion:

- Students who respond to a peer without listening or acknowledging their response.
- Students present an argument without supporting evidence.

## Universal Prompts: Revoice
## Coaching Tips

**Teacher Context**

**Challenge**

- Students aren't listening or connecting to peer's previous responses.

**Action Step**

- Revoice: Prompt students to paraphrase others' reasoning.
    - "If I hear you correctly, you seem to say X. Is that right?"
    - "Are you really saying [paraphrase or re-work their argument to see if they still defend it]?"

**Action Step Overview**

In the early days of discourse, students may talk past or at each other. Encourage attentive listening with revoicing—showing their understanding of what the person shared. There is considerable research on the power of revoicing (see more on Michaels and O'Connor pioneering work in the end notes.[5]) Each time students respond, challenge them to acknowledge their peers' argument with a simple rephrase before adding their own take. Class discussions naturally deepen as students begin to listen and respond more thoughtfully to the ideas in the room.

Watch how high school English teacher Danny Murray uses revoicing in a discussion of Gloria Naylor's *The Women of Brewster Place*.

 WATCH Clip 65: **Universal Prompts—Revoice** (Teaching clip)

Not only is revoicing a tool to encourage students to thoughtfully listen to one another, but at this clip reveals, it can also be used to check for whole-class understanding.

Go Deeper 341

# Key Leadership Moves

**See It**

- Show a video clip of a teacher using revoicing (*Make History* and *Love and Literacy* have additional videos, or film one of your own teachers).
- Utilizing the teacher's lesson plan, live model asking student to rephrase a peer's analysis.

**Plan the Practice**

- Script revoicing prompts in an upcoming lesson plan during the discourse section.

**Do It**

- Role Play, Round 1: With lesson plan in hand, ask students to rephrase or check their understanding of what peer said before responding.
- Role Play Round 2: Enter into full discourse. Role play various students, some who revoice effectively and others who don't, and ask the teacher to identify which students need to be prompted to revoice and to prompt them.

**Real-Time Feedback**

- Whisper prompt: Ask students to paraphrase what the previous student said before responding.
- Model: "Winston, before you respond, can you share what Sarah said in your own words?"
- Model: "Class, I want to remind you to revoice before stating your opinion. I'll model. Demetria, are you saying [rephrase argument]?"

 WATCH Clip 66: **Universal Prompts**
(Key Leadership Move: Real-time Feedback)

# Universal Prompts: Press for Reasoning
# Coaching Tips

**Teacher Context**

**Challenge**

- Students give arguments with limited or no evidence.

**Action Step**

- Ask press for reasoning prompts to push student to elaborate:
  - "Tell me more."
  - "What makes you think that?"
  - "How do you know?"
  - "Why is that important?"

**Action Step Overview**

For a variety of reasons, when a student gets an answer wrong, some teachers move on. They often provide the correct answer or go on to another student to get the answer. Yet if we don't know why the student got the answer wrong, we cannot help him or her correct the misunderstanding. The same challenge occurs when a teacher accepts a correct answer without explanation. That student might have gotten lucky and might not be able to replicate their success.

Using universal prompts helps a teacher unpack the students' thinking. These prompts are triply beneficial: They give the teacher more time to diagnose the error, and they allow students to understand their peers more effectively as well. They also keep a teacher from "rounding up"—adding their own thoughts as to what a student meant—and keep the thinking on the students. Although there are certainly more content-specific ways to respond to error, the universal prompts work well in any content area and are as powerful as they are simple.

During a small group discussion of Julia Alvarez's *In the Time of Butterflies*, middle school English teacher Hadley Westman challenges a student's interpretation a pivotal scene. See how she does it.

 WATCH Clip 67: **Universal Prompts—Press for Reasoning** (Teaching Clip)

Go Deeper 343

Hadley's press for reasoning prompts encourages students to ground their analysis in evidence, which is a critically important move, especially for students who tend to rely on their own experience or beliefs to defend their positions.

### Key Leadership Moves

### See It

- Model how to respond to a student who gives a limited response to prompt. Use the press for reasoning prompts to encourage elaboration and/or justification.

### Plan the Practice

- With the next lesson where discourse appears, predict the types of student responses that will benefit from these prompts: potential wrong answers and correct answers with limited explanation.

### Do It

- Play the roles of three different students: one with a wrong answer, two more with limited answers. Role play a discussion where the teacher practices using each of the prompts.
  - Tell me more. Why/why not?
  - How do you know? Prove it.
  - Why is that important?

- At the end, ask the teachers what they learned about the student's understanding to see how well the teacher diagnosed the error.

### Real-Time Feedback

- Whisper prompt: Ask students to elaborate or to justify their answer with more evidence.
- Model: "Jared, that is an interesting idea. Tell me more. Why or why not?" After modeling, prompt the teacher to do the same with the next limited response.

# Strategies for Coaching: Universal Prompts

| Action Step | See It | Plan the Practice | Do It | Cues for Real-Time Feedback |
|---|---|---|---|---|
| **Revoice** | • Show a video clip of a teacher using revoicing.<br>• Utilizing the teacher's lesson plan, live model asking student to rephrase a peer's analysis. | • Script revoicing prompts in an upcoming lesson plan during the discourse section. | • Role Play, Round 1: With lesson plan in hand, ask student to rephrase or check their understanding of what peer said before responding.<br>• Role Play, Round 2: Enter into full discourse. Role play various students, some who revoice effectively and others who don't, and ask the teacher to identify which students need to be prompted to revoice and to prompt them. | • Whisper prompt: Ask students to paraphrase what the previous student said before responding.<br>• Model: "Winston, before you respond, can you share what Sarah said in your own words?"<br>• Model: "Class, I want to remind you to revoice before stating your opinion. I'll model. Demetria, are you saying [rephrase argument]?" |
| **Press for Reasoning** | • Model how to respond to a student who gives a limited response to prompt. Use the press for reasoning prompts to encourage elaboration and/or justification. | • With the next lesson where discourse appears, predict the types of student responses that will benefit from these prompts: potential wrong answers and correct answers with limited explanation. | • Play the roles of three different students: one with a wrong answer, two more with limited answers. Role play a discussion where the teacher practices using each of the prompts.<br><br>  o Tell me more. Why/why not?<br>  o How do you know? Prove it.<br>  o Why is that important?<br>  o At the end, ask the teacher what they learned about the students understanding to see how well the teacher diagnosed the error. | • Whisper prompt: Ask students to elaborate or to justify their answer with more evidence.<br>• Model: "Jared, that is an interesting idea. Tell me more. Why or why not?" After modeling, prompt the teacher to do the same with the next limited response. |

Go Deeper    345

## Strategically Call Students

> **Teacher Professional Development Goal**
>
> **Strategically Call Students:** To reach all students at their own zone of proximal development, call on students based on their learning need.

There is an art to calling on students during discourse. Many teachers feel most comfortable calling on the most eager students—those with raised hands and/or fully-fleshed out arguments. The challenge here is that those students may fast-forward the discussion past the understanding of the rest of the class, and the conversation devolves into a back-and-forth among the teacher and few select students. No one fully learns in this scenario: Students with a more advanced analysis have it validated, but not challenged, and those who are still making sense of the potential arguments don't have a scaffold to fully participate in the conversation.

In light of this, some teachers lean in the other direction, calling on students who are more reluctant to speak or whose arguments are in the earliest stages. This often slows down the pace of discourse, and the rest of the class may check out as the teacher tries to establish a baseline of understanding. How to strike the balance? Strategically call students.

James Cavanaugh does just that in his middle school Math classroom. Watch how he uses the data he collects during academic monitoring to create his sequence of students for discourse:

 REWATCH Clip 35: **Show Call** (Teaching clip)

Strategic calling allows a teacher to leverage the different levels of comprehension in the room to push overall learning. By intentionally calling struggling students to start the conversation (if you are implementing Academic Monitoring from Phase 2, you will already know who these students are!), every student can access the conversation.

From there, the teacher calls on students with higher levels of understanding only when group sensemaking stalls, returning to the lower levels of understanding to solidify the fundamentals. In the end, whom you call on dictates who does the learning in discourse.

> ## Core Idea
> Whom you call on dictates who does the learning in discourse.

## Findings from the Field: Inclusion and Rigor Go Hand in Hand

"Inclusive and rigorous instruction are not mutually exclusive, but actually two sides to the same coin. Strategically calling on students is the heart of both data driven instruction and culturally responsive teaching. When you proactively determine who to call on, you raise the floor for discourse while ensuring that we hear from all students. This intentionally helps create a pathway to mastery while, most importantly, empowering students to do the real heavy lifting! Strategically calling on students is an integral part of my teaching (and coaching) practice."
—*Danny Murray, Instructional Leader, Newark, NJ*

What follows are the challenges teachers are most likely to face when working to keep discourse in motion:

- The teacher calls on primarily high-achieving students who already know the answer, making it impossible to ascertain if other students are understanding as well.
- Teacher calls on consecutive struggling students and the discussion stalls.
- Discussion ends without the teacher checking to see if initially struggling students have a stronger understanding.

Go Deeper **347**

## Strategically Call Students: Create a Sequence to Call on Students

## Coaching Tips

**Teacher Context**

**Challenge**

- The teacher calls primarily students who already know the answer, and doesn't guarantee that the learning comes from all the students in their class.

- The teacher calls on consecutive struggling students and the discussion stalls.

**Action Step**

- Call on students based on their learning needs (data-driven):
  - Call on students who have responses that are further off or only partially there to unpack the question.
  - If they struggle, call on students whose answers are almost there.
  - If they are easily unpacking, try student who was initially further off.
  - Put it all together: create a sequence of students to call on based on the rigor of each prompt (e.g., first ask partially there student, then further there, then almost there, and so on).

**Action Step Overview**

A perfect complementary action to accessing students' previously learned knowledge is to access the varied levels of learning in the room. The starting point is to identify where the teachers normally err: Do they call primarily on their highest achieving students and the rest are left confused and not needing to think (often the initial new error)? Or do they stick for so long with struggling students that they don't leverage the learning of other students in the room? Once you've identified the error, you can plan the right actions to close the gap.

## Key Leadership Moves

**See It**

- Model: Review student work from previous assignment and create a sequence based on on-track, off-track student performance.

- Watch a model of strategic calling (like James's video here).

348   Get Better Faster 2.0

REWATCH Clip 35: **Guide Discourse—Show Call** (Teaching clip)

**Plan the Practice**

- The key to effective practice is to anticipate the responses students of varying levels will give in class. After identifying the likely responses, script the order of students the teacher will call on during the discourse:
    - Start with a partially there or further off response to see what they can accomplish on their own.
    - Call on a stronger response when the previous students are still struggling to answer.
    - Call on a student whose initial responses were limited when part of the learning has been revealed to ask them to "stamp" the understanding.
- From previous exit tickets, set up the names of students in each group (correct or almost there, partially there, further off) to make it easy to call on those names immediately when needed. (This allow allows you as the instructional leader to be able to monitor when the teacher is calling on the student with the appropriate level.)

**Do It**

- Role-play multiple times, in the following order of complexity:
    - Round 1: First student called on gets it right (forces teacher to keep calling on students with limited understandings to solidify understanding).
    - Round 2: First student gets it wrong; after calling students with stronger responses, struggling students get it right.
    - Round 3: First student gets it wrong, and after calling on students with stronger responses, initial student still gets it wrong.
- For the role play, ideally you'll use actual student names. If not, you can prompt the teachers to mention the type of student they are calling on (e.g., "Agree or disagree? Almost there student.")

**Real-Time Feedback**

- The key to real-time feedback is monitoring student learning during independent practice. Without that, it's difficult to intervene.

Go Deeper

**Tip from a Coach—Use Strategic Calling to Keep Rigor High**

"Strategic calling is all about rigor. When I pay close attention to the work that students are doing, I gain insight into their thinking. With that insight, I can push and challenge the thinking of the class. Sometimes that might be looking for student work that represents an alternative pathway to understanding that might challenge the groupthink and therefore deepen student understanding. Ultimately, I'm thinking about whom I can call on at a given moment that will help to create the most provocative and rigorous discourse in my class. Strategically calling students achieves both aims."

—*Art Worrell, Co-author of Make History and Instructional Leader, Newark, NJ*

REWATCH Clip 53: **Activate Knowledge—Resource**
(Key Leadership Move: See it)

WATCH Clip 68: **Stretch It—Sophisticate**
(Key Leadership Move: Do it)

WATCH Clip 41: **Guide Discourse—Stamp Understanding**
(Key Leadership Move: Do it)

## Strategies for Coaching: Strategically Call on Students

| Action Step | See It | Plan the Practice | Do It | Cues for Real-Time Feedback |
|---|---|---|---|---|
| Create a Sequence to Call on Students | • Model: Review student work from previous assignment and create a sequence based on on-track, off-track student performance.<br>• Watch a model video of a teacher strategically calling. | • Plan the order of students to call on during the discourse:<br>  ○ Start with partially there or further off.<br>  ○ Call on a stronger response when the previous students are still struggling to answer.<br>  ○ Call on a student whose initial responses were limited when part of the learning has been revealed to ask him/her to "stamp" the understanding.<br>• From previous exit tickets, set up the names of students in each group (correct or almost there, partially there, further off). | • Round 1: First student called on gets it right (focus on stamp).<br>• Round 2: First student gets it wrong; after calling on students with stronger responses, struggling students get it right.<br>• Round 3: First student gets it wrong, and after calling on students with stronger responses, initial student still gets it wrong. | • Monitor student work with the teacher to determine who to call on. |

## Stretch It

> ### Teacher Professional Development Goal
>
> **Stretch It:** Coach teachers to prompt students to improve early arguments by adding complexity or perspective.

Teaching is an incredibly complex craft. It requires you to make hundreds of small decisions on the fly every day, and each one has an impact on what children will learn. So, if you, or your teachers, have made it so far along on the Scope and Sequence that they're making daily habits of these actions, take a moment to sincerely congratulate yourself.

Go Deeper

The impact of those particular habits is multiplied by the weight they carry—and by the way they affect every individual student who learns more because they have been set in place.

When you have mastered the structure of discourse, you are now able to move from apprentice to artist. What does that mean? Let's consider a lesson from the artist Michelangelo.

Michelangelo—or, at least, the Michelangelo imagined by Irving Stone in his best-selling *The Agony and the Ecstasy*—wasn't always the celebrated master of painting and sculpture we remember him as today. Like every other artist, Michelangelo began as an apprentice learning the basic skills of his craft.[6] As a young boy, even before he was a formal apprentice, Michelangelo spent time with a stone-cutter and learned the basic skills of hewing blocks of marble from the side of a mountain. When he began his first apprenticeship with a master painter, he had to learn to mix paint colors and make paintbrushes for months before being allowed to apply a single streak of paint to his mentor's fresco—let alone paint on his own. Later, Michelangelo learned to sculpt wax and clay flawlessly before ever carving a piece of marble. Focusing on such menial tasks was excruciating for the young genius, who couldn't wait for the moment when he would bring his most vivid artistic visions to life.

When Michelangelo's chance came to create his own art, the skills he had already mastered served him well. The first piece he carved wasn't David, but it was dramatically more advanced than anything he could have built without serving his time as an apprentice. Even for the most gifted individuals in any profession, some kind of apprenticeship phase—a period of time you spend perfecting the basic skills of the trade under the guidance of an experienced master—will increase your control over your craft, the quality of your work, and the speed at which your work begins to look like an expert's.

Stretch It is all about rising to being a painter of learning. By this point, teachers have learned all the foundational skills they need to begin making the spontaneity of the discussion just as rich a learning ground as the structure of the lecture. Artistry comes into play when we strive to push the conversation to even deeper and more nuanced levels.

---

### Core Idea

Move from mastering the brush stroke to creating a masterpiece.

Stretch It prompts that sophisticate or problematize take students beyond a first-draft analysis. They encourage students to think: more deeply, broadly, and/or granularly about the topic at hand.

---

## Findings from the Field: Stretch Thinking Good to Great

"There are few worse feelings as an educator than being unprepared to expand student thinking when they "got it." Students will consistently amaze us with their mastery and depth of knowledge, so preparing to "stretch it" is essential to pushing rigor and fostering joy in any class! Students love to debate. By exploring the tension in any text or lesson, we kindle that passion. Discourse, and thus student thinking, really soars when students problematize an existing idea by "provoking debate" and "playing devil's advocate." Conversation becomes sticky and memorable when students add complexity by applying different context or exploring hypotheticals. "Stretch-it" transforms students thinking from good to great!"
—*Danny Murray, Instructional Leader, Newark, NJ*

---

Ready to try Stretch-It prompts? Use the following action steps to respond to these common challenges to discourse.

- Student analysis is coalescing around one plausible argument but alternative feasible arguments are not arising in the conversation.

- Student justification of their argument is becoming limited/sloppy because they all agree on the central argument.

- Student arguments are simplistic and lack nuance or complexity

---

## Stretch It: Problematize

## Coaching Tips

**Teacher Context**

**Challenge**

- Student analysis is coalescing around one plausible argument but alternative feasible arguments are not arising in the conversation. OR

Go Deeper     353

- Students' justification of their argument is becoming limited/sloppy because they all agree on the central argument.

**Action Step**

- Problematize the discussion to create tension.
    - Name the debate: "Some of you say X. Some of you say Y. What do you think?"
    - Provoke debate: "[Name] would say [counter-argument]. How would you respond?"
    - Play devil's advocate: "I disagree. I actually think. . ." or "Who can play devil's advocate?"
    - Feign ignorance: "I don't understand. I was thinking. . ."

**Action Step Overview**

Discourse is a boon for developing and sharing ideas. New teachers can push students to develop their arguments further with prompts that problematize. These questions punctuate groupthink by asking students to consider alternatives and hypotheticals that challenge their initial arguments. In the process of thinking through their responses, students can shore up weaker positions and make blind spots visible.

Look at this example from Danny Murray's HS English seminar students on Gloria Naylor's novel *The Women of Brewster Place*. Most students are leaning toward a single reading of the character. Yet one student uses evidence to reach a different conclusion. See how Danny leverages that response to complicate the discourse:

 WATCH Clip 69: **Stretch It—Problematize**
(Teaching clip)

These work incredibly well in every subject. If you think these are only for Humanities classrooms, think again. Here are some STEM examples:

- Algebra class on linear equations and slope:
    - "You say that slope is always constant. What about circles? Do they have a constant slope?"
    - (After some discussion:) "So revise your initial answer: what type of slopes are always constant?" (Linear equations.)
- Physics class on gravity where they have discussed dropping a ball off of a cliff:
    - "You say that gravity makes things move faster. Is that always the case? Can anyone think of a counter-example?" (e.g., throwing a ball up into the air).

- "What about a car going along a road that is completely flat—perpendicular to the force of gravity? What is the impact of gravity on the movement of the car?"
- "Let's revise our initial understanding of gravity."

### Key Leadership Moves

**See It**

- Model a class discussion utilizing a few different prompts to problematize the discussion.

**Plan the Practice**

- Script questions into the lesson plan that build greater conceptual understanding or complexity in response to a limited student answer or a "groupthink" answer.

**Do It**

- Role play the conversation, coaching the teacher to pick the right moment to problematize.

**Real-Time Feedback**

- Model: Name the debate, provoke debate, play devil's advocate, or feign ignorance.

> **Tip from a Teacher—Spark Debate with Stretch It Questions**
>
> "When I first began teaching, I modeled problem-solving techniques for my students and named the rule students should take away from each lesson. This limited students' conceptual understanding and the opportunity to draw conclusions on their own. Learning how to "Stretch" class discussion and provoke debate through questioning increased both classroom engagement and student mastery of material. "Stretch It" questions were a complete game-changer! "Feigning ignorance" or challenging students to "play devil's advocate" got everyone's attention. Prompting students to engage in debate and defend their work brought class to life and made the learning sticky. Now student voice outweighs teacher voice in my classroom. Small, "stretch-it" questions are the ultimate teacher tool for facilitating dynamic student discourse!"
>
> —*Katherine Goett, Teacher and Instructional Leader, Newark, NJ*

# Stretch It: Sophisticate

## Coaching Tips

**Teacher Context**

**Challenge**

- Student analysis is simple and lacks nuance.

**Action Step**

- Sophisticate their argument: prompt to add complexity:
  - Apply within different or new context/perspective: "Consider $2x + 5y = 4$. Does our rule still apply?"
  - Give a hypothetical: "What if. . . ."
  - Press for more convincing evidence: "You've cited some decent evidence for your argument, but there is even more effective evidence that you've overlooked that could deepen your argument. Go back and re-read to find additional evidence."
  - Consider alternatives: "What's another way to interpret this?"
  - Generalize: "So, what's the emerging rule we could apply to all problems like this one?"

**Action Step Overview**

Accepting overly simple analysis doesn't build student thinking. New teachers can push students to add complexity to their arguments with prompts that sophisticate. These questions help students strengthen their initial argument.

High school math teacher Anushae gives a hypothetical example to check for student understanding.

 REWATCH Clip 62: **Model—Check for Understanding** (Teaching Clip)

### Key Leadership Moves

**See It**

- Model: Respond to a surface-level student response with a sophistication prompt.

**Plan the Practice**

- With the next lesson plan in hand, anticipate where students might give simplistic answers or where groupthink might emerge during discourse. Script questions that deepen or broaden their analysis in response to an overly simple student response.

**Do It**

- Practice the discourse:
  - Try it multiple different times, to let different patterns emerge—groupthink, simplistic answers, etc.
  - Prompt the teacher to evaluate the quality of the discourse and choose which of the pre-planned prompts would be most appropriate and use it.

**Real-Time Feedback**

- Model: Apply within different or new context, give a hypothetical, consider alternative, generalize.

**Coaching Examples:**
Humanities:

REWATCH Clip 5: **Stretch It—Sophisticate**
(Key Leadership Move: Real-time feedback)

Math:

WATCH Clip 70: **Stretch It—Sophisticate**
(Key Leadership Move: Do it)

Teaching:

REWATCH Clip 62: **Model—Check for Understanding**
(Teaching Clip)

## Strategies for Coaching: Stretch It

| Action Step | See It | Plan the Practice | Do It | Cues for Real-time Feedback |
|---|---|---|---|---|
| Problematize | • Model a class discussion utilizing a few different prompts to problematize the discussion. | • Script questions into the lesson plan that that build greater conceptual understanding or complexity in response to a limited student answer or a "groupthink" answer. | • Role play the conversation, coaching the teacher to pick the right moment to problematize. | • Model: Name the debate, provoke debate, play devil's advocate, or feign ignorance. |
| Sophisticate | • Model: Respond to a surface-level student response with a sophistication prompt. | • With lesson plan, anticipate where students might give simplistic answers or where groupthink might emerge during discourse. Script questions that deepen or broaden their analysis in response to an overly simple student response. | • Practice the discourse:<br>○ Try it multiple different times, to let different patterns emerge—groupthink, simplistic answers, etc.<br>○ Prompt the teacher to evaluate the quality of the discourse and choose which of the pre-planned prompts would be most appropriate and use it. | • Model: Apply within different or new context, give a hypothetical, consider alternative, generalize. |

These moves to deepen discourse are included in the K-12 Universal Discourse one-pager in the print-ready materials.

## CONCLUSION

When we have prepared students successfully to listen to others, press for reasoning, defend their own thinking, problematize arguments and go deeper, we have prepared them for any career they choose. Whatever paths our students follow, the skills of leading thoughtful discourse will not only serve them well but also empower them to build a better future. By prioritizing discourse when we think about the skills our teachers need, we are putting our students in a position to become the leaders we need.

# Closing: The Pursuit of Excellence

At 16 years old, Sydney McLaughlin-Levrone was one of the most accomplished high school track-and-field athletes in the United States. She backed that up when she made history as one of the youngest athletes in decades to qualify for the 2016 Olympic Games. As she prepared to run the 400-meter hurdles, everyone was buzzing to see what she would accomplish. Although she did her best, she didn't make it out of the semifinals, missing her bid to win an Olympic medal.

For those who follow track and field, you know that the story does not end there. But it is important for us to remember the starting point. It's not about where you start. It's how you finish.

> ### Core Idea
>
> It's not about how you start. It's how you finish.

Over the course of the next eight years, Sydney did the unthinkable. She broke the world record five times at the time of this publication (and certainly many more since then!), winning gold in both the 2021 and 2024 Olympics alongside every other accolade imaginable. Two things propelled her: great coaching and great fellow competitors.

Sydney herself paid homage to Dalilah Muhammad, the former world record holder whom she surpassed in 2021 on her way to gold:

> "Iron sharpens iron. We wouldn't be able to have these world records go back and forth without one another. It's two great athletes pushing each other to be better."[1]

Her sentiments remind me of coach Vince Lombardi's 1959 opening speech to the Green Bay Packers:

"Gentlemen, we are going to relentlessly chase perfection, knowing full well we will not catch it, because nothing is perfect. But we are going to relentlessly chase it, because in the process we will catch excellence. I am not remotely interested in just being good."[2]

Aspiring to get better is what creates excellence. There is no "perfect" teacher—and we can't create one, not in the first 90 days of teaching, not in the first year of teaching, not in 10 years of teaching. But what we can do is embrace a clear pathway to improvement. We can create a better teacher. That is precisely what we do as school leaders and teachers when we identify the most microscopic ways a classroom could improve, when we tackle them one at a time to keep the stream of growth steady and sustainable, and when we role play the moments that matter the most until they're as close to flawless as they can be before the school bell rings again. Each step forward brings us closer to excellence, and stories like Ajanee's.

Ajanee Biggs is the teacher featured on the cover of this book. When she recalls her own development as a first-year kindergarten teacher, she immediately remembers a transformative observation.

As any new teacher, Ajanee was new to teaching phonics. As she was stumbling her way through one of her first lessons, her coach Rachel didn't hesitate. She raised her hand to be invited into the discussion, and then she jumped in to model effective phonics instruction. For Ajanee, it felt like magic, and she couldn't retain all of it. But Rachel was undeterred. As they met for a follow up meeting, they debriefed what Rachel had done. Then they made a plan and practiced the upcoming lesson together.

Over the next few days, the kindergarten students had two phonics teachers: Rachel and Ajanee. Rachel modeled first and Ajanee immediately followed, taking care to match her moves exactly to her coach's. The classroom rang out with the sound of energetic young voices. The two debriefed these lessons, and Ajanee noted the connection between students' high engagement and her own, as well as their improved phonics performance. Their growth spurred on Ajanee. She continued to practice her phonics skills during feedback meetings and began to collaborate with other teachers as well for additional practice.

Fast forward a few months later. Ajanee earned the nickname "Phonics Queen" among fellow teachers, and she eventually mastered other parts of her instruction as well. After a few years, she was coaching her peers and by the time you read this, Ajanee will be welcoming staff to her school as their new principal. "When you have a good coach, there is no limit to what you can do," Ajanee says.

Teach someone to fish, and they fish for a lifetime. Teach a teacher to teach, and the ripple effects are never-ending.

Ajanee's story is one such ripple. But what's exciting is how easy it is to start more of them. With the right coaching, we can create ripple effects everywhere—as the leaders in this book have already shown.

There's no denying it: Chasing perfection is hard work, a cycle that never ends. But it is work that not only makes teachers extraordinarily good at their jobs but also honors the reasons we all became educators in the first place. If we believe in the ability of humans to learn and to grow, perpetuating this cycle of growth from new to master is the *only* logical way we can approach school leadership. There's a poetic as well as a practical beauty to it: The key to granting our students access to a bright future is to give that same gift to their teachers now. The road is a long and steep one, but the excellence we'll catch along the way is its own reward.

Closing: The Pursuit of Excellence **361**

# Appendix: Get Better Faster Coach's Guide

*Quick Reference Guide Aligned to the Get Better Faster Scope and Sequence*

# PHASE 1: PRE-TEACHING

## Phase 1 Management: Develop Essential Routines and Procedures

| Routines and Procedures 101 | | | | |
|---|---|---|---|---|
| Action Step | See It | Plan the Practice | Do It | Cues for Real-time Feedback |
| **Plan and practice critical routines and procedures moment by moment** | • Show a model video of an exemplary classroom routine. If possible, use a video of one of your strongest teachers.<br>• Show an exemplar written routine/ procedure:<br>　○ Connect the written routine to the live model<br>　○ Prompt: "Why was the planning of the routine so important to rolling it out effectively?" | • Complete a template for the key routines in the teacher's classroom (student entry and exit, transitions, materials distribution, and listening).<br>• Plan each moment.<br>• What will the teacher say and do?<br>• What will the students be doing? | • Rehearse every routine in the classroom setting.<br>• Rd 1: Stick to the basics at first: focus on the specific words and actions the teacher will use, such as where they will look and stand, and key ways they could break down the routine into smaller steps for the students. | N/A |

| | | | | |
|---|---|---|---|---|
| | • Do a live model of an effective routine: exaggerate nonverbals and words.<br>• Fully unpack the model: have the teacher break down all the steps of the model before moving to practice. | • What will the teacher do when students don't follow the routine? | • Rd 2: add small moments where students struggle to follow the routine (not too much: you want to build positive muscle memory!). | |
| **Plan and practice the rollout** | • Show a model video or do a live model of an effective routine.<br>• Make sure to unpack all the key components: hook, frame, model, practice. | • Focus on scripting the I Do and What to Do: break it down, pause, repeat piece by piece.<br>• Keep the language positive and enthusiastic, include challenge. | • Rd 1: memorize the rollout speech, then stand up and practice (too much to do both at once!). If teachers are working on this action step in peer groups, have teachers take turns playing the students to make it more authentic.<br>• Rd 2: Add small moments where students struggle to follow the routine. | • If model is ineffective: "Mr. Smith, am I following your model effectively?" (then model the correct actions and narrate what you're doing). |

*(Continued)*

| Confident Presence | | | | |
|---|---|---|---|---|
| Action Step | See It | Plan the Practice | Do It | Cues for Real-time Feedback |
| **Confident stance** | • Watch model video.<br>• Model giving directions with a relaxed posture, then while squaring up and standing still. | • Have new teachers practice delivering the opening routines for the earliest lessons while squaring up and standing still. | • Film the practice—or use a mirror—so that the new teacher can see what they look like while delivering instructions. | • Nonverbal: model exaggerated posture and stance—(e.g., make your posture more erect by pulling back your shoulders and standing up taller). |

| Warm-demander register | • Watch model video of teacher with warm-demander register.<br>• Model giving directions with a warm-demander register.<br>• Show an "anti-model" of what it doesn't look like: before or after model, model the opposite; speak too quickly/ shrilly, monotone. | • Select a scripted lesson routines and procedures. Practice delivering the instructions in a warm-demander register. | • Record the teachers during practice, and review the footage during the check-in so the teachers can hear when they are maintaining a formal register, and when their register begins to become casual/informal.<br>• Practice maintaining a formal tone while delivering a lesson on routines and procedures. Note when the teacher is maintaining a formal register, and when the teacher's register becomes too informal or casual. | • Nonverbal: Combine square up/ stand still gesture with pointing to your mouth to remind the teacher to speak in a formal register. |
|---|---|---|---|---|

## Phase 1 Rigor: Develop Content Expertise and Lesson Plans

| Develop Understanding of Content | | | | |
|---|---|---|---|---|
| Action Step | See It | Plan the Practice | Do It | Cues for Real-time Feedback |
| **Analyze end goal assessment** | • Show the teacher a set of different assessment items all aligned to the standard but with different levels or rigor. Guide to the conclusion that the curriculum doesn't teach you the rigor to which to teach until you define the end game.<br>• Show an example of a teacher's analysis of an assessment question. | • Break down the key knowledge and skills of the end goal assessment.<br>• Use a Know-Show chart or something similar. | • Repeat the process for the teacher with multiple standards covered by the end goal assessment. | • N/A (Action steps that are focused on planning—like this one—should not be coached in the moment of instruction. It could throw off the entire lesson.) |

| Develop/ internalize unit plans | • Show an example of a unit map of another teacher, i.e., how they wrote out the connection between the big ideas of the unit and each individual lesson plan.<br>• Do a think aloud of how to work from a unit plan and see the purpose of each lesson. Emphasize the big ideas and key understandings. | • Review unit-level plans to see how big ideas connect across the content:<br>  ○ Identify and name key concepts and enduring understandings.<br>  ○ Connect concepts across grade spans.<br>• Review independently and then spar with a colleague or with a resource; add whatever is needed to enhance the understanding. | • (A continuation of the planning: Do it and Planning are the same with an action step like this.) | N/A |
| --- | --- | --- | --- | --- |

*(Continued)*

| Develop Effective Lesson Plans 101 | | | | |
|---|---|---|---|---|
| Action Step | See It | Plan the Practice | Do It | Cues for Real-time Feedback |
| **Write precise learning objectives** | • Model a think aloud: Refine an existing objective to make it (1) data-driven (2) manageable and measurable (3) centered around conceptual understanding. | • Pull out upcoming assessments and lesson plans for review. Have all necessary materials on hand.<br>• Plan a full week of upcoming objectives together:<br>  ○ Identify the right end goal from an upcoming assessment.<br>  ○ Break down too-broad objectives to make them manageable for individual lessons.<br>  ○ Rewrite lesson objectives to center them around the big ideas of the content. | • Plan and Do It are identical. | N/A |

| Plan a launch | • Present an exemplar lesson plan with a scripted launch and unpack the purpose of each part of the launch.<br>• Model a think aloud: Plan the knowledge activation activities.<br>• Model think aloud and live model of the Do Now or class oral review. | • Select an upcoming lesson and plan an aligned do now or class oral review or hook.<br>• Script the introduction/routine for the do now or class oral review. | • Deliver the introduction to the do now or class oral review. | • Hold out your palm and point to it with the other hand to indicate to them to go back to their script and follow it. |
|---|---|---|---|---|
| **Create/identify key tasks** | • Model a think aloud with an existing lesson plan/curriculum<br>• Model a think aloud when building a lesson plan from scratch. | • Review existing curriculum or plan to identify the key tasks that students need to do to build conceptual understanding and master the objective.<br>• Build the key tasks for a new lesson plan that align to the objective. | • Plan and Do It are identical. | N/A |

*(Continued)*

| Plan the basic structure of the lesson | • Do a think aloud for planning a model.<br>• Model a think aloud for inquiry. | • Design the model or inquiry for the lesson.<br>• Draft the basic structure of the lesson around that moment. | • Plan and Do It are identical. | N/A |
|---|---|---|---|---|
| Design an exit ticket aligned to the objective | • Model a think aloud: Review upcoming objective and think aloud the process of creating an aligned exit ticket.<br>• Model a think aloud: Review an existing exit ticket against objective and verify that is aligned. | • Plan/revise a week's work of exit tickets. Have the upcoming interim-/year-end assessment questions in hand to help set the rigor of the exit ticket.<br>• Look at previous exit tickets to see where students are struggling and what skills need to continue to be assessed. | • Plan and Do It are identical. | N/A |

| | Internalize Existing Lesson Plans | | | |
|---|---|---|---|---|
| Action Step | See It | Plan the Practice | Do It | Cues for Real-time Feedback |
| **Identify the moment of most productive struggle** | • Think aloud—review the lesson plan and identify the area of most productive struggle. | • Review an upcoming lesson to determine the moment of most productive structure.<br>• Review past exit tickets to anticipate if students will struggle here. | • Plan and Do It are identical. | N/A |
| **Internalize and rehearse key parts of the lesson** | • Think aloud the process of internalizing a section of the lesson. | • Build a lesson internalization routine: Determine when they will spend time each day memorizing key parts of the lesson, how they will practice, and who will be their practice partner (even if their "partner" is as basic as a mirror).<br>• Give the teacher a set time to learn a specific chunk of the lesson cold. | • Have teacher deliver a chunk of the lesson without reading straight off the lesson plan (but referring to it when needed).<br>• Practice one chunk of the lesson at a time. Once teachers have it cold, put those chunks together until they have it completely internalized. | • When the teacher is struggling with the lesson plan, intervene, and cue students to turn and talk. Give the teacher 30–60 seconds to skim the plan before jumping back into the lesson. |

*(Continued)*

Appendix: Get Better Faster Coach's Guide　373

| | | | |
|---|---|---|---|
| **Build time stamps into lesson** | • Model reviewing lesson plan and allotting time to each section | • Write down specific time stamps in their lesson plan. Note which parts of the lesson could be trimmed or cut if teacher is running over. | • Rehearse the lesson with timer in hand. Cut unnecessary language that is slowing them down. | • Nonverbal: Hold up fingers for how many more minutes to spend in that section of the lesson.<br>• Jump in and cue students to turn and talk or work independently. Talk with the teacher for 30–60 seconds to decide what to cut from the lesson and how to adjust timing before jumping back in. |
| **Adjust the lesson plan to target student needs** | • Model think aloud: Review upcoming lesson plan against recent student data.<br>• Model think aloud: Adjust the launch to review/spiral concepts students are missing or need. | • Adapt the upcoming lesson plan to target the knowledge/skill that students need. | • Plan and Do It are identical. | N/A |

| Write an Exemplar | | | | |
|---|---|---|---|---|
| Action Step | See It | Plan the Practice | Do It | Cues for Real-time Feedback |
| **Script the ideal response** | • Model scripting out an ideal written response for an independent practice task, thinking aloud as you do the process. | • Write or revise exemplars for a written-response question in upcoming lessons.<br>• "Spar" with another exemplar: either another teacher's exemplar or experts in the field (e.g., Shakespearean critics).<br>• Break down the exemplar: ID key things the student will need to do to produce a response of the same quality. | • Plan and Do It are identical. | N/A |

## PHASE 2: DAY 1–30

### Phase 2 Management: Rollout and Monitor Routines

| Action Step | What to Do | | | |
|---|---|---|---|---|
| | See It | Plan the Practice | Do It | Cues for Real-time Feedback |
| **Make them bite-sized and chunk them** | • Video: Watch a clip of a teacher giving What to Do Directions: bite-sized, observable, and chunked for clarity.<br>• Unpack the quality of the direction and the pauses. | • Script bite-sized, observable directions for an upcoming lesson. Plan them out word by word.<br>• Provide feedback on clarity before practice: most errors can be fixed before practice. | • Rehearse key directions in the lesson.<br>• Focus on economy of language and the pause between each component of the instruction. | • Model: Give concise direction, using 3–5 words.<br>• Verbal: Could you name the steps for us again?<br>• Verbal: What should students be doing with their/the ___?<br>• Whisper prompt: "When you bring everyone back from this assignment, just say: 'Pencils down. Eyes on me!' No extra words." |

| Check for understanding on complex instructions | • Video: Watch a model video of a teacher checking for understanding.<br>• Live model: Model delivering directions with a check for understanding or a request for students to rephrase. | • Script a check for understanding or a student rephrase after a set of directions. | • Deliver your directions followed by a check for understanding question.<br>• Note: It is valuable to deliver all the directions and not just the check for understanding questions. You can never get too much practice of delivering clear directions. | • Verbal: "Ms. Smith, those directions are so important. Could you call on a student to see if everyone understands?"<br>• Whisper prompt: "Ask a student to restate the instructions to the class." |

(Continued)

| See Your Students | | | | |
|---|---|---|---|---|
| Action Step | See It | Plan the Practice | Do It | Cues for Real-time Feedback |
| **Make eye contact** | • Model: Give instructions to the class and exaggerate your body language to be monitoring the room, e.g., crane neck, angle your body toward different areas of the room, use finger to point to groups/rows.<br>• Model: Have a teacher (as student) exhibit off-task behavior. Make eye contact and redirect behavior. | • Video: Watch recent lesson. Debrief the moment when students begin to go off track. Point out the initial small-scale behaviors. Plan how to see those moments next time.<br>• Have the teacher identify areas in the classroom where student are off-task and the moments in the lesson plan to scan these areas. | • Role play student behavior you want the teacher to be able to catch and correct by scanning. Repeat until the teacher is consistently scanning and identifying off-task behavior.<br>• Have teacher practice maintaining eye contact long enough to note the behavior and see the student stop behavior before looking away.<br>• Start small: Begin with one off-task behavior. Once the teacher notes this and redirects with eye contact, change the target off-task behavior. | • Nonverbal: Gesture toward the area where you want the teacher to notice and redirect off-task behavior.<br>• Nonverbal: Crane your neck to indicate that the teacher should look around the room.<br>• Model: Take over the routine and crane your neck/ scan with your finger while scanning students. |

| Circulate with purpose—move around the room | • Video: Debrief a clip of a teacher circulating the classroom.<br>• Model: Walk purposefully around the room, moving toward groups of desks and individual students as you speak. Pause near these groups/students. | • Identify the areas in the room where off-task behaviors often occur.<br>• Create a set of key spots on the perimeter (think: corners) where you can circulate toward to monitor student work and plan a pathway to walk around the room. | • Simple practice: Practice moving along the pathway while teaching, stopping at areas when disengagement is higher and giving students a nonverbal redirect.<br>• Added complexity: Have the teacher call on imaginary students in different parts of the room and walk away from them, continuing to keep the rest of the class between the teacher and the speaker. | • Nonverbal: Use two fingers to mime legs walking.<br>• Nonverbal: Point to a corner of the room where the teacher should stand.<br>• Nonverbal: Cue the teacher to move away from the student who is speaking. |
| --- | --- | --- | --- | --- |

*(Continued)*

| Circulate with purpose—move away from the student who is speaking | • Model: Have the teacher play the role of a responding student. Move away from the teachers as they speak to stand near different clusters of desks around the room. | • Identify a moment in an upcoming lesson where the teacher will call on a student. Plot three areas in the room where the teacher can move while the student responds. | • Have the teacher pretend to call on an imaginary student. Then, while the imaginary student is responding, you can be playing the part of another student in another part of the room who is off task. The teacher can then practice moving around to remind the other student that he or she are still obligated to pay attention, and, if necessary, to give a silent redirect. | • Nonverbal: Cue the teacher to move away from the student who is speaking. |
| --- | --- | --- | --- | --- |

380   Appendix: Get Better Faster Coach's Guide

| Routines and Procedures 201 | | | | |
|---|---|---|---|---|
| Action Step | See It | Plan the Practice | Do It | Cues for Real-time Feedback |
| **Revise routines** | • Live observation: Go down the hall and watch a teacher who is implementing this routine effectively.<br>• Video: Watch and debrief an exemplary routine. | • Draft a new routine and script directions for the rollout.<br>• Anticipate the challenges: "Where will this break down? How can we revisit so that every student can follow it more easily?" | • Simple practice: Focus practice at the point where the routine has been going wrong. Conduct the role play with you play the student and the teacher rolling out the routine.<br>• Round 2: Role play the student who struggles to follow the routine. Rehearse the first words to say to nonresponsive students.<br>• What to look for during practice: Teaching positioning, Confident Presence and What to Do | • Model: "This is my favorite routine. I want to practice it with all of you. Can I jump in?" |

*(Continued)*

| Do it again | • Video: Watch and debrief video of a teacher cuing students to practice a routine again.<br>• Model: Watch clip of a teacher's lesson. Pause video at first moment of error in routine. Modeling directing students to redo routine. | • Plan each step of the Do it Again sequence:<br>○ Confident Stance<br>○ What to Do<br>○ Give a challenge<br>○ Give a signal to restart routine | • Role-play the revised routine: Make student errors and have the teacher practice pausing the routine, stating the change, and implementing the Do It Again until the routine looks flawless. Pay attention to past action steps; Confident Stance, Warm-Demander Register, What to Do | • Nonverbal: Make a circle with your finger to cue teacher to have students redo routine.<br>• Verbal cue: "Ms. Smith, I know the students can do that better. Let's see how well they can do it."<br>• Model: "Can I show our students what we'd like them to do?" Whisper to the teacher what you are modeling. |

| | | Build Trust and Rapport | | |
| | | Narrate the Positive | | |
| Action Step | See It | Plan the Practice | Do It | Cues for Real-time Feedback |
| --- | --- | --- | --- | --- |
| **Warm welcome** | • Watch video of warm classroom door greeting. Model: Warm greeting at the threshold with the teacher playing the role of the student. | • Plan the steps of an exemplar classroom entry. | • Practice: Doorway entry routine. Focus on the eye contact, smile, and warmth of the greeting. Integrate Seeing Your Students: Make sure the teacher can see the full line of entering students as well as the student already in the classroom. | • Nonverbal: Mime a big smile, point to both eyes and then point to students. |

*(Continued)*

| **Narrate what students do well** | • Video: Watch an exemplary video of a teacher narrating the positive.<br>• Model narrative the positive: use actual student names from the teacher's classroom. | • Watch a clip of teacher's lesson. Notice the positive, observable actions of students that the teacher could name publicly.<br>• Re-write teacher's most frequent negative comments into positive comments.<br>• Script positive narrations after each set of directions in an upcoming lesson plan. | • Role play keeping students on track through positive narration. While practicing, focus not only on the words but also the positive tone in which the teacher delivers. Practice tone until it feels authentic. | • Nonverbal: Index card with a plus sign written on it or sign that says "narrate the positive."<br>• Whisper prompt: "Narrate the positive." |

| | | | |
|---|---|---|---|
| **Praise intellect, not just behavior** | • Video: Watch a video of teacher giving precise academic praise.<br>• Video: Watch clip of teacher's instruction. Model where the teacher could have potentially added precise academic praise in recognition of student work or contribution. | • With an upcoming lesson plan, script moments when the teacher could give precise academic praise that would reinforce student's effort:<br>  ○ Praise process<br>  ○ Praise effort<br>  ○ Praise innovation | • Be the student and have the teacher give precise praise. Role play a questioning sequence in which the teacher specifically praises student thinking. | • Model: Jump in and praise student thinking. "Ms. Smith, can I jump in here? I love what Ezekiel just said. . . ."<br>• Whisper prompt after another academic behavior: "Give precise praise." |
| **Narrate the positive while looking at students who are disengaged** | • Video: Watch a video of teacher who uses narration while looking at off-task student.<br>• Model: Have the teacher be an off-task student. Narrate the positive while looking at teacher/student. | • Script positive narration after a set of direction in an upcoming lesson plan. Note to look at off-task students. Consider standing near disengaged while narrating the positive. Proximity often gets student back on task more quickly, and can be paired with a look. | • Role-play: You play the role of a student and model off-task behavior while the teacher looks at you and narrates the positive actions of another (imaginary) student. | • Whisper prompt: "Look at off-task students while narrating the positive." |

(Continued)

| | Make Authentic Connections | | | |
|---|---|---|---|---|
| Action Step | See It | Plan the Practice | Do It | Cues for Real-time Feedback |
| **Memorize students' names** | • Model: Use student names at the end of a comment or question. | • Review roster to memorize names.<br>• If you have a seating chart, memorize the names in the context of where they sit.<br>• If teacher is still struggling to memorize names, create name tents for every student to reinforce the memorization. | • Practice: Deliver part of the lesson and ask teacher to routinely call on different students by name.<br>• Practice: Point to different seats in the classroom and have teacher call on a student. Then check the seating chart and see if that was accurate. | • Model using student name, "Thank you for sharing your opinion, Carlos." |
| **Make self-to-student connection** | • Video: Show exemplar video of teacher making self-to-student connection. | • Teacher looks at upcoming lessons and identifies moments to make a self-to-student connection. Script to ensure economy of language. | • Practice: Teacher responds to a student comment with a shared struggle, interest, or passion. | N/A |

| Show genuine concern | • Video: Show exemplar video of teacher-student interaction. | • Draft survey to collect important information about students.<br>• Administer survey and record details in a tracker.<br>• Plan when a teacher can mention details at appropriate times.<br>• Plan when a teacher will find a student outside class and plan the conversation they will have with the student. | • Practice: Teacher asks about the well-being of a student whose normal affect is off. | • Whisper prompt: "Julia seems off today. Have you touched base with her?" (If not:) "Why don't you track her down at lunch to see what's up?" |
| --- | --- | --- | --- | --- |

## Phase 2 Rigor: Rollout Academic Routines

| Action Step | Independent Practice | | | |
| --- | --- | --- | --- | --- |
| | See It | Plan the Practice | Do It | Cues for Real-time Feedback |
| **Write first, talk second** | • Show a video of a teacher launching discourse with having everyone write first.<br>• Live model giving a writing task prior to discourse. | • Take out an upcoming lesson plan and ID key moments where students can write before discourse. Script the language to launch the writing task right into the lesson plan.<br>• Do this same task for the remaining lessons of the week by making a quick annotation of "Everybody Writes" in each lesson plan. | • Role-play practice is minimal: it is a matter of simply practicing the launch of the writing task and bringing students back to discussion afterwards. Focus on integrating the previous actions steps around What to Do and See Your Students. | • Raise your hand during class discussion to jump in: "Ms. Smith, I think that is a great prompt. Everyone, grab your pen and take 2 min to jot down your initial response. (Repeat teacher's prompt). You have 2 min. Ready? Go." |

| Implement a daily entry prompt | • Video: Watch a clip of a teacher getting students right to work on the Do Now.<br>• Model: Greet class and give directions to complete the Do Now. | • Write Do Now questions for upcoming lessons: short (three to five minutes to complete), easy to monitor (the teacher can check student work), and aligned to objective. | • Rehearse a start-of-class greeting that will prompt students to begin working on the Do Now. | • N/A |

*(Continued)*

| Use an exit ticket | • Model: Do a think aloud of how to check alignment between the exit ticket, the objective and the other moments of independent practice in the lesson.<br>• Model the implementation of an exit ticket (mostly focusing on exaggerating your model of What to Do and See Your Students). | • Planning and practice will depend on where the teacher is struggling:<br>  ◦ If the challenge is the equality of the exit tickets, write exit tickets that confirm student mastery. Look at the objective, the remaining independent practice and the exit ticket side-by-side to make sure they align in level of rigor.<br>  ◦ If the challenge is the delivery of the exit ticket part of the lesson, spend time on the instructions they give to students during the times, integrating management action: Confident Stance, What to Do, Make Eye Contact. | • Delivery: Spend time on the instructions they give to students during the times, integrating management action: | • N/A |
| --- | --- | --- | --- | --- |

| Academic Monitoring | | | | |
|---|---|---|---|---|
| Action Step | See It | Plan the Practice | Do It | Cues for Real-time Feedback |
| **Create and implement a monitoring pathway** | • Video: Watch clip of a teacher monitoring independent practice (use one of the ones included in this book!).<br>• Sample seating chart of another teacher with students seated to maximize a pathway to reach all of them efficiently. | • Pull out seating charts from other teachers to use as guides and build a seating chart for this teacher's class with data in hand and plan the monitoring pathway: Start with fastest writers and then move to the ones who need more time. | • Practice: test out the seating chart walking around. Revise for anticipated management/off-task behavior. | • Nonverbal or whisper prompt: Cue teacher to use the pre-planned monitoring pathway. |

*(Continued)*

| | | | | |
|---|---|---|---|---|
| **Pen in hand— mark up student work** | • Watch a video of a teacher marking up student work. Debrief how little time is spent with each student and how the teacher prompts efficiently.<br>• Live model: Do a think aloud while modeling academic monitoring: Model key thoughts before, during and after monitoring. | • Create a feedback code: simple cues to write on student work to spur self-correction. | • Practice: Put out a class set of student work on all the desks. Have the teacher monitor the room and write feedback codes on as many papers as possible.<br>• Round 2: Identify ways to go faster. Integrate previous actions: following a clear monitoring pathway, teacher's response tracker template. | • Walk alongside the teacher and debrief as you go:<br>  ○ What are students missing? What prompt could you use?<br>• Jump in to prompt if the student doesn't understand. |

| Gather data while monitoring and prepare to respond | | | | |
|---|---|---|---|---|
| | • Show the teacher an annotated lesson plan/exemplar where the teacher has added trackers for student<br>• Live model: Do a think aloud while modeling academic monitoring and IDing the key gap from the tracker. | • Have the teacher take out the exemplar and annotate for the keys to look for:<br> ○ Humanities: the argument/thesis, evidence, or a writing technique.<br> ○ STEM: a certain formula or critical step in answering a problem<br>• Create the tracker to use and insert it into the exemplar/lesson plan. | • Monitor student work (ideally work from a recent class). Set out papers with student writing on them on desks to monitor and give the teacher a set amount of time to fill in the note-taking template and note the patterns in student responses.<br>• Evaluate the quality of the students' identification of the gap and give them feedback on how to identify the gap more easily. | • Start on your own as instructional leader: Walk the room and determine the pattern in student responses yourself.<br>• Whisper prompt:<br> ○ "What are you seeing in student work?"<br> ○ "What is the pattern/gap?"<br>• If they have incorrect responses, tell them the gap and how you determined it. Then send them back to monitor. |

*(Continued)*

| Guide Discourse 101 | | | | |
|---|---|---|---|---|
| Action Step | See It | Plan the Practice | Do It | Cues for Real-time Feedback |
| **Everybody writes or Show-Call** | • Watch a video on Show-Call.<br>• Live model think aloud: ID the pattern of error, determine which pieces of student work to Show-Call.<br>• Live model: Launch the routine of a Show-Call. | • Look at a set of student work and determine what could be the best pieces of student work to show-call (exemplar versus non-exemplar, two different strategies, or just one exemplar response). | • Practice the What to Do directions when using a Show-Call to launch discourse. | • Walk around the classroom and look for representative student samples that could be used for a Show-Call.<br>• Prompt the teacher:<br>  ○ "What are you seeing?"<br>  ○ "What is the gap?"<br>  ○ "Which pieces of student work could you Show-Call to close the gap?" |

| Technique | | | | |
|---|---|---|---|---|
| **Turn and talk** | • Model think aloud: Identify multiple opportunities in an upcoming lesson for turn and talks.<br>• Model the clear bright lines of launching a turn and talk: setting up, releasing, and bringing students back from a turn and talk. | • Identify moments in upcoming lesson to do a quick turn and talk.<br>• Script the direction for the turn and talk. | • Simple practice: Deliver the instructions for the turn and talk.<br>• Round 2 of practice: Deliver the instructions and redirect off-task students. | • Nonverbal: Point your index fingers toward each other to indicate doing a turn and talk.<br>• Verbal: "Ms. Smith, can students share their responses with the person next to them before sharing out whole group?" |
| **Cold call, then volleyball** | • Model: Cold call student to launch discourse and call on 3–4 students in a row before responding. | • Script names to cold call in lesson plan. | • Practice cold call and volleyball. | • Whisper: "Cold call students."<br>• Nonverbal: Point to another student that teacher should call on after a student responds. |

*(Continued)*

| | | | | |
|---|---|---|---|---|
| **Prompt for and praise basic habits of discussion** | • Live Model: Role play a conversation, prompting to encourage habits of discussion.<br>• Live Model: Role play rolling out a habit of discussion for the students to encourage them to use it:<br>  ○ Hook: explain why this habit is valuable<br>  ○ Frame: tell the students what to look for<br>  ○ Model: Model the habit<br>• Practice: prompt students to use habit. | • Script points in an upcoming lesson to prompt for habits of discussion. | • Practice prompting students when they are not using the habits of discussion using the guide above. | • Verbal: "Camila, how does your comment connect to Eddie's? Do you agree or disagree?" |

| Stamp the key understanding | • Model think aloud: Identify the key takeaways in a lesson plan:<br>○ "What are the key understandings to listen for?"<br>○ Model: "Let's stamp that. What are the key things to remember?" | • Teacher revises lesson plans to include a stamp at the end. | • Role play discourse, giving a variety of answers. Once key understandings have surfaced, teacher asks students to recap and write down the key points of the lesson. | • Verbal: "What should we remember about X? Let's write that down." |

# PHASE 3: DAY 31–60

## Phase 3 Management: Everybody on Board

| Whole Class Reset | | | | |
| --- | --- | --- | --- | --- |
| Action Step | See It | Plan the Practice | Do It | Cues for Real-time Feedback |
| **Plan a whole class reset** | • Show video of a teacher resetting a class.<br>• Live model a whole class reset. | Script the reset word-by-word:<br>• Pause, "Eyes on me."<br>• Narrate the problem and give a direction.<br>• Scan. Wait for 100%. Redirect off-task students.<br>• Narrate the positive.<br>• Continue the lesson. | • Practice reset:<br>  ○ Confidence Presence<br>  ○ What to Do<br>  ○ Make eye contact<br>• Add complexity:<br>  ○ Rd 1: all students "comply" right away.<br>  ○ Rd 2: a few students still don't comply. | • If reset is ineffective, jump in and help lead the reset. Be sure to cede control back to the teacher and affirm their leadership as you do so. |

| Implement an in-the-moment reset | • Show a model video of teacher doing an in-the-moment reset | • Ideally, watch video of the teacher's classroom, and have teacher identify when the engagement is starting to drop and the signs that indicate the lower engagement.<br>• Coach the teacher through the process of scripting a generic in-the-moment reset that could be used in every situation. | • Practice reset:<br>○ Confidence Presence<br>○ What to Do<br>○ Make eye contact<br>• Add complexity:<br>○ Rd 1: all students "comply" right away.<br>○ Rd 2: a few students still don't comply. | • Nonverbal: create a cue for "reset" or show a sign.<br>• Model: "Students, we need to reset ourselves right now." Model a reset for the teacher. |

*(Continued)*

| Engage All Students | | | | |
|---|---|---|---|---|
| Action Step | See It | Plan the Practice | Do It | Cues for Real-time Feedback |
| **Cold call** | • Model from the lesson plan: Follow a scripted question sequence and cold call from the teacher's roster. | • Choose students to cold call in advance. | • Practice: Run through a questioning sequence and strategically cold calling on various students. Leader plays the part of various students. Teacher strategically cold calls. | • Nonverbal: Point at the ideal student for the teacher to cold call. |
| **Pre-call/ warm call** | • Model think aloud: Ask which students are less likely to partici- pate, jot this list as the students to warm call. Model: Discreetly confer with stu- dent and ask that they share their response/thought with the class. Call on student during questioning sequence. | • Choose students for pre-call/warm call in advance. | • Discreetly let a student know you would like them to participate, run through a question- ing sequence and call on that student. | • Whisper: "X has a strong response. Let him know that you'd like him to share with the class." |

| Turn and talk | • Model think aloud: Identify opportunities in an upcoming lesson for a turn and talk.<br>• Model the clear bright lines of launching a turn and talk: Setting up, releasing, and bringing students back from a turn and talk. | • ID moments in upcoming lesson to do a quick turn and talk.<br>• Script your directions for the turn and talk. | • Simple practice: Deliver the instructions for the turn and talk<br>• Round 2 of practice: Deliver the instructions and redirect off-task students. | • Nonverbal: Forefingers turn toward each other. Model: lead a turn and talk and then explain rationale to teacher during the turn and talk. |
|---|---|---|---|---|
| **Use multiple methods to call on students** | • Deliver a segment of the lesson with multiple question techniques. | • Plan a whole group discussion: Note which questions are best suited for cold call, hands, choral response, or turn and talk, | • Role play the discussion following the script the teacher created. Use cold calling, choral response, all hands, turn and talk. | • Nonverbal: Create/Use cue for cold calling, turn and talk, choral response, and all hands. Whisper prompt: "When you call the group back together, start with a choral response followed by a cold call." |

*(Continued)*

| | | | |
|---|---|---|---|
| **Provide supports to students with pre-identified need** | • Show a lesson plan from another teacher with annotations about how to reach students with pre-identified needs.<br>• Do a think aloud on what adjustments to make for students needing more executive functioning or social support. | • Annotate upcoming lesson plans with supports for students with pre-identified needs. | • Practice reinforcing executive function (e.g., timer, checklist).<br>• Practice encouraging social supports: communication strategies, resolve conflict, manage stress. | • If aware of a pre-identified need that can be addressed in the moment, whisper to teacher. |

| Individual Student Corrections | | | | |
|---|---|---|---|---|
| Action Step | See It | Plan the Practice | Do It | Cues for Real-time Feedback |
| **Least-invasive intervention** | • Model: Play the role of teacher. Have the teachers play an off-task student and respond to their behavior with a less invasive technique. Then ask the teacher to remain off-task so that you have to use each of the possible individual corrections in order. | • Choose a common off-task behavior from the classroom. Plan each of the individual corrections and script them on the front of the lesson plan. | • Round 1: Have the teacher redirect the off-task behavior using proximity, eye contact, and a nonverbal. <br> • Round 2: Repeat the practice, but in this case the student remains off task. Use student's name and then a small consequence. <br> • Round 3: Role play multiple students off-task, some requiring only the least-invasive correction and others requiring more. | • Model: Use a Confident Stance near off-task students. <br> • Nonverbal: Point to your eyes and then point at an off-task student or students. <br> • Nonverbal: Mime two legs walking and point to an off-task student or students. <br> • Whisper prompt: "The back table is off task. Use proximity." Whisper prompt: "Samuel is off task again. Give a small consequence." |
| **Close the loop conversations** | • Model a "close the loop" follow up conversation with a student. | • Script follow-up conversation with sample student. | • Practice the follow up conversation. | • Whisper prompt: "Check in with Robert at the end of the lesson." |

## Phase 3 Rigor: Activate Knowledge and Model

| Action Step | Activate Knowledge | | | |
| --- | --- | --- | --- | --- |
| | See It | Plan the Practice | Do It | Cues for Real-time Feedback |
| **Prompt students to access previously learned knowledge** | • Watch a video of a teacher leveraging classroom resources to activate knowledge.<br>• Show a picture of a teacher wall with visual anchors.<br>• Show an exemplar note-taking page from a student notebook.<br>• Model utilizing simple prompts to direct students to their resources. | • ID in lesson plan where students would benefit from a knowledge resource. Add prompts to the lesson plan.<br>• Develop a knowledge tool for the classroom (chart, handout, word wall, etc.). | • Rehearse the part of the lesson where students could get stuck and have the teacher use their prompts to point them to a resource. | • Nonverbal: Point to resources in the room. Whisper prompt: "Ask them to use their knowledge organizer/resources in the room to answer the question." |

404   Appendix: Get Better Faster Coach's Guide

| Use a knowledge organizer (cheatsheet)— all key points on 1–2 pages | • Review a sample knowledge organizer. Recall the cheatsheets the teacher used in college to study: unpack what made them effective. | • Build a knowledge organizer for the unit. <br>• Script activities to review the knowledge organizer in the first 15 minutes of class. | • Role Play the use of the knowledge organizer to set up the class. | • Nonverbal: Point to the knowledge organizer. <br>• Whisper prompt: "Ask them to use their knowledge organizer to answer the question." |
|---|---|---|---|---|
| Retrieve knowledge by applying it | • Model: Revise lesson plan to add application-based knowledge retrieval activities. | • Revise lesson plans to include opportunities for students to apply prior knowledge in new contexts. | • Plan and practice are identical. | N/A |
| Drop knowledge | • Think aloud model: Analyze lesson plan for the key knowledge students need to engage in critical thinking. Note where you can drop this knowledge if student analysis stalls. | • Identify in lesson plan where students will become stuck if they don't have the necessary knowledge. Select the knowledge to provide in this instance. | • Practice: Drop missing piece of knowledge when student problem solving falters. | • Verbal: "Students are missing X information. Drop knowledge so that they can keep doing the deeper thinking." |

*(Continued)*

| Action Step | Model | | | Cues for Real-time Feedback |
| --- | --- | --- | --- | --- |
| | See It | Plan the Practice | Do It | |
| **Narrow the focus** | • Video: See an exemplary clip of teacher modeling a related or same procedure.<br>• Model: Do a think aloud to simplify an overly comprehensive model from an upcoming lesson plan. Make the resulting model 3–5 steps. | • Plan a streamlined model for an upcoming lesson. Reduce the model to 3–5 steps. | • By itself, this is really just a planning task. Integrate with the upcoming action step "Model the thinking, not the procedure" to practice delivering the model. | N/A |
| **Give students a clear listening task** | • Watch a video with an intentional listening or writing task.<br>• Live model: Explain to students what they should be thinking about and doing. Check for student understanding. | • This action is dependent on already developing the model and the key skills that students need to see. Once that is complete, identify the note-taking/listening task that will get students thinking and not just copying. Then check for understanding. | • Practice delivery. | • Verbal Prompt: "Ms. Smith, before you begin your model, I want to make sure the students have their notebooks out to take notes: this is too valuable not to write anything down!" |

| Model the thinking, not the procedure | • Watch a model video: Chosen teacher should clearly exaggerate between teaching voice and think aloud voice.<br>• Live Model: Deliver a concise model that is targeted at student errors. The think aloud should be targeted toward building a greater conceptual understanding.<br>• Model: Emphasize the key points by varying tone and cadence.<br>• Model: Make your thinking visible with an anchor chart or annotations. | • Unpack the errors students have made in recent classes and anticipate what will be challenging with this content.<br>• Then draft the thinking questions you will ask yourself when modeling. Makes sure to have the knowledge resource available (chart, annotations, etc.). | • Practice: Vary tone and cadence of think aloud or model to emphasize key points and be as clear as possible. | • Verbal prompt: "Ms. Smith, that was very interesting. Can you tell me again what you were thinking when you took that step? I want to make sure I understand."<br>• Model: Do a think aloud yourself. |

(Continued)

| Check for understanding after the model | | | |
|---|---|---|---|
| • Video: Show clip of teacher checking for understanding after the model.<br>• Model asking students to identify the thinking skills used in the model. | • Add a check for understanding question after the model. Make sure that the question or task addressed the key points or steps that you want students to remember.<br>• Give students multiple opportunities for independent practice in that lesson and/or upcoming lesson. | • Practice delivery. | • Verbal: "Could someone explain to me how we ___?"<br>• Verbal: "Students, what do we have to remember when we ___?" |

# PHASE 4: DAY 61–90

## Phase 4 Management: Increase the Energy of the Classroom

| Build the Momentum | | | | |
|---|---|---|---|---|
| Action Step | See It | Plan the Practice | Do It | Cues for Real-time Feedback |
| **Create a challenge/ build momentum** | • Watch model video of creating a challenge. Live model 2–3 ways to pose a challenge, using the teacher's own lesson plan to demonstrate where it could happen. | • Script challenges into lesson plan. | • Practice delivery. | • Whisper prompt to add a challenge.<br>• Intervene: "Ms. Smith, that's a pretty nice challenge—normally only 6th graders can accomplish this. Class, are you up to the challenge?" |
| **Warm energy: speak faster, walk faster, vary your voice, and smile (sparkle)!** | • Show model video. Do a live model of a part of the teacher's lesson, highlight the greater speed, voice variation and nonverbals. | • Review the upcoming lesson plan to see how to incorporate warm energy. | • Teach part of upcoming lesson while speaking faster, varying voice, and smiling. | • Nonverbal: point to corners of your mouth to remind teacher to smile, or gesture with your hand to remind him or her to speak more quickly.<br>• Whisper Prompt: "Sparkle! Smile! Jump back into teaching!" |

*(Continued)*

| Pacing | | | | |
|---|---|---|---|---|
| Action Step | See It | Plan the Practice | Do It | Cues for Real-time Feedback |
| **Time yourself** | • Live model: Deliver a portion of the lesson while keeping track of progress using a timer. Set off timer early and model segueing into the next section of the lesson. | • Plan: Review time stamps for each part of the lesson. Script how to move on when the timer goes off and the teacher hasn't finished that section.<br>• Plan where to cut from lesson if falling behind on time. | • Practice lesson with a timer. Rehearse what to do when timer goes off and the teacher isn't finished with that section. | • Nonverbal: Point at watch/wrist when time to move on.<br>• Nonverbal: Give a hand signal of how many more minutes to stay on this activity. |
| **Increase the rate of questioning** | • Deliver a questioning sequence with a consistent, brisk rate. | • Review the questions in an upcoming lesson plan. Plan how many students to call on after each question and when to move onto the next. | • Role play a questioning sequence from an upcoming lesson, keeping track of the rate of questioning. Use real-time feedback. | • Model: Model the questioning pace for the teacher. |

| Use countdowns to work the clock | • Watch model video<br>• Live model using a countdown and/or Bright Lines to transition in a lesson or between lessons. | • Script and practice Bright Lines: Add cues to signal switching between activities: claps, hand gestures, and so on. | • Play the part of students and have teacher transition from one activity to the next using a countdown to work the clock. | • Nonverbal: signal "5-4-3-2-1" with your fingers when it's time for a countdown. |
| --- | --- | --- | --- | --- |
| Call and response | • Live model engaging students in a call and response. Imagine students respond with low energy and have them Do it Again. | • In upcoming lesson plan, identify moments when it would be most useful to implement a choral response. | • Role-play the choral response.<br>• Provide occasional lackluster responses so teacher can practice having students Do it Again for choral response. | • Nonverbal: Create/ Use a cue for choral response. |

*(Continued)*

| Engaged Small Group Work | | | | |
|---|---|---|---|---|
| **Action Step** | **See It** | **Plan the Practice** | **Do It** | **Cues for Real-time Feedback** |
| **Deliver explicit instructions for group work** | • Model delivering explicit directions for group work. Each student should have a job to do. | Script explicit directions for group work. Make sure to consider all the needed components:<br><br>• Materials they will need<br>• Knowledge resources they will need<br>• Where they will make their work visible<br>• Chunk the directions | • Practice delivery. | • Model: Re-establish the small-group work instructions. |
| **Monitor group progress** | • Model think aloud: Set up student work at classroom desks. Circulate through the space and look for visual evidence of student work. Ask yourself: which groups are on track and which aren't? Where do I need to jump in to get them on task or push them further? | • Plan out the visual evidence—exactly what the teacher will want to see on chart paper, in student notebooks, and/or work product—at each stage of the class period. Determine by which time groups should reach each stage. | • Minimal.<br>• Combine with next step (Verbally enforce accountability) to practice redirecting groups who are off track. | • Whisper prompt: look at student work. "What are you noticing? Are they on task and on track?" |

| Verbally enforce accountability | <ul><li>Watch model video.</li><li>Model announcing time checks to groups and redirecting off-task students or groups.</li><li>Think aloud what you are looking for when monitoring the groups:<ul><li>Lack of evidence charted/written</li><li>Pairs that appear to be laughing or talking about something else (even if you cannot be certain from afar)</li><li>Nonverbal body language that suggests off-task behavior</li></ul></li></ul> | <ul><li>Script time checks into the group work section of lesson plans.</li><li>Script the language for an effective reset or individual correction. Incorporate all the keys from previous action steps.</li></ul> | <ul><li>Practice announcing time stamps to groups and verbally redirecting students or groups who are not on-task.</li></ul> | <ul><li>Whisper prompt: Let students know how much time they have left.</li><li>Whisper prompt: "Student/Group X is off task."</li></ul> |
|---|---|---|---|---|

## Phase 4 Rigor: Deepen Discourse

| | Universal Prompts | | | |
|---|---|---|---|---|
| Action Step | See It | Plan the Practice | Do It | Cues for Real-time Feedback |
| **Revoice** | • Show a video clip of a teacher using revoicing.<br>• Utilizing the teacher's lesson plan, live model asking student to rephrase a peer's analysis. | • Script revoicing prompts in an upcoming lesson plan during the discourse section. | • Role Play, Round 1: With lesson plan in hand, ask student to rephrase or check their understanding of what peer said before responding.<br>• Role Play, Round 2: Enter into full discourse. Role play various students, some who revoice effectively and others who don't, and ask the teacher to identify which students need to be prompted to revoice and to prompt them. | • Whisper prompt: Ask students to paraphrase what the previous student said before responding.<br>• Model: "Winston, before you respond, can you share what Sarah said in your own words?"<br>• Model: "Class, I want to remind you to revoice before stating your opinion. I'll model. Demetria, are you saying (rephrase argument)?" |

| Press for reasoning | Model how to respond to a student who gives a limited response to prompt. Use the press for reasoning prompts to encourage elaboration and/or justification. | With the next lesson where discourse appears, predict the types of student responses that will benefit from these prompts: potential wrong answers and correct answers with limited explanation. | Play the roles of three different students: one with a wrong answer, two more with limited answers. Role play a discussion where the teacher practices using each of the prompts:<br>○ Tell me more. Why/why not?<br>○ How do you know? Prove it.<br>○ Why is that important?<br>At the end, ask the teachers what they learned about student understanding to see how well they diagnosed the error. | • Whisper prompt: Ask students to elaborate or to justify their answer with more evidence.<br>• Model: "Jared, that is an interesting idea. Tell me more. Why or why not?" After modeling, prompt the teacher to do the same with the next limited response. |
|---|---|---|---|---|

*(Continued)*

## Strategically Call Students

| Action Step | See It | Plan the Practice | Do It | Cues for Real-time Feedback |
|---|---|---|---|---|
| **Create a sequence to call on students** | • Model: Review student work from previous assignment and create a sequence based on on-track, off-track student performance.<br><br>• Watch a model video of a teacher strategically calling students | • Plan the order of students to call on during the discourse:<br>  ○ Start with partially there or further off.<br>  ○ Call on a stronger response when the previous students are still struggling to answer.<br>  ○ Call on a student whose initial responses were limited when part of the learning has been revealed to ask him or her to "stamp" the understanding. From previous exit tickets, set up the names of students in each group (correct or almost there, partially there, further off). | • Round 1: First student called on gets it right (focus on stamp).<br>• Round 2: First student gets it wrong; after calling on students with stronger responses, struggling students get it right.<br>• Round 3: First student gets it wrong, and after calling on students with stronger responses, initial student still gets it wrong. | • Monitor student work with the teacher to determine who to call on. |

416    Appendix: Get Better Faster Coach's Guide

| Action Step | Stretch It | | | |
| | See It | Plan the Practice | Do It | Cues for Real-time Feedback |
|---|---|---|---|---|
| **Problematize** | • Model a class discussion utilizing a few different prompts to problematize the discussion. | • Script questions into the lesson plan that that build greater conceptual understanding or complexity in response to a limited student answer or a "groupthink" answer. | • Role play the conversation, coaching the teacher to pick the right moment to problematize. | • Model: Name the debate, provoke debate, play devil's advocate, or feign ignorance. |
| **Sophisticate** | • Model: Respond to a surface-level student response with a sophistication prompt. | • Plan and Practice are identical: With lesson plan in hand, anticipate where students might give simplistic answers or group thinking might emerge during discourse. Script questions that deepen or broaden their analysis in response to an overly simple student response. | Practice the discourse:<br>• Try it multiple different times, to let different patterns emerge—groupthink, simplistic answers, etc. Prompt the teacher to evaluate the quality of the discourse and choose which of the pre-planned prompts would be most appropriate and use it. | • Model: apply within different or new context, give a hypothetical, consider alternative, generalize. |

# Notes

## Introduction

1. Lemov, Doug. (2021). *Teach like a Champion 3.0: 63 Techniques That Put Students on the Path to College*, 425–432. Jossey-Bass.
2. Levitan, Shayna. "District Trendline – How are districts observing and providing feedback to teachers?" National Council on Teaching Quality. https://www.nctq.org/blog/How-are-districts-observing-and-providing-feedback-to-teachers. October 13, 2022. Accessed 5/28/2024.
3. Coyle, Daniel. (2009). *The Talent Code*, 1. New York: Bantam Dell.
4. Bryant, Jake, et al. "K-12 teachers are quitting. What would make them stay?" McKinsey & Company. March 2, 2023. https://www.mckinsey.com/industries/education/our-insights/k-12-teachers-are-quitting-what-would-make-them-stay; Linda Darling-Hammond, et al. Policymakers should ring in the New Year with action to end teacher shortages. Learning Policy Institute. Blog Post. January 5, 2023. https://learningpolicyinstitute.org/blog/policymakers-should-ring-new-year-action-end-teacher-shortages; Emma Garcia and Elain Weiss. "U.S Schools struggle to hire and retain teachers." Economic Policy Institute. April 16, 2019. https://www.epi.org/publication/u-s-schools-struggle-to-hire-and-retain-teachers-the-second-report-in-the-perfect-storm-in-the-teacher-labor-market-series/.
5. Ingersoll, Richard, et al. "Seven Trends: The Transformation of the Teaching Force." Updated January 2021.Research Report. Consortium for Policy Research in Education. University of Pennsylvania. https://repository.upenn.edu/cpre_researchreports/

6. Ingersoll, R., Merrill, E., Stuckey, D., Collins, G. & Harrison, B. (2021). "Seven Trends: The Transformation of the Teaching Force," updated January 2021. Research Report. Consortium for Policy Research in Education, University of Pennsylvania, https://repository.upenn.edu/cpre_researchreports/; Kopkowski, Cynthia. "Why They Leave," National Education Association, 2008. http://sullivanclasses.weebly.com/uploads/3/1/1/8/311891113/nea_-why_they_leave.pdf; National Center for Education Statistics, "Teacher Attrition and Mobility: Results from the 2004-05 Teacher Follow-Up Survey," 2007, http://nces.ed.gov/pubs2007/2007307.pdf; http://nctaf.org/wp-content/uploads/2012/01/NCTAF-Cost-of-Teacher-Turnover-2007-policy-brief.pdf; National Commission on Teaching and America's Future "Policy Brief: The High Cost of Teacher Turnover," 2007, http://nctaf.org/wp-content/uploads/2012/01/NCTAF-Cost-of-Teacher-Turnover-2007-policy-brief.pdf

7. Garcia, Emma and Elaine Weiss. "The teacher shortage is real, large and growing, and worse than we thought." March 26, 2019. https://www.epi.org/publication/the-teacher-shortage-is-real-large-and-growing-and-worse-than-we-thought-the-first-report-in-the-perfect-storm-in-the-teacher-labor-market-series/. Accessed 6/5/2024.

8. National Education Association. Report – "5 Ways School Districts Can Better Retrain Educators." https://www.nea.org/resource-library/5-ways-school-districts-can-better-retain-educators. September 30, 2022; Peske, Heather. National Council on Teacher Quality. "Eight ways states can act now to retain an effective, diverse teacher workforce." September 29, 2022. https://www.nctq.org/blog/Eight-ways-states-can-act-now-to-retain-an-effective,-diverse-teacher-workforce.

9. National Institute for Excellence in Teaching. "Why New Teacher Mentoring Falls Shorts, and How to Fix It." chrome-extension://efaidnbmnnnibpcajpcglclefindmkaj/https://www.niet.org/assets/ResearchAndPolicyResources/strengthening-new-teacher-mentoring.pdf. Fall 2021.

10. National Institute for Excellence in Teaching. "New Report Outlines Strategies to Better Support First-Year Teachers." September 9, 2021. https://www.niet.org/newsroom/show/pressrelease/strengthening-new-teacher-mentoring

11. Drake, Graham. District Trendline - "Investing in new teacher orientation and mentoring can produce long-term benefits." National Council on Teacher Quality. https://www.nctq.org/blog/Investing-in-new-teacher-orientation-and-mentoring-can-produce-long--term-benefits September 14, 2023; National Education Administration. "5 Ways School Districts Can Better Retain Educators." https://www.nctq.org/

blog/Investing-in-new-teacher-orientation-and-mentoring-can-produce-long-term-benefits. September 30, 2022; Fall 2021; Ingersoll, Richard. "Beginner Teacher Induction." Phi Delta Kappan. May 2012. V93 N8. Pp. 47–51.

12. National Center for Education Statistics. (2024). "Principal Turnover: Stayers, Movers, and Leavers." Condition of Education. U.S. Department of Education, Institute of Education Sciences. Retrieved 6/5/2024. https://nces.ed.gov/programs/coe/indicator/slb.

13. Cieminski, Amie and Anthony Asmus. "Principal turnover is too high. Principal supervisors can help." Learning Forward: The Professional Learning Association. February 2023. https://learningforward.org/journal/tackling-turnover/principal-turnover-is-too-high-principal-supervisors-can-help/; National Association of Secondary School Principals. NASSP Survey of America's School Leaders and High School Students – 2022. https://survey.nassp.org/2022/#welcome.; Study reissued by the New Teacher Center in 2018. School Leaders Network, "Churn: The High Cost of Principal Turnover," 2014. https://newteachercenter.org/resources/churn-the-high-cost-of-principal-turnover/.1, 12.

14. Kraft, Matthew, John Papay, and Olivia Chi. (2019). "Teacher Skill Development: Evidence from Performance Ratings by Principals." (EdWorkingPaper: 19–97). Retrieved from Annenberg Institute at Brown University: https://doi.org/10.26300/sad5-cz73; Kini, T. and Podolsky, A. (2016). *Does Teaching Experience Increase Teacher Effectiveness?* Palo Alto: Learning Policy Institute http://bit.ly/24hm9dr. June 2016). In a 2013 report, the New Teacher Project covered in great depth the different ways in which individual teachers develop. Specifically, they found that "new teachers perform at different levels and improve at different rates"; that "teachers' initial performance predicts their future performance"; that "multiple measures tend to point to the same conclusion about a teacher's effectiveness"; and, finally, that "a few specific core skills appear to be important to a first-year teacher's success." This underscores both the power of coaching and the need to use any system of coaching in a way that addresses the needs of specific teachers individually, as the Scope and Sequence allows a leader to do. Source: New Teacher Project. Leap Year: Assessing and Supporting Effective First-Year Teachers. 17 April 2013, http://tntp.org/assets/documents/TNTP_LeapYear_2013.pdf.

15. Sample, Ian. "Blow to 10,000-hour rule as study finds practice doesn't always make perfect." *The Guardian.* https://www.theguardian.com/science/2019/aug/21/practice-does-not-always-make-perfect-violinists-10000-hour-rule. August 19, 2019; Valerie Strauss, "Actually, Practice Doesn't Always Make Perfect-New

Study," *Washington Post*, 25 July 2014, http://www.washingtonpost.com/blogs/answer-sheet/wp/2014/07/25/actually-practice-doesnt-always-make-perfect-new-teacher-study/; Collins, Nathan, "Practice Doesn't Always Make Perfect," *Scientific American*, 1 November 2014, http://www.scientificamerican.com/article/practice-doesn-t-always-make-perfect/.

16. A discouraging report from The New Teacher Project underscores the necessity of providing new teachers not only with coaching, but with the right coaching. The Mirage found that although more schools and districts are investing time, money, and energy in teacher training than we tend to assume, this training is all too often unsuccessful. "School systems shouldn't give up on teacher development," the Project concluded, "and they shouldn't cut spending on it, either. Rather, we believe it's time for a new conversation about teacher improvement—one that asks fundamentally different questions about what great teaching means and how to achieve it." Source: The New Teacher Project. The Mirage: Confronting the Hard Truth About Our Quest for Teacher Development. 17 April 2013. http://tntp.org/assets/documents/TNTP-Mirage_2015.pdf

17. Watkins, Michael. (2013). *The First 90 Days: Critical Success Strategies for New Leaders at All Levels*, 1. Boston: Harvard Business School Publishing.

## Chapter 1

1. The JWST was the product of extended collaboration among a team of international contributors (the European Space Agency and the Canadian Space Agency), several NASA centers, and multiple academic and industry partners. For the full list, visit: https://webb.nasa.gov/content/meetTheTeam/team.html

2. The Get Better Faster Scope and Sequence is a living document that has been continuously updated by the collective of school leaders that use it. With more than 100 revisions over the last 10 years, it continues to improve with input from school leaders across the globe who are putting it into action. Here is more detail to the changes. PHASE 1: Develop Content Knowledge is a new first step in the Rigor trajectory. Years of work with new and experienced teachers has shown school leaders that the more deeply teachers understand a given content area, the more skillfully they can instruct and coach students, and this reaps dividends for learning. Although some teachers may enter the profession with a specialized degree in a content area, many others learn the content on the job or in grade-level teams. Both sets of teachers should be coached to deepen their knowledge base over time.

PHASE 2: We've expanded Phase 2 management with a section on building trust and rapport. A classroom that hums with learning is powered by engaged students and their teacher. Educators like Zaretta Hammond, author of *Culturally Responsive Teaching and the Brain*, have pointed to the integral role that positive relationships between teachers and students play in students' academic achievement and resilience. Frontloading relationship-building at the start of the school year creates an atmosphere of trust that makes students more likely to take academic risks and persevere through challenges. It also helps teachers tailor instruction and techniques to students' known interests. Although relationship-building appears early in the sequence, it should be reinforced throughout the school to maintain a positive classroom climate. The second major revision to Phase 2 is in inclusion of Discourse earlier than before. Discourse has been split into Phase 2 (Discourse 101) and Phase 4 (Discourse 201). In the first phase, teachers lay the groundwork for powerful discourse through the implementation of academic routines around student writing, talking, and large group discussion. These build the basic habits of conversation that can be leveraged to make and defend arguments in Phase 4. PHASE 3: Activate knowledge is a new addition to Phase 3 Rigor. Knowledge activation is one of the most powerful tools that teachers have in their toolbox. Not only does it make strong re-teaching possible, but it also makes it more likely that students hang on to new content. Cognitive science research points to several powerful knowledge retrieval techniques (shared in Phase 3) that teachers can leverage in the classroom to fuel students' knowledge retrieval and application. PHASE 4: Discourse (201) takes center stage in this final phase. All of the moves included here are designed to make classroom conversation a space for students to engage in collaborative sense-making. Many of the "Stretch It" moves that followed the four Phases in the original version have been moved here. Lastly, we have renamed some action steps to be clearer and avoid misinterpretation for implementation, for example terms like "teacher radar" and "scanning" have been renamed "see your students" to underscore that the purpose of looking at students is to ensure that everyone is working on task, rather than implying surveillance.

3. Morrison, Toni. (1970). *The Bluest Eye*, pg 2. Holt, Rineheart and Winston.

4. Bambrick-Santoyo, Paul. and Art Worrell (2023). *Make History: A Practical Guide for Middle and High School Instruction*, Pg 45. Jossey Bass.

5. Willingham, Daniel. (2009). *Why Don't Students like School? A Cognitive Scientist Answers Questions about How the Mind Works and What it Means for the Classroom*, Pg 48. Jossey-Bass.

6. Lemov, Doug. (2021). Technique 5: Knowledge Organizer. *Teach like a Champion: 63 techniques that put students on the path to college*, Pg 63. Jossey-Bass.

7. Marzano, Robert, et al. *Effective Supervision*, ASCD, 2011 pg. 9.

8. A variety of authors have been credited with this expression. The earliest trace seems to be George Loomis in the "Michigan School Moderator" in 1902, then Percy Buck in 1944, Francis Mayer in 1963, and Peter Crossley in 1971. Garson O'Toole investigates the origins of the expression in detail at Quote Investigator: http://quoteinvestigator.com/2013/08/29/get-it-right/

9. Wiggins, Grant. and Jay McTighe. (2005). *Understanding by Design*. ASCD.

10. Ross, John A. "Teacher Efficacy and the Effects of Coaching on Student Achievement." *Canadian Journal of Education:* 1992, 17:1, pg 51 and Bennett, B. "The effectiveness of staff development training practices: A meta-analysis." University of Oregon, Eugene, 1987.

11. Several researchers have identified making feedback frequent, or repeated, as the key to making it stick. Sources: Myung, Jeannie, and Krissia Martinez, "Strategies for Enhancing Post-Observation Feedback," Carnegie Foundation for the Advancement of Teaching, July 2013; Sun, Min, Penuel, William, Frank, Kenneth, Gallagher, Alix, and Youngs, Peter, "Shaping PD to Promote Diffusion of Instructional Expertise Among Teachers," Educational Evaluation and Policy Analysis, September 2013.

12. Brown, Brene. (2018). *Dare to Lead*, Pg 48. Random House.

## Chapter 2

1. Ball, Deborah Loewenberg and Francesca M. Forzani. "Building a Common Core for Learning to Teach." American Educator. Summer 2011. https://www.aft.org/ae/summer2011/ball_forzani.

2. If you're familiar with the first edition of *Leverage Leadership*, you may notice that the language we use to describe the components of Living the Learning has been updated. These new terms capture the Living the Learning cycle more straightforwardly. *Leverage Leadership 2.0* (2017) will provide even more details of the new teacher naming!

3. For *Teach Like a Champion*'s professional development resources, visit teachlikeachampion.org. The teacher training modules are available under "Plug and Plays." See also Todd Whitaker and Annette Breaux, *The Ten-Minute In-Service: 40 Quick Training Sessions that Build Teacher Effectiveness*, San Francisco, CA: Jossey-Bass, 2013.

4. Hammond, Zaretta. *Culturally Responsive Teaching and the Brain*. Corwin, 2015.

5. Lemov, Doug. *Teach like a Champion*. Jossey-Bass, 2010, pg. 182.

6. Bambrick-Santoyo, Paul. *Driven by Data 2.0*. Jossey-Bass, 2019, Ch1: Assessment, Pg 21.

7. Bambrick-Santoyo, Paul. *Driven by Data 2.0*. Jossey-Bass, 2019, Ch1: Assessment, Pp 17–49.

8. Bambrick-Santoyo, Paul. *Driven by Data 2.0*. Jossey-Bass, 2019, Ch 1: pp. 20, 29, 30, 36, 37, 39, 41.

9. Leinwand, Steve. Personal interview with the author. 2023.

10. Ermeling, Brad and Genevieve Graff-Ermeling. "Learning to Learn from Teaching: A First-Hand Account of Lesson Study in Japan" International Journal for Lesson and Learning Studies 3, no. 2 (2014):170–191, http://www.marshallmemo.com/issues/da6e777fc93e2de1261d0794d1ab4333/MarshMemo541.pdf.

11. Gauvain, Mary. "Vygotsky's Sociocultural Theory." *Encyclopedia of Infant and Early Childhood Development*, 2009. Pp 404–412. Science Direct. https://doi.org/10.1016/B978-0-12-809324-5.23569-4

12. Bainton, George. *The Art of Authorship*, New York: D. Appleton and Company. 1890. pp. 87–88.

13. Lemov, Doug. *Teach like a Champion*. Jossey-Bass, 2010, page 35.

## Chapter 3

1. If you manage more than 15 teachers—up to 30 teachers—the schedule still looks the same: You just set up a rotation, making sure you see each teacher every other week instead of every week. It doesn't take up any more time. The ratio of 30 teachers to one leader meets the needs of 90 percent of leaders my colleagues and I have met at schools across the country. If you're one of the unique remaining leaders with a greater number of teachers per leader than that, turn to *Lverage Leadership 2.0* (Chapter 3, pp. 132-133) for a set of tips for how to make observation and feedback happen in that context.

2. Walsh, Bill. "A Method for Game Planning." (Undated lecture transcript, approximate year 1983). In the lecture, Walsh describes the counterintuitive value of planning game plays in advanced. Retrieved from http://jameslightfootball.com/2015/04/17/bill-walsh-a-method-for-planning-a-game/.

3. Lemov, Doug. (2021) Technique 20: Do Now. *Teach like a champion 3.0: 63 techniques that put students on the path to college*, 187–194. Jossey-Bass.

4. "Narrate the positive" is a teacher move that falls under a Positive Framing, an approach that seeks to build a classroom environment of trust and positivity. Lemov, Doug. *Teach like a champion: 63 techniques that put students on the path to college.* Jossey-Bass, 2021. Technique 59: Positive Framing, pg 482.

5. Lemov, D. (2021. Technique 26: Exit Ticket). *Teach like a Champion: 63 techniques that put students on the path to college,* 228–233. Jossey-Bass.

6. Lemov, D. (2021. Technique 13: Show-call). *Teach like a Champion: 63 techniques that put students on the path to college,* 120–135. Jossey-Bass.

## Chapter 4

1. These statistics are based on 2022 data. Federal Aviation Administration. "Air Traffic By the Numbers." https://www.faa.gov/air_traffic/by_the_numbers. As of 5/30/2024.

2. These statistics are based on 2022 data. Federal Aviation Administration. "Air Traffic By the Numbers." https://www.faa.gov/air_traffic/by_the_numbers. As of 5/30/2024.

3. Federal Aviation Administration. Transport Airline Accident Library. Douglas DC-8 and Lockheed L-1049 Super Constellation. https://www.faa.gov/lessons_learned/transport_airplane/accidents/N8013U. As of 5/30/2024.

4. Richard DuFour, along with many other educators, has written extensively about the impact of professional learning communities (PLCs) on instruction. Specifically, advocates of PLCs cite the way they help teachers mutually increase their own expertise and the opportunities they create to analyze data and plan re-teaching strategically. Sources: Donohoo, Jenni and Ann T. Mausbach. "Beyond Collaboration: The Power of Joint Work." ASCD. February 1, 2021. Vol.78, No5. https://www.ascd.org/el/articles/beyond-collaboration-the-power-of-joint-work; DuFour, Richard, "How PLCs Do Data Right," *Educational Leadership,* 2015; DuFour, Richard, and Mattos, Mike, "How Do Principals Really Improve Schools?", *Educational Leadership,* 2013; DuFour, Richard, "Work Together, But Only If You Want To," *Phi Delta Kappan,* 2011; Hord, Shirley, "Evolution of the Professional Learning Community," *Journal of Staff Development,* 2008; Sleegers, Peter, de Brok, Perry, Verbiest Fontys, Eric, Moolenaar, Nienke, and Daly, Alan, "Toward Conceptual Clarity: A Multi-dimensional, Multilevel Model of Professional Learning Communities in Dutch Elementary Schools," *Elementary School Journal,* 2013.

5. Lemov, Doug. (2021). Technique 34: Cold Call. *Teach like a Champion: 63 techniques that put students on the path to college*, 282–301. Jossey-Bass.

6. Bambrick-Santoyo, P. and Worrell, A. (2023). *Make history: A practical guide for middle and high school history instruction*, 43–45. Jossey-Bass.

7. Wineburg, Sam. "Unnatural and Essential: the nature of historical thinking." *Teaching History*. no. 129, pp 6-11. *Jstor*, https://www.jstor.org/stable/43259304.

8. Brown, Peter, et al. *Make it stick: The science of successful learning*. Harvard University Press, 2014. Pg. 5.

9. In the late 1880s, psychologist Hermann Ebbinghaus crafted an equation to calculate the rate of forgetting. The results are commonly graphed as the Forgetting Curve. New information is rapidly forgotten as time passes; about 50% of new information is forgotten an hour after learning and this drops to around 80% by day 30. Ebbinghaus's study presumes no prior knowledge or repeated attempts to remember—both of which would impact the rate of forgetting. See Carey, B. (2014). *How we learn: The surprising truth about when, where, and why it happens*, 25–29. Random House.

10. "A Longitudinal Investigation of Directional Relations Between Domain Knowledge and Reading in the Elementary Years" by KyeJin Hwang, Kristen McMaster, and Panayiota Kendeou in *Reading Research Quarterly*, January/February/March 2023 (Vol. 58, #1, pp. 59-77); "Teaching for Transfer Can Help Young Children Read for Understanding" by James Kim and Mary Burkhauser in Phi Delta Kappan, May 2022 (Vol. 103, #8, pp. 20-24)

11. Willingham, Daniel. *Why don't students like school? A cognitive scientist answers questions about how the mind works and what it means for the classroom*, Jossey-Bass. 2010. Pg. 28.

12. Benedict Carey says that many consider forgetting to be the opposite of learning, but it's actually crucial to the way that the brain takes in information, "The harder we have to work to retrieve a memory, the greater the subsequent spike in retrieval and storage strength (learning)." *How We Learn: The Surprising Truth About When, Where, and Why It Happens*. Random House, 2014. P. 38. The book *Powerful Teaching* by cognitive scientist Pooja Agarwal and educator Patrice Bain provides actionable knowledgeable retrieval strategies that teachers can use in any classroom. The related website retrievalpactice.org also includes several downloadable resources.

13. Cognitive load theory examines the intersection between human cognition and instructional practices. Teaching tools like knowledge organizers enhance learning

by decreasing demands on working memory. Instead of struggling to remember a flood of new information, students can quickly access the most critical information within the one-pager as they build their knowledge of a new content area or skill. Knowledge organizers can also include relevant visual information (charts, maps, diagrams, concept maps) and processes; these different formats reinforce recall and retention. Over time, students can also use the knowledge organizer as a study tool, quizzing themselves over its contents, or using strategies like elaboration to draw connections between different pieces of related information, e.g., dates and key figures and events. See the Centre for Education Statistics and Evaluation. *Cognitive Load Theory in Practice: Examples for the Classroom.* New South Wales Government. November 2018. https://education.nsw.gov.au/about-us/education-data-and-research/cese/publications/practical-guides-for-educators/cognitive-load-theory-in-practice. See also Agarwal, Pooja and Patrice Bain. *Powerful Teaching: Unleash the Science of Learning.* Jossey-Bass, 2019 and Miller, Mark. *Impact*: Designing a Curriculum. "Organising knowledge: The purpose and pedagogy of knowledge organizers." September *2018. https://my.chartered.college/impact_article/organising-knowledge-the-purpose-and-pedagogy-of-knowledge-organisers/*

14. Bambrick-Santoyo, Paul and Art Worrell. *Make history: A practical guide for middle and high school history instruction.* Jossey-Bass. 2023. See "Supply (or create) a resource" in Part 2: Build Knowledge for examples of knowledge organizers that can be adapted to different content areas. Pp. 68–71. For more information about knowledge activation and retrieval, read Part 2: Build Knowledge in its entirety, pp. 55–92.

15. This process is called "elaboration, and learners who make multiple connections to new and established knowledge reinforce the process of learning." See Brown, Peter, et al. *Make it stick: The science of successful learning.* Harvard University Press, 2014. Pg. 5–6.

16. Bambrick-Santoyo, P. and Chiger, S. (2021). *Love & literacy: A practical guide for grades 5-12 to finding the magic in literature*, 49–53. Jossey-Bass.

17. Cowan, Nelson. "The magical mystery four: How is working memory capacity limited, and why?" *Curr Dir Psychol Sci.* 2010 Feb 1; 19(1): 51–57. doi: https://doi.org/10.1177/0963721409359277. Johnson, J. Our attention is limited; Our memory is imperfect. *Designing with the Mind in Mind 87–105.* Science Direct. doi:https://doi.org/10.1016/B978-0-12-407914-4.00007-5.

## Chapter 5

1. Steven Johnson. "Where Good Ideas Come From, TED talk" (July 2010), http://www.ted.com/talks/steven_johnson_where_good_ideas_come_from#t-218811

2. Lemov, Doug. *Teach like a champion: 63 techniques that put students on the path to college.* Jossey-Bass, 2021. Pacing, pp. 237–240.

3. Lemov, Doug. *Teach like a champion. 63 techniques that put students on the path to college. Jossey-Bass,* 2021. Pacing, Pg 239.

4. See Part 4: Make Sense of It Through Discourse (pp. 121–152) in *Make History* and Chapter 6: Build Habits of Discourse (pp. 177–203) in *Love and Literacy.* Bambrick-Santoyo, Paul and Art Worrell. *Make History: A Practical Guide for Middle and High School History Instruction.* Jossey-Bass, 2023. Bambrick-Santoyo, Paul and Steve Chiger. *Love and Literacy: A Practical Guide for Grades 5–12.* Jossey-Bass, 2021.

5. A more commonly understood term for revoicing is paraphrasing. The more academic term was coined by O'Connor and Michael, researchers who studied the multiple functions of revoicing as a discourse strategy in the classroom. For more, see: Sarah Michaels and Catherine O'Connor. "Supporting teachers in taking up productive talk moves: The long road to professional learning at scale." International Journal of Education no. 97:166–175. https://doi.org/10.1016/j.ijer.2017.11.003 and "Conceptualizing Talk Moves as Tools: Professional Development Approaches for Academically Productive Discussions." In L.B. Resnick, C. Asterhan and S.N. Clarke (Eds.), *Socializing Intelligence through Talk and Dialogue,* 333–347. https://doi.org/10.3102/978-0-935302-43-1_27.

6. Stone, Irving. *The Agony and the Ecstasy.* Berkley, 1987.

## Closing: The Pursuit of Excellence

1. Lewis, Brian. "Local Stars Sydney McLaughlin, Dalilah Muhammad taking duel to Olympics." *New York Post.* July 20, 2021.

2. First team meeting as Packers coach (1959), reported in Chuck Carlson, *Game of My Life: 25 Stories of Packers Football* (2004), p. 149.

# Index

**A**

Abrams, Katie, 113, 119, 134

Academic achievement, increase, 65

Academic growth, support, 194

Academic habits, initiation, 204

Academic monitoring, 45, 55; coaching strategies, 226–227; data, gathering, 221–222; factors, 213; implementation, 346–347; language, 37; pathway, creation/implementation, 215–217; plan, sample, 56–57; problems, challenges (avoidance), 214; response, preparation, 221–222

Academic routines, rollout, 15–16, 201, 204

Accountability, verbal enforcement, 333–334

Actionable, focus, 3

Action steps, 45; consideration, waterfall analogy (consideration), 41; highest leverage, 30; identification, 79; making, power (focus), 70; management/rigor trajectory, 89–91;

size/precision, impact, 49; teacher usage, 31

Activate knowledge, 286–289

Active learning, 329

Adaptive performance profession, 23–24

Aggressive monitoring, emphasis, 36–37

*Agony and the Ecstasy, The* (Stone), 352

Aha moment, 236

Alvarez, Julia, 343

Analysis: end game anchoring, 249; knowledge, absence, 288

Anchor chart, usage, 303

Annotations, usage, 303

Apprenticeship phase (teaching), 246

AP World History, reference sheet (sample), 293

Archimedes, discovery, 309

Assessment, standards (absence), 249

At-bats, student usage, 305

*Atomic Habits* (Clear), 93

**B**

Back pocket prompts, usage, 340
Backward-plan, 137, 148–149
Bambrick-Santoyo, Paul, 142
Barnett, Josh, 9
Berry, Becky, 68, 97
Biggs, Ajanee, 360–361
Bite-sized action, 31, 42
Bite-sized approach, 3, 24–25, 70–71;
    case study, 38–39; coaching principles
    presentation, 147
Bite-sized directions, 54, 165–167
Bite-sized feedback, 14
Blake, Rachel, 293
*Bluest Eye, The* (Morrison), 46
Bonner, Leslie, 262
Brennan, Sue, 187, 206, 220
Bridges, Nikki, 152
Bright Lines, usage, 326
Brown, Brené, 67
Buddy systems, 9
Building, learning, 237–238
Burnam, Syrena, 114, 199

**C**

Calendar, tool (usage), 152
Call and response, 327–328
Carman-Brown, Ben, 86
Carr, Tera, 71, 225
Carter, Na'Jee, 59–61, 111, 113, 220, 225, 239, 250
Cavanaugh, James, 230, 346, 349
Chalkboard, usage, 332
Champions, practice, 52
Channa, Herminder, 58
Chart paper, usage, 332
Chiger, Steve, 138, 296
Children, education, 318
Circulation, purpose, 173–175
Claps, usage, 326
Classroom: building, 164; conversation,
    strengthening, 235; discussion, 206;
    deepening, 341; energy, increase, 315–316,
    318, 409–413; management: action
    steps criteria, 30–31; habits, 204; reset,
    ability, 40
Clearance takeoff, 398–403
Clear, James, 93
Clock, working, 326–327

Close the loop conversation, 280–281
Coaches, guide, 19–20
Coaching: blueprints, 15, 16, 19, 21; effectiveness,
    importance, 2–3, 26; principles, 14, 17,
    19, 21, 23–24; presentation, 147; routines/
    procedures, strategies, 98; strategies,
    134–135, 143
Coburn, Jesse, 113
Cold call, 228, 305; create/use cue, 274; Guided
    Discourse, 234–235; response, 277–278;
    usage, 269–270, 273
Colombus Day, activate knowledge, 286–287
Complex instructions, understanding
    (checking), 167–168
Confident Presence: coaching strategies, 103–104;
    confident stance, coaching,
    100–101; skills, 99–100; warm-demander
    register, coaching, 102–103
Connections (authentic), 194–200
Content expertise, development, 105–107,
    368–375
Content knowledge, building, 36, 108
Content, understanding (development), 108–114
Contribution, learning, 236–237
Conversation habits, student instruction, 227
Countdown, usage, 326
Counter-example, consideration, 354
Coyle, Daniel, 5
Creativity (enhancement), routines (impact), 94
Cruz, Yanela, 94, 274
Culihan, Marie, 85
Culture of belonging, creation, 186
Culture of care (building), confidence
    (impact), 103
Culture of feedback, creation, 67
Culture resets, 263–264

**D**

Daily data meetings, teacher teams (involvement),
    253–256
Daily entry prompt, implementation, 208–209
*Dare to Lead* (Brown), 67
Data: usage, 115–116; weekly data meetings,
    246–248
Data-driven instructional plan: sample, 155;
    usage, 152
Data Meeting, Coaching Blueprint, 303
Dates, setting, 62

de la Torre, Estrella, 103

Detection/correction, importance, 44

Diaz, Junot, 184, 194

Directions: chunking, 165–166; clarity, providing, 2; short-term result, 4–5

Disagreeing, respectfulness, 228

Discouragement, 2

Discourse: deepening, 36, 336–337, 414–417; rigor skills, 338; early habits, 36; facilitation, teacher role, 339; foundation, formation, 227; fruitfulness/generativity, 229; guiding, routines (creation), 205; usefulness, 354

Discourse Cycle, 228

Disorder, order (impact), 262

Dixon, Knick, 175

Do Now, completion, 326

Dorsey-Carr, Windy, 88

Dowling, Kelly, 81–82, 87, 122, 130

Drop knowledge, 48, 296–297

DuFuor, Richard, 247

Dunbar, Kevin, 309

Dutcher, Julia, 252, 331

## E

Early arguments, improvement, 351

Easterling, Equel, 296

Edwards, Kristie, 119

Ellis, Kimberly, 134

Emerling, Bradley A., 115

Emotional safe space, creation, 156

End game, analysis, 249

End goal: assessment, analysis, 109–111; understanding, response (crafting), 140

End-of-class learning, measure, 206

End-of-year assessment, 42

Engagement techniques, 305

Excellence, pursuit, 359

Executive function, reinforcement, 275

Exemplar: initiation, 248–250, 303; note-taking page, written example, 290, 291; response, 231; sparring, 137; unpacking, power, 250; usage, 221, 248; writing, 136–140, 141–143

Exit ticket: design, 124–125; usage, 210–211

Explicit directions, scripting (process), 331

Explicit instructions, delivery, 330–332

Eye contact, making, 171–173

## F

Federal Aviation Administration (FAA) safety, 245–246

Feedback, 26, 311; alignment, 55; connection, 68; culture, creation, 67–68; delivery, 66–67, 70–75; distinction, 32; frequency, 14, 24, 64, 83, 213; impact, 64; improvement, 29; providing/giving, 20, 45, 55, 156, 212, 246; receiving, 101; scheduling, steps, 148–149; targeting, 30; time allotment, 147; whispering, 73; written feedback, 45

Feedback meeting, 58, 61, 75; format, preview, 156; locking in, 148–149; notes, template, 154; tone, setting, 151–152

Final PD (dress rehearsal), 87–88

*First 90 Days, The* (Watkins), 13

First impression, making, 151

Fitzgerald, F. Scott, 296

Flight pattern adjustment, 282–283, 285, 286

Follow-up/repetition, 53

Foner, Eric, 338

For Inspiration and Recognition of Science and Technology (FIRST) Robotics Competition, 51–52

Forzani, Francesca M., 83

Framing (habit of discourse rollout), 235, 239

Frazier, Denarius, 173

Fritz, Christina, 214, 221, 225

## G

Game, change, 3–7

Gaps: identification, 249; observation, 254; practicing, 60

Get Better Faster (GBF) Scope and Sequence, 35, 42, 52

Get Better Faster (GBF) Sequence, 36, 39, 50; skills, providing, 52; usage, 271, 272

Gile, Amy, 87–88

Goett, Katherine, 355

Gomez, Paula, 304

Good, highlighting, 187

Graff-Emerling, Genevieve, 115

Graham, Vy, 205

Grant, Jaz, 1–5, 248–249, 252

*Great Gatsby, the* (Fitzgerald), 296–297

Griffin, Patricia, 291

Group progress, monitoring, 332–333

Index **433**

Group work. *See* Small-group work:
  instructions, 330
Guided Discourse, 229, 272, 299; coaching: advice,
  230–241; strategies, 242–243; cold call/
  volleyball, 234–235; habits, prompting/
  praising, 236–240; stamp key, 240–241
Guide Discourse, 230–232

**H**

Habits of Discussion: PD goal, 235; prompt/
  praise, 228
Habits, prompting/praising (Guided
  Discourse), 236–240
Halftime meetings, building, 116–117
Hammond, Zaretta, 36
Hand gestures, usage, 72, 326
Handout, usage, 332
Hand signal, giving, 324
Harrison, Benjamin (declaration), 286–287
Harshman, Katie, 100, 186, 268
Harvey, Trennis, 20, 58–59, 61–62, 69–70, 217
Hernandez, Susan, 31, 166, 168, 303
High expectations, 107
Hill, Lisa, 101, 103, 140, 182
Hollis, Brittany, 95, 97, 214
Hooking (habit of discourse rollout), 235, 239
Hypothetical questions, 305, 356

**I**

Ignorance, feigning, 355
Inclusion, rigor (combination), 347
Independent practice: academic routines, 205–207;
  coaching strategies, 211–212; daily entry
  prompt, implementation, 208–209; exit
  ticket, usage, 210–211; incorporation, 204;
  prioritization, 206; student work, 43–44;
  writing/talking sequence, 207–208
Individual student corrections: coaching strategies,
  281–282; student engagement, 40
Ingersoll, Richard, 9
Instant immersion, 15–16, 145; management
  rollout, 376–387; monitoring
  routines, 376–387;
  rollout academic routines, 388–397
Instructional leadership: idea, 6; purpose, 4
Instructions: clarity: absence, impact, 40;
  importance, 3; go-to areas, 45;
  understanding, checking, 167–168
Intellect, praising (positive narration), 189–191

Internal monologue, narration, 304
In-the-moment data: classroom energy, increase,
  409–413; response, 310
In-the-moment reset, implementation,
  265–266
*In the Time of Butterflies* (Alvarez), 343
Iwasko, Alicia, 111

**J**

James Webb Space Telescope, construction/
  success, 25–26, 32, 50
Johnson, Ebonee, 241
Johnson, Steven, 309
Jones, Nikki, 342

**K**

Key Leadership Moves, 232
Knowledge: absence, 288; activation, 36, 48, 285,
  286–289, 404–409; coaching strategies,
  298; drop knowledge, 296–297; knowledge
  organizer, usage, 293–294; knowledge
  retrieval,
  294–296; resource usage, student prompts,
  290–292; foundation, 289; organizer,
  usage, 48, 293–294; retrieval, 36,
  294–296; tool: development,
  292; power, 48
Kotla, Siva, 156

**L**

Language: changes, 36–37; economy, 150;
  learning, 146
Large group class discussion, 271
Launch, planning, 119–120
Leadership, maestro approach, 24
Leaders, problems (creation), 10
Learning: acceleration, 65; coaching, 311;
  improvement, 65, 313; monitoring,
  310–313; objectives,
  writing, 117–119; PD cycle, 20; student
  preparation, 286; time,
  maximization, 329–330
Least invasive intervention, 278–280
Leinwand, Steve, 115
Lemov, Doug, 13, 99, 269, 323
Lesson: adjustment, 116–117; context, 46; design,
  following, 1–2; internalization, 130–131;
  observation, 69; planning, 115;
  productive struggle, identification,

**434** Index

128–130; structure, planning, 122–123; time stamps, building, 131–132

Lesson plans: access, 128; adjustment, 133–134; development, 105–107, 117–121, 124–125, 368–375; strategies, 126–127; identification, 297; internalization, 127–135

Leverage content, knowledge building, 109

Lim, Erica, 37, 54, 175

Listening task, 301–302

Live model, 239

Loewenberg Ball, Deborah, 83

Lombardi, Vince, 360

Look fors, (narrow the focus—model), 303

Loop conversations, closure, 280–281

Losse, Owen, 324

## M

*Make History* (Worrell/Bambrick-Santoyo), 48, 286, 294

Management: issue, determination, 39; routines, rollout/monitoring, 159–160; skills, 15–16, 162, 318; student engagement, 261; teacher mastery, myth, 12; trajectory, 257–261, 314

Marquez, Michelle, 291

Martin, Ashley, 72, 74, 182

Marvania, Neha, 295

Masterpiece, creation, 352

Master teachers, finding, 6

McCarthy, Kristen, 179, 225, 251, 312

McLaughlin-Levrone, Sydney, 359–360

McTighe, Jay, 58

Mentoring programs, impact, 9

Michelangelo, 352

Micro-skills (bite-sized), practice, 4

Mindsets (change), progress (impact), 247

Model: confusion, problem, 300; implementation, 303

Modeling, 299; benefit, 66–67, 74; coaching strategies, 306–307; focus, narrowing, 300–301; habit of discourse rollout, 235, 239; post-model understanding, 305–306; students, listening task, 301–302; thinking, modeling, 302–304

Momentum, building, 319; challenge, creation, 320–321; coaching strategies, 322; teacher PD goal, 319

Monitoring, visualization (difficulty), 214

Monitor routines, 376–387

Monitor the Learning, 310–313

Morrison, Toni, 46–47

Muhammad, Dalilah, 359

Mullins, Jessica, 229

Multi-standard tracker, usage, 222

Murphy, Annie, 86

Murphy, Megan, 340

Murray, Danny, 184, 194, 290, 341, 347, 353–354

## N

Narrate the positive, 86,186–193

Narration, ability, 40

Naylor, Gloria, 341, 354

Newborn, Charles, 247, 253

New teachers: coaching, myths/realities, 11–12; core challenges, 319; focus, reason, 7–10; success, 8–10

Notebook, usage, 290

## O

Observation, scheduling (steps), 148–149

Off-task students: action step, versions, 27–29; challenge, 26–27; reason, 30; redirection, 277; role, playing, 279

One-pagers: consistency, 150; following, 253

On-task behavior, 44

Order, bringing, 262

## P

Pacing: call and response, 327–328; clock, working, 326–327; coaching strategies, 328–329; questioning rate, increase, 325; self-timing, 323–324

Pasricha, Ritu, 60, 150

Peer-to-peer discourse, student thinking (impact), 310

Pelliccio, Emelia, 272, 290

Perfect: component, defining, 53–55

Perfection, chasing, 361

Performance, assessment, 28

Personal organization, tools, 152, 155

Petrosino, Jen, 231

Physical nonverbal cues, usage, 72

Planning: increase, benefits, 163; skipping, 58–59; work, application, 95

Plan, perfecting, 53, 57

Point of failure, occurrence, 25–26

Positive narration, 186–192; ability, 40; coaching strategies, 192–193

Index **435**

Practice: defining, 58–59; experience, contrast, 11; habit of discourse rollout, 235, 239; perfection, 11–12, 60–61; permanence, 60; planning, 53, 55–59, 224; power, 60

Practice-able, 30

Pre-calls, usage, 270–271

Pre-established code, usage, 45

Pre-identified students, equipping, 274–276

Pre-teaching (Summer PD), 14, 17, 81, 88; content expertise, development, 368–375; lesson plans, development, 368–375; routines/procedures, development, 364–367

Principals, profession exit, 10

Problematization, prompts, 353–355

Problem, identification (ability), 40

Problem-solving techniques, modeling, 355

Procedures: coaching strategy, 183; development, 91–92, 93–97; modeling, avoidance, 302; problem, 40; repetition, 181–182

Professional development (PD), 15, 66, 69; bite-sized directions, 54; coaching skills, 83–84; goals, setting, 156; leading, 84–87; practice, absence (problem), 85; summer PD sessions, preparation, 21; training, 83–84

Proficiency, 44

Progress, celebration, 31

Prompting, sophistication (benefits), 312

Prompts, usage, 60

## Q

Quality objective, alignment, 44

Questioning: rate, increase, 325–326; sequence, delivery/role-playing, 325

## R

Rabinowitz, Jessica, 275

Rainbow guide, creation, 20

Randle, Kendra, 164

Rapport, school focus, 185

Real-time feedback, 64–66, 70, 224; benefits, 312; culture, creation, 67; delivery, 71–79; impact, 312; importance, 20; launch, 68–69; loop, closure, 75; planning, 62; rewards, reaping, 67; rollout, 68; transparency, 68; whole-class reset, ineffectiveness, 264

Real-time shifts, creation, 71

Rector, Jesse, 295

Redirections, (off task behavior) design, 278

Response: evolution, 287; scripting, 141–143

Response/thought, sharing, 271

Responsive performance (teaching and other professions), 82

Re-teach, planning/practicing, 248, 252, 255

Revoicing, 341–342; prompts, 342

Rice, Elirah, 95, 97

Rigor, 15–16, 39, 79, 136; case study, 42–44, 46–47; content expertise/lesson plans, development, 105–107; discourse, deepening, 336–337, 414–417; flight pattern adjustment, 282–283; importance, 313; inclusion, combination, 347; rollout academic routines, 388–397; skills, 107, 204, 285, 338; trajectory, 257–261, 285, 314

Roach, Zach, 116, 129, 142, 241, 295

Roberts, Kenya, 129

Rollout: academic routines, 388–397; management routines, 376–387

Routines: coaching strategy, 183; creation, 330; design, 329–330; development, 91–92, 93–97; monitoring, 159–160, 162–163; problems, 94, 262; repetition, 181–182; revision, 179–180; rollout, 159–160, 162–163, 201; academic routines, 388–397; students: following, absence, 39–41; need, 185

Ruiz, Anabel, 97, 128, 225

## S

Saphier, Jon, 13, 116

Schema, foundation, 289

Schools: districts, problems, 8–9; leaders, success, 10

Schrag, Sarah, 297

Schuster, Scott, 50, 271

Scope and Sequence action steps, 31–32; cheat sheet, 80; overview, 33–35; writing, 42

Scope and sequence, importance, 19

Scott, Jr., Michael, 197

See it, Name it, Do it, 84–85, 248

See Your Students, 170–178

Self-timing, 323–324

Shepherd, Toby, 166

Shigenobu, Taro, 73, 241, 311–312

Shigenobu, Taro, 311–312

Short-cycle analysis, 247

Show-Call, 228; Guided Discourse, 230–232

Silent signals, 72

Skill: learning, impact, 2; sequence, 13; teaching, 157–159

*Skillful Teacher, The* (Saphier), 13, 115

Skills: mastery, 11

Small-group work: engagement, 329–330; accountability, verbal enforcement, 333–334; coaching strategies, 335; explicit instructions, delivery, 330–332; group progress, monitoring, 332–333; management, 329; power, 330; skills, utilization, 334; time, productivity, 330

Social supports, 275; encouragement, practicing, 275

Sonnet 65 (Shakespeare), 138–139

Spartak Tennis Club, training (bite-sized), 5

Speed, illusion, 318; creation, 323

Stamp key, understanding, 240–241

Standard, definition (absence), 249

STEM, 35; examples, 354–355

St. Joy, Melissa, 264

Stone, Irving, 352

Stop and jots, usage, 18

Strategic calling, 339; coaching strategies, 351; model, 349; sequence, creation, 348–350

Stretch it, 352; coaching strategies, 358; preparation, 353; problematization, 353–355; prompts, 339; sophisticating, 356–357; strategic prompting, 340

Students: acknowledgment, 173–178; adult-child relationships, forging, 194; analysis, 353; answers, tracking, 213; arguments, 353; justification, 354; at-bats usage, 305; calling on, 273–274, 347; coaching strategies, 351; sequence, creation, 348–350; circulation, purpose, 173–175; connections, making, 195–199; coaching strategies, 200; conversation habits, learning, 227; corrections, 277–278; coaching strategies, 281–282; least invasive intervention, 278–280; loop conversations, closure, 280–281; discourse, quality (measurement), 339; discussions, stalling, 348; disengagement, positive narration, 191–192; engagement, 40, 44, 170, 259, 261, 268; coaching strategies, 276–277; cold call, usage, 269–270; implementing/coaching, 274;

pre-call/warm-call, usage, 270–271; pre-identified students, equipping, 274–276; speed illusion, 323; turn and talk, 271–272; engagement, methods, 273–274; exemplar, 249–250; eye contact, making, 171–173; feedback, giving, 213; gap, 312–313; independent work, review, 212; justification, 353; learning: priority, weekly data meetings (usage), 246–248; teacher prioritization, 66; listening task, 301–302; needs (targeting), lesson plan (adjustment), 133–134; prompting, 351; resource usage prompting, 290–291; responses, scripting, 146; routines, usage, 178–179; speaking, teacher position, 175–176; stalling, 318; strategic calling, 346–347; coaching strategies, 351; sequence, creation, 348–350; struggle, 251; success, 7–8; success, positive narration, 188–189; talking, change, 339; thinking: impact, 310; modeling, 299; prioritization, 206; written response, scripting, 35

Student work: collection, ease, 251; examination, 246–253; making, 217–221; meeting, 247; monitoring, 44; usage, 311

Success, creation, 61–62

Syed, Anushae, 305

## T

*Talent Code, The* (Coyle), 5

Task Management Tracker, usage, 152, 153

Tasks: creation/identification, 120–122; locking, 62

T-chart, creation, 221

Tchsang, Chi, 123

Teachers: actions, examination, 311; action steps, identification, 21, 79; career, trajectory (prediction), 13–14; coaching, need, 4; development, 32; improvement, 313; launch, 33–35; directions, vagueness, 164; feedback, 150; freezing, 83; gap, 313; guidance, 312; instinct, 170; meeting, 21; motivation, 9–10; need, planning, 54; peer practice, 127–128; posture/tone, 100; profession, improvement (needs), 13; real-time changes, 246; shortage, 8; success, 10; teams (leading), weekly/daily data meetings (impact), 253–256; training, 4, 24

Index **437**

Teaching: adaptive performance profession, 23–24; complexity, 351–352; effectiveness, planning (impact), 61; learning, 146; questions, 247; road map, 109; skill learning, impact, 5–6; skills, 89–91, 256, 313–314

*Teach Like a Champion* (Lemov), 13, 99, 136, 269, 323

*Teach Like a Champion 3.0*, 86

*Ten-Minute-In-Service*, 86

Think Aloud, 303; modeling, 125, 233, 272, 332–333

Thinking: modeling, 302–304; understanding, 304; pushing, 340; questions, drafting, 304

Time: blocking, 148–149; calendar prep, 150; saving, 150; stamps, building, 131–132; tracking, tools, 152

Topic, students' background knowledge, 288

Training: occurrence, 84

Trust/rapport, building, 36, 159–160, 162–163, 184

Turn and talks, 271–273, 305, 330; launching, modeling, 272; listening, 228

Tymkowych, Kim, 86

**U**

Unit plans, development/internalization, 111–114

Universal prompts, 339, 340–341; coaching strategies, 345; reasoning, 343–344; revoicing, 341–342

U.S. teachers, profession exit, 8–9

**V**

Values, practice, 14, 24, 51, 63, 83, 147

Verbal interventions, 333

Verrilli, Jamey, 185

Videos, usage, 18, 342

Vision, crafting, 88

Visual cues, usage, 72

Visual tool, usage, 332

Voice, tone (dropping), 320

Volleyball, 234–235

**W**

Walsh, Bill, 162–163

Warm calls, usage, 270–271

Warm energy, sparkle, 321

Warm welcome, positive narration, 187–188

Watkins, Michael D., 13

Weekly Data Meeting (WDM): discussions, 247; power, 251; student learning, priority, 246–248; teacher teams, involvement, 253–256

Weekly meeting notes, usage, 152

Weekly planning meetings, usage, 20

Westman, Hadley, 343

What-To-Do directions, 2, 37, 54, 85, 164–169, 331

*Where Good Ideas Come From* (Dunbar/Johnson), 309

Whisper prompt, 72–74, 280, 292, 294, 321

Whiteboard, usage, real-time feedback, 76; instruction, 332

Whole-class discussion, 329–330

Whole-class reset, 41–42; coaching strategies, 267; ineffectiveness, 264; in-the-moment reset implementation, 265–266; planned whole class reset, 263–264; scripting, 265; teacher PD goal, 262

Whole-class understanding, 341

Whole-group discussion, planning, 274

*Why Don't Students Like School* (Willingham), 288

Wiggins, Grant, 58

Willingham, Daniel, 288

Wineburg, Sam, 286

Wolf, Brittany, 235

*Women of Brewster Place, The* (Naylor), 341, 354

Worrell, Art, 48, 66, 240, 286, 289, 338–339, 350, 357

Writing: gesture, 72; Guided Discourse, 230–232

Written feedback, 45